Poststructuralist Agency

Poststructuralist Agency

The Subject in Twentieth-Century Theory

GAVIN RAE

EDINBURGH
University Press

Edinburgh University Press is one of the leading university presses in the UK. We publish academic books and journals in our selected subject areas across the humanities and social sciences, combining cutting-edge scholarship with high editorial and production values to produce academic works of lasting importance. For more information visit our website: edinburghuniversitypress.com

© Gavin Rae, 2020, 2021

Edinburgh University Press Ltd
The Tun – Holyrood Road, 12(2f) Jackson's Entry, Edinburgh EH8 8PJ

First published in hardback by Edinburgh University Press 2020

Typeset in 10/13 ITC Giovanni Std by
IDSUK (DataConnection) Ltd

A CIP record for this book is available from the British Library

ISBN 978 1 4744 5935 8 (hardback)
ISBN 978 1 4744 5936 5 (paperback)
ISBN 978 1 4744 5938 9 (webready PDF)
ISBN 978 1 4744 5937 2 (epub)

The right of Gavin Rae to be identified as the author of this work has been asserted in accordance with the Copyright, Designs and Patents Act 1988, and the Copyright and Related Rights Regulations 2003 (SI No. 2498).

CONTENTS

Preface vi

    Introduction 1

Part I. Decentring the Subject

1. Deleuze, Differential Ontology and Subjectivity 33
2. Derrida's *Différance*: Deconstruction and the Sexuality of Subjectivity 62
3. Foucault I: Power and the Subject 88
4. Foucault II: Normativity, Ethics and the Self 116

Part II. Turning to the Psyche

5. Butler on the Subjection of Gendered Agency 143
6. Lacan on the Unconscious Subject: From the Social to the Symbolic 167
7. Kristeva on the Subject of Revolt: The Symbolic and the Semiotic 191
8. Castoriadis, Agency and the Socialised Individual 219

    Conclusion 247

Bibliography 252
Index 273

PREFACE

That poststructuralist thinkers have offered a number of radical critiques of the subject has long been acknowledged. Their framework has, however, been criticised for seeking to annihilate and/or decentre the subject to the extent that agency – meaning autonomous intentional action – is not possible. This criticism is built on two premises: first, poststructuralist thought decentres the subject to think of it in founded rather than foundational terms. Second, the decentred subject is understood to be a *determined* effect of pre-personal structures and processes. While I agree that poststructuralist thinking does, indeed, decentre the subject, I argue that this critical process is combined with a regenerative one whereby the founding, constituting subject is replaced by a founded, constituted subject, and crucially that this rethought subject is understood to be merely *conditioned*, rather than determined, by pre-personal structures and processes. Furthermore, I maintain that poststructuralist thinkers are aware of the implications that this rethinking has for the question of agency and offer substantial and heterogeneous proposals to resolve it.

From this, I defend four fundamental claims: 1) The question of the subject is central to poststructuralist thinking by virtue of its attempt to decentre the subject from the foundational status it has long had within Western philosophy. 2) Poststructuralist thinkers are aware of the implications that this rethinking has for the question of agency and propose heterogeneous 'solutions' to account for it. 3) It is those poststructuralists inspired by (Lacanian) psychoanalysis who offer the most logically sophisticated and subtle rethinking of the founded subject as it relates to the question of agency, with 4) Cornelius Castoriadis providing the most detailed account by virtue of his insistence that it be thought in terms of a nexus of ever-changing configurations of social, symbolic and psychic components.

With this, I contribute to our understanding of poststructuralism and each of the thinkers engaged with, show the important role that psychoanalytic theory plays within poststructuralist thought, and demonstrate that poststructuralist thought is able to decentre the subject while coherently explaining how agency is possible.

This is fully developed in the text, but at this stage I am happy to acknowledge that this book forms part of the activities of the Conex Marie Skłodowska-Curie Research Project 'Sovereignty and Law: Between Ethics and Politics' (2013-00415-026), co-funded by the Universidad Carlos III de Madrid, the European Union's Seventh Framework Program for Research, Technological Development and Demonstration under Grant Agreement 600371, The Spanish Ministry of the Economy and Competitivity (COFUND2013-40258), The Spanish Ministry for Education, Culture, and Sport (CEI-15-17), and Banco Santander. Information about the project can be found at https://sovereigntyandlaw.wordpress.com/.

Chapter 1 includes rewritten material that first appeared in 'The Political Significance of the Face: Deleuze's Critique of Levinas', *Critical Horizons: A Journal of Philosophy and Social Theory*, 17.3/4, 2016, pp. 279–303; Chapter 2 includes rewritten material that was first published in 'Disharmonious Continuity: Critiquing Presence with Sartre and Derrida', *Sartre Studies International*, 23.2, 2017, pp. 58–81; while rewritten aspects of Chapters 6 and 7 appear in 'Maternal and Paternal Functions in the Formation of Subjectivity: Kristeva and Lacan', forthcoming in *Philosophy and Social Criticism*; I thank the publishers for permission to include that material here. A short version of Chapter 8 was presented at the 'Poststructuralism: Past, Present, Future' conference held at the Universidad Complutense de Madrid on 6–7 March 2019; I thank the participants for their questions and queries.

At Edinburgh University Press, I would once again like to thank Carol Macdonald for her support for the project and, along with her assistant Kirsty Woods, her help in bringing it to publication; the anonymous reviewers for their very helpful comments on the original text; and Andrew Kirk for his careful copy-editing. Closer to home, *mil gracias otra vez a* Emma for her continuing encouragement, discussions and support. This book is dedicated to Toran, our newly arrived 'wee screaming monster' (see Chapter 8) who, despite (or probably because of) all attempts at socialisation, thankfully continues to exercise his agency at every opportunity, including at our newly established 2 a.m. *fiestas*!

Introduction

The poststructuralist paradigm has become one of the dominant modes of inquiry in the humanities and social sciences, to the extent that, as Françoise Dosse explains, 'it is no longer even possible to think without taking the structuralist revolution into account'.[1] This is not to say that it has been universally accepted. Among mainstream theorists, poststructuralism is often associated with contradiction, hyperbole, lack of clarity and vacuity. Although it is true that poststructuralist writers are unlikely to win any praise for their writing style,[2] a large part of this is due to the challenge that these writers set themselves; namely, to contest many of the foundational assumptions upon which much mainstream Western (political) philosophical thought is and has been based. To do so, they do not simply reconfigure pre-existing concepts, but go further by disrupting and undermining the concepts, categories and ways of thinking that have long dominated. For those trained in and focused on traditional forms of thought, this can be too much. One of the sub-aims of this book, however, is to show that if we are willing to delve patiently into the works of various poststructuralist thinkers, not only is their position subtle and developed, but it tends to be able to provide a sophisticated response to many of the queries and questions raised against them.

As its name suggests, *post*structuralism developed out of debates taking place within 1960s French structuralism, itself a development from linguistics and, in particular, Ferdinand de Saussure's *General Course in Linguistics*, published posthumously by his students in 1916.[3] Saussure's linguistic theory is complicated, but the pertinent point for us is the emphasis it places on the relationships inherent in the generation of meaning. Rather than hold that meaning is ahistoric, tied substantially to each signifier, or simply representative of an external object, Saussure argues that meaning is generated from the relations between two signifiers and, crucially, that this relation is not grounded in a third mediating moment. Instead, he explains that

> *in the language itself, there are only differences.* Even more important than that is the fact that, although in general a difference presupposes positive terms between which the difference holds, in a language there are only differences, *and no positive terms.* Whether we take the signification or the signal, the language includes neither ideas nor sounds existing prior to the linguistic system, but only conceptual and phonetic differences arising out of that system. In a sign, what matters more than any idea or sound associated with it is what other signs surround it. The proof of this lies in the fact that the value of a sign may change without affecting either meaning or sound, simply because some neighbouring sign has undergone a change.[4]

As Lionel Bailly explains, for Saussure, 'it is the relation of the Sign (the word) to the code of signification (the language) that accords it meaning, rather than a simple correspondence with an external object',[5] a position that emphasises the immateriality, or abstract nature, of the linguistic signifier. For Saussurean linguistics, therefore, meaning is generated from the nature and structure of the *relations* between signs.

Structuralists took this over to claim that structure is determinate for meaning but finite: the meaning of a sign changes depending on its relation, but there are only so many combinations that it can enter into. As structuralist thought developed philosophically, the limitations of this position became apparent. First, even if it is accepted that meaning is generated from the relations between signs, it is not evident that these are finite. Second, structuralist analyses tended to imply that the relationship between the signifiers is a symmetrical one, with each side being just as important as the other. There was liberating intent behind this: all of a sudden, those aspects that had previously been downgraded were considered to be just as important as those that had previously been privileged. However, it gradually became apparent that it was quite possible for meaning to be generated from an *asymmetric relation*, wherein the importance or contribution of each side is unequal. This spawned significantly more relational combinations than the symmetric structuralist understanding permitted and, in so doing, destabilised meaning to an even greater degree than the structuralist conception did or could. Third, whereas structuralism was taken to insist on a finite number of possible combinations and, by extension, meanings, the question of the closure inherent in this understanding was increasingly attacked. By emphasising logical (and metaphysical) openness, poststructuralist thinkers insisted that structures change and morph in a multiplicity of ways, not all of which can be foreseen.[6]

This ties into the fourth major critique of the structuralist position: its fetishisation of structure. As Saul Newman explains,

> [t]he virtue of structuralism was that it avoided essentialist understandings, in which identity and experience were seen as being grounded in an objective intelligible 'substance' or 'reality' that was internal to it – the 'thing in itself.' Structuralism showed that there was no such thing as the 'thing in itself,' and this was because the structure was so totalising and determining, it could be seen as a kind of essence in itself. In other words, structuralism came increasingly be seen as a new form of essentialism or foundationalism, in which identity was once again founded on an absolute ground.[7]

By insisting that meaning is generated by and from relations, which in turn are conditioned by specific structures, structuralist thought usurped the privileged role historically given to essence and subjectivity[8] and replaced it with a privileging of structure. In so doing, however, it simply changed the focus so that rather than insist that the subject constitutes structures, structures were taken to be constitutive of the subject. Therefore, despite its insistence that the fact that meaning is generated relationally undermines any privileging of a singular point or principle, structuralism nevertheless continued to give foundational importance to 'structure'. It is at this moment that *poststructuralism* arises.

Instead of overcoming the continuing (implicit) foundationalism inherent in structuralism by returning to a pre-structuralist understanding grounded in a fixed ahistoric essence, poststructuralism took the relationality of structuralism to its radical conclusion: if meaning is generated from (a)symmetric relations, then the structure itself must be radically ever-changing and open-ended. All unity, consistency and stability must be questioned and undermined whenever and wherever it arises. As Todd May explains, instead of continuing to operate through a structure/subject divide, poststructuralism

> dissolves the subject/structure dichotomy altogether by substituting for both a concept that might be called 'practices.' What is of interest to the poststructuralists is neither the constituting interiority of the subject nor the constituting exteriority of structures, but instead the interlocking networks of contingent practices that produces 'subjects' and 'structures.'[9]

However, instead of simply being a destructive form of thinking, I will show that this negative moment is accompanied by a *positive* aspect that aims to reconstruct identity and the difference–identity relation in non-essentialist terms.

Of course, that poststructuralist thought rejects essentialism causes the commentator who attempts to define 'it' significant problems. The best we can do is point to particular conditions or approaches shared, usually in heterogeneous ways, by thinkers normally associated with poststructuralism. Judith Butler and Joan W. Scott summarise this nicely when they explain that '[i]f the reader [tries] to discover what "poststructuralism" is, she will be frustrated and, perhaps, disconcerted. Poststructuralism is not, strictly speaking, *a position*, but rather a critical interrogation of the exclusionary operations by which "positions" are established.'[10] Whereas Western philosophical thought has long affirmed a fixed substance to ground its conclusions in ahistoric foundations, poststructuralism offers heterogeneous critiques of this assumption to ground thought in difference or, put more simply, pure change. By attacking the assumptions that have long grounded thought, poststructuralists aim to undermine any claim to permanence, identity or ahistoric truth. This even extends to the label 'poststructuralist', which was questioned by many of the thinkers associated with it, and, indeed, included in this study.[11]

This book is not a history of poststructuralism[12] and so I have not aimed to discuss every figure who could potentially be included. However, while this account does not claim to be exhaustive, the thinkers discussed are extensive and demonstrate the heterogeneity of 'poststructuralism'. There is, however, one figure – Luce Irigaray – whose exclusion perhaps stands out, especially given the inclusion of other feminist poststructuralists such as Judith Butler and Julia Kristeva. The reason for this is simple: as fascinating and important as Irigaray's work has been and arguably continues to be, she is not included because although she offers an account of subjectivity thought from sexuality, she does not offer an explicit account of agency in the way that the other thinkers included here do.[13]

On the other hand, the inclusion of Cornelius Castoriadis and Jacques Lacan might also be thought to be contentious. After all, for a long time Lacan was associated with structuralism, an assessment based primarily on the reduction of his thinking to the differential relations inherent in his conception of the symbolic, which were taken to structure all else and form a closed totality. Castoriadis, for example, bases his critique of Lacan on this understanding. The start of the new millennium, however, witnessed a new wave of Lacanian scholarship that criticised this 'structuralist' reading for ignoring the third Lacanian register – the real – which emphasises that which cannot be symbolised, and by focusing on this third register concluded that Lacan's thinking affirms discontinuity, difference, plurality, openness and so on.[14] It is this later reading (which has become the standard one) that brings Lacan into the poststructuralist orbit and so warrants his inclusion here.

In relation to the inclusion of Castoriadis, I follow a long line of commentators who have associated his thinking with (post-)structuralism. Axel Honneth, for example, ties Castoriadis to the structuralist trajectory, albeit negatively, by claiming that 'Castoriadis . . . follows structuralism [as] a point of departure', only to subsequently insist that his thought is tied to it because Castoriadis follows the structuralists in holding that social change is 'an impersonal occurrence' of anonymous processes.[15] Similarly, Jürgen Habermas claims that Castoriadis's thought ends up as 'another variant of poststructuralism'.[16] While Honneth and Habermas make the association pejoratively, it nevertheless supports the inclusion of Castoriadis in this study. More positively, Suzi Adams insists that Castoriadis joins the poststructuralists because he mirrors their return to Freud 'to develop his own thoughts', while Johann Michel recognises the problem but includes Castoriadis within poststructuralism by noting that he remains tied to structuralism, namely through his conflictual bond with Lacanian psychoanalysis, but 'adopts a strategy of "surpassing without conserving"' it.[17] As such, Castoriadis is 'post'-structuralist in both a temporal and a conceptual sense in so far as he develops, without strictly adhering to, the fundamental premises of structuralist thought. Warren Breckman, however, helpfully settles the matter by showing the ways in which Castoriadis and other poststructuralist thinkers overlap:

> Vehement as Castoriadis's comments could be, his relationship to [post-]structuralism was in fact not merely a matter of drawing a rigid battle line. Indeed, his work entwined constructively with the broad shift in thinking represented most prominently by Levi-Strauss and Lacan. He too rejected the idea that we have unmediated access to reality; he too rejected the idea of a sovereign conscious subject for whom language is a transcendent medium of expression. He too believed that society is a symbolic construction made up of significations, and he spoke of 'structures' shaping the material forms and mentalities of instituted society. That he shared many of the premises of structuralism makes it all the more intriguing, both theoretically and historically, that he worked his way toward such different conclusions.[18]

Besides the similarities mention by Breckman, I would also point to the common rejection of fixed essence and ahistoricism, and the concomitant emphasis on flux and change. As such, just because Castoriadis comes to different conclusions than other authors normally associated with poststructuralism does not mean that he cannot be associated with them; after all, the poststructuralist paradigm is highly heterogeneous. Indeed, I will argue that it is precisely because he comes to different conclusions that Castoriadis's inclusion is valuable.

Another contentious issue that arises relates to the question of what I mean by 'poststructuralism'. After all, discussing 'poststructuralist agency' requires some idea of what 'poststructuralism' delineates. This is, however, a complicated topic not only because of the heterogeneity of the positions tied to 'it' and because, as noted, a number labelled as 'poststructuralist' have openly hesitated about the term, but also because one of the defining features of the poststructuralist paradigm is a rejection of a defining 'essence' or 'identity'. In response, and while I am mindful of the heterogeneity of the positions staked out by the different thinkers included, I simply use the term 'poststructuralism' as a hermeneutic tool to engage with and develop the argument of the book: namely, that contrary to long-standing and widespread critiques, poststructuralist thought engages extensively with the problems of the subject and (autonomous, intentional) agency and, in so doing, offers a number of increasingly radical conceptions of the subject to rethink (intentional) agency in historical non-essentialist terms. For this reason, I will not treat poststructuralism as offering or describing a definitive homogeneous programme orientated towards a particular end, but as a *style of thinking*, adopted, to different degrees and in different ways, by thinkers who engage with the question of ontological identity and presence to call their privileging into question. As a rough starting point, this manner of thinking aims to affirm radical heterogeneity and change over homogeneity and ahistoricism.

This has implications for all areas of thought, but to get started it will be helpful to mention three. First, poststructuralism, broadly understood, insists that reality is a historical construction resulting from alterations in the pre-personal, anonymous structures and processes subtending the manifestations of the phenomenal world. Rather than adopt a two-world approach, wherein the world of appearance is grounded in a hidden essential one, poststructuralist thinkers emphasise that thinking occurs immanently to historically contingent (pre-personal) forces and structures. Therefore, to understand an issue requires that we take a close and very particular look at its actual appearance, which will, so they contend, reveal it to be shaped by constantly changing differential forces or processes. To understand an 'entity' requires that we comprehend the composition of those ever-changing differential forces and the relationship between them.

Second, poststructuralists take over the structuralist affirmation of relationality but radicalise it by recognising that relations are asymmetric, with their unequal distribution bringing forth the question of power. Rather than think of power, or force, as a possession of an agent, poststructuralist thought implicitly takes over the Nietzschean premise that the world is a

> [m]onster of energy, without beginning, without end; a firm, iron magnitude of force that does not grow bigger or smaller, that does not expend itself but only transforms itself; as a whole, of unalterable size, a household without expenses or losses, but likewise without increase or income; enclosed by 'nothingness' as by a boundary; not something blurry or wasted, not something endlessly extended, but set in a definitive space as a definite force, and not a space that might be 'empty' here or there, but rather as force throughout, as a play of forces and waves of force, at the same time one and many, increasing here and at the same time decreasing there; a sea of forces flowing and rushing together, eternally changing, eternally flooding back, with tremendous years of recurrence, with an ebb and a flood of its forms; out of the simplest forms striving toward the most complex, out of the stillest, most rigid, coldest forms toward the hottest, most turbulent, most self-contradictory . . . as a becoming that knows no satiety, no disgust, no weariness.[19]

The basic idea is that struggle and contestation are constitutive of the ontological structures of reality. This struggle may not be apparent, but it is always rumbling away in the background, shaping and reshaping reality. So, whereas Western anthropocentrism[20] has tended to maintain that individual agents are the ground of things, poststructuralists maintain that we have to turn away from this anthropocentrism to recognise that things and individual actions are effects of the pre-personal forces and structures subtending them.

Third, the most obvious ways in which poststructuralist thought challenges traditional thinking is found in its analysis of subjectivity. Rather than a substantial being that precedes its actions, choosing how and when to act, poststructuralism affirms that the subject is an effect of pre-personal, differential structures. This undermines the conception of the subject (defined by essentialist traits, egoism and unencumbered autonomy) dominant in Western (modern) thinking because, as Adriana Cavarero explains, it 'causes the isolated, sealed, perfect shape of the ego to collapse into the vortex of multiple fragments that succeed in nullifying all of the possible spatial patterns of the scene (there is no centre nor periphery any longer)'.[21] Again, the ways in which this takes place are heterogeneous depending on the thinker in question, but all poststructuralists agree that the subject must be displaced from the foundational status long afforded it and rethought from and through the differential structures and processes subtending it. Whereas this offers a radical critique of past thinking on the subject, it also brings forth the question that motivates this book: are poststructuralists able to offer a coherent account of autonomous, intentional agency to complement their radical critiques of the foundational subject?

The Problem of Poststructuralist Agency

Although accepting that poststructuralists offer radical critiques of the subject, various criticisms from different schools of thought have long argued that they do so by sacrificing agential autonomy. From an existentialist perspective, for example, Jean-Paul Sartre continuously rejected structuralist critiques of humanism and binary logic, suggesting in a 1966 interview published in *L'Arc* that they had emptied their analyses of what he considered to be essential: a certain emphasising of the subject and approach to history, and a confrontation with traditional philosophy on its terms.[22] In contrast, Sartre continues to insist on the primacy of the subject who chooses how to interact with a more or less conditioning world. The implicit point for him is that without this primary position, resistance or political action is simply not possible.[23]

Luc Ferry and Alain Renaut take a slightly different line of attack that questions the totalising nature of the poststructuralist critique of the subject: 'the error or illusion shared by all the philosophical currents to which the ideal type of the sixties can be applied, the error of assimilating those forms of subjectivity and of believing it could massively denounce *all* subjectivity or *all* humanism'.[24] Their point is twofold: the poststructuralist critique is mistaken in prophesying the coming end of the subject *and*, linked to this, poststructuralist thought continues to depend upon a certain conception of subjectivity. It therefore fails in its stated aim of overcoming the subject to offer an ontological analysis based on pre-personal differential relations. With this, Ferry and Renaut defend a similar point to the one that motivates this book; the difference, however, is that they understand that poststructuralism aims to overcome *all* forms of subjectivity to focus solely on the pre-personal differential ontological relations subtending entities and so criticise the continuing dependence and affirmation of subjectivity. In contrast, I argue that this is a mistaken, though often repeated, understanding of the purpose behind poststructuralist thought, which does not so much aim to overcome all forms of subjectivity as rethink a certain conception of the constituting foundational subject to offer an alternative based on a constituted founded subject. As a consequence, the various poststructuralist thinkers do not aim to leave the subject behind *per se*, but aim to abandon a particular conception of the subject to reconceive of it based on a 'prior' foundation.

Nevertheless, a variety of thinkers from critical theory and feminism have also questioned the reconceptualised notion of the subject offered, claiming that it is inadequate and/or is not logically permitted by the poststructuralist critique of the constituting founding subject. Jürgen Habermas, for example, engages with Foucault and Castoriadis, claiming that the former's conception of power is badly flawed, in so far as it is constructed around the same binary opposition as the tradition rejected, but simply inverts the aspect traditionally privileged:

> Foucault abruptly reverses power's truth-dependency into the power-dependency of truth. Then foundational power no longer need be bound to the competences of acting and judging subjects – power becomes subjectless. But no one can escape the strategic constraints of the philosophy of the subject merely by performing operations of reversal upon its basic concepts.[25]

Based on this, Habermas concludes that 'Foucault cannot do away with all the *aporias* he attributes to the philosophy of the subject by means of a concept of power borrowed from the philosophy of the subject itself.'[26] By providing a subjectless conception of power, Habermas charges that Foucault provides no means for effecting social change: 'the danger of anthropocentrism is banished only when under the incorruptible gaze of genealogy, discourses emerge and pop up like glittering bubbles from a swamp of anonymous processes of subjugation'.[27] On this reading, Foucault's conception of power does away with any form of political action, which is held to be an effect of random alterations to the underlying power relations.

Even when poststructuralists do offer conceptions of autonomous agency, Habermas critically questions them. For example, he recognises that Castoriadis affirms a notion of autonomy, but rejects it because he thinks that it is too individually orientated, leaving 'no room for an intersubjective praxis for which socialized individuals are *accountable*. In the end, social praxis disappears in the anonymous hurly-burly of the institutionalization of ever new worlds from the imaginary dimension.'[28] Although I will argue that this conclusion is based on a simplification and erroneous presentation of Castoriadis's position, Habermas suggests that Castoriadis gets round the problem of agency by simply reaffirming a monadic substance-based conception of subjectivity, before criticising Castoriadis for ignoring the social constitution of individual agency.

Axel Honneth has been somewhat more sympathetic to poststructuralist thought, specifically in its Derridean form, for its so-called ethical turn towards justice and, indeed, uses it to criticise Habermas's discourse ethics,[29] but he has been a vociferous critique of other aspects of poststructuralist thought.[30] For example, he repeats Habermas's critique of the role that the Foucaultian subject is capable of playing to bring about change:

> Since [Foucault] wanted to describe the genesis of structure of thought from the estranged perspective of structuralism as an anonymous activity of the formation of identity, as a subjectless appearance and disappearance of scientific discourses, he had to leave unanswered the question whether the constitution of new contents of knowledge and forms of thought is to be derived from the chance impulses of a blind history of events or from the specific constellation of a historical situation.[31]

Indeed, Honneth goes further by claiming to identify a tension that runs throughout Foucault's analysis, which, on the one hand, makes the subject a 'fictive unity generated either by anonymous rules of discourse or produced by violent strategies of domination',[32] while, on the other hand, continuing to emphasise the suffering, domination and harm imposed on the subject by repressive historical structures. Honneth argues that the first ontological position cancels out the possibility of the second ethical critique: 'although everything in his critique of the modern age appears concentrated on the suffering of the human body under the disciplinary action of the modern apparatus of power, there is nothing *in* his theory which could articulate this suffering *as* suffering'.[33] Having emptied the subject of all properties to make it an effect of ever-changing power relations, there is, strictly speaking, nothing unified that suffers. On this argument, the choice facing poststructuralism is a stark one: either reconceptualise the subject around some form of identity and so weaken, if not abandon, its ontological focus on differential processes, or affirm its ontological analysis and so abandon 'the idea of individual autonomy because one can no longer simply state in what way the subject is to attain a higher degree of self-determination or transparency'.[34]

Commentators from a certain strand of feminist theory – one that insists on the foundational importance of an unbending (sexed) body – have also long attacked poststructuralist analyses, arguing that their focus on pre-personal ontological forces and processes undermines the socio-historical embeddedness of individuals and/or rejects the fundamental sexual difference between men and women.[35] As a consequence, it not only projects a flawed conception of subjective agency, but is also unable to offer a theoretical standpoint from which to fight repression, domination and injustice.

Toril Moi offers one of the earliest types of this critique. Focusing on Foucault, she argues that he offers a conception of power relations that prevents any escape from power and, in so doing, undermines the possibility of a feminist critique of patriarchy. For Moi, Foucault's conception of power provides a 'sado-masochistic spiral of power and resistance, which circling endlessly in heterogeneous movement, creates a space in which it will be quite impossible convincingly to argue that women under patriarchy constitute an oppressed group, let alone develop a theory of their liberation'.[36] As I will show, however, this does significant disservice to Foucault's notion of power, which explicitly distinguishes power from patriarchal forms of domination.[37] While Foucault rejects the notion that it is possible to offer a theory of liberation from power *per se*, if by this is meant a theory that frees the individual from all forms of power, there is no reason why patriarchal manifestations of power relations cannot be resisted.

Moi's second critique attacks the Foucaultian locus of resistance: 'If we return to our original question: "what resists powers?", it would seem that Foucault can give no answer at all. His celebratory account of the pleasure of power degenerates into a kind of pan-powerism where "power" has becomes a nebulous, mystical element beyond the reach of human reason.'[38] With this, Moi identifies the crux of the argument that is typically made against the notion of poststructuralist agency: by focusing on subtending power relations and forces, poststructuralist thought is unable to identify the locus of change or, in this case, resistance. As a consequence, political change seems to magically and mystically appear regardless of human action.

Moi's critique is extended by Nancy Hartsock, who wonders why, just when women are starting to question the rules and norms of patriarchal domination, the notion of the unified subject that permits such a question is suddenly under attack. While denying that she is proposing a conspiracy, Hartsock suggests that poststructuralists do not offer a *critique* of domination *per se*, but are part of a continuing aspect of Western thinking that perpetuates subtle and cunning modes of thinking that reinstantiate patriarchal domination by undermining the categories of 'men' and 'women' that would permit a critique of such domination.[39] From this general critique of what she takes to be 'poststructuralism', she focuses on Foucault's notion of power to argue that, by insisting that power relations subtend all entities and cannot be thought as a possession or in zero-sum games, it 'makes it very difficult to locate discrimination, including discrimination in gender relations'.[40] The problem is that 'his account makes room only for abstract individuals, not women, men, or workers'.[41] Her proposed solution is 'to engage in the historical, political, and theoretical process of constituting ourselves as subjects as well as objects of history'.[42] Beyond the question of how this differs from Foucault's historically informed analysis, the obvious issue arising from Hartsock's proposal is that it presupposes a foundational (and binary sexed) subject that constitutes itself, thereby denying the need for a historical or theoretical analysis of the conditions accompanying that process. Nevertheless, for Hartsock, the process appears to be an individual one based, presumably, on the agent's will. It therefore not only simply ignores the poststructuralist critique, but seems to return to a pre-structuralist conception of the foundational subject.

Kate Soper complements these critiques by rejecting the supposed asexuality of the poststructuralist subject. By focusing on pre-personal ontological forces or discourses, she argues that poststructuralists are unable to account for the actual differences between 'men' and 'women'. Whereas poststructuralists argue that these terms are discursive and, to greater or lesser degree, constructed, Soper insists on an ahistoric sexual difference between the two sexes that is based on certain ontological differences. As a consequence, she claims that, whereas men and women may experience events, '*all* men and *all* women are subject to them *differently*'.[43] With this, Soper not only (implicitly) reverts to a sex/gender essentialism – in so far as each sex is defined by different ahistoric essential characteristics – but also remains within a binary gender opposition that excludes alternative categories, such as transgender. Soper's use of a gender essentialism to attack poststructuralist thought reverts, then, to a pre-structuralist understanding and so – despite her affirmation to the contrary – does not engage with poststructuralism on its own terms.

One feminist critique that does aim to engage with poststructuralist thought on its own terms is Seyla Benhabib's critique of Judith Butler's work. Benhabib doubts 'whether Butler's performative theory of the constitution of gender identity can do justice to the complexities of the onto-genetic origins of gender in the human person' or, indeed, 'lead us to rethink a new configuration of subjectivity'.[44] The basic problem is, so Benhabib affirms, that Butler's conception of the onto-genesis of the subject is too thin: 'what mechanisms and dynamics are involved in the developmental process through which the human infant, a vulnerable and dependent body, becomes a distinct self with the ability to speak its language and the ability to participate in the complex social process which define its world?'[45] That Butler notes that the subject is formed discursively leads Benhabib to question 'how can one by constituted by discourse without being determined by it?',[46] especially given that Butler seems to reject any form of essentialism or pre-discursive features that may be said to escape and so resist the dominant discourse. Without such an account of the subject, it is unclear 'what enables the self to "vary" the gender codes such as to resist hegemonic discourses? What psychic, intellectual, or other sources of creativity and resistance must we attribute to human subjects for such variation to be possible?'[47] For Benhabib, Butler simply does not have the conceptual tools to explain how the subject, formed through power relations and discourses, can effect political action to resist and reconfigure those relations.

This issue forms part of Martha Nussbaum's infamous critique of Butler's thinking, which starts with complaints about the 'ponderous' nature of Butler's writing, Butler's treatment of the other which Nussbaum feels is not sufficiently nuanced, and the obscurity and lack of logical force to Butler's arguments.[48] However, Nussbaum's two major critiques are orientated against Butler's perceived lack of a normative stance to guide political action and her performative theory of the self. Regarding the former, Nussbaum questions 'Butler's naïvely empty politics'[49] in which subversion for subversion's sake is celebrated. This strictly negative approach to politics is held to be simply incapable of producing a nuanced analysis that distinguishes between forms of subversion that improve an individual's material conditions and those that do not. Because she does not offer a normative stance and, indeed, rejects all normative stances because they are held to reduce heterogeneity to a singular discourse or sign, Nussbaum claims that Butler can, at most, only guide political action negatively – it must subvert already existing power structures and relations – but cannot produce positive political norms to create an alternative. By celebrating all action that subverts dominant norms, Butler, and on Nussbaum's telling poststructuralists generally, cannot legitimately criticise anything. As a consequence, Butler ends up affirming political subversion for its own sake. The danger in taking this position, however, is that it can end up 'collaborat[ing] with evil' just because it is subversive.[50]

Furthermore, Nussbaum maintains that Butler's constructionist-performative analysis empties the subject of all the attributes that would allow it to contribute to fighting repression. There are two aspects to this. First, Nussbaum (mis)reads Butler's performative theory of the subject as entailing an aesthetic performance and then questions the political effectiveness of her performative theory:

> Parodic performance is not so bad when you are a powerful tenured academic in a liberal university. But here is where Butler's focus on the symbolic, her proud neglect of the material side of life, becomes a fatal blindness. For women who are hungry, beaten, raped, it is not sexy or liberating to reenact, however paradoxically, the conditions of hunger, illiteracy, disenfranchisement, beating, and rape. Such women prefer food, school, votes, and the integrity of the body.[51]

While critical of the proposals that she understands Butler to put forward, Nussbaum also questions whether the Butlerian subject is actually capable of effecting performative gestures. After all, her subject is so empty that it is not clear where the agency emanates from. Thus, while admitting that 'Butler does in the end want to say that we have a kind of agency, an ability to undertake change and resistance', Nussbaum asks: 'but where does this ability come from, if there is no structure in the personality that is not thoroughly power's creation?'[52] Without an in-built structure divorced, to whatever degree, from power structures and social norms, Butler cannot show how the subject can fight repression or injustice. As such, her thought leads to 'hip quietism' in which 'we [simply] ought to wait to see what the political struggle itself throws up, rather than prescribe in advance to its participants'.[53]

Nussbaum's polemic is rather unsubtle and totalising,[54] but it does represent a certain, almost dominant, perception about poststructuralist thinking from within mainstream (liberal) theory that tends to reject it *tout court*. A more nuanced critical analysis has been provided by feminist writers more sympathetic to the poststructuralist position. Lois McNay, for example, offers a general critique of poststructuralist thinking on the subject that is developed from and accompanied by a number of specific critiques of various poststructuralist thinkers. For example, she laments the focus that, she argues, poststructuralist thinkers have placed on processes of subjection and subjugation, claiming that this implies a 'negative moment'[55] with regard to the issue of identity construction. Her fundamental problem with such an approach is that it offers a 'passive conception of the subject' that is accompanied by 'an etiolated conception of agency which cannot explain how individuals may respond in an unanticipated or creative fashion to complex social relations'.[56]

Second, the poststructuralist critique is understood to depend upon a dispersed notion of identity, whether from power relations, symbolic discourse or ontological forces and processes, which results in 'subjectivity becom[ing] a free-floating and atemporal entity which lacks historical depth or *durée*'.[57] Thus, in relation to psychoanalytic approaches to poststructuralism, such as that provided by Lacan, McNay complains that 'although the destabilising form of the category of the unconscious points to ways in which the internalisation of the law of the symbolic can be resisted, a more substantive account of agency beyond the individualist terms of a libidinal politics is foreclosed'.[58] Similarly, in relation to Butler's work, McNay charges that 'agency remains an abstract structural potentiality which is sufficiently undifferentiated that it becomes difficult, for example, to distinguish whether an act is politically effective or not given that all identity is performatively constructed'.[59] The implicit point being that a more socio-historically differentiated account of subjective agency is required.

The Argument

These are by no means all the lines of critique that have been proposed against poststructuralist thinking on the subject and agency, but I have spent some time outlining them to show both their historical longevity and, indeed, their diverse nature. After all, it might be thought that, if such a diverse group of commentators, coming from different theoretical positions and 'schools' of thought, agree on this point, there must be something to it. For the purposes of this book, I understand that the common charge implicitly linking these disparate individuals is that, while poststructuralists desire to alter our understanding of the world, their critiques of anthropocentric essentialism, at both symbolic and material levels, empty the subject of all possibilities for autonomous, intentional agency.

To further clarify what this means, it is helpful to follow Nathan Widder in holding that, minimally speaking, '[t]he subject may loosely be defined in terms of a being whose relation-to-self is sufficient for it to recognise and represent – or, perhaps better, to "re-cognise" and "re-present" – itself as a unified point of reference in relation to its agency',[60] with 'agency' being a mode of subjectivity wherein the subject is capable of intentionally effecting its own movements and thoughts. The question then becomes whether poststructuralist thought is capable of offering a conception of subjectivity that permits agency. If, as the critics discussed charge, poststructuralist thought makes the subject a determined effect of pre-personal structures and processes, does this not undermine the possibility that the subject can act on or against the pre-personal structures that ground it? After all, any individual action would simply be an effect of those pre-personal processes. To Karl Marx's famous dictum that 'the philosophers have only *interpreted* the world in various ways, the point is to *change* it',[61] its critics charge that the poststructuralist position cannot effect change; the philosophers, or anyone else for that matter, must simply wait for the pre-personal ontological or discursive relations and structures constituting reality to change. Poststructuralists affirm radical change, all the while undermining any form of individually determined action that could bring it about.

The overall aim of this book is to defend poststructuralism against this charge. One way of achieving this would be to dissolve the problem by claiming that it is premised on a particular conception of the political rejected by the poststructuralists approach; namely, one whereby political change is simply premised on the actions of a foundational autonomous agent. That poststructuralists claim that the subject is an effect of pre-personal differential ontological processes means that the notion of politics accompanying it also has to change; it can no longer be premised on autonomous, intentional, agential action. This disarms the critique by rejecting its basic premise that political action is and should be based on the intentional agency of a founding subject. Instead, it calls for a new conception of politics, one that ties political change to ontological alterations and, in so doing, means that if political change occurs, it does so irrespective of individual intentional input. The problem with such an approach, however, is that it 1) is unlikely to convince those not already convinced by the poststructuralist critique, and 2) reduces politics to ontology. For these reasons, this book takes a different, arguably more challenging, approach that aims to meet the critique on its own terms by showing that poststructuralist thinkers do engage with the question of agency and, indeed, offer numerous conceptions of human intentional agency to meet the charge laid against it; namely, that their critique of the foundational subject prevents them from offering a logically coherent account of agency that allows subjects to purposefully engage in (political) action to bring about the transformation(s) that poststructuralist thinkers affirm.

Strangely, this issue has been relatively ignored in the literature, with commentators either content to ignore or simply bypass it to descriptively, rather than critically, outline what each poststructuralist thinker engaged with affirms politically. Etienne Balibar and Caroline Williams are among the few to take it up, with both pointing out that the so-called death of the subject so often attributed to poststructuralist thinkers has been misunderstood and/or greatly exaggerated.[62] Balibar's contribution is, however, limited to a single article, thereby preventing him from engaging with specific poststructuralist thinkers to show how this manifests itself in their thinking, while Williams's book-length study aims to show the persistence of the subject in twentieth-century French philosophy. For all its merits, it is not, then, orientated by and to the same problematic that motivates this study – which is to show that, contrary to its critics, poststructuralist thought offers a coherent theory of intentional agency – and in holding that the subject persists, comes dangerously close to claiming that the subject is somehow desperately hanging on for dear life against attempts to remove it from thought.

Rather than hanging on for its life, I argue that 'the subject' is integral to poststructuralist thought, which, following Balibar's suggestion, is conditioned by a 'simultaneous operation of *deconstruction* and *reconstruction of the subject*, or deconstruction of the subject as *arche* (cause, principle, origin) and reconstruction of subjectivity as an *effect*, or in yet another formulation, a passage from constitutive to constituted subjectivity'.[63] Poststructuralist thought does not, then, aim to annihilate the subject as is often taken to be the case, but *deposes* a specific conception of the subject, where 'it' is held to be the foundation or constituting entity for all else, to rethink or reconstitute the subject in terms of a constituted effect of pre-personal/subject sources. As a consequence, while poststructuralist thought may reject the notion of an *unencumbered* agent who exists outside of socio-historical context to freely choose how to act in and on the world, this does not mean that *agency per se* is abolished. Rather, we have to rethink the nature of and scope for agential action from a subject that is constituted rather than constituting.

My fundamental argument, therefore, is that rather than simply discard the subject as an effect of pre-personal relations or processes, poststructuralist thinkers, albeit in different ways, aim to *depose* one dominant form of subjectivity so as to *propose* another, with this alternative thought as a constituted effect of the ontological premises of poststructuralism (differential, multiple, non-essentialist and non-substantial, continuously becoming, and so on). Having shown that poststructuralism rethinks the subject, I respond to the related question of whether there is a way for poststructuralist thought to defend itself against the charge that its reliance on pre-individual processes and structures undermines individual intentional (political) agency. In other words, does poststructuralist thought lead, as a number of its critics complain, to political quietism?

To reject this notion, I show that it is based on a particular conception of poststructuralism, gleaned from a narrow selection of authors and texts often outlined in caricature. Furthermore, critics base their analysis on two conceptual errors. First, they tend to confuse 'effect' with 'determine' so that when poststructuralist thinkers are understood to decentre the subject by making it an *effect* of a prior process (social, historical, discursive and so on), their critics understand that they are claiming that the subject is *determined* by those pre-subject processes. I will argue that this is a consequence of a reductive or particularly uncharitable reading or hermeneutical errors regarding the handling of key texts.

Second, critics tend to conflate 'unencumbered agency' with 'agency' so that when poststructuralists reject the former, based as it is on a notion of a constituting subject who exists outside socio-historic-symbolic structures, their critics argue that this disqualifies *all* forms of agency. However, to claim that *unencumbered* agency is the only kind possible is to depend upon a particularly reductionist understanding of the concept. After all, as Mark Bevir explains, 'to deny that subjects can escape from all social influence is not to deny that they can act creatively for reasons that make sense to them'.[64] That subjects emanate from others does not necessarily mean that they are determined by that source. As Amy Allen points out, 'children are shaped from birth by the practice, beliefs, and superior power of their parents. However, no one who actually has children will think for a second that this statement implies that children have no agency or will but are instead completely determined and controlled by their parents.'[65] Building on this, I argue that, while poststructuralist thinkers reject the notion of an unencumbered, constituting subject, they replace it with a notion of an embedded constituted subject – which is understood to be an effect of pre-personal socio-historical-symbolic processes – that is able to intentionally act, to varying degrees, *within* its conditioning environment.

However, while I show that each of the thinkers engaged with continues to (often implicitly) insist that the subject is capable of action, the responses provided as to how this is possible are often problematic. There are a variety of reasons for this that will be outlined as I proceed, but the disagreements point to a cleavage within poststructuralist thinking based on its relationship to psychoanalysis and the unconscious. While recognising that Deleuze, Derrida and Foucault undertake extensive engagements with psychoanalytic theory,[66] my argument is guided by the contention that they do not sufficiently or coherently discuss or incorporate the notion of the psyche and, in particular, the conscious–unconscious split into their rethinking of the subject, with the consequence that they struggle to satisfactorily account for how their decentred subject is capable of intentional agency to effect its pre-personal 'foundations'.

In contrast, those poststructuralists, such as Butler, Castoriadis, Kristeva and Lacan, who do explicitly split the subject from the psyche and distinguish between the conscious and unconscious are better able to engage with the question of how the decentred subject is capable of such agency. By explicitly incorporating the unconscious into their explanations, they decentre the (conscious) subject and start to develop the conceptual distinctions to explain how such a subject can be conditioned by pre-personal structures and processes, but still choose how to act in relation to them. However, I argue that in the case of Butler, Kristeva and Lacan, this splitting does not go far enough and so fails to resolve the issue of how the subject who is *unconsciously* conditioned by pre-personal structures and processes is also able to (*consciously*) choose how to react to them.

In contrast, I argue that Castoriadis surmounts this objection because he does not just split the subject from the psyche and distinguish between the conscious and unconscious; he also splits the unconscious so that it is defined by a part that internalises the social norms that allow it to function and survive in society *and* an asocial fluctuating monadic 'core' that contests that socialisation and, in being distinct from the socialised part, allows the subject to choose how to act in relation to its social norms. While this appears to establish and depend upon a problematic ontological opposition between the psychic monadic core and social norms, Castoriadis's acceptance of a limited form of psychic asociality is understood in terms of processes and so remains consistent with the poststructuralist critique of foundationalism, essentialism and substantive identity, while he shows that the pseudo-totality that is the human being works to overcome the psyche/society opposition. I argue, therefore, that his conception offers the most developed poststructuralist account of agency because it produces a sophisticated, multidimensional account of the constituted subject and complements it with a detailed, subtle and heterogeneous analysis of the conditions that permit the *embodied* subject to act autonomously despite being conditioned by pre-personal (socio-historic-symbolic) forces and processes.

Chapter Structure

To outline this, the book is divided into two parts distinguished by those poststructuralist thinkers who offer *primarily* ontologically and socially orientated analyses (Part I) and those who offer psychoanalytically orientated ones (Part II). However, to reiterate, my argument is *not* that the thinkers engaged with in Part I ignore or are not interested in psychoanalysis or questions of the psyche; it is that, at the very least, they do not incorporate its insights into their positive conceptions of the subject with the same emphasis that the thinkers engaged with in Part II do. Furthermore, to muddy the structural division further, those authors included in Part II also recognise, focus on and incorporate the socio-historic-symbolic insights found in the non-psychoanalytical accounts of Part I. I divide the authors in this way for organisational and hermeneutical reasons to most clearly develop and outline my claim that because the thinkers in Part II most fully and explicitly take into consideration the psyche as part of their reconstruction of the subject, they provide the more sophisticated and subtle analyses of the decentred subject's capacity for intentional agency.

Furthermore, within each part, the thinkers are not placed chronologically, but in terms of conceptual coherence. This is particularly the case in Part II, where, for example, the chapter on Butler is placed before that on Lacan because, even though he precedes her historically, *conceptually* her thinking combines Foucault's socio-historical analysis with Freudian psychoanalysis to pave the way for the privileging of psychoanalytical categories and approaches found in the later chapters on Lacan, Kristeva and Castoriadis. Similarly, Castoriadis comes after Kristeva even though he historically preceded her because I argue that he offers a more *conceptually* satisfactory response to the question of poststructuralist agency.

Part I, entitled 'Decentring the Subject', is composed of four chapters. Chapter 1 engages with Gilles Deleuze's critique of the foundational Cartesian subject as thought from and through his privileging of difference. The affirmation of difference (over identity) is often understood to be the defining motif of poststructuralist thought, with Deleuze's thinking being particularly important to this endeavour. Starting with Deleuze's thinking on this matter, including its implications for any questioning of subjectivity and agency, not only demonstrates the radicality of his critique – it aims at nothing other than a complete overhaul of the categories of Western philosophy – but also sets the scene for subsequent thinkers who also affirm the fundamental importance of difference. I first show that Deleuze aims to undermine the notion of the foundational, essentialist subject to rethink the subject from difference, before, second, engaging with whether this permits a coherent account of intentional agency. While noting that this question has garnered significant contemporary debate, I conclude that Deleuze's positive comments on the topic are simply too ambiguous and indeterminate to be taken as offering a definitive account of agency, while, in any case, he appears to purposely reject the anthropocentrism that underpins the question of whether the subject thought from difference is capable of autonomous, intentional agency. Instead, he asks for a radical reformulation of the question in terms of the pre-personal ontological 'singularities' structuring reality, rather than of the subject that is their effect. As such, Deleuze is unable to offer an adequate response to the question motivating this volume, not necessarily due to a failing in his thinking, but because he *purposely* rejects any formulation of the question in terms of subjectivities and, by extension, intentionality.

However, whereas Deleuze privileges difference over the identity that he maintains has traditionally been used to think subjectivity, Jacques Derrida (Chapter 2) criticises this inversion, claiming that it does not go far enough in deconstructing the logic of the identity model. Rather than privilege 'identity' or 'difference', Derrida insists that there is a 'prior' moment that makes possible the opposition between these terms. Terming this *différance* and using 'it' to rethink the subject – a discussion that also brings to the fore the relationship between sexuality and subjectivity as mediated through Heidegger's thinking – Derrida reaffirms the deconstruction of one historically dominant form of subjectivity to stimulate a rethinking (rather than abandonment) of subjectivity. I argue, however, that he simply says too little on what the resultant subject entails and little, if anything, on the question of agency, tending to simply take it for granted that the subject can 'choose' how to act.

I complement these two chapters with two on Foucault, showing how he moves the decentring of the subject away from the ontological concerns prevalent in Deleuze and Derrida to social-historical concerns based in a specific conception of power relations. To this end, Chapter 3 turns to Foucault's earlier 'archaeological' and 'genealogical' works to outline their significance for the question of 'the subject' and show that it is wrong to claim, as many critics have, that Foucault simply makes the subject an effect of power relations. Through a detailed textual analysis, I identify that Foucault holds that, while the subject is an effect of power relations, this does not mean that the subject is *determined* by them. Rather, the individual is held to be a relay point through which power relations flow and, as such, is capable of redirecting those power relations. Foucault is, then, the first thinker engaged with who explicitly argues that the decentred subject is capable of agency.

Chapter 4 extends this by focusing on Foucault's later work, where he builds on his early decentring of the subject to rethink the *self* as being capable of self-constitution. This affirms his earlier claim that the subject-as-self is not just conditioned by power relations, but can also choose how to act in relation to them. Ultimately, however, I argue that his account of what permits such agency is simply too thin to adequately account for its possibility. The chapters on Derrida and Foucault also engage with the question of sexuality to counter the charge that poststructuralist thought ignores sexuality and the sexual difference, while in so doing also preparing the way for the engagement with later feminist poststructuralist accounts in Chapters 5 (Butler) and 7 (Kristeva).

Having shown that Deleuze, Derrida and Foucault do not simply aim to annihilate the subject but rethink it in founded rather than founding terms and even start to account for how agency is possible within these terms, Part II, entitled 'Turning to the Psyche', transitions to psychoanalytically orientated accounts to argue that these provide the strongest engagement with the question of how a decentred subject is capable of agency. To ease the transition between the two parts and approaches, Chapter 5 deals with Judith Butler's analysis because she takes off from Foucault's account of power relations but combines it with insights from Freudian psychoanalysis. I first outline her critique of the essentialist, substantial subject to show that her theory of performativity maintains that the subject is conditioned by social norms, linguistic structures and the body. I then show that she also brings the question of the unconscious into the discussion – a concept that will take on increasing importance in subsequent chapters – before outlining what this means for her account of agency to argue that, for Butler, agency is defined by and from the disjunction between the social and psyche.

In making this claim, I counter two dominant, but contradictory, critiques of Butler's work: 1) that she cannot offer an account of agency because she holds that socio-symbolic norms *determine* the subject; and 2) that she does offer an account of agency, but it is too thin, which has led to the further claim that she must rely on a form of transcendence that she otherwise rejects. I argue against 1), but take up a qualified version of 2) by agreeing that her account of agency is too thin. While she decentres the subject from a foundational position, and maintains that the constituted subject continues to be capable of agency, we need a far more precise and subtler conception of where intentional agency is located 'within' the subject to permit it to actually act once the site for agency has been opened by the constantly changing alterations in the socio-symbolic systems it is an effect of and inhabits.

While Butler develops her analysis from insights gained from Freud and is critical of Lacanian psychoanalysis, I argue that it is Lacan's thinking that contributed most to 'the' poststructuralist rethinking of the subject and, by extension, agency. For this reason, Chapter 6 turns to Lacan to first outline his critique of the Cartesian subject, before moving to his famous real, symbolic and imaginary schema. I argue that the Lacanian subject is a consequence of the entwinement of the three registers, with their interrelationship constantly and momentarily configuring itself into bursts of agency that permit the subject to act in ways that are not predefined by its symbolic conditions. However, I conclude by showing that Lacan is simply not sufficiently clear on the mechanics of agency: while the lack of the real accounts for how agency is possible for a subject conditioned by and resulting from symbolic relations, it does not adequately explain how the disruption caused to the symbolic realm by the lack of the real subsequently permits the subject to decide – or whatever mechanism this takes place through – to act in a positive expressive form.

Chapter 7 moves from Lacan's to Kristeva's account of the subject, an analysis that is largely conducted *against* the former. Two differences stand out. First, Kristeva returns to Freud to claim, contra Lacan, that the unconscious is defined by drives rather than language. Second, she criticises Lacan's account of the symbolic, claiming that it ignores the semiotic, by which she means non-conceptual signification. Putting the two critiques together allows Kristeva to argue that the subject is always in process due to the complex amalgamation of drives, semiotic and symbolic significations, and social norms. I link this to her political analysis and, in particular, her critique of the impact that contemporary capitalist society has on the psyche. Kristeva holds that, historically, the psyche's development meant that it was marked by negativity, which provided the subject with some independence from the social norms it was embedded within. This independence was crucial to permit the subject to 'freely' express itself. Kristeva warns, however, that contemporary capitalist society has undermined this negative space, with the consequence that psychic space and hence freedom has shrunk. Her solution is to search for new semiotic forms of revolt to reopen the division between the psyche and social to enact non-conceptual and non-instrumental forms of expression.

It is here that the question of agency enters Kristeva's analysis. While her clinical work depends upon the subject being capable of acting to change itself, she never provides a detailed discussion of agency or of how and where it fits into her schema. This has given rise to a debate in the literature between those who defend Kristeva by claiming that she does offer a theory of agency that shows how the subject can effect social change and those who claim that she does not. I side with the latter by arguing that the former do not actually identify what agency entails for Kristeva, but simply conflate it with her theory of the subject-in-process. As a consequence, and despite her conceptual innovations, Kristeva depends on a theory of agency that her analysis of the subject-in-process is too thin to support.

Chapters 1–7 chart the main trajectories through which poststructuralist thinkers have both decentred the subject from its long-held foundational role *and* attempted to reconstruct the subject from what results. While these show that the poststructuralist paradigm is far more sophisticated than is typically appreciated with regard to the subject – the subject is not simply decentred, but is rethought as an embodied socio-symbolic being – they also link the discussion to the issue of autonomous, intentional agency. I have, however, claimed that the various 'solutions' proposed have been, in some way, structurally problematic because the notion of agency offered is underdeveloped, inconsistent with other aspects of the proponent's thought, or relies upon a conception of the subject that is too thin to permit such agency.

In contrast, Chapter 8 turns to the work of Cornelius Castoriadis, who, I argue, develops an embodied and socially-symbolically embedded notion of the subject that is also sufficiently conceptually thick to offer a sophisticated, subtle and coherent analysis of how such a subject is capable of intentional agency. To outline this, I show that Castoriadis splits the subject between an initial psychic monad – the ontological core of the psyche that he also calls the 'little screaming monster'[67] – and the *individual*, with the latter resulting from the socialisation of the former that is necessary to ensure the subject's survival. Part of the process of successfully socialising the psyche monad is to find avenues *within* the social-historical formation whereby the autonomy of the psychic monad can express itself. In this way, Castoriadis not only insists that the socialised individual must continue to act, but that such agency is integral to the well-being of the subject.

This does, however, lead back to the question of whether it is logically possible for Castoriadis to claim that the socialised individual is capable of such agency. In response, I suggest that Castoriadis introduces a conceptual innovation. Whereas psychoanalytically orientated poststructuralists, such as Butler, Kristeva and Lacan, focus on the psyche, split it between the conscious and unconscious, and focus on the latter, Castoriadis goes one step further by also splitting the unconscious between what might be called the 'socialised unconscious', 'housing' the social norms and values learned and incorporated from the socialisation process, and the 'primal unconscious which is the monadic core of the psyche'[68] that always remains distinct from the former. With this split, Castoriadis is able to show that, while the subject is embodied and socially founded and embedded, there is a part of the subject's psyche – itself always in flux – that remains distinct from its social norms to permit and explain how the socialised individual is capable of autonomously and intentionally choosing its actions.

The concluding chapter provides a brief overview of the argument to show that, contrary to their critics, the issue of the subject and the question of agency are central, if at times problematic, topics for poststructuralist thinkers and that Castoriadis provides the most sophisticated response to them. I subsequently go on to clarify the normativity inherent in poststructuralist thinking to start to respond to the question of the type of politics permitted, depended upon and indeed affirmed from this.

Notes

1. François Dosse, *History of Structuralism, Volume 1: The Rising Sign, 1945–1966*, trans. Deborah Glassman (Minneapolis, MN: University of Minnesota Press, 1997), p. xxiii. Dosse collapses 'poststructuralism' into structuralism; a not uncontroversial move. For example, Tilottama Rajan (*Deconstruction and the Remainders of Phenomenology: Sartre, Derrida, Foucault, Baudrillard* [Stanford, CA: Stanford University Press, 2002]) explicitly seeks to distinguish between them, all the while further differentiating each from 'deconstruction', while Craig Lundy ('From Structuralism to Poststructuralism', in Benoît Dillet, Iain MacKenzie and Robert Porter [eds], *The Edinburgh Companion to Poststructuralism* [Edinburgh: Edinburgh University Press, 2013], pp. 69–94) argues that they are different but related, in so far as 'poststructuralism' is understood to be a particular transformative out-growth of 'structuralism'.
2. Famously, in 1998 Judith Butler was awarded the (short-lived) Bad Writing award by the journal *Philosophy and Literature* (see Denis Dutton, 'The Bad Writing Contest: Press Releases, 1996–1998', http://www.denisdutton.com/bad_writing.htm [accessed 22 August 2017]).

3. Jacques Derrida suggests that 'poststructuralism' is an American invention, 'a word unknown in France until its "return" from the United States' ('Letter to a Japanese Friend', trans. David Wood and Andrew Benjamin, in *Psyche: Inventions of the Other, Volume 2*, ed. Peggy Kamuf and Elizabeth Rottenberg [Stanford, CA: Stanford University Press, 2008], pp. 1–6 [p. 3]).
4. Ferdinand de Saussure, *Course in General Linguistics*, ed. Charles Bally, Albert Sechehaye and Albert Riedlinger, trans. Roy Harris (Chicago: Open Court, 1986), p. 118.
5. Lionel Bailly, *Lacan* (London: OneWorld, 2009), p. 23.
6. The classic text on this issue is Jacques Derrida, 'Structure, Sign, and Play in the Discourse of the Human Sciences', in *Writing and Difference*, trans. Alan Bass (New York: Routledge, 2001), pp. 351–70.
7. Saul Newman, *Power and Politics in Poststructuralist Thought: New Theories of the Political* (Abingdon: Routledge, 2005), p. 5.
8. For the purposes of narration and because the meaning of these terms depends upon a whole conceptual apparatus that differs from thinker to thinker, I will, at this point, resist offering a guiding definition of this term, all the while using the terms 'subjectivity' and 'subject' interchangeably. This will change when I engage with how these concepts are conceptualised by the various poststructuralists.
9. Todd May, *The Political Philosophy of Poststructuralist Anarchism* (University Park, PA: Pennsylvania State University Press, 1994), pp. 77–8.
10. Judith Butler and Joan W. Scott, 'Introduction', in Judith Butler and Joan W. Scott (eds), *Feminists Theorize the Political* (Abingdon: Routledge, 1992), pp. xiii–xvii (p. xiv).
11. For example, Michel Foucault famously proclaimed '[l]et me announce once and for all that I am not a structuralist, and I confess, with the appropriate chagrin, that I am not an analytic philosopher. Nobody is perfect' ('Sexuality and Solitude', in *Ethics: Subjectivity and Truth, Essential Works of Foucault, Volume 1, 1954–1984*, ed. Paul Rabinow, trans. Robert Hurley et al. [London: Penguin, 1997], pp. 175–84 [p. 176]). As noted, Jacques Derrida was also uneasy about the term 'poststructuralism', noting that it was not heard in France until the theories of those associated with 'it' had been introduced to American academia and subsequently returned to France. For Derrida, then, 'poststructuralism' exists, but in a particular culturally specific sense as an American invention ('Letter to a Japanese Friend', p. 3). Julia Kristeva also notes the ambivalent status of the term 'poststructuralism' by, on the one hand, denying that the thinkers usually associated with the term were sufficiently theoretically homogeneous to permit their grouping, but, on the other hand, recognising that, despite this, the impact that they had on French intellectual life 'lends these writings their apparent cohesiveness and perhaps justifies the notion of a "poststructuralist group"' ('Julia Kristeva Speaks Out', in *Julia Kristeva: Interviews*, ed. Ross Mitchell Guberman [New York: Columbia University Press, 1996], pp. 257–70 [p. 259]).

12. The classic history of this movement is François Dosse's two-volume *History of Structuralism, Volume 1: The Rising Sign, 1945–1966*; and *Volume 2: The Sign Sets, 1967–Present*, trans. Deborah Glassman (Minneapolis, MN: University of Minnesota Press, 1997).
13. For one of the very few accounts that have tried to reconstruct Irigaray's thinking to point to a conception of agency therein, see Miri Rozmarin, 'Living Politically: An Irigarayan Notion of Agency as a Way of Life', *Hypatia*, 28.3, 2013, pp. 469–82.
14. See, for example, Lorenzo Chiesa, *Subjectivity and Otherness: A Philosophical Reading of Lacan* (Cambridge, MA: MIT Press, 2007); Adrian Johnston, *Time Driven: Metapsychology and the Splitting of the Drive* (Evanston, IL: Northwestern University Press, 2005); Slavoj Žižek, *Interrogating the Real* (London: Continuum, 2005); Alenka Zupančič, *Ethics of the Real: Kant and Lacan* (London: Verso, 2000).
15. Axel Honneth, 'Rescuing the Revolution with an Ontology: On Cornelius Castoriadis's Theory of Society', *Thesis Eleven*, 14.1, 1986, pp. 62–78 (pp. 69, 71).
16. Jürgen Habermas, 'Excursis on Cornelius Castoriadis: The Imaginary Institution', in *The Philosophical Discourse of Modernity: Twelve Lectures*, trans. Frederick Lawrence (Cambridge: Polity, 1987), pp. 327–35 (p. 333).
17. Suzi Adams, *Castoriadis's Ontology: Being and Creation* (New York: Fordham University Press, 2011), p. 84; Johann Michel, *Ricoeur and the Poststructuralists: Bourdieu, Derrida, Deleuze, Foucault, Castoriadis*, trans. Scott Davidson (New York: Rowman and Littlefield, 2015), p. 124.
18. Warren Breckman, *Adventures of the Symbolic: Post-Marxism and Radical Democracy* (New York: Columbia University Press, 2013), p. 98. It is important to note that Breckman does not distinguish between 'structuralism' and 'poststructuralism', but runs them together. Nevertheless, I suggest that Breckman's comments on Castoriadis's relation to 'structuralist' thought more accurately describe Castoriadis's bond to the way of thinking, with its emphasis on dynamic structures, fluidity, symbolic meaning, the decentred subject and so on, that are shared, albeit heterogeneously, by the style of thinking and, indeed, group of thinkers usually called 'poststructuralist'.
19. Friedrich Nietzsche, *Will to Power*, ed. Walter Kaufmann, trans. Walter Kaufmann and R. J. Hollingdale (New York: Vintage, 1968), §1067.
20. For an overview of Western anthropocentrism, see Gavin Rae, 'Anthropocentrism', in Henk ten Have (ed.), *Encyclopedia of Global Bioethics* (Dordrecht: Springer, 2014), pp. 1–12.
21. Adriana Cavarero, 'Inclining the Subject: Ethics, Alterity, and Natality', in Jane Elliott and Derek Attridge (eds), *Theory after 'Theory'* (Abingdon: Routledge, 2011), pp. 194–204 (p. 194).
22. Jean-Paul Sartre, 'Jean-Paul Sartre Répond', *L'Arc*, 30, October 1966, pp. 87–96.
23. For a discussion of Sartre's thinking, see Gavin Rae, *Realizing Freedom: Hegel, Sartre, and the Alienation of Human Being* (Basingstoke: Palgrave Macmillan, 2011).

24. Luc Ferry and Alain Renaut, *French Philosophy of the Sixties: An Essay on Antihumanism*, trans. Mary H. S. Cattans (Amherst, MA: University of Massachusetts Press, 1990), p. 31.
25. Jürgen Habermas, 'Some Questions concerning the Theory of Power: Foucault Again', in *The Philosophical Discourse of Modernity: Twelve Lectures*, trans. Frederick Lawrence (Cambridge: Polity, 1987), pp. 266–93 (p. 274).
26. Ibid., p. 274.
27. Ibid., p. 268.
28. Ibid., p. 330.
29. Axel Honneth, 'The Other of Justice: Habermas and the Ethical Challenge of Postmodernism', in Stephen K. White (ed.), *The Cambridge Companion to Habermas* (Cambridge: Cambridge University Press, 1995), pp. 289–324.
30. For a good overview of Honneth's critique of poststructuralism, see Robert Sinnerbrink, 'Power, Recognition, and Care: Honneth's Critique of Poststructuralist Social Philosophy', in Danielle Petherbridge (ed.), *Axel Honneth: Critical Essays* (Leiden: Brill, 2011), pp. 177–206.
31. Axel Honneth, 'Foucault and Adorno: Two Forms of the Critique of Modernity', trans. David Roberts, *Thesis Eleven*, 15.1, 1986, pp. 48–59 (p. 51).
32. Ibid., p. 59.
33. Ibid., p. 59.
34. Axel Honneth, 'Decentred Autonomy: The Subject after the Fall', in *The Fragmented World of the Social: Essays in Social and Political Philosophy*, ed. Charles W. Wright (Albany, NY: State University of New York Press: 1995), pp. 261–71 (p. 262).
35. It goes without saying that this critique of poststructuralist thought is not representative of all strands of feminist thinking. As we will see, Judith Butler and Julia Kristeva develop feminist theory (albeit in different ways) from poststructuralist positions, as do Hélène Cixous and Luce Irigaray. Indeed, Cixous, Irigaray and Kristeva are often grouped together under the label 'French feminists'. For an overview of French feminism, see Christine Delphy, 'The Invention of French Feminism: An Essential Move', *Yale French Studies*, 97, 1987, pp. 190–221; and on the relationship between feminist theory and poststructuralism, see Claire Colebrook, 'Feminist Criticism and Poststructuralism', in Gill Plain and Susan Sellers (eds), *A History of Feminist Literary Criticism* (Cambridge: Cambridge University Press, 2007), pp. 214–34.
36. Toril Moi, 'Power, Sex, and Subjectivity: Feminist Reflections on Foucault', *Paragraph*, 5, 1985, pp. 95–102 (p. 95).
37. Michel Foucault, 'Discussion of "Truth and Subjectivity"', in *About the Hermeneutics of the Self: Lectures at Dartmouth College, 1980*, ed. Henri-Paul Fruchard and Daniele Lorenzini, trans. Graham Burchell (Chicago: University of Chicago Press, 2016), pp. 93–126 (p. 115).
38. Ibid., p. 101.
39. Nancy Hartsock, 'Foucault on Power: A Theory of Women?', in Linda Nicholson (ed.), *Feminism/Postmodernism* (New York: Routledge, 1990), pp. 157–75 (pp. 163–4).

40. Ibid., p. 167.
41. Ibid., p. 167.
42. Ibid., p. 170.
43. Kate Soper, 'Feminism, Humanism, and Postmodernism', *Radical Philosophy*, 55.1, 1990, pp. 11–17 (p. 16).
44. Seyla Benhabib, 'Subjectivity, Historiography, and Politics', in Seyla Benhabib, Judith Butler, Drucilla Cornell and Nancy Fraser (eds), *Feminist Contentions: A Philosophical Exchange* (Abingdon: Routledge, 1995), pp. 107–26 (p. 108).
45. Ibid., p. 109.
46. Ibid., p. 110.
47. Ibid., p. 110.
48. Martha Nussbaum, 'The Professor of Parody: The Hip Defeatism of Judith Butler', *The New Republic*, 22 February 1999, pp. 37–45 (pp. 38, 39).
49. Ibid., p. 43.
50. Ibid., p. 45.
51. Ibid., p. 43.
52. Ibid., p. 41.
53. Ibid., pp. 45, 42.
54. For a defence of Butler against Nussbaum's criticisms, see Ori J. Hernstein, 'Justifying Subversion: Why Nussbaum Got (the Better Interpretation of) Judith Butler Wrong', *Buffalo Journal of Gender, Law, and Social Policy*, 18, 2010, pp. 43–73.
55. Lois McNay, *Gender and Agency: Reconfiguring the Subject in Feminist and Social Theory* (Cambridge: Polity, 2000), p. 2.
56. Ibid., p. 161.
57. Ibid., p. 17.
58. Ibid., p. 8.
59. Ibid., p. 46.
60. Nathan Widder, 'How Do We Recognise the Subject?', in Benoît Dillet, Iain MacKenzie and Robert Porter (eds), *The Edinburgh Companion to Poststructuralism* (Edinburgh: Edinburgh University Press, 2013), pp. 207–26 (p. 207).
61. Karl Marx, 'Theses on Feuerbach', in Karl Marx and Frederick Engels, *Marx and Engels Collected Works*, Volume 5 (London: Lawrence and Wishart, 2010), pp. 6–8 (p. 8).
62. Etienne Balibar, 'Structuralism: A Destitution of the Subject?', *differences: A Journal of Feminist Cultural Studies*, 14.1, 2003, pp. 1–21; Caroline Williams, *Contemporary French Philosophy: Modernity and the Persistence of the Subject* (London: Continuum, 2001). She repeats the same argument in 'Structure and Subject', in Benoît Dillet, Iain MacKenzie and Robert Porter (eds), *The Edinburgh Companion to Poststructuralism* (Edinburgh: Edinburgh University Press, 2013), pp. 189–206.
63. Balibar, 'Structuralism', p. 10.
64. Mark Bevir, 'Foucault, Power, and Institution', *Political Studies*, 47.2, 1999, pp. 345–59 (p. 358).

65. Amy Allen, 'The Anti-Subjective Hypothesis: Michel Foucault and the Death of the Subject', *Philosophical Forum*, 31.2, 2000, pp. 113–30 (p. 120).
66. Deleuze critically engages most extensively with psychoanalysis in Gilles Deleuze and Félix Guattari, *Anti-Oedipus*, trans. Robert Hurley, Mark Seem and Helen R. Lane (London: Continuum, 2004). Out of the three authors mentioned here, Derrida is perhaps the figure who has taken the greatest interest in and conducted the most extensive engagement with psychoanalytic theory. His most explicit and extended discussions are found in Jacques Derrida, *Archive Fever: A Freudian Impression*, trans. Eric Prenowitz (Chicago: University of Chicago Press, 1996) and *Resistances of Psychoanalysis*, trans. Peggy Kamuf, Pascale-Anne Brault and Michael Naas (Stanford, CA: Stanford University Press, 1998). Besides the early texts, published in 1954, 1961 and 1963 respectively, concerning the practices and discipline of psychiatry – Michel Foucault, *Mental Illness and Psychology*, 2nd rev. edn (Berkeley, CA: University of California Press, 2008); Michel Foucault, *History of Madness*, ed. Jean Khalfa, trans. Jonathon Murphy (New York: Routledge, 2009); and Michel Foucault, *The Birth of the Clinic: An Archaeology of Medical Perception* (New York: Vintage, 1994) – Foucault also engages with psychoanalysis in *The Order of Things: An Archaeology of the Human Sciences* (New York: Vintage, 1994), pp. 373–8.
67. Cornelius Castoriadis, 'Power, Politics, Autonomy', in *Philosophy, Politics, Autonomy: Essays in Political Philosophy*, ed. David Ames Curtis (Oxford: Oxford University Press, 1991), pp. 143–74 (p. 148).
68. Cornelius Castoriadis, *The Imaginary Institution of Society*, trans. Kathleen Blamey (Cambridge, MA: MIT Press, 1998), p. 298.

Part I

Decentring the Subject

CHAPTER 1

Deleuze, Differential Ontology and Subjectivity

Gilles Deleuze is the poststructuralist who is closest to what might be called the 'traditional' problems and approaches of philosophy. As he happily explains in a 1990 letter to Jean-Clet Martin, 'I consider myself a classic philosopher . . . I believe in philosophy as system.'[1] This is not to say that he defends traditional conclusions. Rather, he aims to radically reorientate thought away from its historical privileging of identity and its accompanying representational model of thought – what he calls the 'image of thought'[2] – to an ontology and style of thinking based on a privileging of difference. This affirmation of difference over the identity that has long dominated Western thinking is often taken to be a foundational claim of poststructuralist thought. Rather than appeal to and depend upon an ahistoric, fixed, substantial, singular essence or principle to define things, one of the recurring themes of poststructuralist thought is that it is necessary to think of them as differentiated and differentiating. Deleuze offers a particularly sophisticated engagement with and justification for such an approach that involves the development of a radically innovative methodology that aims at nothing other than a complete revolution in Western thought.

Given the foundational nature of Deleuze's critique of identity, it is not surprising to find that it has implications for the subject. Whereas the subject has historically been thought to be defined by a fixed, ahistoric essence and, since Descartes, has been assumed to be the foundation of thought, Deleuze's affirmation of difference decentres the subject and, in so doing, radically undermines the foundationalism and essentialism that have traditionally been attributed to it. Politically speaking, he advocates a movement away from ahistoric, universal goals, teleological historical processes and, generally speaking, a 'macro' approach to political change, to a 'micro' one in which the focus turns to the continuous alterations to the ontological underpinnings of political regimes, as a means of undermining any affirmation of the legitimacy of a single political regime.[3] There is no question that this ontological approach offers a radically different conception of politics than the agent-centred version dominant in traditional political theory. By making change an ever-present aspect of the ontological underpinnings of political configurations, Deleuze argues that, no matter how stable they might appear to be, political regimes are actually unstable amalgamations of forces that constantly undermine their stability and any claim to universality or identity.

The issue that arises relates to the role and place of the subject in instantiating political change. To outline this, I focus on Deleuze and Guattari's analysis of the face because it is here that the relationship between his differential ontology, questioning of subjectivity and insistence on the need for political activism come clearly to the fore.[4] I argue that Deleuze's analysis affirms the fundamental claim of his differential ontology; namely, that instead of being established on a fixed ground or the actions of a foundational subject, ontological change, upon which subjectivity and political change depend, is a consequence of alterations to the pre-personal matrix of differential relations subtending their explicit actual manifestations. Rather than being instantiated *by* individuals, change occurs in spite of them, and, at most, *through* them.

As a consequence, various commentators have concluded that Deleuze and Guattari reject the notion of subjective agency that might actively direct ontological-political change. Instead, they focus on the virtual–actual relationship, wherein the former term relates to the differential, intensive fluctuations that subtend and generate actual beings. From this, the charge is that, according to Deleuze and Guattari, actual beings are simply passive effects of the pre-personal virtual differential relations subtending them. Peter Hallward, for example, explains that '[t]he crucial point is that all of the productive, differential or creative force . . . stems from the virtual creating alone, and not from the actual creature',[5] while Brian Massumi concludes that it signifies that 'what we think of as "free," "higher" functions, such as volition, are apparently being performed by autonomic, bodily reactions occurring in the brain but outside of consciousness . . . but prior to action and expression'.[6] While recognising that this undermines the long-standing notion of a foundational constituting subject, these commentators conclude that it does so at the expense of subjective intentional agency.

The fundamental problem with such an approach, however, is that, on a number of occasions, including in his work on faciality, Deleuze does appear to claim that political change can be instantiated *by* subjects. As a consequence, other commentators have argued that there is a conception of agency inherent in Deleuze's ontology, although they disagree on what this entails. Jane Bennett, for example, recognises that Deleuze and Guattari insist on the importance of 'a vital impetus, conatus, or clinamen',[7] but maintains that this is not transcendent to the actual; rather, it is immanently expressed through actual beings, who can therefore interact with and affect how they are manifested. She does, however, also maintain that actual beings are never individuated, but always depend 'on the collaboration, cooperation, or interactive interference of many bodies and forces'.[8] As a consequence, humans are not individuated beings choosing how to interact with their environment, but are intimately tied to other non-human beings to form assemblages of vital, heterogeneous materialities.[9] For Bennett, then, agency is built into Deleuze's account, but it is located at the level of human–non-human assemblages rather than at the level of an individual (human) being.

Jon Protevi, however, questions this. While he agrees with Bennett that Deleuzian agency is based on the notion of assemblages and that the Deleuzian subject is an amalgamation of human and non-human actualities, he nevertheless continues to affirm a privileged place for human agency. To do so, he considers the ways in which 'bodies, minds, and social settings are intricately and intimately linked'.[10] While affirming that human subjects are constitutively entwined with their social settings, Protevi also claims that Deleuze 'do[es] not neglect the subjective level', with the consequence that 'subjectivity [must] be studied both in its embodied subjectivity and in terms of the distribution of affective cognitive traits in a population'.[11] Contra Bennett, therefore, Protevi maintains that the human subject, as an assemblage of human and non-human aspects, is both a vehicle for agency brought about by the interactions of the parts of the assemblage and capable of intentional agency to affect its assemblage.

The fundamental issue with Protevi's conclusion, however, is that, strictly speaking, he does not make it by appealing to the work of Deleuze, instead using insights from Husserlian phenomenology and contemporary philosophy of emotions. This gives rise to the question of whether Deleuze actually offers such a theory of intentional subjective agency. Sean Bowden has recently taken up this issue to argue that, in the *Logic of Sense*,[12] Deleuze affirms, not an assemblage account of agency as Bennett and Protevi contend, but an *expressive* one that explains how the non-foundational subject is capable of intentional agency.[13] However, while recognising that Bowden draws attention to a little-known aspect of Deleuze's thinking to show that he does, at least, point to an account of intentional agency, I argue that Bowden's position depends on a number of contentious hermeneutical moves, while Deleuze's position is ultimately too underdeveloped to adequately explain how the differential subject is capable of such agency. As a consequence, and despite Bowden's insights, Deleuze's account of subjective agency falls into an antinomy, in so far as it can be read as offering an account that privileges the insights of his differential ontology to make subjects and political change effects of pre-personal processes *or* as holding that subjects can and must choose to act in a particular way to effect specific ontological and political alterations.

By way of conclusion, I show that, in a late text,[14] Deleuze was given the opportunity to clarify how these two pieces fit together when he was asked precisely this question as part of his response to the issue of who comes after the subject. Rather than doing so, he simply reiterates that the subject is to be replaced by pre-personal, pre-individual singularities; a retort that, despite his comments on how to deal with faciality and occasional affirmation of intentional agency, confirms that political change is an effect of pre-individual ontological changes. This undermines the essentialist, foundational subject and, indeed, offers a radically different notion of politics, but it does so at the expense of providing a fully *coherent* account of how the resultant decentred, founded subject is capable of autonomous intentional agency to effect that political change.

Differential Ontology

Originally published in 1968, *Difference and Repetition* was Deleuze's first main work. Prior to this, he had written a number of monographs on different philosophers, including Bergson, Hume, Kant, and Nietzsche, but, as he notes in the Preface to the English translation of *Difference and Repetition*, there is a big difference between writing about someone else and writing philosophy.[15] Only in the latter do 'we trim our own arrows, or gather those which seem to us the finest in order to try to send them in other directions, even if the distance covered is not astronomical but relatively small'.[16] Deleuze's ambition in *Difference and Repetition* is not, however, small. As noted, it aims at nothing other than a fundamental re-evaluation of the logic that has dominated Western philosophy. More specifically, he claims that

> the majority of philosophers ha[ve] subordinated difference to identity or to the Same, to the Similar, to the Opposed or to the Analogous: they ha[ve] introduced difference into the identity of the concept, they ha[ve] put difference in the concept itself, thereby reaching a conceptual difference, but not a concept of difference.[17]

Rather than think difference from identity, or hold that identity is differential, Deleuze's aim is twofold: first, to think 'difference in itself', before, second, thinking from difference, thereby undermining the traditional image of thought that has reduced being to an abstract universal category.[18] The aim, in other words, is 'to think difference in itself independently of all the forms of representation which reduce it to the Same, and the relation of different to different independently of those forms which make them pass through the negative'.[19] The basic coordinates through which Deleuze undertakes this task are being as becoming, difference-in-itself, multiplicity and the virtual–actual movement.

At the beginning of *The Science of Logic*, Hegel argues that the opposition between being and nothing is reconciled through the transition to becoming.[20] This marks an important point in the history of philosophy. Prior to this, and, indeed, when time had been recognised, it had tended to be subsumed under or devalued in favour of an atemporal substantial essence. Hegel's reintroduction of the importance of becoming was particularly significant to Martin Heidegger's affirmation of the close relationship between being and time,[21] while Heidegger's influence on Deleuze ensured that the latter agreed that being must not be thought substantially, but as becoming. Deleuze's novelty is to explicitly break with any notion of a linear process of becoming by questioning not only *what* the becoming of being entails, but also *how* being becomes. This leads to a study of difference, which, as noted, is understood not as an analysis of conceptual difference – the difference between concepts – but as the interrogation of the concept of difference itself.[22]

To do so, Deleuze moves beyond empirical differences to 'imagine something that distinguishes itself – and yet that from which it distinguishes itself does not distinguish itself from it'.[23] Rather than something that creates different things, he affirms a logic of autopoietic 'self'-distinction where 'difference is made, or makes itself'.[24] Instead of being an effect of identity, difference is that which generates identity. To develop this, he returns to medieval scholasticism and, in particular, the concept of univocity to explain that 'being is univocal'.[25] To understand what is at stake here we have to differentiate between 'univocity' and 'equivocity'. The latter holds that 'being' is said in different senses across all beings, which appears to accord with Deleuze's effort to affirm difference. However, Deleuze claims that equivocity is underpinned by a particular logic of identity where being is understood as a thing that subsequently finds expression in different ways. Rather than thinking from difference, equivocity thinks from a single point that becomes different.

Univocity, on the other hand, holds that being is said of the same sense in each of its expressions. While this appears to reduce each sense to a single point, Deleuze's innovation is to claim that the sense that is expressed univocally is difference: 'Being is said in a single and same sense of everything of which it is said, but that of which it is said is different: it is said of difference itself.'[26] Being as difference is, then, said differently in each expression. Crucially, the univocal expression of being takes place prior to its appearance and so requires that we identify 'how a prior field of individuation within being conditions at once the determination of species of forms, the determination of parts and their individual variations'.[27]

Thinking difference-in-itself has, then, to occur through two activities. First, there must be a movement from emphasising extensive difference-in-kind – that is, the objective, extensive differences between entities – to focusing on difference-in-degree, entailing the univocal difference lying 'behind' difference-in-kind. This prior field of individuation is not singular or static, but differential. Second, Deleuze claims that such a move entails a turn to a particular empiricism. This is not a primitive empiricism focusing on simple differences between individuated objects, but a 'superior empiricism'[28] that attends to the transcendental conditions generating each object. Only when 'empiricism becomes transcendental' will it focus on 'the very being *of* the sensible: difference, potential difference and difference in intensity as the reason behind qualitative diversity'.[29] By focusing on the processes that produce entities rather than the superficial appearance of the entities themselves, we will see that 'difference is behind everything, but behind difference there is nothing'.[30] It should be emphasised that when Deleuze talks of 'behind' the world, he is not introducing a two-world metaphysics; 'being is difference itself',[31] which expresses itself immanently through entities.

To understand this, a word is needed on Deleuze's use of the notion of Ideas. This is part of his attempt 'to overturn Platonism'.[32] For Deleuze, Platonism is the doctrine that most successfully reduces difference to identity in the form of the One and insists upon a representational model of thought wherein the truth of a representation depends upon its representational approximation to the Idea of the thing being discussed. To overcome both, Deleuze distinguishes between two senses of the Platonic Ideas. First, there is the traditional interpretation that distinguishes and compares the appearance of an object to its ahistoric essence. Given his rejection of the notion of ahistoric essences, it should be no surprise to find that Deleuze rejects this interpretation. As such, he affirms a second interpretation wherein there are multiple Ideas, each of which is different from others. The Idea of Red, for example, is different to the Idea of Blue. This permits Deleuze to claim that Ideas are different in kind and are that from which actual entities emanate. The key point, however, is that the difference-in-kind of the Ideas is a consequence of an intensive (self-generating) process of differentiation. Difference-in-itself is, then, also differentiating.

This realisation brings Deleuze to distinguish between differentiation and differenciation, a distinction that also ties into the one between the virtual and actual: 'we call the determination of the virtual content of an Idea differentiation; we call the actualisation of that virtuality into species and distinguished parts differenciation'.[33] A multiplicity is formed when a virtually differentiated Idea actualises itself into differenciated form. Thus, virtuality is a non-spatio-temporal pre-individuated field from which spatio-temporal individuated entities result. This does not have to happen, meaning that Ideas can and do exist in virtual form without ever being actualised: an 'Idea may be completely determined (differentiated) and yet lack those determinations which constitute actual existence (it is undifferenciated, not yet even individuated)'.[34] If, however, Ideas are to be actualised, they must move from their pre-individuated virtual form to a spatio-temporal actual one. This occurs through differenciation, meaning that it is never the same process nor does it conform to a prior model. It emanates from differences in intensive difference, thereby ensuring that no process of actualisation is ever the same nor are the actualities created.

Indeed, it is important to note that Deleuze claims that what results from this process is not an entity, but a multiplicity. The concept 'entity' is rejected because it implies a totalisation and wholeness that contravenes the emphasis that Deleuze places on differential becoming. 'Multiplicity', in contrast, denotes that being's different/ciation occurs along multiple lines simultaneously. There is no centre binding these. Furthermore, the entities created take on a particular form: rather than being a whole composed of parts, they are a fluid, heterogeneous becoming that 'has no need whatsoever of unity in order to form a system'.[35] For this reason, Deleuze notes that there are three main aspects to multiplicities: 1) absence of any prior identity or unity, 2) reciprocity of the various elements so that no element exists independently or apart from the others, and 3) the various lines of flight are bound by multiple connections rather than a single point.[36] That they are tied together heterogeneously means that the different/ciation process can burst out in unexpected ways at any moment. As a consequence, 'multiplicity' denotes a form of organisation defined by pure, spontaneous, open-ended, different/cial becomings.

There is obviously much more to Deleuze's ontology,[37] including the descriptions of the various parts, than I have focused on here, but this broad overview is sufficient to highlight the challenge that he poses to thinking that is grounded in a fixed identity or essence. Instead he claims that being as difference is differentiated into different Ideas that exist in an undifferenciated, non-extensive, non-determinate virtual realm. These virtual Ideas emanate from differences in degree of intensive difference and are real without being actual and are made actual by differenciating themselves into extensive spatio-temporal form. This actualisation process occurs differently each time and so creates a multiplicity that is different to its virtual Idea, other virtual Ideas, and other actualities. The key issue is that this movement is not imposed from outside, but is 'internal' to being itself. With regard to the subject, Deleuze's ontology teaches us that it is not defined by a fixed, ahistoric identity or essence. Rather, it is a multiplicity resulting from a process of constant different/cial becoming and is an effect of the pre-individuated virtual–actual movement rather than any individual choice or action. This is clearly seen from his analysis of faciality (undertaken primarily with Félix Guattari, but also with Claire Parnet), which, in turn, brings forth the question of subjective (intentional) agency.

Difference and the Face

Deleuze's differential ontology, as outlined in *Difference and Repetition*, forms the basis for his subsequent thought. This is not to say that there are not substantial alterations or changes. The most substantial of these arise from a rethinking of identity and, indeed, its reincorporation within his analysis. The reason for this is complicated, but, put simply, it is caused by the recognition that difference cannot be thought in-itself, but continues to cling to a form of identity. Thus, while in *Difference and Repetition*, Deleuze calls for 'a new image of thought – or rather, a liberation of thought from those images which imprison it',[38] Emma Ingala argues that he came to appreciate that thought could not do away with all images and, by extension, identity. Rather than simply replace a model of thought based on identity for one based on difference, she claims that Deleuze and Guattari came to see the two as being in continuous, uneasy relation.[39] To affirm difference over identity is not, then, to depart from identity *per se*, but to depart from a particular conception of identity, while continuing to depend upon an alternative.

I have elsewhere[40] argued that this is implicit in the analysis of difference in *Difference and Repetition*, but it becomes explicit throughout Deleuze's writings from around the 1970s onwards and is particularly evident from the relationship between de-territorialisation and re-territorialisation. I will return to this issue, but, very simply, de-territorialisation is associated with difference and disrupts identity. That disruption does not, however, stay as pure disruption or difference; it re-territorialises and so takes on a form or identity that must, in turn, be de-territorialised. The point is that there is no binary opposition between difference and identity; Deleuze and Guattari come to offer a far more sophisticated, entwined understanding of the two, wherein each passes into the other. This relationship is also clearly seen from their analysis of the face, a topic tied to the question of subjectivity.

While Deleuze and Guattari discuss the face in numerous texts,[41] the most condensed analysis is found in the seventh plateau of *A Thousand Plateaus*; a plateau that needs to be read in conjunction with the fifth plateau, where Deleuze and Guattari explicitly link signification to the face,[42] and, to a degree, the sixth plateau, where they discuss the body without organs. The next most substantial discussion of it is found in *Francis Bacon: The Logic of Sensation* where Deleuze distinguishes between the head-body and the face to explain that the face cannot be located in, is not part of, nor is it reducible to, the body.[43] The face is not synonymous with the physical features of the body. It does not actually express any part of the body, but overcodes and so distorts the body. '[T]he face is a structured, spatial organization that conceals the head',[44] meaning that the body, as Deleuze and Guattari understand the term, and, by extension, the head, precedes the face. Nevertheless, as the signification of a 'hidden' essence, Deleuze and Guattari claim that, once it is produced, it acts as a signifier for the entire being, including the body.[45] Because it succeeds the body, the face is not a 'natural' occurrence, but a semiotic construction designed to reveal the body in a particular fashion. It is for this reason that, for Deleuze and Guattari, the face is intimately connected to conceptuality, politics, power and repression.

To properly understand this, we have to briefly turn to their important notion of the 'body without organs', which describes the intensive, differential 'possible' traits that give rise to an actual, extensive, physical body. For Deleuze and Guattari, every actual body is subtended by a variety of limited, differential traits, habits and features. As such, its actual characteristics do not exhaust the 'being' of the multiplicity because there is always a virtual aspect to each that entails a changing reservoir of 'potential' traits which are made actual in a particular manner.[46] The 'body without organs' is the term that Deleuze and Guattari use to describe the 'underlying' virtual 'realm' that is actualised into spatio-temporal extensive multiplicities.[47] As such, the body without organs is the intensive differential flux of virtuality from which the actual differenciated physical body is created. The face overcodes this changing actual body with a homogeneous identity. At the same time, however, the face is not autonomous from the virtual body without organs, but only arises if the virtual aspect that subtends it permits this. In turn, the face overcodes the actual body that results from the virtual aspect. This process is not homogeneous and so it is necessary to uncover the regimes of signifying power grounding the being, form and meaning of the face.

To develop this, Deleuze and Guattari claim that the face lies at the intersection of a white wall/black hole matrix, whereby the white wall of signification is the outer manifestation of the black hole of subjectivity.[48] With this, they tie the face to representation, in so far as the outer white wall of the face conceals while pointing towards an 'inner' essential subjectivity to be faithfully represented. Given Deleuze's rejection of the representational model of thought upon which this understanding depends – an outer appearance representing an inner truth – it is no surprise to discover that he is deeply critical of the face.[49]

But the face does not simply emanate from this inner/outer representational model. Deleuze also emphasises that there are different types of face. This is not something as banal as pointing to the empirical 'truth' that we each have a different face and, indeed, can 'put on' different faces at different times. It is an ontological point, emanating from his affirmation of difference. As we have seen, Deleuze claims that being's differential becoming ensures that each manifestation of 'the' transcendental difference that 'grounds' actualities is always different and continues to different/ciate. Each manifestation of difference is never unitary, but always multiple. As a consequence, there is not one face, but multiple faces, each of which emanates from different political systems of signification.

Developing this in *Cinema 1*, Deleuze differentiates between reflective faces, which are composed of features that are grouped under one, eternal thought, and intensive faces, which entail autonomous actions that break through, or at least alter, their limits.[50] Daniel W. Smith points out that the difference seems to be that the reflective face is somewhat reactive and static in so far as it is marked by the minimum of movement and alteration. Intensive faces, however, are associated with vitality and alteration, meaning that they continuously change and pass into new formations.[51] By distinguishing between reflective and intensive faces, Deleuze reveals that the face is far more complicated and multidimensional than its mere empirical manifestation would suggest. It is marked by intensive and extensive movement, staticisity, reflection and, as we will see, power and conceptual signification.

By overcoding the body without organs, Deleuze and Guattari link the face to de-territorialisation, which describes the processes that '"make" the body an animal or human organism'.[52] This needs to be explained, however, because de-territorialisation can take three forms. *Relative* de-territorialisation describes the process whereby the component parts of an organism alter as part of its becoming. As Deleuze and Guattari explain, 'it concerns the historical relationship of the earth with the territories that take shape and pass away with it, its geological relationship with eras and catastrophes, its astronomical relationship with the cosmos and the stellar system of which it is a part'.[53] In other words, relative de-territorialisation describes the way the territory of the organism alters, changes and becomes through the alterations to the relations between its parts.

While Deleuze and Guattari note that the human head implies a de-territorialisation that creates something else relative to the animal, they claim that 'the face represents a far more intense, if slower, de-territorialisation', which they call *absolute* de-territorialisation.[54] This severs the linkages holding the component parts of the object together to create something fundamentally distinct from it. Deleuze and Guatarri claim that the face entails this form of de-territorialisation because 'it removes the head from the stratum of the organism, human or animal, and connects it to other strata, such as significance and subjectification'.[55] The face abandons the concrete to privilege the absolutely de-territorialised (abstract) realm of significance and subjectification. For example, the face overcodes the concrete body with signs that point to an abstract truth or essence to define the body from that abstraction.

Things are not quite as simple as this, however, because Deleuze and Guattari recognise positive and negative forms of absolute territorialisation.[56] Negative absolute de-territorialisation is intimately connected to subjectivity, in so far as it entails the abandonment of concrete reality for an abstract subjective construction that does not express the concreteness of being's differential onto-genesis. For example, they explain that 'de-territorialisation is *absolute* when the earth passes into the pure plane of immanence of a being-thought, of a Nature-thought of infinite diagrammatic movements'.[57] It entails the abandonment of the concrete for the construction of an abstraction which is taken to reveal the 'truth' of the concrete. This form of absolute de-territorialisation is negative because it moves from the difference of the concrete to the universal identity of the abstract, which it subsequently imposes on to being's rhizomic becoming. In contrast, the positive form of absolute de-territorialisation, which Deleuze and Guattari mention without discussing in any depth, involves an absolute de-territorialisation that, rather than impose identity on to the object, takes its cue from the novelty inherent in being's rhizomic becoming.[58] While Deleuze and Guattari emphasise that the face is related to negative absolute de-territorialisation, we will see that they also recognise that the face is related to the positive form.

Deleuze claims that, because it distinguishes between an outer appearance and a hidden, inner, essential black hole of subjectivity, the encounter with the face is one of distortion and, to a degree, deception meant to act as a 'megaphone'[59] that signals to others both the 'inner' nature of the face in question and the appropriate way to act socially. Importantly, the face is not imposed on to the body without organs by another concrete individual, nor can it be reduced to an economic formation or ideological superstructure.[60] The face emanates from a particular social assemblage, one that requires a face to function.[61] As such, 'the face is a politics'.[62]

Because it is intimately related to a political regime, Deleuze and Guattari hold, contra Levinas, that the face is not that which is most personal or that brings individuals together;[63] the face divides, in so far as it delineates who/what is acceptable to the regime and who/what is not. As a consequence, Deleuze and Parnet insist that 'nothing is less personal than a face'.[64] Importantly, however, as an overcoded system of signification, the face is capable of transmitting many meanings based on the needs of the political regimes it is located within and emanates from. The conclusion drawn is that, as a socially produced overcoding of the body without organs, the face is not 'natural' to the human, nor is it the apotheosis of the human. As an imposition which distorts the free-flowing intensive difference that is the human multiplicity, Deleuze and Guattari explain that the face is 'the inhuman in human being'.[65]

To engage with the types of regimes that require a face, Deleuze outlines the nature of signification and its relationship to the political to show which types of society require and therefore code their social assemblage facially. This leads to a tripartite division between primitive, counter-signifying and post-significatory societies. The primitive is closest to nature and, indeed, signifies *through* nature. As a consequence, this type of society 'fosters a pluralism or polyvocality of forms of expression that prevents any power takeover by the signifier and preserves expressive forms particular to content; thus forms of corporeality, gesturality, rhythm, dance, and rite coexist heterogeneously with the vocal form'.[66] Rather than a particular focal point from which order and meaning emanate linearly, primitive societies involve multiple circulations that re-enforce certain sedimented social norms and actions.

In contrast, counter-signifying societies proceed not by natural associations, but through number and arithmetic. Emphasising number leads to a particular form of social organisation entailing 'arrangements rather than totals, distributions rather than collections, which [operate] more by breaks, transitions, migration, and accumulation than by combining units'.[67] There is, in other words, 'less' rhythmic flow to this sense of signification and 'more' order, rationality, calculability and instrumentality. Post-signifying systems are distinguished from primitive and counter-signifying societies by virtue of being tied to the creation of subjectivity. The post-signifying regime creates the ego and, having created it, then attributes meaning to this creation.[68] Because the face lies at the intersection between subjectivity and signification, it is dependent on regimes of signification that create subjectivity and is therefore located in post-signifying regimes.

This is not to say, however, that post-signifying regimes create the same face or utilise the face in the same manner. To show this, Deleuze, in conjunction with both Guattari and Parnet, identifies, discusses and differentiates between the Pharaonic and Hebraic systems of faciality. Deleuze and Parnet explain that the former Pharaonic system is despotic and operates through 'specific regimes of signs in so far as it expresses a state of fluxes and intensities'.[69] This is not a linear, top-down regime of physical force, but a circular configuration of signs which re-enforce one another. As a consequence, this social assemblage re-enforces its power structure through an endogenous play of signs where each sign refers to the next to re-enforce both. While there is a centre – which Deleuze and Parnet describe as being the despot or God, his temple or house – this centre instantiates and, in turn, is re-enforced by a system of signification that is disseminated throughout the social body. Within this system of signification, the ruler's face is 'an exposed face seen straight on, black hole on a white wall'.[70] The ruler does not hide but is manifested through his face, which is always visible and directly experienced. However, while the visual immediacy of the face may make it appear to be transparent, the ruler's face signifies the black hole of subjectivity, meaning it is anything but transparent. While the despotic Pharaoh rules and appears in immediate form, what is presented with him is the mystery of the black hole; his unconstrained subjectivity defines him and ensures that he is not constrained in any way, a 'freedom' that lends itself to despotism.

In contrast to the relatively sedimentary Pharaonic system built around a specific socio-geographic locale, the Hebraic system of signification detaches itself from the imperial network of the Pharaonic system to pit 'the most authoritarian of subjectivities against despotic significance'.[71] Rather than orientate itself around a fixed spatio-temporal despotic location, the Hebraic system is defined by subjectivity orientated around and from 'the most fundamental or extensive event in the history of the Jewish people: the destruction of the Temple'.[72] The loss of the Temple does not, however, mean the loss of the unitary focal point of signification. The focal point becomes ineffable: God is both nowhere and everywhere.

At least two consequences result from this. First, the loss of the Temple is accompanied by the incapacity to pinpoint blame. The notion of misfortune comes to the fore, but rather than being externally focused (i.e. our misfortune is caused by another specific thing), it becomes internalised, whereby it is transformed from a negative loss into a positive aspect of the individual's subjectivity. Second, Deleuze and Guattari claim that the loss of the Temple is accompanied by a profound nostalgia for the certainty of the Pharaonic system, with the result that there is renewed focus on re-establishing a King and Temple to 'find the face of God again'.[73]

There is, as a consequence, a movement from a despotic regime to an authoritarian one, in which, rather than a system of various signs which exist polymorphously, there exist 'little blocs of signs, which [line] up along an endless straight line, marking on it a succession of processes, of finished segments, each with a beginning and an end'.[74] Rather than an endogenous force that binds the system together, there is now one definitive exogenous authoritative event that not only authors all else, but is that to which all else is returned. It must be remembered, however, that the definitive event is marked by a sense of loss, meaning that it is not present and so does not designate an immediate spatio-temporal 'thing' as in the Pharaonic system. Losing its spatio-temporal manifestness means that the Hebraic founding event becomes both indeterminate and 'eternal'.

Whereas the Pharaonic system is heterogeneous because it is marked by the immediate subjectivity of the despot and is re-enforced by the entire social assemblage, the Hebraic system proceeds linearly from the authoritative event and is homogeneous because it is always returned to the authoritative event. With this, 'faciality undergoes a profound transformation'.[75] While the Pharaonic system emphasises the determinate face of the despot, in the Hebraic system 'God averts his face, which must be seen by no one; and the subject, gripped by a veritable fear of the god, averts his or her face in turn. The averted faces, in profile, replace the frontal view of the radiant face.'[76]

The loss of the Temple entails, then, a loss of God's presence, which does not mean a loss of God. God now averts his face and becomes 'hidden' so that an 'indefinite postponement'[77] marks the experience of the face. Whereas the Pharaonic face is manifested immediately, explicitly and determinately, yet alters continuously to replicate the Pharaoh's (black hole of) subjectivity, the Hebraic face, while ineffable and indeterminate, attains a fixed, homogeneous meaning. While it may be thought that the heterogeneity of the Pharaonic face permits more options, Deleuze and Guattari claim that the opposite is the case. The Pharaonic face is thoroughly repressive in that it limits meaning to that imposed by the Pharaoh. In contrast, the Hebraic face is both repressive, in that it limits meaning to the ineffable loss of God's face, and strangely expressive in that it uses the lost event to structure new lines of flight that are always bound to its lost founding event. This indeterminateness means that the Hebraic face is homogeneous in its source but heterogeneous in its effects, which are always given meaning from its homogeneous source.

Combating the Face

We have seen that Deleuze, with Guattari and Parnet, explains how the face operates in relation to the body and subjectivity: it overcodes the former with a particular semiotic system, which, in turn, creates and supports a particular notion of subjectivity. The few commentators who have focused on Deleuze and Guattari's notion of the face have tended to take an uncritical, descriptive approach to it.[78] In contrast, in what follows, I will take a critical approach that first turns to the prescriptive aspect inherent in their analysis, before going on to evaluate it in relation to Deleuze's differential ontology and the question of individual intentional agency.

To understand the prescriptive aspect of Deleuze and Guattari's analysis of the face, we have to remember that it describes 1) the *transcendental conditions* of the face, and 2) the impact that the *experience* of the face can have on the one experiencing it. While the former reveals that the face overcodes the body without organs with an identity, the experience of the face can undermine this attempt by, somewhat paradoxically, pointing towards and so revealing the 'possibility' subtending the body without organs that the identity of the face is supposed to conceal. The reasoning behind this is under-developed but it appears to emanate from two different, but related, directions. The first is the recognition that the face is a sign. While it projects an identity, the face is not permanent but contingent, thereby leaving open the possibility that it can be abolished or, at least, altered. Second, in his descriptions of different *experiences* of the face, Deleuze, on at least two occasions, recognises that there is something special about the face, in so far as it can reveal possibilities to the one experiencing it. This does not mean that the face is possibility or that it is linked to possibility, but that, because the face is the actual manifestation of one virtual–actual configuration, any alterations to it point towards different expressions of the virtual realm 'underpinning' actuality and, by extension, to different actualities.

Exploring this further, Deleuze, in *Difference and Repetition*, claims that the manifestation of one particular face – the terrified face – 'expresses a possible world'.[79] The experience of the terrified face shakes its recipient out of their complacency, thereby opening up (an) alternative(s). The relationship between terror, possibilities and the face is also found in *What is Philosophy?*, where Deleuze and Guattari describe how a frightened face is encountered: 'the other person appears here as neither subject nor object but as something that is very different: a possible world, the possibility of a frightening world'.[80]

By identifying that the transcendental conditions of the face entail a form of political signification that aims at identity and homogeneity, and showing that the experience of the face can point to the virtual 'possibilities' it aims to cover over, Deleuze and Guattari not only reveal that the face's overcoding can undo itself, but also highlight the role that fear plays in the overcoming of political repression. Their point seems to be that the experience of a particular face can undermine the sense of homogeneous identity that the face aims at because the experience of terror has such 'affective' significance that the individual experiences a change from one state to another, and is thus brought to recognise both the changing nature of the signifying face and his own becoming. By breaking up the identity inherent in the face, the terror that results from the experience of a frightened face can bring out the virtuality inherent in the body without organs that 'underpins' it.[81]

The face does not, then, simply manifest itself in one particular way and in so doing represent that particular message; it points towards the possibilities, options and transformations inherent in the virtual realm subtending it. Therefore, the political 'programme' proposed by Deleuze and Guattari aims to free the face from the repressive consequences of identity by 'unlocking' the virtuality subtending it. They therefore exhort us 'lose one's identity, one's face . . . One has to disappear to become unknown',[82] a strategy that may result in madness,[83] but which is necessary to escape the oppression of the face. Indeed, they insist that 'the face has a great future, but only if it is destroyed, dismantled',[84] a claim echoed by Deleuze and Parnet's insistence that we must 'undo the face, unravel the face'.[85]

Importantly, this is not simply 'an aesthete's adventure'[86] based on playing with identity/ies or, as in the works of Francis Bacon, offering a pictorial manifestation of dismantled faces. It entails a politics, whereby the 'possibility' of the virtual that subtends actual faces is released. Crucially, however, Deleuze goes to great pains to reject the idea that the dismantling of the face 1) entails a return to a 'primitive', pre-signifying regime, 2) can be achieved by assuming a mask, such as pretending to be another, and 3) aims simply to annihilate the face; the de-territoriliasation/re-territorialisation structure means that each de-territorialisation necessarily requires and entails a re-territorialisation. But given the different forms of de-territorialisation, and that the positive form of absolute de-territorialisation aims to affirm the differential becoming of the body without organs, it does not seem inappropriate to suggest that this is the aim of Deleuze's affirmation of action that dismantles the face.

To achieve this, Deleuze and Guattari talk, not of annihilating, destroying, overcoming or replacing the face, but of creating 'probe-heads'[87] that will bore into the signifying identities of the face to poke holes in its stratifications and significations to reveal and so express the virtual body without organs 'lying beneath' the face. For this reason, Richard Rushton's claim that 'the face is virtual' is inaccurate.[88] The face is not virtual; it emanates from the virtual (body without organs), but is a distorting overcoding of virtuality. It is the *body without organs*, not the face, that delineates the virtual being of the multiplicity that is made actual through a physical body, which can then be overcoded with a face. By sending probe-heads into its virtual 'underpinnings', Deleuze and Guattari aim to reveal alternative positive creative possibilities that, in turn, will form 'strange new becomings, new polyvocalities'.[89]

While Deleuze does not and, given his critique of representation, cannot provide a detailed blueprint for political action based on cuttings or the launching of probe-heads, his insistence that the political is intimately connected to signification means that Deleuzian political action must entail a rethinking of the signification of the face, with this contributing to a transformation that brings us away from a privileging of identity to a thinking that explores and affirms difference.[90] Importantly, Deleuze recognises that the de-territorialisation/re-territorialisation structure means that faciality (= identity) cannot be fully overcome. This does not, however, mean that we must simply accept that we have to adopt a fixed identity. We must learn to move between different identities which are only ever partially adopted. As Deleuze puts it, we need to 'be a little alcoholic, a little crazy, a little suicidal, a little of a guerrilla'.[91] The ambition is to push the boundary of actuality to express the 'possibilities' of the virtual subtending it without ever falling into the pure chaos of virtuality without any actuality. In this way, the identity of actuality is continually disrupted by the difference of virtuality. Subjectivity takes on identities that are continuously disrupted to reveal new possibilities from the virtual subtending them. There is no universal, general rule that can determine what this entails or when it can and will happen; it is a micro-politics of experimentation specific to each virtual–actual movement.

Agency and the Subject

Deleuze's questioning of subjectivity through his differential ontology and analysis of the face is certainly radical, calling into question any notion of a clear and simplistic identity. The fundamental problem that his analysis throws up relates to the processes that disrupt identity. As I have shown, Deleuze does not argue against all forms of identity, but comes to accept a partial and temporary form of identity that is always disrupted by the actualisation of the virtual subtending it. This necessarily occurs from the dynamics of the different/cial ontological structures subtending actuality, which are constantly changing and becoming anew. As Deleuze explains in *Foucault*, 'there never "remains" anything of the subject, since he is to be created on each occasion, like a focal point of resistance, on the basis of the folds which subjectivise knowledge and bend each power'.[92] There is, then, a strong sense that any regime of signification that creates a face is almost immediately undermined by its own differential constitution. This also implies that individuals who are subject to the regime of the face do not need to do anything to undermine it; the face is constantly undermined by its ontological structure.

The problem, of course, is that Deleuze and Guattari/Parnet do appear to offer the subject a role in overcoming faciality and, indeed, prescribe a form of action necessary for this to occur. As we saw, they suggest that the subject adopt multiple identities, play with them and, indeed sink probe-heads into the virtual that subtends them to release alternative configurations. This, however, requires some form of agency – meaning autonomous intentional action – on the part of subjects. While I have previously noted that a number of commentators (Bennett, Protevi) have attempted to explain what this entails by appealing to an 'assemblage' theory of agency, but disagree on whether this takes non-human (Bennett) or human (Protevi) form, I will focus on the 'expressive' account provided by Sean Bowden, which, in contrast to the assemblage version, explicitly aims to show that, in the *Logic of Sense*, Deleuze offers a particularly innovative explanation of and for individual intentional agency.

Bowden explains that '[t]he key idea behind the expressive conception of agency is that actions are in some sense primary in relation to the intentions that animate them'.[93] This distinguishes it from 'voluntarist' accounts, wherein 'intentions are thought of as primary in relation to actions'.[94] For the voluntarist position, 'there are two separate elements of actions: a physical movement, and an intention that temporally precedes and causes this movement'.[95] Furthermore, for the voluntarist, the agent has 'a privileged and unrevisable access to this prior and causally efficacious intention, which is accordingly more or less fully specified in the agent's mind'.[96] According to Bowden, Deleuze's expressive account of agency, on the contrary, maintains that 'an agent's intention is not incorrigibly known by the agent, and is not artificially separable from the action itself, such as this unfolds, and produces effects, in shared or public space'.[97]

To defend this, Bowden explains that Deleuze distinguishes between 'the realm of bodies in general with their relative, causal activity and passivity, and their particular physical, biological and even psychological states' and 'the realm of "what happens" – the realm of *events* in general – which are uniformly characterised as impassive, incorporeal and impersonal happenings'.[98]

As a consequence, for Deleuze, events are distinct from corporeal things and 'exist only as the expressed or expressible sense of propositions'.[99] By distinguishing absolutely between corporeal bodies and incorporeal events in this manner, Deleuze appears to undermine the possibility that the former can affect the latter. Incorporeal events generate corporeal bodies, with the consequence that corporeal bodies appear to be incapable of affecting the incorporeal event that makes them happen.

Bowden notes, however, that in the 'Twenty-first Series of the Event'[100] of *The Logic of Sense*, in one of the few places where Deleuze explicitly discusses intentional agency, he rejects the notion that the primacy of incorporeal events should lead to resignation or *ressentiment* on the part of actual bodies. Instead, he proposes a conception of 'willing the event'[101] that appears to allow corporeal bodies to affect the event by way of an intentional action (= agency). Bowden warns, however, that this requires that we follow a number of conceptual moves. In particular, it must be recognised that Deleuze's conception of 'willing the event' does 'not consist in causing some particular, intended action, clearly conceived of prior to the act'.[102] Rather, it 'consist[s] in willing the "sense-event" from which our determined actions are inseparable, *but where this sense-event also creates in us our willing*'.[103] The basic point is that, for Deleuze, actual corporeal bodies are a combination of the incorporeal event that brings them forth and the sense attributed to them. The incorporeal event that brings forth corporeal bodies is different to but inseparable from the sense attributed to that actual event to give it meaning. Having been brought forth, the corporeal body can subsequently 'spiritually will'[104] the sense (= meaning) attributed to the event that brought it forth. Importantly, the 'spiritual will' is different to the corporeal or 'organic will',[105] in so far as it 'does not precede the event and its expression'.[106] Rather, '[t]he event and its expression ... determine the [spiritual] will',[107] which subsequently and retroactively, through the sense attributed to it, impacts on and shapes the event.

Therefore, while events generate corporeal beings, it is not the case that the latter are passive and determined effects of the former. Bowden suggests that Deleuze has a far more complicated, paradoxical and entwined understanding of the event–sense relation in which, although events make sense possible, they are not 'complete' until attributed with sense. Because of the entwinement of events and sense, the retrospective creation and imposition of sense on to the event that generated it can be described as a particular form of expressive agency that, in a very particular way, affects the event. For this reason, an agent's intention (as manifested *through* their attribution of sense to the event) is both grounded in the event that brought it forth and, as a consequence, an expression of the event that founded it.

Importantly, Bowden claims that the creation of sense and, by extension, the attribution of agency is a thoroughly social, rather than individual, endeavour that takes place through others who 'are themselves "out there" in their multiply-interpretable actions'.[108] As a consequence, '[a]n action will count as being the action of a particular agent in so far as both this agent, and other agents, are able to recognise him or her in that action', with '[t]hese interpretations and recognitive processes tak[ing] place in a shared expressive medium or language which is not already given or fixed but is always being produced'.[109] This reaffirms Bowden's claim that, according to Deleuze, the attribution of sense to an event cannot be said to precede the event, nor can it be said to be an individual act; the sense attributed to an event not only results immanently through and from the event that brought it forth to retroactively impose meaning on to the event and, in so doing, 'complete' the event, but is also the consequence of mobile, heterogeneous social interactions rather than individual imposition. Bowden concludes that this clarifies what Deleuze means by willing and how this relates to his insistence that the realm of events is ontologically distinct from the realm of psychological or corporeal causes, all the while pointing to a particularly innovative understanding of intentional agency wherein, rather than preceding actions (= events), 'the intentions which are said to lie behind our actions (including our expressive actions) . . . retrospectively appear as "effects" of the sense-event taking place in our shared expressive medium'.[110]

Bowden's argument is certainly innovative, not only shedding light on the content of a number of obscure passages in the *Logic of Sense* that have received scant attention in the literature, but also identifying that a particular Deleuzian account of agency is possible and, indeed, developing what it might look like. However, his approach suffers from at least two significant problems. First, as Bowden notes, because his account is, at best, 'implicit'[111] to Deleuze's statements in the *Logic of Sense*, it depends upon a charitable reading that accepts a number of additional points that, strictly speaking, are not included in Deleuze's text. To give but one example, Bowden notes that the notion of 'recognition' inherent in his claim that, for Deleuze, 'an action will count as mine in so far as both I and others are able to recognise me in that action' depends on 'the word "recognition" that is simply not part of the Deleuzian vocabulary'.[112] Bowden gets round this by distinguishing between recognition in the sense of 'correctly grasping a pre-given identity', which is rejected by Deleuze, and recognition understood 'as the acknowledgement of a normative or social status, as when we recognise or acknowledge another person's right to something even when there is no objective fact of the matter to which to refer', to claim that the latter 'is not incompatible' with aspects of Deleuze's analysis.[113] Regardless of whether or not we agree that such a distinction is acceptable and, indeed, can be accurately applied to Deleuze's thinking, the paucity and obscurity of Deleuze's comments on the question of agency in *The Logic of Sense* mean that developing Bowden's point requires a particularly charitable hermeneutical strategy on the part of the reader; one that may not be forthcoming or that may lead to an alternative interpretation of the 'same' passage(s).

Second, this links to another problem with Bowden's methodological strategy relating to his insistence that *The Logic of Sense* must be read in isolation from other Deleuzian texts. This is a long-standing question within Deleuzian scholarship that pits those who affirm Deleuze's insistence that he is a systematic philosopher to conclude that there is a certain consistency or unity across his works[114] against those, such as Bowden, who assert Deleuze's affirmation of difference to conclude that each of his texts is a self-contained, systematic work of philosophy that deals with a particular problem and constructs concepts in a particular way to respond to that particular problem.[115] If, as Bowden contends, Deleuze's texts must be read individually so that the conclusions of one cannot be transposed to another, it is unclear whether the conclusions that Bowden gleans from *The Logic of Sense* can be said to offer a Deleuzian account of agency *per se*. As Bowden himself admits, it appears that the account of agency offered in *The Logic of Sense* can, at most, be said to offer a particular conception of agency to respond to a particular conceptual problem posed in a particular way. This is problematic because Bowden notes that the texts subsequent to *The Logic of Sense*, in particular *A Thousand Plateaus*, entail 'a seismic shift in Deleuze's thinking about action and agency'.[116] For Deleuze's defenders, this indicates that the question of whether a Deleuzian conception of agency is possible is still very much a live one; for his detractors, it points to and is symptomatic of the ambiguity that marks Deleuze's *oeuvre* on this issue.

Conclusion: Questioning the Subject

Interestingly, in 1989 Deleuze was invited to clarify this ambiguity in his contribution to the collection of essays edited by Eduardo Cadava, Peter Connor and Jean-Luc Nancy, translated (in 1991) as *Who Comes after the Subject?*[117] His brief response begins by clarifying that 'a philosophical concept fulfils one or more *Functions* in fields of thought that are themselves defined by internal variables. There are also external variables (states of things, moments of history) in a complex relationship with the *internal variables* and the functions.'[118] As a consequence, 'a concept is not created and does not disappear at whim, but to the extent that new functions in new fields dismiss it relatively'.[119] Thus the generation or abandonment of a concept arises from the structures and fields that generated and used it in the first place.

Importantly, 'the concept of the subject does not escape these rules'.[120] Its creation resulted from particular problematics and structural relations, but

> [f]or a long time, it fulfilled two functions. First, it was a universalizing function, in a field where the universal was no longer represented by objective essences but by noetic or linguistic acts . . . Second, the subject fulfill[ed] a function of individuation in a field where the individual [could] no longer be a thing or a soul, but a person, a living and lived person, speaking and spoken to (I–You).[121]

Having maintained that the concepts 'subject' and, by extension, 'subjectivity' were created to resolve a particular historical problematic in a specific way based on a certain set of assumptions, Deleuze suggests that the conditions that generated the concepts 'subject/subjectivity' have changed, so that it is the concept 'singularity' that is now important. This 'should not be understood as something opposing the universal but any element that can be extended to the proximity of another such that it may obtain a connection'.[122] In turn, he suggests that the conceptual alteration that brings us from 'subject' to 'singularity' has been and has to be accompanied by the creation of other concepts, including 'assemblage' and 'arrangement', that 'indicate a discharge and distribution of singularities'.[123] These 'form a transcendental field without a subject. The multiple becomes the noun, multiplicity, and philosophy becomes the theory of multiplicities that refer to no subject as a pre-established unity.'[124]

Deleuze is here affirming the basic coordinates of his differential ontology: pre-personal structures and processes take precedence over any notion of an entity that transcends them to offer the possibility of affecting them from the outside. Indeed, he speculates that 'types of individuation that are no longer persona have imposed themselves'.[125] Rather than think from the first or second person, he advocates a pre-personal stance summarised by his statement that '[w]e believe that the notion of the subject has lost most of its interest *in favour of pre-individual singularities and non-personal individuations*'.[126] Deleuze is here doing more than simply rejecting the notion of the (autonomous) subject. He is trying to develop an alternative based around the notion of a pre-personal singularity. This echoes a point he makes in the 1972 essay 'How Do We Recognize Structuralism?':

structuralism is not at all a form of thought that suppresses the subject, but one that breaks it up and distributes it systematically, that contests the identity of the subject, that dissipates it and makes it shift from place to place, an always nomad subject, made up of individuations, but impersonal ones, or of singularities, but pre-individual ones.[127]

Although this points to the need to orientate the question of agency towards the notion of 'singularity' that has replaced 'subjectivity' as the point of focus, the key issue for our purposes is not necessarily *who* Deleuze claims comes after the subject, but whether this 'who' is capable of effecting the change that his political prescription regarding the face demands; that is, whether 'it' is capable of intentionally and autonomously sinking probe-heads into the virtual subtending it and/or adopting multiple changing identities, and so on. When we turn to this issue, we see that, although Deleuze clearly wants to rethink the language and problems of the subject, agency and politics, in trying to develop this through a sophisticated affirmation of difference he affirms pre-personal structures and processes to the extent that any agential action to intentionally bring it about is *explicitly* undermined.

Those who criticise poststructuralist thought for being unable to produce a coherent account of how the decentred subject is capable of agency appear, then, to be vindicated with regard to Deleuze's thinking, although it must be noted that this is not because of a failing on his part, but is because he purposely maintains the strong claim that the subject is an uninteresting and useless concept surpassed by the importance of pre-personal differential structures. As such, he does not seek to show how the decentred subject is capable of agency, but subsequently fail to do so; he advocates the dissolution of the subject in the name of pre-personal singularities. This is a radical conclusion, but, for all its merits, it is unlikely to win over those not already predisposed to its move. For this reason, I noted in the Introduction that I would be evaluating the various poststructuralist positions based on the critique affirmed against them; namely, whether their decentring of the subject is capable of coherently accounting for autonomous intentional agency. Against that criterion, subjective agency is the question where Deleuze's differential ontology (purposely) runs up against its limits.

Notes

1. Gilles Deleuze, 'Letter-Preface to Jean-Clet Martin', in *Two Regimes of Madness: Texts and Interviews, 1975–1995*, ed. David Lapoujade, trans. Ames Hodges and Mike Taormina (New York: Semiotext(e), 2007), pp. 365–7 (p. 365).

2. Gilles Deleuze, *Difference and Repetition*, trans. Paul Patton (New York: Columbia University Press, 1994), p. 129.
3. The literature on Deleuze and politics has recently grown substantially. For a detailed discussion of Deleuze's micropolitics, see Nathan Widder, *Political Theory after Deleuze* (London: Continuum, 2012), esp. ch. 5. A multi-dimensional analysis is found in the essays collected in Ian Buchanan and Nicholas Thoburn (eds), *Deleuze and Politics* (Edinburgh: Edinburgh University Press, 2008), and a general overview is offered in Paul Patton, *Deleuze and the Political* (Abingdon: Routledge, 2000).
4. Félix Guattari (1930–92) was a psychoanalyst and long-time collaborator of Gilles Deleuze.
5. Peter Hallward, *Out of this World: Deleuze and the Philosophy of Creation* (London: Verso, 2006), p. 28.
6. Brian Massumi, *Parables for the Virtual: Movement, Affect, Sensation* (Durham, NC: Duke University Press, 2002), p. 29.
7. Jane Bennett, *Vibrant Matter: A Political Ecology of Things* (Durham, NC: Duke University Press, 2010), p. 21.
8. Ibid., p. 21.
9. Ibid., p. 21.
10. Jon Protevi, *Political Affects: Connecting the Social and the Somatic* (Minneapolis, MN: University of Minnesota Press, 2009), p. xi.
11. Ibid., p. xi.
12. Gilles Deleuze, *The Logic of Sense*, ed. Constantin V. Boundas, trans. Mark Lester with Charles Stivale (New York: Columbia University Press, 1990).
13. Sean Bowden, '"Willing the Event": Expressive Agency in Deleuze's *Logic of Sense*', *Critical Horizons*, 15.3, 2014, pp. 231–48; Sean Bowden, 'Normativity and Expressive Agency in Hegel, Nietzsche, and Deleuze', *Journal of Speculative Philosophy*, 29.2, 2015, pp. 236–59; Sean Bowden, 'Tragedy and Agency in Hegel and Deleuze', in Craig Lundy and Daniella Voss (eds), *At the Edges of Thought: Deleuze and Post-Kantian Philosophy* (Edinburgh: Edinburgh University Press, 2015), pp. 212–28; Sean Bowden, 'Human and Nonhuman Agency in Deleuze', in Jon Roffe and Hannah Stark (eds), *Deleuze and the Non/Human* (Basingstoke: Palgrave Macmillan, 2015), pp. 60–80. I will focus on the first article, while drawing material from the others as and when necessary.
14. Gilles Deleuze, 'A Philosophical Concept . . .', in Eduardo Cadava, Peter Connor and Jean-Luc Nancy (eds), *Who Comes after the Subject?* (Abingdon: Routledge, 1991), pp. 94–5. Reprinted as 'Response to a Question of the Subject', in *Two Regimes of Madness: Texts and Interviews, 1975–1995*, ed. David Lapoujade, trans. Ames Hodges and Mike Taormina (New York: Semiotext(e), 2007), pp. 353–5. All references are to the former version.
15. Gilles Deleuze, *Bergsonism*, trans. Hugh Tomlinson and Barbara Habberjam (New York: Zone Books, 1988 [1966]); Gilles Deleuze, *Empiricism and Subjectivity: An Essay on Hume's Theory of Human Nature*, trans. Constantin V. Boundas (New York: Columbia University Press, 2001 [1966]); Gilles Deleuze, *Kant's*

Critical Philosophy, trans. Hugh Tomlinson and Barbara Habberjam (Minneapolis, MN: University of Minnesota Press, 1984 [1963]); Gilles Deleuze, *Nietzsche and Philosophy*, trans. Hugh Tomlinson (New York: Columbia University Press, 2006 [1962]).
16. Deleuze, *Difference and Repetition*, p. xv.
17. Ibid., p. xv.
18. Ibid., pp. xv, xvi.
19. Ibid., p. xix.
20. Georg W. F. Hegel, *The Science of Logic*, trans. and ed. George Di Giovanni (Cambridge: Cambridge University Press, 2010), p. 59.
21. Martin Heidegger, *Being and Time*, trans. John Macquarrie and Edward Robinson (Oxford: Blackwell, 1962). This is despite Heidegger's ongoing critique of Hegel. See, for example, Martin Heidegger, *Hegel's Phenomenology of Spirit*, trans. Parvis Emad and Kenneth Maly (Bloomington, IN: Indiana University Press, 1988), and Martin Heidegger, *Hegel*, trans. Joseph Arel and Niels Feuerhahn (Bloomington, IN: Indiana University Press, 2015).
22. Deleuze, *Difference and Repetition*, p. 27.
23. Ibid., p. 28.
24. Ibid., p. 28.
25. Ibid., p. 35.
26. Ibid., p. 36.
27. Ibid., p. 38.
28. Ibid., p. 57.
29. Ibid., pp. 56, 57.
30. Ibid., p. 57.
31. Ibid., p. 64.
32. Ibid., p. 59.
33. Ibid., p. 207.
34. Ibid., p. 279.
35. Ibid., p. 182.
36. Ibid., p. 183.
37. For a detailed analysis of Deleuze's ontological categories, see Gavin Rae, *Ontology in Heidegger and Deleuze* (Basingstoke: Palgrave Macmillan, 2014), ch. 6.
38. Deleuze, *Difference and Repetition*, p. xvii.
39. Emma Ingala, 'Of the Refrain (The Ritornello)', in Jeffery Bell, Henry Somers-Hall and James Williams (eds), *A Thousand Plateaus and Philosophy* (Edinburgh: Edinburgh University Press, 2018), pp. 190–205.
40. For more on this, see Gavin Rae, 'Traces of Identity in Deleuze's Differential Ontology', *International Journal of Philosophical Studies*, 22.1, 2014, pp. 86–105.
41. Gilles Deleuze, *Cinema 1: The Movement-Image*, trans. Hugh Tomlinson and Barbara Habberjam (Minneapolis, MN: University of Minnesota Press, 1994), p. 260; Gilles Deleuze and Félix Guattari, *What is Philosophy?*, trans. Hugh Tomlinson and Graham Burchell (New York: Columbia University Press, 1994), pp. 17–19; Gilles Deleuze, 'On *A Thousand Plateaus*', in *Negotiations:*

1972–1990, trans. M. Joughin (New York: Columbia University Press, 1995), pp. 25–35 (p. 26); Gilles Deleuze, *Francis Bacon: The Logic of Sensation*, trans. Daniel W. Smith (Minneapolis, MN: University of Minnesota Press, 2002), p. 19; Gilles Deleuze and Claire Parnet, 'On the Superiority of Anglo-American Literature', in *Dialogues II*, trans. Hugh Tomlinson and Barbara Habberjam (New York: Continuum, 2002), pp. 27–56; Gilles Deleuze and Claire Parnet, 'Dead Psychoanalysis: Analyse', in *Dialogues II*, trans. Hugh Tomlinson and Barbara Habberjam (London: Continuum, 2002), pp. 57–92; Gilles Deleuze and Félix Guattari, *A Thousand Plateaus*, trans. Brian Massumi (London: Continuum, 2004), pp. 123–64, 185–211.

42. Deleuze and Guattari, *A Thousand Plateaus*, p. 127.
43. Deleuze, *Francis Bacon*, p. 19.
44. Ibid., p. 19.
45. Deleuze and Guattari, *A Thousand Plateaus*, p. 189.
46. I have alternated between 'possibility' and 'potentiality' in the description of the virtual and, indeed, placed quotation marks around each to try to show that the virtual is not, strictly speaking, associated with either. The virtual is distinguished from 1) possibility, because it has a reality of its own whereas Deleuze claims that reality is added to possibility to make it real, and 2) potential, because Deleuze claims that potential entails a becoming that occurs within fixed parameters. The virtual, in contrast is, *pace* possibility, real and, *pace* potential, 'an' open-ended rhizomic becoming. In relation to 1), see Gilles Deleuze, 'Immanence: A Life', in *Two Regimes of Madness: Texts and Interviews, 1975–1995*, ed. David Lapoujade, trans. Ames Hodges and Mike Taormina (New York: Semiotext(e), 2007), pp. 388–94 (p. 392), and Deleuze, *Difference and Repetition*, pp. 191, 208; and on 2), see Gilles Deleuze, 'Bergson, 1859–1941', in *Desert Islands and Other Texts*, ed. David Lapoujade, trans. Mike Taormina (New York: Semiotext(e), 2004), pp. 22–31 (p. 30).
47. Deleuze and Guattari, *A Thousand Plateaus*, pp. 166, 169–70. See also Gilles Deleuze and Félix Guattari, *Anti-Oedipus*, trans. Robert Hurley, Mark Seem and Helen R. Lane (London: Continuum, 1984), pp. 9–11.
48. Deleuze and Guattari, *A Thousand Plateaus*, p. 186.
49. Deleuze, *Difference and Repetition*, p. 262.
50. Deleuze, *Cinema 1*, pp. 89–91.
51. Daniel W. Smith, 'A Life of Pure Immanence: Deleuze's "Critique et Clinique"', in *Essays on Deleuze* (Edinburgh: Edinburgh University Press, 2012), pp. 189–221 (p. 205).
52. Deleuze and Guattari, *A Thousand Plateaus*, p. 191.
53. Deleuze and Guattari, *What is Philosophy?*, p. 88.
54. Deleuze and Guattari, *A Thousand Plateaus*, p. 191.
55. Ibid., p. 191.
56. Ibid., p. 149.
57. Deleuze and Guattari, *What is Philosophy?*, p. 88.
58. Deleuze and Guattari, *A Thousand Plateaus*, p. 149.

59. Ibid., p. 199.
60. Ibid., p. 194.
61. Ibid., p. 201.
62. Ibid., p. 201.
63. For a discussion of Levinas's notion of the face, see Gavin Rae, *The Problem of Political Foundations in Carl Schmitt and Emmanuel Levinas* (Basingstoke: Palgrave Macmillan, 2016), ch. 7.
64. Gilles Deleuze and Claire Parnet, 'A Conversation: What is it? What is it for?', in *Dialogues II*, trans. Hugh Tomlinson and Barbara Habberjam (London: Continuum, 2002), pp. 1–26 (p. 16).
65. Deleuze and Guattari, *A Thousand Plateaus*, p. 189.
66. Ibid., p. 130.
67. Ibid., p. 131.
68. Ibid., p. 131.
69. Deleuze and Parnet, 'Dead Psychoanalysis', pp. 80, 79.
70. Ibid., p. 78.
71. Deleuze and Guattari, *A Thousand Plateaus*, p. 135.
72. Ibid., p. 135.
73. Ibid., p. 136.
74. Deleuze and Parnet, 'Dead Psychoanalysis', p. 79.
75. Deleuze and Guattari, *A Thousand Plateaus*, p. 136.
76. Ibid., p. 136.
77. Ibid., p. 136.
78. See, for example, the discussions in Eugene W. Holland, *Deleuze and Guattari's A Thousand Plateaus* (London: Bloomsbury, 2013), pp. 85–8; Brent Adkins, *Deleuze and Guattari's A Thousand Plateaus: A Critical Introduction and Guide* (Edinburgh: Edinburgh University Press, 2015), pp. 108–19; Nathan Widder, 'Year Zero: Faciality', in Jeffrey A. Bell, Henry Somers-Hall and James Williams (eds), *A Thousand Plateaus* (Edinburgh: Edinburgh University Press, 2018), pp. 115–33.
79. Deleuze, *Difference and Repetition*, p. 260.
80. Deleuze and Guattari, *What is Philosophy?*, p. 17.
81. This is reminiscent of Hegel's description of the role that fear plays in the overcoming of the master–slave dialectic, whereby fear of the master brings the slave to recognise that negativity is an aspect of his being and so reveals that he is not simply the thing that his position as a slave indicates. While Deleuze would no doubt reject the affirmation of negativity inherent in Hegel's description, Hegel's point does seem to support Deleuze's claim that transformative possibility emanates from the experience of terror. See Georg W. F. Hegel, *Phenomenology of Spirit*, trans. A. V. Miller (Oxford: Oxford University Press, 1977), p. 17.
82. Deleuze and Parnet, 'A Conversation', p. 16.
83. Deleuze and Guattari, *A Thousand Plateaus*, p. 208.
84. Ibid., p. 190.

85. Deleuze and Parnet, 'A Conversation', p. 17.
86. Deleuze and Guattari, *A Thousand Plateaus*, p. 208.
87. Ibid., p. 210.
88. Richard Rushton, 'What Can a Face Do? On Deleuze and Faces', *Cultural Critique*, 51, spring 2002, pp. 219–37 (p. 226).
89. Deleuze and Guattari, *A Thousand Plateaus*, p. 211.
90. On this point, see Simone Bignall, 'Dismantling the Face: Pluralism and the Politics of Recognition', *Deleuze Studies*, 6.3, 2012, pp. 389–410 (p. 390).
91. Deleuze, *The Logic of Sense*, p. 157.
92. Gilles Deleuze, *Foucault*, ed. and trans. Seán Hand (London: Continuum, 1999), p. 87.
93. Bowden, 'Human and Nonhuman Agency in Deleuze', p. 75.
94. Ibid., p. 75.
95. Ibid., p. 75.
96. Ibid., p. 75.
97. Ibid., p. 75.
98. Bowden, '"Willing the Event"', p. 234.
99. Ibid., p. 234.
100. Deleuze, *The Logic of Sense*, pp. 148–53.
101. Ibid., p. 149.
102. Bowden, '"Willing the Event"', p. 237.
103. Ibid., p. 237.
104. Deleuze, *The Logic of Sense*, p. 149.
105. Ibid., p. 149.
106. Bowden, '"Willing the Event"', p. 237.
107. Ibid., p. 237.
108. Ibid., p. 238.
109. Ibid., p. 238.
110. Ibid., p. 242.
111. Bowden, 'Normativity and Expressive Agency in Hegel, Nietzsche, and Deleuze', p. 249.
112. Bowden, '"Willing the Event"', p. 245.
113. Ibid., p. 245.
114. In many respects, this is the approach adopted throughout this chapter, in so far as it synthesises a number of Deleuze's texts. See also my *Ontology in Heidegger and Deleuze*, ch. 9.
115. Bowden, '"Willing the Event"', p. 232.
116. Bowden, 'Tragedy and Agency in Hegel and Deleuze', p. 213.
117. Eduardo Cadava, Peter Connor and Jean-Luc Nancy (eds), *Who Comes after the Subject?* (Abingdon: Routledge, 1991).
118. Gilles Deleuze, 'A Philosophical Concept . . .', p. 94.
119. Ibid., p. 94.
120. Ibid., p. 94.
121. Ibid., p. 94.

122. Ibid., p. 94.
123. Ibid., p. 95.
124. Ibid., p. 95.
125. Ibid., p. 95.
126. Ibid., p. 95.
127. Gilles Deleuze, 'How Do We Recognize Structuralism?', trans. Melissa McMahon and Charles J. Stivale, in *Desert Islands and Other Texts*, ed. David Lapoujade, trans. Mike Taormina (New York: Semiotext(e), 2004), pp. 170–92 (p. 190).

CHAPTER 2

Derrida's *Différance*: Deconstruction and the Sexuality of Subjectivity

Writing at around the same time as Deleuze, Jacques Derrida represents another strand of poststructuralist thought that differs subtly, but importantly, from Deleuze's, especially as it relates to the notion of the subject.[1] Whereas Deleuze rejects the historical privileging of identity and, instead, aims to think difference-in-itself, Derrida undertakes a critique of Heidegger's notion of the ontological difference to argue that what is more important is to think the difference – or as Derrida will call it for reasons to be explained, '*différance*'[2] – *between* difference and identity. However, while both Deleuze and Derrida emphasise pre-personal structures thought from difference/*différance*, Deleuze aims to abandon the notion of 'the subject' to analyse 'singularities', whereas I will show that Derrida aims to rethink the notion from *différance*; a position that accepts that 'the subject/subjectivity' will continue to play a key role in future Western thinking.

To do so, I first identify the basic coordinates of Derrida's notion of *différance*, as outlined in his 1968 essay of the same title,[3] before demonstrating what it means for the subject. This is important because, as Caroline Williams notes, 'the theorisation of the concept of the subject is central to deconstruction [and] has been a key component of Derrida's thinking from the 1960s'.[4] However, whereas many see Derrida as privileging *différance* in itself, with the consequence that they maintain that he aims simply to rethink the subject in terms of division, disruption and deferment,[5] I argue that *différance* is what might be called a constellation concept for Derrida, in so far as it acts as the nexus that binds multiple tasks and heterogeneous perspectives to offer a particularly complex conception of a particular issue. Instead of simply thinking 'the subject' from *différance*, in 1983's '*Geschlecht I*: Sexual Difference, Ontological Difference',[6] Derrida goes further by tying this relation to the question of sexuality also thought from *différance*. In so doing, he brings the question of sexuality firmly to the forefront of his rethinking of the subject and points to a political programme aimed at overcoming the logic of patriarchy. It does, however, lead to the question of who or what questions sexuality? It is here that the problematic motivating this book comes to the fore: Derrida affirms the primacy of *différance* to undermine the notion of a constituting subject, but it is unclear whether this means that the subject becomes merely an effect of the pre-personal structures and relations of *différance*, or whether Derrida continues to offer the possibility that the *différantial subject* can act autonomously and intentionally despite, on his telling, 'agency', like the subject, appearing to be grounded in and an effect of *différance*.

Derrida takes up this issue in the 1988 interview with Jean-Luc Nancy entitled '"Eating Well," or the Calculation of the Subject'.[7] While he aims to clarify the nature of 'who' comes after the 'subject' and what this 'after' means, the fundamental problem that results is that he, on the one hand, appeals (once more) to Heidegger's analysis of *Dasein* to suggest that, in the same way that *Dasein* substantialises itself in gender form through a mysterious process, so too will the reformulated 'subject', thereby permitting it to play a role in establishing the affirmation of *différance*. But, on the other hand, because Derrida holds that *différance* grounds all, the reconstituted 'subject' must be an effect of *différance*, thereby appearing to undermine the previous claim that the 'subject' can constitute itself and so effect (political) change. Derrida does not satisfactorily reconcile these two positions, with the consequence that it is not clear how he would adequately and consistently meet the charge that motivates this book; namely, to show how the constituted subject is capable of intentional agency to affect that which constitutes it.

Différance

On 27 January 1968 Jacques Derrida delivered a lecture to the Société française de philosophie titled 'Différance'. In it, he gives a rather programmatic overview and clarification of a, if not *the*, fundamental concept of his thinking: *différance*. The topics covered in the lecture are multiple, but a key feature running through it is the primacy of *différance* as opposed to difference (Deleuze), nothingness (Hegel and Sartre), human consciousness (Husserl and Kant) or being (Heidegger). The latter issue and figure were particularly important for the development of Derrida's thinking; indeed, it is from Heidegger's ontological difference that Derrida develops the notion and primacy of *différance*.[8]

Heidegger's ontological difference delineates the difference between being and entities. As he explains, 'being cannot have the character of an entity'[9] and so 'being, as that which is asked about, must be exhibited in a way of its own, essentially different from the way in which entities are discovered'.[10] Thought that focuses on entities and facts about them is called ontic. However, thought 'remains . . . naïve and opaque if in its researches into the being of entities it fails to discuss the meaning of being in general'.[11] Heidegger spent the rest of his career trying to outline what this entails and how ontic and ontological analyses relate to one another, an inquiry that required a famous methodological *kehre*.

Whereas *Being and Time* claims that one entity, human being or *Dasein*[12] is capable of raising the question of the meaning of being, with the consequence that Heidegger starts with an inquiry into *Dasein* to reveal being, he subsequently recognised that such an approach is too ontic, in so far as it makes an analysis of being dependent on first understanding *Dasein*. To correct this, he turned to study being as a precursor to revealing ontic beings. The most famous and extended discussion of this takes place in the 'Letter on Humanism'.[13] For Heidegger, this turn instantiated a new form of humanism, one in which human being is understood as the 'shepherd of being'[14] rather than its foundation.

Derrida starts his engagement with Heidegger from the relationship between being and human being.[15] For our purposes, two criticisms stand out. First, in the famous essay 'The Ends of Man', Derrida claims that Heidegger does not break with the metaphysical tradition because his analysis remains too humanistic and, indeed, continues to affirm the tradition's emphasis on unity as manifested through his obsessive affirmation of the meaning of the question of being; one that, for Derrida, is based on a 'proper' and so singular questioning that will lead to a final, correct answer.[16]

Second, Derrida insists that Heidegger simply came to the wrong conclusion from his analysis of the ontological difference. By claiming that entities can only be understood through an inquiry into their being, Heidegger maintains the fundamental importance of being when, for Derrida, it actually reveals that being, in so far as it is only revealed through its difference from entities, depends upon and emanates from difference. Difference, or as he would come to write it for reasons that will be shortly outlined, *différance*, is, then, 'in a certain and very strange way . . . "older" than the ontological difference or than the truth of being'.[17] Thus, identity is not overcome by engaging with the question of the meaning of being, but by affirming the difference (between being and entities) upon which Heidegger's questioning of being depends.

With this, Derrida establishes a different frame of reference for overcoming identity. Whereas Heidegger affirms being as a means to understand human being – whether this is through a study of a privileged human as in his pre-*kehre* writings or from a prior study of being post-*kehre* is largely irrelevant for current purposes – Derrida effects a movement to the non- or pre-individual difference inherent 'in' the relations between 'things' to explore how this *necessarily* disrupts and undermines identity. For Derrida, any claim to identity results from a failure to appreciate that reality is actually an effect of differential relations.

While it might be thought that Derrida is here simply affirming the same conclusion as Deleuze, he is actually offering a subtle but important critique of Deleuze. Whereas Deleuze claims that overcoming the historical affirmation of identity requires that we think of difference as and from difference, Derrida maintains that this merely inverts the privileged term within the identity–difference economy that has dominated Western thinking. As such, it does not challenge the *logic* that has structured that thinking, nor is it capable of recognising that this economy is dependent upon the 'difference' or 'between' that binds, all the while distinguishing, the two terms in the economy. However, while the two terms are bound by their difference, Derrida cannot term that relationality 'difference', because 'difference' is one of the terms of the relation. A 'thing' cannot be part of a non-hierarchical heterogeneous economy, while being that which grounds the economy because the latter creates a hierarchy disqualified by the former premise. But neither can it be taken to be a foundational or transcendent third term that grounds the relation because this would risk reintroducing a metaphysics of transcendence and substance that, following Heidegger, Derrida criticises and rejects. Instead, Derrida maintains that what permits the relation and, indeed, generates the parts of the relation must be wholly immanent to the relation itself and, indeed, nothing other than a relation. To describe this, Derrida introduces the term *différance*.

The first thing to note is that *différance* is not a 'word nor a concept'.[18] It is a relation, one that accompanies all presence but is itself never present. Indeed, while 'it is read, or it is written . . . it cannot be heard',[19] a position that, in privileging the written over the spoken, continues Derrida's critique of logo-phonocentrism.[20] The 'a' of *différance* plays a special role, in so far as it 'is not heard; it remains silent, secret and discreet as a tomb'.[21] That it cannot be heard, spoken or defined does not, however, mean that it does not exist, nor does it diminish its importance. Rather, it is that which is undefinable, but also that which is most important.

The reasoning for this will become clear as we proceed, but Derrida is following the structuralist mantra that meaning is relational rather than substantial. As we saw in the Introduction, Saussure claims that sense emanates, not from concepts, but from the relations between concepts.[22] It is the difference between concepts that is crucial for the generation of sense. Derrida accepts Saussure's basic point, but criticises him for limiting its applicability to semantics. For Derrida, *différance* does not only refer to the 'play of differences within language but also the relation of speech to language'.[23]

Différance is therefore different to 'difference'. Simply affirming the latter risks turning 'difference' into a singular category that generates all other concepts or entities. This would reinstantiate the logic of onto-theology, albeit one that privileges 'difference' over 'God' or 'being' or any other concept, that has traditionally been privileged. For this reason, Derrida warns that

> [d]*ifférance* is not only irreducible to any ontological or theological – onto-theological – reappropriation, but as the very opening of the space in which ontotheology – philosophy – produces its system and its history, it includes ontotheology, inscribing it and exceeding it without return.[24]

Différance is not an onto-theological concept because – while Derrida is aware that his descriptions will often 'resemble those of negative theology, occasionally even to the point of being indistinguishable from negative theology'[25] – *différance* rejects negative theology's dependence on a single foundation. However, *différance* cannot be thought in terms of 'existence [or] essence. It derives from no category of being, whether present or absent.'[26] As that which gives rise to the presence–absence relation, *différance* cannot be defined by either. It 'exceeds the alternative of presence and absence'.[27]

With this, Derrida notes that *différance* 'is the condition for the possibility and functioning of every sign', it 'is in itself a silent play' and 'the difference which establishes phonemes and lets them be heard remains in and of itself inaudible, in every sense of the word'.[28] *Différance* is never present and so never announces itself, not because it is nothing, but because *différance* is not defined by being or nothing; 'it' is that which makes the difference between being and nothing possible. These categories are effects of *différance* and so cannot turn in on themselves to reveal that which grounds them, especially because those foundations do not present themselves.

Crucially, while *différance* subtends the being–nothing economy, it is not opposed to this economy. Opposing *différance* to the being–nothing economy would create a binary opposition between the being of that economy and the *non*-being of *différance* that, somewhat paradoxically, would 'collect' *différance* into the logic of binary opposition and, by extension, the restrictions of ontology. It would not, then, ask about the differential relations that subtend and so give meaning to ontological categories. Derrida is aware that thinking this is an 'uneasy and uncomfortable'[29] task, but claims that it is imperative that we recognise that *différance* is not defined by ontological categories, nor by its difference/opposition to them; it describes the differential relations that 1) distinguish ontological categories and 2) generate the meaning of those categories. As Derrida puts it, 'difference is not a distinction, an essence, or an opposition, but a movement of spacing, a "becoming-space" of time, a "becoming-time" of space, a reference to alterity, to a heterogeneity that is not first a matter of opposition'.[30] *Différance* subtends all oppositions. So, to summarise, because opposition is fundamental to ontology (being versus nothing, for example), Derrida claims that *différance* is *not* an ontological concept. *Différance* highlights the differential *logic* that gives rises to and continues to define the relations between ontological categories.

The problem is that it is all too easy to slip back into a logic of ontological opposition. For example, if we think of *différance* as an activity that generates entities, *différance* would be thought from the active/passive matrix and so inscribed *within* a restricted economy. *Différance*, however, is 'beyond every kind of limit: whether it is a matter of cultural, national, linguistic, or even human limits'.[31] It is that which comes logically and not temporally 'prior' to the being–nothing relationship specifically and binary oppositions generally, with the consequence that it cannot be understood in opposition to anything or in terms of an oppositional logic such as that which underpins the being–nothing and active–passive relationships. Indeed, as that which makes relations between concepts possible, *différance* is never manifest and 'cannot be exposed' because 'one can expose only that which at a certain moment can become *present*, manifest, that which can be shown, presented as something present, a present-being in its truth, in the truth of a present or the presence of the present'.[32] Only its effects are presented and, even then, their meaning is always deferred.

Developing this, Derrida turns to the etymology of *différance* to explain that it is composed of two aspects: first, a temporal aspect linked to deferment, which ensures that its meaning is always reserved and continuously put off until later. This is accompanied by a spatial aspect linked to differentiation that ensures that 'it' is never identical with itself or anything else, cannot be discerned, and is always other.[33] Importantly, *différance* is nothing other than this continual process of 'self-'division. It is this that lies behind 'the difference marked in the "differ( )nce" between the *e* and the *a*',[34] 'difference' and 'différance'. This does not point to a 'third' mediating term between difference and *différance*, but reveals the structure of differential relations themselves: they are always differentiated and differentiating; a movement that is intrinsic to *différance* rather than that which must be generated external to it. As Derrida explains in an interview with Antoine Spire,

> [i]n *différance*, it's not just about time but also about space. It's a movement in which the distinction between space and time has not yet come about: spacing, becoming-space of time and becoming-time of space, *differentiation*, process of production of differences and experience of absolute alterity.[35]

Différance is, then, the source of opposition and signification, but because origin has traditionally implied foundation, which is, of course, denied by the deferred differentiation of *différance*, Derrida insists that 'the name "origins" no longer suits it'.[36] *Différance* cannot be located in a source, even one defined by nothingness, but is that from which being and nothing emanate, without this point of emanation being, in fact, a point or an origin. It will also be remembered that it is differentiated/ing and so inherently multiple and unstable.

Derrida is clearly walking a very thin line here, but his overall point is to emphasise that entities do not emanate from a particular act nor from categories traditionally associated with being. They emanate from a becoming that, by virtue of the nature of that becoming, does not and cannot be thought from a point of origin. For this reason, he explains that

> we will designate as *différance* the movement according to which language, or any code, any system of referral in general, is constituted 'historically' as a weave of differences. 'Is constituted,' 'is produced,' 'is created,' 'movement,' 'historically' etc., necessarily being understood beyond the metaphysical language in which they are retained, along with all their implications.[37]

Importantly, Derrida claims that those who privilege human consciousness or action to account for the break-up of identity or the effecting of change fail to understand that such action is grounded in *différance*. For this reason, he explains that 'presence – and specifically consciousness, the being beside itself of consciousness – [is posited] no longer as the absolutely central form of being but as a "determination" and as an "effect"'.[38]

Although the primary orientation of Derrida's affirmation of *différance* is to deconstruct the categories and logic that subtend traditional metaphysics, he points out that it also has significant political importance. We have, however, to understand this in a particular way. Derrida is not a rule-based or systematic political theorist. While he will later come to affirm politics of justice, hospitality and cosmopolitanism,[39] there is no systematic political programme offered. His thinking on the political is always deconstructive, undermining any claim to an authoritative foundation to open spaces for alternatives or those excluded. *Différance* therefore 'governs nothing, reigns over nothing, and nowhere exercises any authority. It is not announced by any capital letter. Not only is there no kingdom of *différance*, but *différance* instigates the subversion of every kingdom.'[40]

Two issues stand out from this. First, *différance* undermines authoritarian claims to truth and monolithic political and social structures upon which such authority rests by showing that these are composed of moving relations that are, as a consequence, historical, unstable and contestable. Second, the political consequences of *différance* and, indeed, *différance* itself are not the result of a subjective decision or action; they emanate from the pre-individual deferring–differentiation movement inherent in *différance*. Not only does this appear to make subjectivity an effect of *différance*, thereby undercutting any singular foundational point for political action, but it also seems that subjective action to disrupt political structures is impossible or irrelevant; these structures are always already undermined by the difference–deferment structure of *différance*. Derrida's analysis of *différance* leads, then, to the question of the relationship between *différance* and subjectivity. I take this up in the next two sections, first through the mediation of his analysis of sexual difference, before turning to the question of what happens to the subject from this deconstruction.

Différance and the Sexual Difference

I noted in the Introduction that one of the criticisms levelled against poststructuralism by a certain strand of feminist critique relates to its lack of focus on issues to do with sex or gender. According to this line of attack, poststructuralist thought removes all socio-historical and/or biological marks from the subject, with the consequence that poststructuralist analyses are unable (and, for some, unwilling) to discuss sex/gender. Whatever the truth of this with regard to other poststructuralist thinkers, this is not the case with Derrida. As Elizabeth Grosz notes,

> Derridean deconstruction [poses] a series of the most difficult challenges to the self-conception of feminist theories, challenges – not simply critiques or objections – that . . . [raise] questions about the status of subversion, the position of subordination, and the possibilities of transgression that feminists now need to address if feminism is to remain a viable and effective political force into the twenty-first century.[41]

It is, therefore, not just that Derrida talks explicitly about sex and the sexual difference, but that he does so in a way that challenges any notion of a strict binary opposition between two sexes to, in so doing, open up the logic that can be used to think about sex(uality). As I aim to show, this rethinking of sexual difference is built from and on his notion of *différance*.

In 1983 Derrida published '*Geschlecht I*: Sexual Difference, Ontological Difference', which deals with the question of sexuality in Heidegger's fundamental ontology. Derrida starts by noting that

> [o]f sex, one can readily remark, yes, Heidegger speaks as little as possible, perhaps he has never spoken of it. Perhaps he has never said anything, by that name or the names under which we recognise it, about the 'sexual relation,' 'sexual difference,' or indeed about 'man-and-woman.'[42]

Given that the discussion of *Dasein* in *Being and Time*, for example, does not discuss sexuality, '[o]ne might conclude ... that sexual difference is not an essential trait, that it does not belong to the essential structure of *Dasein*. Being-there, being *there*, the *there* of being as such, bears no sexual mark.'[43] But no sooner does it appear as if the matter is settled than Derrida exclaims 'And yet!',[44] thereby indicating that there is more going on than meets the eye (so to speak). In particular, he notes that in the lecture course – translated as *The Metaphysical Foundations of Logic* – given at Marburg in 1928, the year after *Being and Time* was published, Heidegger addresses the issue of the relationship between *Dasein* and sexuality. In particular, Heidegger explains that 'the term "man" was not used for that being which is the theme of the analysis. Instead, the neutral term *Dasein* was chosen.'[45] Indeed, he goes on to affirm that 'the peculiar *neutrality* of the term "Dasein" is essential, because the interpretation of this being must be carried out prior to every factual concretion. This neutrality also indicates that Dasein is neither of the two sexes.'[46] As a consequence, fundamental ontology does not and, indeed, cannot engage with the specific facticity of each entity, but must be conducted from a neutral basis.

Sexuality and the sexual difference must, then, be put aside for the ontological analysis into the being of *Dasein* to proceed. The significance of the positing of this originary neutrality is twofold: *epistemologically*, it ensures that the analysis of the meaning of being proceeds from how being reveals itself in its becoming rather than from any categories that are imposed on to it from the tradition; *ontologically*, it secures being's pure becoming because it confirms that the becoming is not constrained or contained within *a priori* structures. It is for this reason that Heidegger explains that turning to originary neutrality is not to affirm an abstract void. Instead, it recognises and announces 'the potency of the *origin*, which bears in itself the intrinsic possibility of every concrete factual humanity'.[47] Strictly speaking, '[n]eutral Dasein is never what exists; Dasein exists in each case only in its factical concretion . . . [N]eutral Dasein is . . . the primal source of intrinsic possibility that springs up in every existence and makes it intrinsically possible.'[48] Prior to sexual designation 'lies', according to Heidegger, a neutral *Dasein*, which 'harbours the intrinsic possibility for being factically dispersed into bodiliness and thus into sexuality'.[49]

From this discussion, Derrida first focuses on Heidegger's claim that its neutrality 'indicates that Dasein is neither of the two sexes'.[50] Derrida is somewhat perplexed by this: what happened between the publication of *Being and Time* in 1927, where it is not mentioned, and the lecture course in 1928 where 'it figures . . . at the forefront of the traits to be mentioned'?[51] Derrida's response is that this turn permits Heidegger to posit a particular conception of sexuality: 'if *Dasein* is neutral, and if it is not man (*Mensch*), the first consequence to draw out from this is that it does not submit to the binary partition one most spontaneously thinks of in such a case, namely, "sexual difference"'.[52] Thus, if *Dasein* does not mean 'man', its neutrality 'designates neither "man" nor "woman"'.[53]

Second, Derrida holds this to be important because it points towards a particular transition from the originary (ontological) neutrality of *Dasein* to ontic sexual difference: 'the sexless neutrality does not desexualise; on the contrary, its *ontological* negativity is not deployed with respect to *sexuality itself* (which it would instead liberate), but with respect to the marks of difference, or more precisely to *sexual duality*'.[54] Heidegger does not start from sexual designation and then remove sex to achieve the neutrality of *Dasein*. He starts from the neutrality of *Dasein*, claiming that it is 'the primordial positivity and potency of the essence',[55] to open up the possibilities for ontic sexual expression. Thus,

> [i]f *Dasein* as such belongs to neither of the two sexes, that does not mean that it is deprived of sex. On the contrary: here one must think of a pre-differential, or rather a pre-dual, sexuality – which, as we shall later, does not necessarily mean unitary, homogeneous, and undifferentiated.[56]

Prior to the ontic, sexual, male–female difference lies a more fundamental, non-dualistic sphere described, by Heidegger, as neutral: 'the a-sexuality [of *Dasein*'s neutrality] does not signify in this instance the absence of sexuality – one could call it the instinct, desire or even the libido – but the absence of any mark belonging to one of the two sexes'.[57] Prior to all ontic sexual designation lies a 'realm' of non-sexual neutrality that becomes ontically sexualised:

> beginning with that sexuality, more originary than the dyad, one may try to think at its source a 'positivity' and a 'potency' that Heidegger is careful not to call 'sexual,' fearing no doubt to reintroduce the binary logic that anthropology and metaphysics always assign to the concept of sexuality.[58]

The pre-sexual 'realm' does not conform to the male–female dyad of 'traditional' sexuality; ontic sexuality is generated from a 'prior' neutrality.

This, of course, requires an explanation of how the pre-sexual, non-dyadic structure becomes ontically sexualised. Derrida's (and Heidegger's) response is rather disappointing: 'by some strange yet very necessary displacement, sexual division itself leads us to negativity'.[59] While neither Derrida nor Heidegger can explain it, Derrida does note that the 'positivity' that generates the movement towards ontic sexuality can descend into negativity, by which he means opposition, so that ontic sexuality is defined by a logic of versus. This 'sexual binarity'[60] nullifies the openness that defines the original neutrality by constraining its expression within a restricted economy.

Crucially, the creation of a sexual binary does not simply bind two sexualities together in opposition; it creates an imbalance, wherein one is privileged over the other, thereby creating a 'discrimination belonging to one or the other sex . . . that destines (to) or determines a negativity that must then be accounted for'.[61] As Derrida explains: 'when sexual difference is determined by *opposition* in the dialectical sense . . . one appears to set off "the war between the sexes"; but one precipitates the end with the victory going to the masculine sex'.[62] Overcoming this binary opposition requires a return 'to the originarity of *Dasein*, of this *Dasein* said to be sexually neutral [so that], "original positivity" and "potency" [*puissance*] can be recovered'.[63] This presumably will break the restriction inherent in the dyad to permit an alternative form of sexual difference and relationship, one that accords with the open androgyny of *Dasein*'s originary ontological indeterminacy.

As Heidegger notes, however, this is not a return to an 'egocentric individual, the ontic isolated individual'.[64] *Dasein*'s neutrality, removed from any ontic designations, does not lead to a pure, unencumbered egoism. Nor is it 'identical with the vagueness of a fuzzy concept of a "consciousness as such"'.[65] While it 'does imply a peculiar isolation of the human being', it does not refer to an individual who 'is the centre of the world. Rather, it is the *metaphysical isolation* of the human being.'[66] Heidegger's use of 'metaphysics' here is somewhat problematic because he will increasingly come to see metaphysics as the problem to be overcome,[67] but, in this instance, it simply refers to pre-factical *Dasein*; 'something' that can never exist *per se*, but must be thought to explain ontic *Dasein*.

Importantly, 'Dasein harbours the intrinsic possibility for being factically dispersed into bodiliness and thus into sexuality'.[68] It is from its metaphysical isolation and the factical neutrality this implies that *Dasein* is subsequently embodied, through a process of dispersal, into a particular facticity and sexuality. As Derrida explains, 'the sequence proposed by Heidegger seems very clear: the dispersing multiplicity is not primarily due to the sexuality of the body; it is bodiliness itself, the flesh, the *Leiblichkeit*, that originally draws *Dasein* into dispersion and *thus* into sexual difference'.[69] The dispersion into facticity must not be understood negatively or as some loss of a previous 'paradise'. The 'metaphysical' neutrality of '*Dasein* is not an empty abstraction drawn from or in the sense of the ontic . . . but rather what is the authentic concreteness of the origin, the "not-yet" of factical dissemination'.[70] In other words, the neutrality of *Dasein* is the 'prior' that must be expressed factically. It does not, then, describe a glorious origin, but a transcendental condition of facticity. For this reason, the 'dissociated being, un-bound, or de-socialised . . . is not a fall or an accident . . . It is an originary structure of *Dasein* that affects it – along with a body, and *thus* with sexual difference – with multiplicity and unbinding.'[71]

The implications of the relationship between the originary neutrality of *Dasein* and its expression in ontic facticity are striking: 'Assigned to a body, *Dasein* is separated in its facticity, subjected to dispersion and division (*zersplittert*), and concomitantly (*ineins damit*) always disunited, disaccorded, split, divided (*zwiespältig*) by sexuality into a particular sex (*in eine bestimmte Geschlechtlichkeit*).'[72] Far from being grounded in unity or identity, the neutrality of *Dasein* reveals an originary domain 'prior' to any identity or sexuality marked as difference or opposition. This neutrality cannot take on the form of an identity, but is expressed as one once it is dispersed into facticity. Derrida's overarching point is that Heidegger's conception of *Dasein* points to a conception of human being that is differential and constituted by absence: *Dasein* is split from its own facticity, but also expressed factically through its diversion and dispersion in a particular body and sexuality, which themselves are varied. Any facticity adopted continues to be 'underpinned' by the originary 'neutral' *différance* that permits different facticities to arise.

To outline this, Heidegger distinguishes between 'multiplicity' and 'multiplication'.[73] Specifically, he recognises that '"dispersion," "disunity" sound negative at first, (as does "destruction"), and negative concepts such as these, taken ontically, are associated with negative evaluations', before clarifying that 'here we are dealing with something else, with a description of the multiplication (not "multiplicity") which is present in every factically individuated Dasein as such'.[74] From the perspective of a privileging of unity – which Heidegger claims has dominated Western thinking – any valorisation of multiplication or multiplicity takes us away from the One and so is understood negatively. For Heidegger, however, there never is 'a' One that is simply multiplied: being is multiplication and, for this reason (and anticipating Deleuze, who makes the same claim forty years later without ever mentioning Heidegger), 'multiplicity belongs to being itself'.[75] Being as multiplicity means that 'in its metaphysically neutral concept, Dasein's essence already contains a primordial *bestrewal* [*Streuung*], which is in a quite definite respect a *dissemination* [*Zerstreuung*]'.[76]

From this, Derrida explains that '*Dasein* never relates to *one* object, to a single object. If it does, it is always in the mode of abstraction or abstention with regard to other beings that always co-appear at the same time.'[77] *Dasein* is not a unity that experiences a multiplicity of objects; the multiplicity of *Dasein* makes possible the multiple objects it experiences: 'it is the originary, disseminal structure, the dispersion of *Dasein*, that makes possible this multiplicity'.[78] *Dasein* comes to existence through an act of auto-dispersion, wherein it becomes manifest ontically through an initial dissemination. This is not done to it, but is the process through which *Dasein* 'obtains' a factical existence. This 'transcendental dispersion',[79] according to Derrida, 'belongs to the essence of *Dasein* in its neutrality'.[80] This essence is linked to the notion of thrown-ness, which, for Derrida, is linked to both the transcendental dispersion that permits ontic expression and the fact of ontic expression itself. *Dasein* is thrown to a particular form of transcendental dispersion, which becomes manifest through and in a specific factical thrown-ness. Thus, the spatial expression of *Dasein* depends on the prior thrown-ness linked to the transcendental dispersion defining its neutrality. *Dasein* is never a unity or identity; it is always unstable and dispersed. It is here that Derrida returns to the issue of sexual difference.

To do so, he notes that the question of sexual difference is tied to the neutrality of *Dasein*, and, by extension, the ontological difference and Heidegger's fundamental ontology. That *Dasein* is neutral and tied to dispersion reveals it to be dispersed *into* the sexual difference. There is, therefore, 'no properly sexual predicate [that] refer[s] back, in its meaning, to the *general* structures of *Dasein*'.[81] From this, Derrida draws two conclusions. First, sexuality is not essential or ontological, but is an ontic construction resulting from how the ontological difference and neutrality of *Dasein* are manifested factically. Any understanding of sexuality is discursive, in so far as it 'evoke[s] remoteness [*éloignement*], the inside and the outside, dispersion and proximity, the here and the there, birth and death, the between-birth-and-death, being-with and discourse'.[82] That it is discursive means that it is constructed, rather than biologically determined. Sexual identity and orientation 'are all determinations that are derived from and occur after the *Dasein*'.[83]

Second, this constructivism 'opens thinking to a sexual difference that would not yet be sexual duality, difference as dual'.[84] That being is multiplicity, with *Dasein* understood as a 'metaphysical neutral[ity]'[85] that is dispersed into facticity, including sexuality, brings Derrida to point out that multiple forms of sexual difference are possible. There is the sexual difference understood as dyadic opposition, a relation which, as we saw, is defined by negativity, in so far as sexuality is limited to two options, one of which is held to be the negative of (and subordinate to) to the other. But the neutrality of *Dasein* subtending its factical dispersion means that other forms of sexual difference are possible: 'in leading back to dispersion and multiplication (*Zerstreuung, Mannigfaltigung*), might one not begin to think of a sexual difference (without negativity, let us be clear) that would not be sealed by the two?'[86] Rather than dyadic opposition, we are led to a different notion of sexual *différance* based on the affirmation of the *différance* of each aspect.

Derrida is, in other words, pointing out that sexuality does not need to conform to a binary opposition, but can take different forms '[b]eyond the binary difference that governs the decorum of all codes, beyond the opposition feminine/masculine, beyond bisexuality as well, beyond homosexuality and heterosexuality which come to the same thing'.[87] For this reason, he suggests that it is better to 'speak . . . of sexual *differences*, rather than of just one difference'.[88] This not only requires a rethinking of the concepts 'man' and 'woman' but also a re-examination of 'the line of cleavage between the two sexes';[89] an endeavour that clearly has ethical-political intent aimed at undermining the dominant patriarchal conceptions of sexuality and the notion of *a* sexual difference. As Derrida puts it,

> I would like to believe in the multiplicity of sexually marked voices. I would like to believe in the masses, this interminable number of blended voices, this mobile of non-identified sexual marks whose choreography can carry, divide, multiply the body of each 'individual,' whether he be classified as 'man' or as 'woman' according to the criteria of usage.[90]

Derrida's engagement with Heidegger's notion of the ontological difference and comments on sexuality are important, then, not simply because they correct the common assumption that Heidegger says nothing about sexuality,[91] but because they show that Heidegger recognises that sexuality is tied intimately to the ontological difference and, in particular, the analytic of *Dasein* that is constitutive of *Being and Time*. By revealing that sexual differences result from a prior asexuality, Derrida aims to undermine any notion of an essential or biological sexuality. Sexuality is immanently constructed from the ontological neutrality or indeterminateness that 'precedes' *Dasein*'s facticity. It also undermines conceptions of sexual difference thought in terms of patriarchal opposition, points to an alternative non-oppositional notion of sexual difference, and suggests that sexuality is and should be thought of and, indeed, celebrated for being fluid and differential. It does, however, lead to one particularly pertinent question. If the scaffolding supporting both the identity of that questioned (= sexual difference) and (the being/sex of) the questioner (= subject) are effects of *différance*, is it actually possible for a *subject* to turn back on itself to intentionally question its foundations, reveal the *différantial* neutrality subtending it, and express it in alternative ways, or is it the case that such action is only ever the result of the pre-personal movements inherent in *différance*? In short, the question of *who* is doing the questioning comes to the fore; an issue that ties Derrida's affirmation of *différance* to the question of intentional agency.

Beyond the Subject

In 1988 Derrida responded to this issue in an interview given to Jean-Luc Nancy entitled '"Eating Well," or the Calculation of the Subject'. His comments are important because they point to the figure that comes 'after' the deconstruction of the subject and reveal much about Derrida's thinking on the topic more generally. Briefly engaging with the content of this interview will then determine the extent to which an agent – whatever form this takes – continues to adhere to Derrida's thinking, as well as determining the degree to which such an agent is capable of effecting the political and epistemological changes that Derrida's deconstruction of identity and affirmation of *différance* demands.

Given Derrida's deconstruction of the subject, the question of 'who comes after the subject' is, as he notes, an interesting one because it is premised on a number of assumptions, including the nature of 'after' and the assumption that it is an agent of some sort, not a thing (which would require the designation 'what') that succeeds it. However, for Derrida, these two questions depend upon a certain 'confused'[92] understanding of recent French thinking:

> the question 'who comes *after* the subject'... implies that for a certain philosophical opinion today, in its most visible configuration, something named 'subject' can be identified, as its alleged passing might also be identified in certain identifiable thoughts or discourses.[93]

Derrida maintains that the question of the passing of the subject is frequently understood as a desire to *annihilate* the subject completely. It is from this premise that the question of 'who' comes *after* the subject is established, in so far as it is based on a certain temporal rupture and binary opposition between subjectivity and, what we might call, post-subjectivity.

The problem, according to Derrida, is that no such annihilation took place:

> Did Lacan 'liquidate' the subject? No. The decentred subject of which he speaks certainly doesn't have the traits of the classical subject (and even here, we'd have to take a closer look...), though it remains indispensable to the economy of the Lacanian theory. It is also correlate of the law.[94]

We will return to Lacan in Chapter 6, but Derrida also mentions Althusser, who 'seeks to discredit a certain authority of the subject only by acknowledging for the instance of the "subject" an irreducible place in a theory of ideology',[95] and Foucault, who offers 'a history of subjectivity that, in spite of certain massive declarations about the effacement of the figure of man, certainly never consisted in "liquidating" the Subject'.[96] For these thinkers, 'the subject can be re-interpreted, restored, re-inscribed, it certainly isn't "liquidated"'.[97] By pointing to these instances, Derrida questions how these figures have been read, undermines the notion that the 'subject' can simply be removed, and clarifies that the deconstruction of the subject does not entail the annihilation of the subject *per se*, but affirms the abandonment of the classical, or Cartesian, notion of subjectivity (understood as individuated, autonomous, prior to all structures and so on), and its replacement with an alternative thought from *différance*.

To develop this, Derrida again returns to Heidegger's notion of *Dasein* to suggest that

> *Dasein* cannot be reduced to a subjectivity, certainly, but the existential analytic still retains the formal traits of every transcendental analytic. *Dasein*, and what there is in it that answers to the question 'Who?' comes to occupy, no doubt displacing lots of other things, the place of the 'subject,' the cogito or the classical '*Ich denke*.'[98]

Dasein is not subjectivity, but occupies the place that the subject long had: it is the concept around which Heidegger's analysis, in *Being and Time*, revolves and retains a number of features traditionally associated with subjectivity: 'freedom, resolute-decision . . . a relation or presence to self, the "call" [*Ruf*] toward a moral conscience, responsibility, primordial imputability or guilt [*Schuldigsein*], etc.'[99] With the notion of *Dasein*, Heidegger does not simply leave behind subjectivity, but reconfigures it. This accords with Heidegger's claim – one that Derrida takes over – that a trace of metaphysics, of which subjectivity is a key component, will continue to inform that which will overcome it.[100]

Heidegger's notion of *Dasein* is, then, one way in which a form of post-subjectivity – which, to reiterate, does not mean the abandonment of subjectivity but only the overcoming of a particular way of thinking about the subject – could be thought. For this reason, Derrida continually returns to this concept in his analyses of *différance* and sexual difference. It does, however, lead to two problems: 'first: what becomes of those problematics that seemed to presuppose a classical determination of the subject (objectivity, be it scientific of other – ethical, legal, political, etc.), and second: who or what "answers" to the question "who?"'[101]

Derrida is somewhat evasive in response to both questions, but he does suggest that 'I would keep the name provisionally as an index for the discussion', before going on to clarify that he does not 'see the necessity of keeping the word "subject" at any price',[102] thereby indicating that there will be a transitional phase wherein the nature and name of the 'place' long occupied by the signifier 'the subject' will be worked out. Such a transition must not start with a direct analysis of the subject, but from the nature of the question itself:

> I note first of all in passing that to substitute a very indeterminate 'who' for a 'subject' overburdened with metaphysical determinations is perhaps not enough to bring about any decisive displacement. In the expression *the question 'Who'?* the emphasis might well later fall on the word 'question.' Not only in order to ask *who* asks the question or *on the subject of whom* the question is asked [so much does syntax decide the answer in advance], but to ask if there is a subject, a 'who,' before being able to ask questions about it.[103]

There are at least two issues of importance here. First, with the suggestion that the real issue is not the subject *per se*, but the syntax that generates the notion of the subject, Derrida moves the discussion away from 'the subject' to the pre-personal linguistic structures subtending 'the subject'. This, however, leads to the second issue: 'who' is the one moving from a questioning of the subject to the questioning of the syntax that generates 'the subject'? On the one hand, it seems to be the individual called 'Derrida' who is intentionally calling for that movement to the pre-personal level, but 'Derrida' then claims that such action is dependent on the configuration of the pre-personal syntax generating the problematic. If this is accurate, the movement is, in many respects, a random gift of *différance*. If, however, it is not, then Derrida has to explain how that is possible.

Perhaps realising this, Derrida goes on to outline some of the features of the approach that he would adopt to rethink subjectivity. He is clear that 'the relation to self, in this situation, can only be difference, that is to say alterity, or trace. Not only is the obligation not lessened in this situation, but, on the contrary, it finds in it its only possibility, which is neither subjective nor human.'[104] To clarify what this means, he asks 'what, in the structure of the classical subject, continues to be required by the question "Who?"'[105] His response navigates a complex system of different logics. He does not advocate that the subject be overcome by simply returning to a reconfigured conception of subjectivity based in identity, unity and will.[106] This strategy is an impossible one for the simple reason that 'there has never been The Subject for anyone, that's what I wanted to begin by saying. The subject is a fable.'[107]

That the subject is a fable does not, however, undermine its force or reality. The fable has long structured (philosophical) discourse; we have, in other words, become accustomed to it. Given this, it cannot simply be surgically removed from our lexicon. As a consequence, Derrida maintains that we must rethink the 'who' in terms of *différance*:

> The singularity of the 'who' is not the individuality of a thing that would be identical to itself, it is not an atom. It is a singularity that dislocates or divides itself in gathering itself together to answer to the other, whose call somehow precedes its own identification with itself.[108]

There are at least two ways to interpret this statement: 1) the 'who' is a unity thought in terms of *différance* and so is constantly breaking up, dissolving to reunite itself before dispersing again. This version has the advantage of permitting autonomous action; after all the 'who' gathers itself from *différance* to (momentarily) constitute itself as a unity. The disadvantage is that it is not clear how this fits in with Derrida's claim that *différance* grounds such a unity. Alternatively, 2) it could mean that the 'who' be thought of as an effect of *différance* but somehow plays a role in constituting itself from *différance*. The advantage of this understanding is that it accords with Derrida's conception of the fundamental importance of *différance*. The disadvantage is that there is an inherent ambiguity within it: the 'who' is both a passive effect of *différance and* is capable of facilitating its own creation through *différance*.

Derrida does not so much resolve this issue as offer a number of comments that complicate it substantially. For example, he again emphasises Heidegger's notion of *Dasein*:

> I believe in the force and the necessity (and therefore in a certain irreversibility) of the act by which Heidegger *substitutes* a certain concept of *Dasein* for a concept of subject still too marked by traits of the being as *vorhanden, and hence by an interruption of time,* and insufficiently questioned in its ontological structure.[109]

He goes on to note that Heidegger's notion of *Dasein* still contains a certain singularity and suggests that this feature 'seems to be common just as much to transcendental idealism, to speculative idealism as the thinking of absolute subjectivity'.[110] This singularity will, then, continue to mark the 'who', although the form that this singularity takes will be different. Specifically, because Derrida insists it must be thought from *différance*, the 'who'

> cannot be absolutely stabilised in the form of the subject. The subject assumes presence, that is to say sub-stance, stasis, stance. Not to be able to stabilise itself *absolutely* would mean to be able *only* to be stabilising itself: relative stabilisation of what remains *unstable,* or rather *non-stable*.[111]

The 'who' will not, then, form a fixed, atemporal unity, but will be conditioned by a process of stabilisation that never achieves full stable totality.

The key point from this discussion is the suggestion that the 'who' stabilises itself from *différance*. Derrida once more points to Heidegger's analysis of *Dasein*: 'The *Da* of *Dasein* singularises itself without being reducible to any of the categories of human subjectivity (self, reasonable being, consciousness, person), precisely because it is presupposed by all these.'[112] As Derrida identifies from the relationship between *Dasein* and sexuality in Heidegger's early thinking, prior to ontic sexual determinations lies a process that *Dasein* does to itself from its 'initial' indeterminate neutrality understood in terms of *différance*. That 'subjectivity' is an effect of certain processes indicates that we have to focus on the processes that generate 'the subject', rather than on the 'subject' *per se*. The question is not, then, who comes *after* the subject, but, as Derrida's questioner puts it: 'Who comes before the subject . . . ?'[113] Derrida agrees, but only if '"before" no longer retains any chronological, logical, [or] even ontologico-transcendental meaning, if one takes into account, as I have tried to do, that which resists here the traditional schema of ontologico-transcendental questions'.[114] Derrida's questioner tries to pin him down on this issue, explaining that 'I still do not understand whether or not you leave a place for the question "Who?" Do you grant it pertinence or, on the contrary, do you not even want to pose it, do you want to bypass every question . . . ?'[115]

Rather than evasion, Derrida explains that his position is one of caution. It is all too easy to respond to the question in a definitive sense, but such action risks, unintentionally, reaffirming the metaphysical postulates of a strict identity or binary opposition between a subject that acts or one that is acted upon. Even Heidegger's notion of *Dasein* is problematic because it is based 'on . . . oppositions that remain insufficiently interrogated',[116] such as the relationship between the human (which is reserved for *Dasein*) and non-human. For Derrida, however, rethinking 'the subject' cannot be done from and within such a restricted economy. The assumptions underpinning 'subjectivity' have 'to go through the experience of a deconstruction' constituted by 'ceaselessly analysing the whole conceptual machinery' supporting it.[117] This is a constant process that is not simply 'done to' the subject, but, in so doing transforms 'the subject'. Thus,

> [i]f we still wish to speak of the subject – the juridical, ethical, political, psychological subject, and so forth – and of what makes its semantics communicate with that of the subject of a proposition (distinct from qualities, attributes viewed as substance, phenomena, and so on) or with the theme or the thesis (the subject of a discourse or of a book), it is first of all necessary to submit to the test of questioning the essential predicates of which all subjects are the subject.[118]

These are diverse, but they centre on the notion of 'being-present [*étant-present*]: presence to self – which implies . . . a certain interpretation of temporality; identity to self, positionality, property, personality, ego, consciousness, will, intentionality, freedom, humanity etc.'[119] This questioning 'itself offers neither the first nor the last word',[120] but is key to the process through which the subject will be deconstructed, and a reconfigured 'post-deconstructive'[121] conception of subjectivity revealed.

Conclusion

Derrida's response to the question of subjectivity is, then, suggestive, open-ended and multifaceted. He does not so much provide an answer to the question of 'who' succeeds the deconstructed subject as provide a number of partial suggestions, culminating in the demand that we constantly question the presuppositions underpinning any conception offered to undermine any notion of identity that might cling to it. Only this will ensure that the 'who' is thought from and as *différance*. It is not clear, however, whether and how this accords with his claim that the unstable 'identity' of the 'who' comes about from a process that it, in part, contributes to. Indeed, such questioning gives rise to the issue of 'who' engages with this topic: Derrida's questioning of identity seems to depend upon an agent who asks the questions, but his analysis of *différance* and discussion of the transition from subjectivity to 'post-subjectivity' are simply not sufficiently clear on whether this is permitted by *différance*, or, if it is, the process through which it takes place.

Indeed, as we saw, Derrida's favourite responsive technique is one of pseudo-evasion; the question must always be referred to the prior assumptions subtending it. *Conceptually speaking*, there is nothing wrong with this. It can allow an engagement with issues that are often too quickly overlooked. But, at the same time, it simply does not explain 1) how the transition from subjectivity thought as identity to post-deconstructive subjectivity can be made, 2) who makes the transition, and 3) how the 'who' thought from *différance* can be an effect of *différance* and yet 'precede' or transcend *différance* to effect its expression and so contribute to its own singularisation. Derrida's analysis of subjectivity is, then, far more complicated and subtle than is usually appreciated, but he struggles to conceive of what the 'subject' thought from *différance* 'looks' like and, indeed, how it can affect the expression of *différance* despite 'itself' being an effect of *différance*. Although this is perfectly in keeping with the deferred nature of *différance*, it does leave us with a partial, tension-filled explanation that affirms political change from the actions of a reconstituted agent, all the while also holding that such agential action is a consequence of the pre-personal structures and changes of *différance*.

Notes

1. For more extensive discussions of the Deleuze–Derrida relation, see Bruce Baugh, 'Making the Difference: Deleuze's Difference and Derrida's *différance*', *Social Semiotics*, 7.2, 1997, pp. 127–46; Gordon C. F. Bearn, 'Differentiating Derrida and Deleuze', *Continental Philosophy Review*, 33.4, 2000, pp. 441–65; the essays collected in Paul Patton and John Protevi (eds), *Between Deleuze and Derrida* (London: Continuum, 2003); and Kir Kuiken, 'Deleuze/Derrida: Towards an almost Imperceptible Difference', *Research in Phenomenology*, 35, 2005, pp. 290–308.

2. Jacques Derrida, 'Différance', in *Margins of Philosophy*, trans. Alan Bass (Chicago: University of Chicago Press, 1982), pp. 3–27 (p. 3).
3. Ibid., pp. 3–27.
4. Caroline Williams, *Contemporary French Philosophy: Modernity and the Persistence of the Subject* (London: Continuum, 2001), p. 133.
5. See, for example, Peter Dews, *Logics of Disintegration: Post-Structuralist Thought and the Claims of Critical Theory* (London: Verso, 1987), pp. 38–41; Bruce Baugh, *French Hegel: From Surrealism to Postmodernism* (Abingdon: Routledge, 2003), ch. 4, esp. pp. 134–40; Fanny Söderbäck, 'Being in the Present: Derrida and Irigaray on the Metaphysics of Presence', *Journal of Speculative Philosophy*, 27.3, 2013, pp. 253–64; Simon Lumsden, *Self-Consciousness and the Critique of the Subject: Hegel, Heidegger, and the Post-structuralists* (New York: Columbia University Press, 2014), pp. 145–9.
6. Jacques Derrida, '*Geschlecht I*: Sexual Difference, Ontological Difference', trans. Ruben Bevezdivin and Elizabeth Rottenberg, in *Psyche: Inventions of the Other, Volume 2*, ed. Peggy Kamuf and Elizabeth Rottenberg (Stanford, CA: Stanford University Press, 2008), pp. 7–26. This text is developed from an engagement with Heidegger's ontological difference, outlined in 1927's *Being and Time*, trans. John Macquarrie and Edward Robinson (Oxford: Blackwell, 1962), as it relates to the clarificatory analytic of *Dasein* found in the 1928 lecture course translated as *The Metaphysical Foundations of Logic*, trans. Michael Heim (Bloomington, IN: Indiana University Press, 1984). Interestingly, Heidegger's questioning of the meaning of being in *Being and Time*, although not the 1928 lecture course, also provides the stimulus for the development of Luce Irigaray's thinking on sexual difference and, by extension, poststructuralist feminist theory. While there are substantial differences between Derrida's and Irigaray's reading of Heidegger, informed in no small part by the substantial differences inherent in their respective projects, the fact that both look to Heidegger to develop their thinking on the relationship between subjectivity and sexuality not only discloses the fundamental role that he plays in the development of poststructuralist attempts to rethink the subject, but also reveals that the question of sexuality plays a particularly important function in this endeavour; a significance that will be confirmed once we turn to the thought of Judith Butler in Chapter 5 and Julia Kristeva in Chapter 7. Irigaray's most sustained engagement with Heidegger is found in *The Forgetting of Air in Martin Heidegger*, trans. Mary Beth Mader (London: Athlone, 1999). For a comparative discussion of Derrida's and Irigaray's projects, especially as they relate to their readings of Heidegger, see Ellen T. Armour, 'Questions of Proximity: "Women's Place" in Derrida and Irigaray', *Hypatia*, 12.1, 1997, pp. 63–78; Claire Colebrook, 'The Trope of Economy and Representational Thinking: Heidegger, Derrida, and Irigaray', *Journal of the British Society for Phenomenology*, 28.2, 1997, pp. 178–91; Söderbäck, 'Being in the Present'; and Anne van Leeuwen, 'Sexuate Difference, Ontological Difference: Between Irigaray and Heidegger', *Continental Philosophy Review*, 43.1, 2013, pp. 111–26.

7. Jacques Derrida, '"Eating Well," or the Calculation of the Subject', in Eduardo Cadava, Peter Connor and Jean-Luc Nancy (eds), *Who Comes after the Subject?* (Abingdon: Routledge, 1991), pp. 96–119. Reprinted as '"Eating Well," or the Calculation of the Subject', trans. Peter Connor and Avital Ronell, in *Points . . . Interviews, 1974–1994*, ed. Elizabeth Weber, trans. Peggy Kamuf et al. (Stanford, CA: Stanford University Press, 1995), pp. 255–87. References are to the latter version.
8. For example, in 1964 and 1965, Derrida gave a lecture course on Heidegger's re-raising of the question of the meaning of being at the École Normale Supérieure. See Jacques Derrida, *Heidegger: The Question of Being and History*, ed. Thomas Dutoit with the assistance of Marguerite Derrida, trans. Geoffrey Bennington (Chicago: University of Chicago Press, 2016).
9. Heidegger, *Being and Time*, p. 23.
10. Ibid., p. 26.
11. Ibid., p. 31.
12. Ibid., pp. 32–4.
13. Martin Heidegger, 'Letter on Humanism', trans. Frank A. Capuzzi and J. Glenn Gray, in *Basic Writings*, ed. David Farrell Krell (London: Harper, 1977), pp. 217–65.
14. Ibid., p. 245.
15. For a fuller, critical discussion of Derrida's critique of Heidegger, see Gavin Rae, 'Authoritarian and Anthropocentric: Examining Derrida's Critique of Heidegger', *Critical Horizons: A Journal of Philosophy and Social Theory*, 16.1, 2015, pp. 27–51.
16. Jacques Derrida, 'The Ends of Man', in *Margins of Philosophy*, trans. Alan Bass (Chicago: University of Chicago Press, 1982), pp. 111–36 (p. 124).
17. Derrida, 'Différance', p. 22.
18. Ibid., p. 3.
19. Ibid., p. 3.
20. See Jacques Derrida, *Of Grammatology*, rev. edn, trans. Gayatri Chakravorty Spivak (Baltimore, MD: Johns Hopkins University Press, 1997), especially Part I, ch. 1.
21. Derrida, 'Différance', p. 4.
22. Saussure, *Course in General Linguistics*, p. 118.
23. Derrida, 'Différance', p. 15.
24. Ibid., p. 6.
25. Ibid., p. 6.
26. Ibid., p. 6.
27. Ibid., p. 20.
28. Ibid., p. 5.
29. Ibid., p. 12.
30. Jacques Derrida and Elizabeth Roudinesco, 'Politics of Difference', in *For What Tomorrow . . . A Dialogue*, trans. Jeff Fort (Stanford, CA: Stanford University Press, 2004), pp. 20–32 (p. 21).

31. Ibid., p. 21.
32. Derrida, 'Différance', pp. 5–6.
33. Ibid., p. 8.
34. Ibid., p. 5.
35. Jacques Derrida and Antoine Spire, '"Others are Secret because they are Other"', in *Paper Machine*, trans. Rachel Bowlby (Stanford, CA: Stanford University Press, 2005), pp. 136–63 (p. 150).
36. Derrida, 'Différance', p. 11.
37. Ibid., p. 12.
38. Ibid., p. 16.
39. While Derrida deals with these topics in a number of places, good starting points are, respectively, Jacques Derrida, 'Force of Law: The "Mystical Foundation of Authority"', in *Acts of Religion*, ed. Gil Andjar (Abingdon: Routledge, 2002), pp. 231–98; Jacques Derrida, *Of Hospitality*, trans. Rachel Bowlby (Stanford, CA: Stanford University Press, 2000); and Jacques Derrida, *On Cosmpolitanism and Forgiveness*, trans. Mark Dooley and Michael Hughes (Abingdon: Routledge, 2001).
40. Derrida, 'Différance', pp. 21–2.
41. Elizabeth Grosz, 'Ontology and Equivocation: Derrida's Politics of Sexual Difference', *Diacritics*, 25.2, 1995, pp. 115–24 (p. 115).
42. Derrida, 'Geschlecht I', p. 7.
43. Ibid., p. 10.
44. Ibid., p. 10.
45. Heidegger, *The Metaphysical Foundations of Logic*, p. 136.
46. Ibid., p. 136.
47. Ibid., p. 137.
48. Ibid., p. 137.
49. Ibid., p. 137.
50. Ibid., p. 137.
51. Derrida, 'Geschlecht I', p. 13.
52. Ibid., p. 13.
53. Ibid., p. 13.
54. Ibid., p. 14.
55. Heidegger, *The Metaphysical Foundations of Logic*, p. 137.
56. Derrida, 'Geschlecht I', p. 14.
57. Jacques Derrida, 'Choreographies', trans. Christie V. McDonald, in *Points . . . Interviews, 1974–1994*, ed. Elizabeth Weber, trans. Peggy Kamuf et al. (Stanford, CA: Stanford University Press, 1995), pp. 89–108 (p. 104).
58. Derrida, 'Geschlecht I', p. 14.
59. Ibid., p. 14.
60. Ibid., p. 15.
61. Ibid., p. 15.
62. Derrida, 'Choreographies', pp. 100–1.

63. Derrida, 'Geschlecht I', p. 15.
64. Heidegger, *The Metaphysical Foundations of Logic*, p. 137.
65. Ibid., p. 140.
66. Ibid., p. 137.
67. For a discussion of this, see Gavin Rae, *Ontology in Heidegger and Deleuze* (Basingstoke: Palgrave Macmillan, 2014), ch. 4.
68. Heidegger, *The Metaphysical Foundations of Logic*, p. 137.
69. Derrida, 'Geschlecht I', p. 18.
70. Ibid., p. 18.
71. Ibid., p. 18.
72. Ibid., p. 18.
73. Heidegger, *The Metaphysical Foundations of Logic*, pp. 137–8.
74. Ibid., p. 137.
75. Ibid., p. 138.
76. Ibid., p. 138.
77. Derrida, 'Geschlecht I', p. 19.
78. Ibid., p. 20.
79. Heidegger, *The Metaphysical Foundations of Logic*, p. 138.
80. Derrida, 'Geschlecht I', p. 21.
81. Ibid., p. 26.
82. Ibid., p. 26.
83. Derrida, 'Choreographies', p. 103.
84. Derrida, 'Geschlecht I', p. 26.
85. Heidegger, *The Metaphysical Foundations of Logic*, p. 138.
86. Derrida, 'Geschlecht I', p. 26.
87. Derrida, 'Choreographies', p. 108.
88. Derrida and Spire, '"Others are Secret because they are Other"', p. 154.
89. Derrida, 'Choreographies', p. 105.
90. Ibid., p. 108.
91. On this point, see, for example, S. L. Bartky, 'Originative Thinking in the Later Philosophy of Heidegger', *Philosophy and Phenomenological Review*, 30.3, 1970, pp. 368–81; and Tina Chanter, 'The Problematic Normative Assumptions of Heidegger's Ontology', in Nancy J. Holland and Patricia Huntington (eds), *Feminist Interpretations of Martin Heidegger* (University Park, PA: Pennsylvania State University Press, 2001), pp. 73–108.
92. Derrida, '"Eating Well," or the Calculation of the Subject', p. 255.
93. Ibid., p. 255.
94. Ibid., p. 256.
95. Ibid., p. 256.
96. Ibid., p. 256.
97. Ibid., p. 257.
98. Ibid., p. 258.
99. Ibid., p. 258.

100. See, for example, Martin Heidegger, *On Time and Being*, trans. Joan Staumbaugh (London: Harper, 1972), p. 28; and Martin Heidegger, *Contributions to Philosophy (From Enowing)*, trans. Parvis Emad and Kenneth Maly (Bloomington, IN: Indiana University Press, 1999), pp. 122–3. For a discussion of the notion of 'trace' in Heidegger, see Rae, *Ontology in Heidegger and Deleuze*, pp. 102–15.
101. Derrida, '"Eating Well," or the Calculation of the Subject', p. 258.
102. Ibid., p. 258.
103. Ibid., p. 260.
104. Ibid., p. 261.
105. Ibid., p. 261.
106. Ibid., pp. 265–6.
107. Ibid., p. 264.
108. Ibid., p. 261.
109. Ibid., p. 266.
110. Ibid., p. 267.
111. Ibid., p. 270.
112. Ibid., p. 271.
113. Ibid., p. 271.
114. Ibid., p. 271.
115. Ibid., p. 271.
116. Ibid., p. 273.
117. Ibid., pp. 272, 274.
118. Ibid., p. 274.
119. Ibid., p. 274.
120. Ibid., p. 274.
121. Simon Critchley, 'Post-deconstructive Subjectivity?', in *Ethics–Politics–Subjectivity: Essays on Derrida, Levinas, and Contemporary French Thought* (London: Verso, 1999), pp. 51–82 (p. 70).

CHAPTER 3

Foucault I: Power and the Subject

Close to both Deleuze and Derrida – he famously commented that 'perhaps one day, this century will be known as Deleuzian',[1] while he was the latter's professor – Michel Foucault, nevertheless, departs from both in a number of important ways. Perhaps the most significant of these, especially for our purposes, is that rather than ground his analysis in a specific, albeit heterogeneous, ontological notion of difference/*différance*, Foucault disrupts and undermines claims to ahistoric universality by offering a historical approach – whether as 'archaeology' or 'genealogy' – that examines past discourses to bring to light the 'hidden' structures generating them (as in archaeology) or the changing socio-historical practices and distributions of power relations subtending them (as in genealogy). The methodology may be different, and indeed changes throughout Foucault's writings, but the key point is that he shares Deleuze's and Derrida's interest in exposing and undermining any claim to universality, essentialism, ahistoricism and substantial identity.

While he died relatively young in 1984, it is customary to note that he left behind a diverse corpus that is usually split between the 'archaeological' period of the 1960s, the 'genealogical ' writings of the 1970s and the 'technologies of the self' musings of the 1980s. There is much debate regarding the difference and relationship between these three periods, including whether they are, in fact, distinct. For example, one dominant reading holds that Foucault moved from archaeology to genealogy due to the failure of the former to adequately account for history and, indeed, the role that non-discursive practices play in generating and supporting dominant discourses.[2] It should be noted, however, that Foucault suggested in the 1975–76 lecture course *Society Must Be Defended* that the two methodologies are complementary: 'Archaeology is the method specific to the analysis of local discursivities, and genealogy is the tactic which, once it has described these discursivities, brings into play the desubjugated knowledges that have been released from them.'³ The relationship between Foucaultian genealogy and his later work on the technologies of the self is a further issue that complicates the reception of his work.

My approach to these issues is split across this chapter and the next and suggests that these periods and approaches, while diverse and heterogeneous, are orientated from and around the same problematic. As Foucault puts it in the 1982 interview 'The Subject and Power':

> I would like to say . . . what has been the goal of my work during the last twenty years. It has not been to analyse the phenomena of power, nor to elaborate the foundations of such an analysis. My objective, instead, has been to create a history of the different modes by which, in our culture, human beings are made subjects . . . Thus, it is not power, but the subject, that is the general theme of my research.[4]

I will, therefore, focus on the implications that Foucault's three periods or forms of analysis have for the notion of the subject to show that his treatment of the topic is remarkably homogeneous.

In this chapter, I will focus on what Foucault's archaeological and genealogical approaches have to say about the subject to establish the parameters of the debate. This will show that there is a commonality to both, in so far as they reject the notion that the subject is foundational or constituting. The first part of the chapter briefly outlines the arguments found in the archaeological writings of the 1960s, including *The Order of Things*, *The Archaeology of Knowledge* and 'What is an Author?', where Foucault explicitly proposes arguments or statements that appear to affirm the death of the subject.[5] The longer second part, composed of multiple sections, shows that this focus continues in the genealogical writings of 1970s, especially *Discipline and Punish*, the 1976 lecture series *Society Must Be Defended* and *History of Sexuality, Volume 1*.[6] There are obviously differences between the two periods, but I will argue that both *aim* not to annihilate the subject *per se*, but to undermine the notion of the primacy of the subject. The third part draws this out fully by engaging with the dominant interpretation of his works that holds that by thinking the subject from power relations, Foucault suggests that the subject is determined by them.[7] On this reading, there is no way for the subject to act in an intentional manner to affect the structure of power relations, meaning that intentional agential political action is excluded by Foucault's analysis of power. I offer two arguments to dismiss this interpretation. First, it misunderstands the nature of the subject that Foucault attacks. Rather than attacking all forms of the subject, he is, in fact, only rejecting the notion of an essentialist, unencumbered, constituting subject. Second, it confuses 'effect' with 'determine' and so fails to recognise that just because the subject is an effect of power relations does not mean that it is determined by them.

Following from these two points, I conclude that Foucault's conception of the relationship between power relations and the subject is not a linear one that passes from the former to the latter, but sees the two as being intertwined, albeit with an emphasis on the former. The subject is an effect of power relations but also actively participates in and affirms those practices that emanate from and support that power configuration. But at the same time, it is not fully determined by those power relations and so is able to reflect on and act in accordance with or against them. As a consequence, Foucault's theory of power relations deposes the dominant conception of the constituting foundational subject to reconceptualise it in terms of a constituted subject, located within a socio-historical sphere of moving power relations, who is capable of affecting the flow of the power relations constituting it. With regard to the problematic that motivates this book, his analysis of the power–subject relation does not, then, prevent or preclude intentional action to effect political change. The subsequent chapter builds on this insight by arguing that his later analysis of the *self* outlines how the self should develop and orientate itself within its socio-historical situatedness.

Affirming the Death of the Subject

In 1966 Foucault published *Les Mots et les choses*, translated as *The Order of Things*. This marked both a continuation of and a departure from his previous writings, which had focused on the history of psychiatry and especially the categorisation of mental illness.[8] The 1966 text aims to point out and examine the subtending structures that shape discourse and knowledge. Foucault terms this approach 'archaeology' to designate that it excavates beneath the surface appearance of language to outline its subtending structures. This does not simply relate to the grammatical rules and logic of language, but to the discursive norms, practices of acceptability and ways of looking at things that inform grammatical rules and logic. As he explains in the 1966 interview with Raymond Bellours:

> By 'archaeology' I would like to designate not exactly a discipline but a domain of research, which would be the following: in a society, different bodies of learning, philosophical ideas, everyday opinions, but also institutions, commercial practices, and police activities, mores – all refer to a certain implicit knowledge [*savoir*] special to this society. This knowledge is

profoundly different from the bodies of learning [*des connaissances*] that one can find in scientific books, philosophical theories, and religious justifications, but it is what makes possible at a given moment the appearance of a theory, an opinion, a practice.[9]

Based on this presupposition, *The Order of Things* identifies and charts the structure of knowledge from the Renaissance up to the present, meaning 1960s France. The basic argument is that knowledge within this period was not unitary and homogeneous. Rather, it was underpinned by different underlying structural systems or *epistemes*; namely, the classic and modern periods, with Kant understood as the key pivot point between them. The fundamental issue for our purposes is the claim that the notion of 'man' arose from a particular *episteme* and point in time:

> Before the end of the eighteenth century, *man* did not exist – any more than the potency of life, the fecundity of labour, or the historical density of language. He is a quite recent creature, which the demiurge of knowledge fabricated with its own hands less than two hundred years ago: but he has grown old so quickly that it has been only too easy to imagine that he had been waiting for thousands of years in the darkness for that moment of illumination in which he would finally be known.[10]

Foucault is quick to point out that this does not mean that the human being or species did not physically exist prior to this; it points to the idea that 'man' as an epistemic category did not exist: in classic knowledge, 'our conception of man ... had no basis ... and no place',[11] 'there was no epistemological consciousness of man as such'.[12] From this, he clarifies that the invention of the epistemic category 'man' had two consequences: 'man' was held 'to be ... at the foundation of all positivities and present, in a way that cannot even be termed privileged, in the element of empirical things'.[13] In other words, 'man' was taken to be the foundation of all other things and one object to be studied among others, a configuration that brought forth the rise of the human sciences. Foucault charts the importance of the concept 'man' throughout the nineteenth century before suggesting that it, along with the notion of God, was gradually questioned, most notably by Nietzsche.[14] He goes on to suggest that this critical process continued into the twentieth century before concluding 'that man is in the process of disappearing'.[15]

Foucault draws two conclusions from this. First, man is not a constant aspect of human knowledge, an assessment that calls into question any notion that 'man' is singularly important or foundational. Second, he affirms that 'man' is not an old concept, but rather 'an invention of recent date'.[16] The point is both to counter the notion that 'man' has been an important concept historically and, indeed, has been that which grounds knowledge historically, all the while re-enforcing his critique of the anthropocentric pretensions of modern knowledge. Indeed, he goes beyond this by claiming that this recent invention is perhaps 'nearing its end',[17] as a consequence not of an individual decision, but of changes to the *episteme* subtending knowledge.

This conclusion is frequently taken to describe a normative call to arms, wherein, far from simply describing historical events, Foucault is proposing the death or annihilation of 'man'. There are at least two reasons to be wary of this narrative. First, Beatrice Han-Pile points out that Foucault never actually says this; his words are far more hesitant and tentative regarding this issue;[18] and, second, Emma Ingala notes that the final metaphor – 'man would be erased, like a face drawn in sand at the edge of the sea'[19] – indicates that Foucault does not simply think that man will be abolished, but in the same way that water erases a drawing in the sand to permit a clean slate for another drawing, so the erasure of man permits a space to rethink that category.[20] The point – one that underpins the argument of this chapter – is that, even if Foucault is held to advocate the disappearance of man, this does not necessarily entail its obliteration; the sand–sea metaphor indicates that there is more going on.

This is seen when we turn to *The Archaeology of Knowledge*, published in 1969, which seeks to formalise Foucault's understanding of the archaeological method. He outlines more fully the methodological principle that systems of thought and knowledge are governed by rules that exist beneath the level of grammar and logic inherent in those systems, and that it is those subterranean rules that generate and govern the rules of language. With this, and continuing the point made in *The Order of Things*, he reaffirms his prior decentring of consciousness, the subject and (hu)man. Rather than being the foundation of knowledge-systems, man/consciousness/the subject is an epistemic construction dependent upon the subterranean rules generating and subtending discourse.[21]

Foucault does, however, go beyond this, in so far as he refines his target. Supporting my previous argument that his comments at the end of *The Order of Things* do not necessary relate to the desired annihilation of man *per se*, Foucault confirms that he is not seeking to annihilate the subject *per se*, but only 'the founding function of the subject'[22] that has been understood to structure, generate and support knowledge since the eighteenth century. For the first time, we see Foucault explicitly distinguishing between different versions of the subject. Far from seeking the annihilation of the subject, he seeks to undermine the notion of the *founding subject* by showing that it is a construction of subtending discursive rules.

Foucault takes up and extends this issue in the essay 'What is the Author?', published in the same year as *The Archaeology of Knowledge*. While there seems nothing more obvious than the notion that a text is a consequence of an author – after all, the author is generally held to generate the problem, the conclusion to it, and the arguments to support said conclusion, not to mention that he or she is the one who sits down to structure and write the piece – Foucault sets out 'to deal solely with the relationship between text and author and . . . the manner in which the text points to this figure that, at least in appearance, is outside it and antecedes it'.[23]

Foucault's argument is premised on the notion that the act or nature of writing has changed: rather than being an expression of a subject, he claims that writing has become 'a question of creating a space into which the writing subject constantly disappears'.[24] As a consequence, writing can no longer be taken to reveal what an author wants to say, but must be understood as an autonomous act that opens up new spaces. By highlighting 'the disappearance – or death – of the author', Foucault engages with the consequences that might accrue from this, before warning about the ways in which the notion of the author as founder of the text might be inadvertently or implicitly slipped back into discourse.[25]

While this seems to support the notion that Foucault affirms the death of the author and, by extension, the subject, it is important to note that he clarifies that the thesis about the disappearance of the author/subject does not amount to a simple annihilation. Rather, it leaves a space that necessitates a rethinking. As he warns,

> [i]is not enough . . . to repeat the empty affirmation that the author has disappeared. For the same reason, it is not enough to keep repeating that God and man have died a common death. Instead, we must locate the space left empty by the author's disappearance, follow the distribution of gaps and breaches, and watch for the openings this disappearance uncovers.[26]

This can be interpreted in the strong sense whereby the removal of the author/subject as the foundation of the text opens up gaps and new ways to engage with the text that do not and should not reintroduce any notion of the author/subject. Alternatively, it can be interpreted in a weak sense, whereby the author/subject loses their previously held foundational role, but still has a place – yet to be determined – within the order of things. Towards the end of the text, Foucault clarifies that he affirms the latter option: the author/

subject is displaced from their foundational role and understood to perform 'a certain role with regard to narrative discourse, assuring a classification' that 'permits one to group together a certain number of texts, define them, differentiate them from and contrast them to others. In addition, it establishes a relationship among the texts.'[27] Rather than being placed as the generator of the text, the author is reconceived as a function, or effect, of that text; 'his' name binds the text together, but in a way that emanates from the text itself rather than from the author, understood as consciousness or subject.

Without engaging with the validity of this claim, and, indeed, recognising that there is obviously far more to this text than I have touched on, this brief outline reveals that Foucault's archaeological method not only engages substantially with the notion of the subject, but, more importantly, does not simply call for its abolition. Foucault aims to displace the subject from the originating, founding role given to it by the epistemic alterations that coalesced into a new *episteme* in the eighteenth century to reconceptualise the subject as an effect of discourse. This treatment continues, albeit with a different methodological approach, throughout his genealogical writings.

From Discourse to Power

The movement to genealogy arose from the perceived limitations of the archaeological method. While archaeology was very effective at charting the structure of different discursive regimes, including their historical significance, it could not explain why one episteme became dominant or, indeed, why dominant *epistemes* were replaced. It also reduced knowledge to the abstraction of linguistic structures and so seemed to downplay concrete practices. Genealogy was meant to remedy these shortcomings by 1) tracing the movement between *epistemes* by focusing on the role that power relations play in generating the rules of discourse, and 2) moving from discursive rules and regulations to practices to re-enforce, in so doing, the concrete embodiment of discourse.[28]

The first extended application of the genealogical method is found in *Discipline and Punish*, published in 1975, a work that examines the changes that have taken place in the structure and means of punishment from the eighteenth century. Starting with a vivid description of the punishment meted out to the regicide Damiens on 2 March 1757, Foucault takes issue with the notion that punishment has become kinder or less imposing. Instead, he argues that the means of punishing those judged to have committed a crime has altered away from relying on *punishment* by direct physical imposition by the sovereign on the body of the guilty party towards a more insidious, totalising, everyday *discipline* involving practices such as measurement of time and action, normalisation of judgement and examination. The aim is to mould, regulate and normalise the population, rather than simply punish individuals.

There are many facets to this, but one of the key issues relates to the role that the body plays in punishment/discipline: 'One no longer touched the body, or at least as little as possible, and then only to reach something other than the body itself.'[29] Rather than aim to alter or punish through the imposition of physical pain,

> a whole army of technicians took over from the executioner, the immediate anatomist of pain: warders, doctors, chaplains, psychiatrists, psychologists, educationalists; by their very presence near the prisoner, they sing the praises that the law needs: they reassure it that the body and pain are not the ultimate objects of its punitive action.[30]

This is important for at least two reasons. First, it demonstrates Foucault's renewed interest in embodiment; a topic crucial for his own theory, but also for our purposes, in so far as it demonstrates that the poststructuralist challenge to the subject is not simply dependent upon abstract linguistic or ontological structures and processes. The poststructuralist subject is embodied.

Second, it points to the role that power relations play in forming the subject. As Foucault explains, the point is to 'make the technology of power the very principle both of the humanisation of the penal system and of the knowledge of man'.[31] Rather than starting from the perspective of linguistic rules and suggesting that the subject is an effect of them, Foucault argues that the subject is an effect of power relations and, in *Discipline and Punish*, uses the changing nature of juridical punishment to show how the subject is both formed and maintained. With this, Stuart Elden points out that the differences between *The Archaeology of Knowledge* and *Discipline and Punish* are stark, not just revealing a methodological change but also a theoretical reorientation away from abstract issues towards political engagement: 'if *The Archaeology of Knowledge* [i]s a methodological treatise, *Discipline and Punish* [i]s a call to arms'.[32]

Explaining the relationship between power and the body, Foucault notes that he is not pointing to a simple unilinear flow whereby power is forced on to the body. Rather, 'the body becomes a useful force only if it is both a productive body and a subjected body'.[33] Power is not manifested on the body as an external force; there is at play a 'political technology of the body'[34] that operates with or without direct violence. Rather than being located in one place or defined by a straightforward top-down imposition,

Foucault affirms a whole array of subterranean networks and fields of force that coalesce to form bodies and subjects in specific ways. 'This technology is diffuse, rarely formulated in continuous, systematic discourse; it is often made up of bits and pieces; it implements a disparate set of tools or methods.'[35]

Importantly,

> it cannot be localised in a particular type of institution or state apparatus. For they have recourse to it; they use, select or impose certain of its methods. But, in its mechanisms and its effects, it is situated at a quite different level. What the apparatuses and institutions operate is, in a sense, a micro-physics of power, whose field of validity is situated in a sense between these great functionings and the bodies themselves with their materiality and their forces.[36]

With the notion of a 'micro-physics of power', Foucault points to the theoretical underpinnings that shape his analysis. Rather than referring to a property or substance, power relations entail 'a strategy' with 'its effects of domination . . . attributed not to "appropriations", but to dispositions, manoeuvres, tactics, techniques, functionings'.[37] Crucially, these relations are not harmonious, but 'constantly in tension, in activity', with the consequence that we must think of them as 'a perpetual battle rather than a contract regulating a transaction or the conquest of a territory'.[38]

To understand power relations further, Foucault points to three key aspects. First, 'power is exercised rather than possessed; it is not the "privilege", acquired or preserved, of the dominant class, but the overall effect of strategic positions'.[39] Foucault is obviously distancing himself from Marxist class struggle. Second, 'power is not exercised simply as an obligation or a prohibition on those who "do not have it"; it invests them, is transmitted by them and through them; it exerts pressure upon them, just as they themselves, in their struggle against it, resist the grip it has on them'.[40] This is a key stipulation: power is not just negative, it also produces and, indeed, is that which constitutes or founds all else, including the subject. However, we should not think that power relations are singular or homogeneous. Doing so risks reaffirming the logic of fixed foundations that supports Western thought. For this reason, Foucault's final stipulation is that power relations 'are not univocal; they define innumerable points of confrontation, focuses of instability, each of which has its own risks of conflict, of struggles, and of an at least temporary inversion of the power relations'.[41]

From this theoretical framework, Foucault proceeds with his historical analysis. To do so, he notes that up until the end of the eighteenth century, punishment was based on, among other factors, corporeal punishment and was underpinned by the idea that, in breaking the law, the criminal had challenged the power of the sovereign.[42] Punishment was then a way of reasserting sovereign power and warning others about the appropriate forms of social conduct. The public execution was 'understood not only as a judicial, but also as a political ritual . . . It [wa]s a ceremonial by which a momentarily injured sovereignty [wa]s reconstituted. It restore[d] that sovereignty by manifesting it at its most spectacular.'[43] By imposing itself on the body of the condemned, the sovereign reasserted and demonstrated his power for all to see. Thus, the condemned was the location from, around and through which the power of the sovereign was manifested. Power relations in this schema are hierarchical, confrontational and based on explicit physical imposition: the body of the condemned, in particular its debasement, is the locus whereby power relations are played out.

Somewhat paradoxically, however, this generated the fundamental problem with this form of power relations: on the one hand, 'in calling on the crowd to manifest its power, the sovereign tolerated for a moment acts of violence, which he accepted as a sign of allegiance, but which were strictly limited by the sovereign's own privileges'.[44] However, on the other hand, this (controlled) release of popular violence against the condemned could quite easily turn against the sovereign by, for example, '[p]reventing an execution that was regarded as unjust, snatching a condemned man from the hands of the executioner, obtaining his pardon by force, possibly pursuing and assaulting the executioners, in any case abusing the judge and causing uproar against the sentence'.[45] This anticipates Foucault's later point that power is never simply repressive, but always manifests forms of resistance.

Foucault notes that the potential for rebellion against the sovereign was the undoing of this form of punishment; an undoing that occurred remarkably quickly. By the end of the eighteenth century, 'the public execution [had become] intolerable'.[46] This is not to say that it disappeared completely, but that it was no longer the principal form of punishment or had the same standing in society: 'it [had become] dangerous, in that it provided a support for a confrontation between the violence of the king and the violence of the people'.[47] In turn, this was accompanied by a specific epistemological movement.

Appealing to his earlier archaeological work, Foucault explains that the late eighteenth century witnessed epistemic changes that gave rise to the notion of 'man', who was held to have a specific dignity or humanity. Drawing on this, punishment moved away from public torture to kill or physically break the condemned to the re-education and redemption of man in accordance with his 'inner' humanity.[48] That the prisoner could be redeemed set up the question of how his behaviour was to be altered.

Foucault responds that this required a complete rearrangement of how the guilty party was approached, treated, housed and engaged with. There was classification, calculation, minute tweaks of punishment into ever subtler and more constant forms, and the objectification of the criminal as an object to be worked on. All these indicate, so Foucault claims, that the criminal was not simply to be physically punished, but 'known according to specific criteria'.[49] In turn, this was underpinned by a new configuration of power, based on 'the supersession of the punitive semio-technique by a new politics of the body'.[50]

Foucault's discussion of the various ways in which this occurred is detailed and fascinating, but one of its key components was the creation of a particular space – the prison – where the body of the prisoner could be worked on most efficiently.[51] Punishment, therefore, went from being a public spectacle on the scaffold to a private endeavour performed by specialised technicians who would regulate and train the body and actions of the prisoner to rehabilitate him into the 'correct' norms of society.[52]

In turn, this depended on a new understanding of the body: rather than a mere object, this alteration 'was the moment when the art of the human body was born',[53] in which

> [w]hat was ... being formed was a policy of coercions that act upon the body, a calculated manipulation of its elements, its gestures, its behaviour. The human body was entering a machinery of power that explores it, breaks it down and rearranges it. A 'political anatomy', which was also a 'mechanics of power', was being born.[54]

The subject created was a disciplined one, who, through this discipline, simply 'knew' how to act. He or she did not have to act out of fear of punishment from the sovereign, but acted in a certain way because they had been conditioned to hold that it was 'right'. This behaviour, outlook and body were the gestation of years of subtle mechanisms of training: '[t]hey were at work in secondary education at a very early date, later in primary schools; they slowly invested the space of the hospital: and, in a few decades, they restructured the military organisation'.[55]

Importantly, these mechanisms were structured around 'meticulous, often minute, techniques'[56] that transmitted the required codes of behaviour and appearance at every moment. Far from being blunt instruments of coercion, '[d]iscipline is a political anatomy of detail'.[57] This, in turn, required a new understanding and approach to time so that an individual's actions and behaviour could be measured and appropriately controlled. Indeed, Foucault notes that the notion of 'the individual' was dependent on this new approach to time, based as it was on serialisation and the movement of discrete moments.⁵⁸ As a consequence, the form of power relations known as

> [d]iscipline 'makes' individuals; it is the specific technique of power that regards individuals both as objects and as instruments of its exercise. It is not a triumphant power, which because of its own excess can pride itself on its omnipotence; it is a modest, suspicious power, which functions as a calculated, but permanent economy. These are humble modalities, minor procedures, as compared with the majestic rituals of sovereignty or the great apparatuses of the state.⁵⁹

Humble they might have been, but they were effective in creating disciplined, normalised individuals. This was not a one-off event, but a continuous process of correction, occurring through constant exposure and examination.⁶⁰ Rather than a society of spectacle,⁶¹ Foucault claims that disciplinary society is one of constant 'surveillance'⁶² and normalisation through the judgement of that which is witnessed. Nevertheless, the key point for present purposes is that '[t]he individual [is] a reality fabricated by this specific technology of power ... called "discipline"'.⁶³ That the individual is a consequence of power relations means that

> [w]e must cease once and for all to describe the effects of power in negative terms; it 'excludes', it 'represses', it 'censors', it 'abstracts', it 'masks', it 'conceals'. In fact, power produces, it produces reality; it produces domains of objects and rituals of truth. The individual and the knowledge that may be gained of him belong to this production.⁶⁴

Foucault struggled with the question of what it means to say that the subject is produced by power in the rest of his writings. To outline this, commentators tend to move from *Discipline and Punish*, published in 1975, to the first volume of *The History of Sexuality*, published in 1976.⁶⁵ The problem in doing so, however, is that this ignores the lecture course – translated as *Society Must Be Defended* – that Foucault gave at the beginning of 1976, prior to the publication of the first volume of *The History of Sexuality*. This course is important for current concerns because in it Foucault 1) relates power relations directly to politics, thereby reaffirming the political nature of his thought, 2) engages with the nature of power relations by engaging with whether they should be thought in terms of war, and 3) deepens his understanding of the ways in which power relations shape and create individuals by showing that alongside the disciplinary power relations outlined in *Discipline and Punish* arose, in the nineteenth century, another form of power relations called biopower.[66]

Power as War

The lecture course tries to offer 'a noneconomic analysis of power', where power is not thought in terms of pure repression or intentional action, but as 'primarily, in itself, a relationship of force'.[67] This does, however, raise the question of the nature of the force relations, to which Foucault responds that instead of thinking in 'functional terms as the reproduction of the relations of production, [we should] be analysing it first and foremost in terms of conflict, confrontation, and war?'[68] In the interview 'Truth and Power', given the same year (1976) as the lecture course, Foucault justifies this move by explaining that 'it is astonishing to see how easily and self-evidently people talk of warlike relations of power or of class struggle without ever making it clear whether some form of war is meant, and if so what form'.[69] *Society Must Be Defended* is Foucault's attempt to respond to these issues.

Foucault identifies 'two grand hypotheses' about power.[70] First, contemporarily speaking, analyses have tended to hold that 'power is essentially that which represses'.[71] Foucault insists, however, that this is a very traditional conception of power that seems inadequate to conceptualise the dynamics of power-force. He calls it 'Reich's hypothesis', which is opposed to another – termed 'Nietzsche's hypothesis' – that seeks to analyse power in terms of conflict and war.[72] Thus, if Reich's hypothesis holds that power is repressive, Nietzsche's hypothesis claims that 'power is war, the continuation of war by other means'.[73] With this, Foucault inverts Carl von Clausewitz's famous dictum to 'say that politics is the continuation of war by other means'.[74]

This leads to three points. First, political organisation is structured according to and from war and, indeed, was instantiated at a particular moment when the structure of war was transposed to politics.[75] Second, politics must be understood in terms of war; that is, shifting alliances, movements, oppositional struggles and so on.[76] Third, and most controversially, politics is dependent on 'a trial by strength in which weapons are the final judges'.[77] The implication is that 'the last battle would put an end to politics' because it 'would at last . . . suspend the exercise of power as continuous warfare'.[78] This final point would, ultimately, prove highly problematic for Foucault, who, very quickly, rejected the notion that war and, hence, power could somehow come to an end in a moment of great political refusal.[79]

Nevertheless, by inverting Clausewitz's dictum to hold that politics is war by other means, Foucault points out that he is committing himself to the problem of war: 'I would like to try to see the extent to which the binary schema of war and struggle, of the clash between forces, can really be identified as the basis of civil society, as both the principle and motor of the exercise of political power.'[80] There is much to this, but I will focus on the outline of power relations undertaken in the second lecture, dated 14 January 1976, because it is here that Foucault deepens his understanding of what power means, especially as it relates to subjectivity.

The second lecture deals primarily with the question of the relationship between war and power by examining juridical sovereignty, a topic that will bring Foucault to the issue of disciplinary power. Foucault notes that, in the West, 'the elaboration of juridical thought has essentially centred around royal power since the Middle Ages'.[81] Even when law was subsequently divorced from royalty, the question of law was still orientated around its relation to the royal sovereign. As such, Foucault claims that 'the king was the central character in the entire Western juridical order'.[82] Foucault's problems with this conclusion are multiple, but, very simply, he explains that the question of law should not be thought in terms of sovereignty, but in terms of domination and its relationship to subjugation.

To defend this, he asks that we observe a number of methodological precautions. First, the focus must not be on a central point where power is held to originate or where diverse phenomena are reduced to a unitary position. Instead, we should focus on the regional, minor forms through which power is exposed and revealed.[83] Second, we should not 'analyse power at the level of intentions of decisions, not . . . try to approach it from inside, and not . . . ask the question . . . So who has power?'[84] Power cannot be reduced to intentional consciousness. Third, rather than a top-down model located from a subject, Foucault suggests that we try 'to discover how multiple bodies, forces, energies, matters, desires, thoughts, and so on are gradually, progressively, actually and materially constituted as subjects, or as the subject'.[85] Again we see Foucault arguing for a constituted rather than a constituting subject. Fourth, power cannot be reduced to an ideological construct. This might be part of it, but power relations are related to and revealed through concrete practices.[86] Finally, power must not be understood 'as a phenomenon of mass and homogeneous domination – the domination of one individual over others, of one group over others, or of one class over others'.[87] Rather than being understood as a possession, power 'must be analyzed as something that circulates, or rather as something that functions only when it is part of a chain'.[88] Referring this back to the issue of the subject, Foucault explains that

> power is exercised through circuits and individuals do not simply circulate in those networks; they are in a position to submit to and exercise this power. They are never the inert or consenting targets of power; they are always its relays. In other words, power passes through individuals. It is not applied to them.[89]

That individuals are relays can mean at least two things: first, the subject is a passive point through which power passes as it moves to another point, or, second, the relay point plays an active role in directing or redirecting the exercise of power. Following Amy Allen,[90] I understand that the second sense describes Foucault's position and defend this by pointing to his claim that individuals 'are in a position to submit to *and exercise this power*'.[91] It is therefore an error to think of the individual 'as a sort of elementary nucleus' that exists prior to power or as 'some multiple, inert matter to which power is applied, or which is struck by a power that subordinates or destroys individuals'.[92] Rather,

> one of the first effects of power is that it allows bodies, gestures, discourses, and desires to be identified and constituted as something individual. The individual is not, in other words, power's opposite number; the individual is one of power's first effects. The individual is in fact a power-effect, and at the same time, and to the extent that he is a power-effect, the individual is relay: power passes through the individuals it has constituted.[93]

When this is combined with the claim that the subject plays an active role in the distribution of power relations, we see that, for Foucault, the constituted subject is capable of intentionally redirecting those relations and so exercising power through its actions.

The latter part of Foucault's lecture ties this conceptualisation of power relations back to the question of juridical sovereignty by pointing out that thinking of power in terms of networks, flows, microscopic movements and domination is at odds with the top-down, linear, subject-based notion of power that underpins the traditional notion of juridical sovereignty. Foucault affirms the network model, claiming that it can be used to understand and conceptualise historical movements; namely, the challenge to juridical forms of sovereign power that arose in the seventeenth and eighteenth centuries. As we saw in *Discipline and Punish*, this time-period was constituted by the movement that associated punishment with torture to the episteme that associated it with discipline. It is here that the lecture course and the earlier text meet.

Crucially, however, in later lectures, Foucault pushes beyond the disciplinary mode of power to a new mode – 'biopolitics'[94] – that exists simultaneously with the disciplinary but that regulates whole populations. In turn, this will subsequently give way to the notion of 'governmentality'.[95] Biopolitics does, nevertheless, act as the hinge that binds yet separates the notions of 'disciplinary power' in *Discipline and Punish* and 'governmentality' in Foucault's later works.

Power and Sexuality

So far we have seen that Foucault's genealogy of power relations examines historical modes of punishment and the question of sovereignty. The third line of inquiry through which he outlines his genealogical approach to power is sexuality. *The History of Sexuality* is spread across four volumes: volumes 1–3 were originally published in 1984, with the latter two volumes usually included in his later 'technologies of the self' phase, as is volume 4, which was published posthumously in 2018 against Foucault's express wishes.[96] The first volume, in particular, continues the inquiry into power relations. Two aspects stand out from it. First, Foucault develops a particular historical narrative around sexuality from the seventeenth to the twentieth centuries that undermines the notion that power is simply repressive. In so doing, he bolsters his claim that power is defined by a domination–resistance tension. That power is never able to determine its effect and automatically produces resistance is important for my subsequent argument that the subject constituted by power relations is always able to subvert them. From this, Foucault, second, develops a detailed schematic clarification of his conception of power relations that collects and develops the scattered comments he makes on the topic in *Discipline and Punish* and *Society Must Be Defended*.

The problem motivating Foucault's study of sexuality is what he calls the 'repression hypothesis', which describes the apparent changes in the way that sexuality operates within discourse from the seventeenth to the nineteenth centuries.[97] Whereas in the former period, '[s]exual practices had little need of secrecy; words were said without undue reticence, and things were done without too much concealment; one had a tolerant familiarity with the illicit',[98] by the nineteenth century, a different approach dominated:

> Sexuality was carefully confined; it moved into the home. The conjugal family took custody of it and absorbed it into the serious function of reproduction. The legitimate and procreative couple laid down the law. The couple imposed itself as model, enforced the norm, safeguarded the truth, and reserved the right to speak while retaining the principle of secrecy.[99]

On the one hand, this seems to re-enforce Foucault's point that different configurations arise from the shifting power relations subtending society. If this were all that he was pointing to, Foucault's study would be an interesting engagement with the question of sexuality in Western society between these centuries. He goes further, however, by explicitly and extensively engaging with the resistances that the repressive hypothesis generate(d).

To do so, he charts a history of the changes that took place in discourse about sex in the eighteenth and nineteenth centuries, paying particular attention to the various attempts to manage or regulate sex. From this, he links his historical narrative to his analysis of power relations and, indeed, his previous lecture course. The repressive hypothesis is based on a top-down hierarchical conception of power – the sovereign model of power, where power comes from the top and is imposed through repression on that which is beneath it. If power operated like this, the only way to defeat or subvert it would be to resist it with a Great Refusal; action that, as Foucault pointed out in *Discipline and Punish*, must elicit a response from the sovereign.

As a consequence, Foucault suggests that we need a new understanding of power relations, one that 'no longer takes law as a model and a code'.[100] While he pointed to what this might look like in his previous genealogical studies, it is in the first volume of *The History of Sexuality* that Foucault's most explicit and detailed comments on the topic are found. Foucault starts by clarifying that 'by power, I do not mean "Power" as a group of institutions and mechanisms that ensure subservience to the citizens of a given state'.[101] Nor does he agree with Hannah Arendt's insistence that power is opposed to violence, or that power refers to a possession that one group has over others.[102] Rather,

> power must be understood in the first instance as the multiplicity of force relations immanent in the sphere in which they operate and which constitute their own organization; as the process which, through ceaseless struggles and confrontations, transforms, strengthens, or reverses them; as the support which these force relations find in one another, thus forming a chain or a system, or on the contrary, the disjunctions and contradictions which isolate them from one another; and lastly, as the strategies in which they take effect, whose general design or institutional crystallization is embodied in the state apparatus, in the formulation of the law, in the various social hegemonies.[103]

Power is, then, for Foucault, multifaceted and multidimensional. It finds expression in different ways, flowing through all its effects. However, while power is omnipresent, this is 'not because it has the privilege of consolidating everything under its invincible unity, but because it is produced from one moment to the next, at every point, or rather in every relation from one point to another'.[104] Power is not, then, a substance transcending its manifestations, but is 'constituted' by moving relations and is expressed immanently through the things it founds.

From this, Foucault outlines a further five characteristics of power. First, 'power is not something that is acquired, seized, or shared', but is a constant 'interplay of nonegalitarian and mobile relations'.[105] Second, '[r]elations of power are not in a position of exteriority with respect to other types of relationships (economic production, knowledge relationships, sexual relations), but are immanent in the latter'.[106] Because they are immanent to their expression, power is inherently productive. As Foucault states elsewhere:

> If power were never anything but repressive, if it never did anything but to say no, do you really think one would be brought to obey it? What makes power hold good, what makes it accepted, is simply the fact that it doesn't only weigh on us as a force that says no; it also traverses and produces things, it induces pleasure, forms knowledge, produces discourse.[107]

Third, '[p]ower comes from below; that is, there is no binary and all-encompassing opposition between rulers and ruled at the root of power relations'.[108] It is not that Foucault fails to recognise that divisions in society exist, but that he holds that any such divisions are the manifestation of the splits that define power relations. These are mobile and constantly changing, as are their effects. Fourth, 'power relations are both intentional and nonsubjective'.[109] While there is a purpose or aim to them, this does not result 'from the choice or decision of an individual subject'.[110] Thus, while 'the logic is perfectly clear, the aims decipherable ... it is too often the case that no one is there to have invented them'.[111] Foucault is again criticising the notion of the constituting subject. Finally, '[w]here there is power, there is resistance, and yet, or rather consequently, this resistance is never in a position of exteriority in relation to power'.[112] Resistance arises immanently from the play of forces 'constituting' power relations. There is not one site of resistance nor can power be overcome once and for all; 'points of resistance are present everywhere in the power network'.[113]

From this short schema, Foucault spends the rest of the first volume of *The History of Sexuality* showing how this undermines both the central premise of the repressive hypothesis and the notion of sovereign power upon which that hypothesis depends. For our purposes, however, his discussion of power relations in this text is important because it not only clarifies what he means by this notion, but also demonstrates that power is not located in the subject; power precedes the subject, delineating the constantly shifting, mobile relations from which the subject is generated and sustained. The exact nature of the power–subject relationship in Foucault's thinking is, however, a contentious one in the literature. The debate is orientated around the fundamental issue motivating this inquiry: in making the subject an effect of power relations, does Foucault not undermine any possibility that the subject may intentionally act to influence the power relations constituting it? In other words, does Foucault's notion of power relations not prevent the possibility of autonomous agential action?

Conclusion: Power and the Subject

The dominant interpretation of the relationship between Foucault's conceptions of power relations and the subject has been a critical one: in making the subject an effect of power relations, it is argued that he does not have the means to permit subjects to intentionally act against the power relations constituting them. As a consequence, the subject becomes something akin to an irrelevant victim of forces beyond its control. Charles Taylor, for example, complains that Foucault's account of power relations 'leaves us with a strange kind of Schopenhaurian will, ungrounded in human action'.[114] The basic problem with Foucault's position, on Taylor's telling, is that, in making the subject an effect of power relations, it undermines the subject's autonomy. As Taylor explains, however, 'there *must* be something between total subjectivity, on the one hand, holding that there are no undersigned patterns in history and the strange Schopenhaurian-without-the-will in which Foucault leaves us'.[115]

Jürgen Habermas makes two critical points. First, Foucault's insistence on the primacy of constantly moving power relations 'cannot lead to a way out of the philosophy of the subject, because the concept of power that is supposed to provide a common denomination for the contrary semantic components has been taken from the repertoire of the philosophy of the subject itself'.[116] As a consequence, Foucault's attempt to remove the subject from the equation must fail because he aims to achieve this while using the terminology of the tradition to be overcome. Second, Habermas claims that by privileging power relations and claiming that they are everywhere and subtend everything, Foucault's account lacks explanatory force. Rather, 'discourses emerge and pop up like glittering bubbles from a swamp of anonymous processes of subjugation'.[117] Overcoming these problems requires, on Habermas's telling, that we abandon Foucault's model to reintroduce a form of agency or rational subject into the constituting process.

In contrast to Habermas's assumption that Foucault aims to remove the subject from the equation, Peter Dews recognises that Foucault maintains the subject, although he ultimately agrees with Habermas that Foucault privileges power relations to the extent that 'subjects are entirely constituted by the operation of power'.[118] As a consequence, subjects are unable to resist the power relations subtending them, a position that Lois McNay echoes when she complains that 'the emphasis that Foucault places on the effects of power upon the body results in a reduction of social agents to passive bodies and does not explain how individuals may act in an autonomous fashion'.[119]

These assertions are, however, built on a number of problematic assumptions regarding Foucault's project. The fundamental premise underpinning Taylor's and Habermas's critiques is that Foucault aims to remove the subject from the equation entirely, while Dews's and McNay's position is based on the notion that because the subject is an effect of power relations, it must be determined by them. In what follows, I show that these premises are based not only on a one-dimensional interpretation of Foucault's thinking, but also conceptual conflations that fail to accurately portray or understand his position regarding the power–subject relation. Once we pay attention to a wider array of comments that Foucault makes on precisely these issues, we will see that he offers a far more nuanced understanding of the power–subject relation that continues to permit subjective agency.

My first argument refers to the premise underpinning Taylor's and Habermas's critiques; namely, that Foucault aims to annihilate the subject. As I have argued throughout this chapter, this is simply not the case. From his earliest archaeological writings, Foucault rejects one conception of the subject – the constituting, founding subject – to rethink the notion, first from a privileging of discourse and subsequently from his conception of power relations. As he clarifies in the 1977 interview 'Truth and Power': 'One has to dispense with the constituent subject, to get rid of the subject itself, that's to say to arrive at an analysis that can account for the constitution of th[is] subject within a historical framework.'[120] When we recognise that he is not trying to annihilate the subject *per se*, the criticisms that he fails to do so make little sense. His is a rethinking of the subject, rather than its abandonment.

To be sure, Foucault was aware that his early formulations concerning the disappearance or death of the subject were problematic. As he explains in a 1978 interview, he came to recognise that the way that he had presented the so-called death of man in *The Order of Things* was problematic on two counts. First, he 'made the mistake of presenting this death as something that was underway in our era'.[121] Second, and more importantly for present purposes, he recognised that he presented an analysis that was too one-dimensional and linear. In claiming that man was premised on the order of discourse, he made it appear that man was determined by discourse, thereby forgetting that

> in course of their history, men have never ceased to construct themselves, that is, to continually displace their subjectivity, to constitute themselves in an infinite, multiple series of different subjectivities that will never have an end and never bring us in the preserve of something that would be 'man.'[122]

Subjects are perpetually engaged in action that constitutes objects which, in so doing, alters the power relations that constitute subjects. The subject is not, then, a passive recipient of discursive structures or power relations, but also plays a role in the manifestation of those structural relations. There is, in other words, a feedback loop, so that changes to discourse/power relations do not lead to the termination of the subject, but to new configurations and new subjectivities that subsequently influence the dispersion of power relations.

The question now arises as to whether it is possible for Foucault to consistently claim that the subject is constituted by power relations while also holding that the subject can influence their expression. According to the interpretations of Dews and McNay, Foucault's conception of power relations maintains that they constitute the subject so completely that they leave no room for subjective intentional agency. This argument is, however, based on two different, but related, conceptual slippages: first, between 'effect' and 'determine' and, second, between 'unencumbered autonomous agency' and 'autonomous agency'.

The first (effect–determine) slip describes the way(s) in which power relations imbue and underpin the subject. Those critical of Foucault's analysis of power relations claim that in making the subject an effect of power relations, he means that the subject is *determined* by those relations and so is unable to resist or affect them. However, this interpretation is based on a very simplistic and narrow conception of power relations that, in the 1977 interview 'Power and Strategies', Foucault explicitly rejects. While noting 'that power *is* "always already there," that one is never "outside" it, that there are no "margins" for those who break with the system to gambol in', he goes on to claim that '[t]o say that one can never be "outside" power does not mean that one is trapped and condemned to defeat no matter what'.¹²³ Power is everywhere and the subject is an effect of power relations, but

> there is . . . always something in the social body, in classes, groups and individuals themselves which in some sense escapes relations of power, something which is by no means a more or less docile or reactive primal matter, but rather a centrifugal movement, an inverse energy, a discharge.¹²⁴

In many respects, this is a direct consequence of Foucault's claim that power always creates resistance. This is not because of a subjective decision or act, but is inherent in the play of forces that condition power relations. They are productive and so create subjects, while, through this production, creating the conditions for resistance to that productive movement. It is through this structural movement that the possibility for subjective agency arises.

This, however, depends upon untangling a second conceptual slippage; namely, the failure to distinguish between 'unencumbered autonomous agency' and 'autonomous agency', an issue that refers us back to the question of the type of subject that Foucault rejects. Mark Bevir suggests that 'unencumbered autonomy' refers to the notion of a subject that 'would be able, at least in principle, to have experiences, to reason, to adopt beliefs, and to act, outside of all social contexts. [It] could avoid the influence of any norms and techniques prescribed by a regime of power/knowledge.'¹²⁵ As Bevir notes, '[t]his concept of the autonomous subject resembles the idea of a "sovereign" founding subject that Foucault vehemently rejects'.¹²⁶ In contrast, autonomous agents

> exist only in specific social contexts, but these contexts never determine how they try to construct themselves. Although agents necessarily exist within regimes of power/knowledge, these regimes do not determine the experiences they can have, the ways they can exercise their reason, the beliefs they can adopt, or the actions they can attempt to perform.¹²⁷

To repeat, whereas his critics take Foucault to be affirming the death of all subjectivity, he is, in fact, only arguing against one conception of it – the unencumbered, constituting, founding subject – that he maintains has dominated Western thought since the seventeenth century. As Bevir points out, however, 'a rejection of [unencumbered] autonomy need not entail a rejection of agency: we can say the subject always sets off against a social background that influences him and still insist he then can reason and act in creative, novel ways so as to modify this background'.[128]

Support for this understanding is found in Foucault's explicit rejection of the autonomous, founding subject, his affirmation that power relations effect without determining the subject, his insistence that individuals are relays who exercise and so influence the course of the power relations constituting them, and his claim that we have to 'account for the constitution of the subject within a historical framework'.[129] When read in this manner, Foucault does not maintain that the subject is a passive effect of power relations. As he explains in the late interview 'The Ethics of the Concern for Self as a Practice of Freedom', 'the idea that power is a system of domination that controls everything and leaves no room for freedom cannot be attributed to me'.[130]

Contrary to how his critics often read him, then, Foucault does not argue for the death of the subject *per se*, but for the rejection of a particularly dominant conception of the autonomous, constituting subject, and he does so by drawing attention to the way(s) in which the subject is a constructed effect of both discourse and power relations. This constituted subject is not, however, *determined* by its subtending discursive structures and field of power relations; it is capable them of acting to affirm, combat or alter them. Rather than produce a detailed investigation of the mechanisms 'within' the subject that permit such action, for Foucault the question now becomes how the subject *should* act; an issue that requires that we 'promote new forms of subjectivity through the refusal of th[e] kind of individuality that has been imposed on us from several centuries'.[131] Foucault's response to this issue forms the basis for his later writings on the self.

Notes

1. Michel Foucault, 'Theatrum Philosophicum', in *Aesthetics: Essential Works of Foucault 1954–1984, Volume 2*, ed. James D. Faubion (London: Penguin, 2000), pp. 343–68 (p. 343).
2. Hubert L. Dreyfus and Paul Rabinow, *Michel Foucault: Beyond Structuralism and Hermeneutics*, 2nd edn (Chicago: University of Chicago Press, 1983), pp. 79–103.
3. Michel Foucault, *Society Must Be Defended: Lectures at the Collège de France, 1975–1976*, ed. Mauro Bertani and Alessandro Fontana, trans. David Macey (London: Penguin, 2003), pp. 10–11.
4. Michel Foucault, 'The Subject and Power', in *Power: Essential Works of Foucault 1954–1984, Volume 3*, ed. James D. Faubion (London: Penguin, 2002), pp. 326–48 (pp. 326–7).

5. Michel Foucault, *The Order of Things: An Archaeology of the Human Sciences* (New York: Vintage, 1994); Michel Foucault, *The Archaeology of Knowledge*, trans. A. M. Sheridan Smith (New York: Vintage, 2010); Michel Foucault, 'What is an Author?', trans. Josué V. Harari, in *Aesthetics: Essential Works of Foucault 1954–1984, Volume 2*, ed. James D. Faubion (London: Penguin, 2000), pp. 205–22.
6. Michel Foucault, *Discipline and Punish: Birth of the Prison*, trans. Alan Sheridan (New York: Vintage, 1995); Michel Foucault, *A History of Sexuality, Volume 1: An Introduction*, trans. Robert Hurley (New York: Vintage, 1990).
7. This argument, or a variation of it, is found in Charles Taylor, 'Foucault on Freedom and Truth', in *Philosophical Papers 2: Philosophy and the Human Sciences* (Cambridge: Cambridge University Press, 1985), pp. 152–84 (pp. 165, 172, 173–4); Jürgen Habermas, 'Some Questions concerning the Theory of Power: Foucault Again', in *The Philosophical Discourse of Modernity: Twelve Lectures*, trans. Frederick Lawrence (Cambridge: Polity, 1987), pp. 266–93 (pp. 268, 274); Peter Dews, *Logics of Disintegration: Post-structuralist Thought and the Claims of Critical Theory* (London: Verso, 1987), pp. 190, 225; Lois McNay, *Foucault and Feminism: Power, Gender, and Agency* (Cambridge: Polity, 1992), p. 3.
8. In 1954, 1961 and 1963 respectively, Foucault published *Mental Illness and Psychology*, 2nd rev. edn (Berkeley, CA: University of California Press, 2008); *History of Madness*, ed. Jean Khalfa, trans. Jonathon Murphy (Abingdon: Routledge, 2009); and *The Birth of the Clinic: An Archaeology of Medical Perception* (New York: Vintage, 1994).
9. Michel Foucault, 'The Order of Things', in *Aesthetics: Essential Works of Foucault 1954–1984, Volume 2*, ed. James D. Faubion (London: Penguin, 2000), pp. 261–8 (p. 261).
10. Foucault, *The Order of Things*, p. 308.
11. Foucault, 'The Order of Things', p. 264.
12. Foucault, *The Order of Things*, p. 309.
13. Ibid., p. 344.
14. Ibid., p. 385.
15. Ibid., p. 385.
16. Ibid., p. 386.
17. Ibid., p. 387.
18. Beatrice Han-Pile, 'The "Death of Man": Foucault and Anti-Humanism', in Timothy O'Leary and Christopher Falzon (eds), *Foucault and Philosophy* (Oxford: Wiley-Blackwell, 2010), pp. 118–42 (p. 135).
19. Foucault, *The Order of Things*, p. 387.
20. Emma Ingala, 'Catachresis and Mis-Being in Judith Butler and Etienne Balibar: Contemporary Refigurations of the Human as a Face Drawn in the Sand', *Literature and Theology*, 32.2, 2018, pp. 142–60.
21. Foucault, *The Archaeology of Knowledge*, pp. 11–14.
22. Ibid., p. 12.
23. Foucault, 'What is an Author?', p. 205.
24. Ibid., p. 206.

25. Ibid., pp. 207, 209–10.
26. Ibid., p. 209.
27. Ibid., p. 210.
28. Foucault's most condensed, but extensive, discussion of 'genealogy' is found in Michel Foucault, 'Nietzsche, Geneaology, History', trans. Donald F. Bouchard and Sherry Simon, in *The Foucault Reader*, ed. Paul Rabinow (New York: Vintage, 2010), pp. 76–100. For an extended discussion of Foucault's notion and use of genealogy, see Colin Koopman, *Genealogy as Critique: Foucault and the Problems of Modernity* (Bloomington, IN: Indiana University Press, 2013).
29. Foucault, *Discipline and Punish*, p. 11.
30. Ibid., p. 11.
31. Ibid., p. 23.
32. Stuart Elden, *Foucault: The Birth of Power* (Cambridge: Polity, 2017), p. 2.
33. Foucault, *Discipline and Punish*, p. 26.
34. Ibid., p. 26.
35. Ibid., p. 26.
36. Ibid., p. 26.
37. Ibid., p. 26.
38. Ibid., p. 26.
39. Ibid., p. 26.
40. Ibid., p. 27.
41. Ibid., p. 27.
42. Ibid., pp. 41, 47.
43. Ibid., pp. 46–7.
44. Ibid., p. 59.
45. Ibid., pp. 59–60.
46. Ibid., p. 73.
47. Ibid., p. 73.
48. Ibid., p. 74.
49. Ibid., p. 102.
50. Ibid., p. 103.
51. Ibid., p. 115.
52. Ibid., p. 131.
53. Ibid., p. 137.
54. Ibid., p. 138.
55. Ibid., p. 138.
56. Ibid., p. 139.
57. Ibid., p. 139.
58. Ibid., p. 160.
59. Ibid., p. 170.
60. Ibid., pp. 179, 192.
61. Guy Debord, *The Society of the Spectacle*, trans. Donald Nicholson-Smith (New York: Zone Books, 1995).
62. Foucault, *Discipline and Punish*, p. 217.

63. Ibid., p. 194.
64. Ibid., p. 194.
65. For example, Mark Bevir suggests that 'Foucault's *Discipline and Punish* [i]s an attempt to analyse the way power works on the body through external controls, and his *History of Sexuality* [i]s an attempt to analyse the way it does so through internal controls' ('Foucault and Critique: Deploying Agency against Autonomy', *Political Theory*, 27.1, 1999, pp. 65–84). The problem with this suggestion is that it sets up a binary structure between the two texts, when I understand that in each, Foucault is trying to show, albeit in different ways, how power relations work both in relation to the 'external' body and the 'internal' values that normalise the individual.
66. For a detailed discussion of Foucault's analysis of power in this lecture course, especially as it relates to the question of sovereign violence, see Gavin Rae, *Critiquing Sovereign Violence: Law, Biopolitics, Bio-Juridicalism* (Edinburgh: Edinburgh University Press, 2019), ch. 5.
67. Foucault, *Society Must Be Defended*, pp. 14, 15.
68. Ibid., p. 15.
69. Michel Foucault, 'Truth and Power', trans. Robert Hurley, in *Power: Essential Works of Foucault 1954–1984*, ed. James D. Faubion (London: Penguin, 2002), pp. 111–33 (p. 124).
70. Foucault, *Society Must Be Defended*, p. 16.
71. Ibid., p. 15.
72. Ibid., p. 16.
73. Ibid., p. 15.
74. Ibid., p. 15.
75. Ibid., p. 15.
76. Ibid., p. 16.
77. Ibid., p. 16.
78. Ibid., p. 16.
79. Foucault, *A History of Sexuality, Volume 1*, pp. 92–102.
80. Foucault, *Society Must Be Defended*, p. 18.
81. Ibid., p. 25.
82. Ibid., p. 27. This understanding lies behind his famous assertion that 'we need to cut off the king's head' (Foucault, 'Truth and Power', p. 122).
83. Foucault, *Society Must Be Defended*, pp. 27–8.
84. Ibid., p. 28.
85. Ibid., p. 28.
86. Ibid., p. 33.
87. Ibid., p. 29.
88. Ibid., p. 29.
89. Ibid., p. 29.
90. Amy Allen, *The Politics of Our Selves: Power, Autonomy, and Gender in Contemporary Critical Theory* (New York: Columbia University Press, 2008), p. 55.
91. Foucault, *Society Must Be Defended*, p. 29, emphasis added.
92. Ibid., p. 29.

93. Ibid., pp. 29–30.
94. Ibid., p. 43.
95. See, for example, Michel Foucault, *On the Government of the Living: Lectures at the Collège de France, 1979–1980*, ed. Michel Senellart, trans. Graham Burchell (Basingstoke: Palgrave Macmillan, 2014).
96. Michel Foucault, *A History of Sexuality, Volume 2: The Use of Pleasure*, trans. Robert Hurley (London: Penguin, 1985); Michel Foucault, *A History of Sexuality, Volume 3: The Care of the Self*, trans. Robert Hurley (London: Penguin, 1985); Michel Foucault, *Histoire de la sexualité, IV: Les aveux de la chair*, ed. Frédéric Gros (Paris: Gallimard, 2018).
97. Foucault, *A History of Sexuality, Volume 1*, p. 10.
98. Ibid., p. 3.
99. Ibid., p. 3.
100. Ibid., p. 90.
101. Ibid., p. 92.
102. Ibid., p. 92; Hannah Arendt, *On Violence* (New York: Harvest, 1970). For a comparison of Arendt's and Foucault's conceptions of power, see Amy Allen, 'Power, Subjectivity, and Agency: Between Arendt and Foucault', *International Journal of Philosophical Studies*, 10.2, 2002, pp. 131–49.
103. Foucault, *A History of Sexuality, Volume 1*, pp. 92–3.
104. Ibid., p. 93.
105. Ibid., p. 94.
106. Ibid., p. 94.
107. Foucault, 'Truth and Power', p. 120.
108. Foucault, *A History of Sexuality, Volume 1*, p. 94.
109. Ibid., p. 94.
110. Ibid., p. 95.
111. Ibid., p. 95.
112. Ibid., p. 95.
113. Ibid., p. 95.
114. Taylor, 'Foucault on Freedom and Truth', p. 172.
115. Ibid., p. 172.
116. Habermas, 'Some Questions concerning the Theory of Power', p. 274.
117. Ibid., p. 256.
118. Dews, *Logics of Disintegration*, p. 190.
119. McNay, *Foucault and Feminism*, p. 3.
120. Foucault, 'Truth and Power', p. 118.
121. Michael Foucault, 'Interview with Michel Foucault', in *Power: Essential Works of Foucault 1954–1984, Volume 3*, ed. James D. Faubion (London: Penguin, 2002), pp. 239–97 (p. 275).
122. Ibid., p. 275.
123. Michel Foucault, 'Power and Strategies', in *Power/Knowledge: Selected Interviews and Other Writings 1972–1977*, ed. Colin Gordon, trans. Colin Gordon, Leo Marshall, John Mephan and Kate Soper (New York: Pantheon, 1980), pp. 134–45 (pp. 141–2).

124. Ibid., p. 138.
125. Bevir, 'Foucault and Critique', p. 67.
126. Ibid., p. 67.
127. Ibid., p. 67.
128. Ibid., p. 68.
129. Foucault, 'Truth and Power', p. 118.
130. Michel Foucault, 'The Ethics of the Concern for Self as a Practice of Freedom', trans. P. Aranov and D. McGrawth, in *Ethics: Essential Works of Foucault 1954–1984, Volume 1*, ed. Paul Rabinow (London: Penguin, 2000), pp. 281–301 (p. 293).
131. Foucault, 'The Subject and Power', p. 118.

CHAPTER 4

Foucault II: Normativity, Ethics and the Self

While I noted in the previous chapter that Foucault's work was always based on the notion that the subject was capable of agential action, his work from the 1980s until his untimely death in 1984 is marked by a turn to an explicit questioning of the self as part of an extended engagement with the ways in which the agent is capable of acting within the constraints of the power relations subtending it. There is, then, a focus in his later work on the practices that an agent can autonomously adopt and how these both accord with and depart from the dominant discursive practices of its society. For this reason, Foucault's later works explicitly take up the question that motivates this volume; namely, how the subject that has been decentred from its foundational constituting role is capable of intentional agency to affect that which constitutes it.

Foucault's questioning of this issue depends upon and was made possible by at least three conceptual modifications. First, he alters his conception of power so that the emphasis is no longer on the network of pre-personal force relations that generate individuals, but the relations between individuals: 'the characteristic feature of power is that some men can more or less entirely determine other men's conduct – but never exhaustively or coercively'.[1] This is not to say that the relationship between individuals is a 'nude'[2] one of pure force. It is 'organised following certain principles and according to certain techniques, to certain objectives, to certain tactics and so on'.[3] These structural components create and re-enforce power differentials that favour one individual over others. These are never absolute or ahistoric, but demonstrate how individuals both exist within asymmetric power relations and are capable of acting within those constraints. The question then becomes how individuals are to act with regard to the power relations that structure their relationships with others. With this, Foucault explains how individual action reshapes power relations. As a consequence, and in relation to the claim that institutions and ideas have no power themselves, he responds that '[i]t's obvious, no?'; they 'have power to the extent that they are ruled by people'.[4] Rather than holding that the subject is an effect of pre-personal structures, he highlights the agency that individuals 'have' 'within' those pre-personal structures and relations.

Second, this is accompanied by the introduction of an important distinction between 'power' and 'domination' wherein 'the category of power is the larger, and in this category you can find relations of domination, which are the most simple, the most violent power relations'.[5] Domination arises when the fluidity of power relations becomes 'fixed in such a way that they are perpetually asymmetrical and allow an extremely limited margin of freedom'.[6] Foucault gives the example of women in the eighteenth century, who, despite having quite a few options through which to express power within a conventional marriage, 'were still in a state of domination in so far as these options were ultimately only strategems that never succeeded in reversing the situation'.[7] By distinguishing between 'power' and 'domination', Foucault nuances his account of power and shows that these relations, which are always constituted by force, can reify into pseudo-permanent asymmetries that cause structural forms of domination that substantially limit the freedom of the individuals existing in and through them.

Third, having decentred the subject from its foundational role, Foucault's attempt to describe the agency of this decentred subject leads him from the subject to the *self*. The reason for this change is both linguistic, in so far as he notes that the word 'self' is not found in French, which is unfortunate 'because … it's a good word',[8] and conceptual, in so far as it allows him to distinguish his position from the foundationalism of 'the philosophy of the subject',[9] all the while denoting 'the kind of relation that the human being as a subject can have and entertain with himself'.[10] In other words, Foucault recognises that it is not enough to simply decentre the subject from its foundational position. This risks leaving the subject as a passive effect of pre-personal structures. To counter this, he shows that the subject is capable of acting on itself to effect its existence.

To engage with the ways in which the self makes itself, Foucault undertakes a 'genealogy of the modern subject as a historical and cultural reality – which means as something that can eventually change'.[11] In particular, he returns to the ancient Greeks to show that, for them, the self develops itself through the adoption of specific practices. With this, Foucault hopes to achieve three ends. 1) To show that, for the ancient Greeks, the ethical subject was premised not on adherence to universal rules, but from and around specific conducts and practices that were individual and contextual. The tendency within contemporary society to appeal to universal rules and means–end instrumental rationality is, as a consequence, a historical, particularly Christian, product; a conclusion that disrupts its claim to universal legitimacy. 2) To develop a contextual, practice-based ethics to complement his previous focus on the 'techniques of production, techniques of signification or communication, and techniques of domination' with one that emphasises what he calls the '"technologies of the self"'[12] that describe the practices through which the self acts to make and remake itself within, but also against, the techniques of production, signification and domination that it exists 'within'. And, from this, 3) to point to a conception of normativity from and with which to structure and orientate future agential political action.

This last issue is controversial – although it is crucial to understanding Foucault's later works – because one of the standard criticisms of Foucault, and the poststructuralist position generally, is that he/it offers no logically consistent form of normativity to direct or justify individual action.[13] Certainly Foucault appears to reject any need to affirm a norm to guide action, noting that 'I never behave like a prophet – my books don't tell people what to do'[14] and 'there is always something ludicrous in philosophical discourse when it tries, from the outside, to dictate to others, to tell them where their truth is and how to find it, or when it works up a case against them in the language of naïve positivity'.[15] Despite this, I will argue that Foucault's later work does offer a normative framework to orientate future action, based around a particular approach to practices of the self in which we create a 'politics of ourselves'.[16] Specifically, he names three *principles* that guide ethical action: 'refusal, curiosity, and innovation'.[17]

The key to my argument is to distinguish between two senses of normativity, termed here 'the normativity of universal *a priori* rules', in which normativity is understood in a formal, positive, juridical sense that determines in advance what is and is not acceptable, and 'normativity as an open practical principle', which describes a general principle that guides, without determining, individual action and that leaves it up to the individual to determine how to affirm that principle. Foucault rejects the former, but embraces the latter through his affirmation that the self should be open to trying out different practices to determine, via trial and error, what works or is simply acceptable, in that moment, for each self. Foucault's normative ethics affirms, then, not a formal juridical universalism, but an ethic of practice-based openness that manifests itself in and through a self-willingness to morph into and adopt different approaches to the everyday challenges and circumstances that individuals find themselves in.

This, however, leads to the second line of critique historically aimed at Foucault's later thinking – one that I will, somewhat paradoxically, deal with first – namely, that his attempt to develop an aesthetics of the self based on individual action not only undermines his previous decentring of the self, but also abandons all socio-political concern in favour of an ethics of pure individual self-creation and experimentation.[18] While I showed in the previous chapter that it is a mistake to claim that Foucault abandoned but subsequently returned to the fondational subject, in this chapter I appeal to a number of comments that he makes that explicitly demonstrate the social nature of the aesthetic self.

From Subject to Self

In 1980 Foucault gave two lectures at Dartmouth College where he clarified his thinking and in so doing started to outline a new line of research orientated from and around the question of the relationship between subjectivity and truth that would occupy him for the remaining years of his life. He starts by reaffirming his opposition to 'the philosophy of the subject' that dominated European philosophy after the Second World War and that 'set as its task *par excellence* the foundation of all knowledge and the principle of all signification as stemming from the meaningful subject'.[19] Although he is taking aim at Husserlian phenomenology and Sartrean existentialism, he links both to Descartes to reveal that his critique is actually orientated against the logic governing modern philosophy. With this, he reaffirms my argument from the previous chapter that he was not criticising the subject *per se*, but a particular form and logic of the subject; namely, the foundational, constituting subject. This rejection does, however, open a space from and through which to rethink the subject.

In the 1981 lecture 'Sexuality and Solitude', he follows Jürgen Habermas's insistence that subjectivity is conditioned by

> three major types of technique: the techniques that permit one to produce, to transform, to manipulate things; the techniques that permit one to use sign systems; and finally, the techniques that permit one to determine the conduct of individuals, to impose certain ends or objectives. That is to say, techniques of production, techniques of signification or communication, and techniques of domination.[20]

However, Foucault notes that

> there is another type of technique . . . that permit[s] individuals to effect, by their own means, a certain number of operations on their own bodies, their own souls, their own thoughts, their own conduct, and this in a manner so

as to transform themselves, modify themselves, and to attain a certain state of perfection, happiness, purity, supernatural power. Let us call these techniques 'technologies of the self.'[21]

It is not, then, sufficient simply to study the techniques of domination, wherein the subject is effected by power structures and relations; 'one must [also] take into consideration . . . techniques of the self'[22] by examining 'those forms of understanding which the subject creates about himself'.[23] For this reason, Foucault explains that '[h]aving studied the field of power relations taking techniques of domination as a point of departure, I would like, in the years to come, to study power relations starting from the techniques of the self'.[24] Indeed, in the 1982 text 'Technologies of the Self', he even claims that he '[p]erhaps . . . insisted too much on the technology of domination and power', before reaffirming his interest in 'the interaction between oneself and others, and in the technologies of individual domination, in the mode of action that an individual exercises upon himself by means of the technologies of the self'.[25]

Crucially, Foucault never gives up his previous analysis of power; rather, he refines and complements it by inquiring into the ways in which the subject acts within these power relations. This, in turn, leads him away from a biopolitical analysis, which focuses on the ways in which power makes the body, to governmentality, which delineates 'the encounter between the technologies of domination of others and those of the self'.[26] He chooses 'sexuality' as the medium through which to explore the different practices in which the self constitutes itself because

> [s]exuality is part of our behaviour. It's part of our world freedom. Sexuality is something that we ourselves create – it is our own creation, and much more than the discovery of a secret side to our desire. We have to understand that with our desires, through our desires, go new forms of relationships, new forms of love, new forms of creation. Sex is not a fatality; it's a possibility for creative life.[27]

Sex is not, on Foucault's telling, an urge or desire, but a form of self-creation and self-expression. To study it is to analyse how we create and express ourselves; an analysis that reveals how the self is created through social practices. But Foucault goes on to explain that 'the problem is not to discover in oneself the truth of one's sex, but, rather, to use one's sexuality henceforth to arrive at a multiplicity of relationships'.[28] This does not mean that he simply advocates that we take on as many sexual partners as we can, but that we examine our sexual practices to open them to multiple forms to explore as full a variety of them as we are comfortable doing.

In the 1984 interview 'The Ethics of the Concern for Self as a Practice of Freedom', Foucault admits that he has not got very far in outlining the ways in which this occurs,[29] but his study of ancient forms of sexual techniques and practices does not simply describe historical sexual practices; it also has philosophical and political importance, in so far as it identifies different (sexual) practices to those that govern the contemporary world to reveal that options other than those currently dominant are possible. This is part of his normative affirmation of practical openness and experimentation rather than the closure and exclusion inherent in practices based on adherence to pre-established universal moral rules.

What Foucault finds fascinating about the ancient Greeks is that the technique governing their lives was so very different to the instrumental rationality that dominates contemporary European society or the ethic of renunciation he associates with Christianity. They practised an 'arts of existence',[30] by which he means

> those intentional and voluntary actions by which men not only set themselves rules of conduct, but also seek to transform themselves, to change themselves in their singular being, and to make their life into an *oeuvre* that carries certain aesthetic values and meets certain stylistic criteria.[31]

According to Foucault, the Greeks shaped their practices from and around 'a precept: *epimeleisthai sautou*, "to take care of yourself," to take "care of the self," "to be concerned, to take care of yourself"'.[32] The notion of care of the self 'was the mode in which individual freedom – or civic liberty, up to a point – was reflected [*se réfléchie*] as an ethics'[33] and depended upon and fed into a whole system of knowledge, practices and values. It was a holistic system within which the individual had specific obligations to himself and others. This notion has largely been ignored in the history of Greek thought as the Delphic imperative 'know thyself'[34] has been privileged, but the Delphic imperative is dependent upon the prior care of self: 'In Greek and Roman texts, the injunction of having to know oneself was always associated with the other principle of the care of the self, and it was that need to care for oneself that brought the Delphic maxim into operation.'[35]

There were many facets through which the ancient Greeks understood the notion of care of self, and Foucault produces extensive descriptions of these in the second and third volumes of the *History of Sexuality*, but one of the key general points identified is that for the ancient Greeks,

> sexual activity was perceived as natural (natural and indispensable) since it was through this activity that living creatures were able to reproduce, the species as a whole was able to escape extinction, and cities, families, names, and religions were able to endure far longer than individuals, who were destined to pass away.³⁶

Furthermore, sexuality was configured around a whole set of practices and norms to do with the nature of the community and the desire to contribute to life after one had died. The logic surrounding sexuality was not prohibitive, but orientated towards the question of its proper use or application. It was necessary to do it 'correctly' for the 'right' reasons:

> Foods, wines, and relations with women and boys constituted analogous ethical material; they brought forces into play that were natural, but that always tended to be excessive; and they all raised the same question: how could one, how must one 'make use' (*chrēsthai*) of this dynamics of pleasures, desires, and acts? A question of right use.³⁷

The notion of *chrēsis aphrodisiōn*, or the right use of pleasures, had two senses. First, it denoted a period of time of the year or life where it was considered good to engage in sexual activity. Second, it referred to the way 'in which an individual managed his sexual activity, his way of conducting himself in such matters, the regimen he allowed himself or imposed on himself, the conditions in which he accomplished sexual acts, the share he allotted them in his life'.³⁸ We might call this second sense an individual's style of sexual activity.

What is important about this second sense is that it is not based on a universal norm or law: 'It is not a question of what was permitted or forbidden among the desires that one felt or the acts that one committed, but of prudence, reflection, and calculation in the way one distributed and controlled his acts.'³⁹ It was obviously necessary to respect 'the laws and customs of the land, to keep from offending the gods, and to heed the will to nature', but the practices were not determined by laws or even 'a clearly defined code'.⁴⁰ 'It was more a question of a variable adjustment in which one had to take different factors into account: the element of want and natural necessity; that of opportuneness, which was temporal and circumstantial; that of the status of the individual himself.'⁴¹ Far from being defined by rigid, universal laws that determined and dictated individual sexual behaviours, there was a flexibility and specificity to sexual activity that had to be continually negotiated, to be 'adapted to suit the user and his personal status'.[42] This did not mean that there were no laws, but the way in which they were adhered to and practised was based on a *'technē* or "practice," a *savoir-faire* that by taking general principles into account would guide action in its time, according to its context, and in view of its ends'.[43]

As a consequence, the individual did not turn him or herself into an ethical subject by following universal principles or universalising the principles that informed their action; 'he did so by means of an attitude and a quest that individualised his action, modulated it, and perhaps even gave him a special brilliance by virtue of the rational and deliberate structure his action manifested'.[44] This points to a particular form of sexual practice that is very different to the Christian one. However, Foucault rejects the notion of a fundamental rupture between the ancient Greeks and Christianity. There are similarities between the ways in which the two structured discourse on sexuality, although these are masked by the fact that their component pieces are not only configured differently but are also orientated towards different ends.[45] On the one hand, for example, Foucault holds that 'Christian asceticism and ancient philosophy are placed under the same sign: that of the care of the self. The obligation to know oneself is one of the central elements of Christian asceticism.'[46] On the other hand, however, the Christian notion of care for self is based on different practices and attains an alternative signification than it does for the ancient Greeks. Whereas the ancient Greeks saw sexuality as a natural act necessary for procreation and the continuation of the species, its Platonic heritage brought Christianity to hold that the natural world is that which 'must be renounced in order to gain access to another level of reality'.[47] All bodily pleasures are, then, to be forsaken. This, in turn, ensured that the Greek care for self 'was readily denounced as a form of self-love, a form of selfishness or self-interest in contradiction with the interest to be shown in others or the self-sacrifice required'.[48]

From the Christian perspective, then, the ways in which the Greeks went about caring for themselves by experimenting with different forms of self-expression based on circumstances, need and time was ultimately narcissistic and egoistical. Christians stressed the need to get away from the ego by renouncing bodily pleasures to, in so doing, live a 'purer' spiritual relation (with God). This renunciation of the body was accompanied by the affirmation of the 'inner' life and, with it, specific practices of the self: 'forms of attention, concern, decipherment, verbalization, confession, self-accusation, struggle against temptation, renunciation, spiritual combat, and so on'.[49] The Christian model of renunciation also creates and depends upon a whole range of affirmative practices and a specific attitude, including a network of institutional practices, such as the monasteries, where such practices could be closely controlled. In turn, confession of transgressions came to the fore to reveal and support the importance of power hierarchies wherein individuals were placed under the supervision of an institutional hierarchy that punished, supported and moulded the individual based on predetermined rules of conduct.

These were completely absent from the Greek conception of care for the self which was 'much more orientated towards practices of the self and the question of *askēsis* than toward codifications of conducts and the strict definition of what is permitted and what is forbidden'.[50] Whereas the Christian sense of asceticism maintains that pleasure is a negative to be renounced, the Greek sense of '*ascesis* is something else: it's the work that one performs on oneself in order to transform oneself or make the self appear, which, happily, one never attains'.[51] The key point that Foucault draws is that '[n]o technique, no professional skill can be acquired without exercise; neither can one learn the art of living, the *tekhnē tou biou*, without an *askēsis* which must be taken as a training of oneself by oneself'.[52] Both the Greek and Christian ethics of care for self contain this moment of self-discipline and training; indeed, it must be part of all ethics of the self because it is the process through which 'one attempts to develop and transform oneself, and to attain to a certain mode of being'.[53]

Different types of care of the self are possible because Foucault notes that they are constructed from and around four aspects. First, there is 'the ethical substance [*substance éthique*]'[54] that implicitly underpins any view of the self. For example, Foucault explains that 'from the Kantian point of view, intention is much more important than feelings [whereas] from the Christian point of view, it is desire . . . [and] [f]or the Greeks, the ethical substance was acts linked to pleasure and desire in their unity'.[55] 'The second aspect is . . . the mode of subjectivation [*mode d'assujettissement*], that is, the way in which people are invited or incited to recognize their moral obligations.'[56] This is tied to the social norms and power discourses and relations within which the subject exists which define acceptable ways of behaving, acting and so on. In turn, this is linked to the question of how a particular ethical code substantiates and grounds its claims, such as whether it appeals to emotion, natural law, reason, theology or some alternative to ultimately ground its claims. The third aspect refers to the agency through which 'we can change ourselves in order to become ethical subjects'.[57] Among other things, it outlines how we moderate our actions and decide what we are to be, including how we are to create this. For Foucault, this is the moment of self-transformation through the regulation of one's own behaviour – '*asceticism* in a very broad sense'.[58] The fourth aspect refers to the *telos* of the ethical subject: to what end is it directed? 'For example, shall we become pure, or immortal, or free, or masters of ourselves, and so on?'[59] This is the aspect of the ethical system that sets the ethical norms that ground the agent's asceticism.

Foucault's history of sexuality aims to show how these aspects find expression through the ethical systems of the ancient Greeks and Christianity. By identifying that each configured the respective aspects differently, he highlights that they had different approaches to sexuality and, by extension, different ways of training the self. In particular, he looks to the ancient Greeks for an alternative ethics because theirs is so radically different to the model of renunciation constitutive of Christianity and the instrumental rationality of modern ethics. The purpose is not to simply reaffirm the Greek model. After all, their ethic was exclusionary, in that it was only enacted by a very small proportion of the population,[60] and is clearly not suitable for the complexities of modern societies: 'you can't find the solution of a problem in the solution of another problem raised at another moment by other people'.[61] What it can do, however, is disrupt the certainty of modern ethical codes, showing that they are not the only ones available.

This is important because Foucault notes that we in the West have become used to thinking of our ethics, everyday life, economy and politics as being intertwined in a delicate balance where to change one aspect is to risk ruin. He asks us to disentangle these relations by 'get[ting] rid of this idea of an analytical or necessary link between ethics and other social or economic or political structures'.[62] Through this disentanglement, the ethical options available to the self are opened. To take advantage of this, Foucault warns against 'a codification of acts ... [or] a hermeneutics of the subject', to instead suggest an ethics that takes inspiration from the Greek's 'stylization of attitudes and ... aesthetics of existence'.[63] From this, he points to the following normative prescription: the self should be guided by an (initial) openness to all practices, with the validity of each being determined by the individual, based on their specific context.

The Question of Sociality

One of the most frequently cited objections to Foucault's affirmation of an aestheticisation of the self is that it is a purely individualistic account of ethical subjectivity that lacks any awareness of social commitments or consideration for others. Richard Wolin, for example, claims that 'Foucault's standpoint favours either an attitude of narcissistic self-absorption or one of outwardly directed, aggressive self-aggrandisement. In neither case is there a discernible trace of human solidarity, mutuality, or fellow-feeling.'[64] Peter Dews echoes this by complaining that 'it is difficult to see how in contemporary society any such turn towards an aesthetics of existence could be anything other than a re-enforcement of social tendencies towards atomisation'.[65] Pierre Hadot suggests that by affirming the aestheticisation of the self, 'Foucault might have been advancing a cultivation of the self which was too purely aesthetic – that is to say, I fear, a new form of dandyism, a late twentieth-century version', while Ranier Rochlitz complains about the lack of universality in Foucault's account, and Alexandros Kioupkiolis objects to his failure to understand and account for the cultural dimension of social existence.[66]

This line of critique is, however, based on a simplistic reading of Foucault's position that fails to properly understand the embedded nature of the Foucaultian self. Foucault makes this clear in a number of comments that explicitly address this issue. For example, in the 1983 interview 'On the Genealogy of Ethics', he specifically responds to the question of whether his ethics is simply one of self-absorption by distancing himself from 'the Californian cult of the self [in which] one is supposed to discover one's true self, to separate it from that which might obscure or alienate it'.[67] There simply is no authentic, true self to be found or worked on; rather, there is a self to be invented and created, which is a social act.

The sociality inherent in Foucault's understanding of ethics is developed through his analysis of what it meant to freely care for oneself in ancient Greece. This was not an individual act, but an inherently socio-political one, not only because to have the status of 'free' was contrary to having the status of 'slave' and 'a slave has no ethics',[68] but also because a free self was intimately tied to practices of moderation and acceptability. To be free required that 'with respect to oneself one establishe[d] a certain relationship of domination, of mastery, which was called *arkhē*, or power, command'.[69] That the free self was in command of itself meant that it was not simply orientated to the satisfaction of its own desires, which would put it in thrall to them. Freedom for the ancient Greeks was not understood in terms of atomisation and independence, but in terms of the individual's embeddedness within social practices: 'The freedom that needed establishing and preserving was that of the citizens of a collectivity of course, but it was also, for each of them, a certain form of relationship of the individual with himself.'[70]

While the organisation of the city, its laws, education and the comportment of its leaders were crucial in creating and sustaining the 'correct' individual behaviours, 'the freedom of individuals, understood as the mastery they were capable of exercising over themselves, was indispensable to the entire state'.⁷¹ The social embeddedness of the individual and the symbiotic relationship between the state and the individual points to the notion that individual freedom requires a certain form of self-control and moderation.⁷² It is, then, linked to 'knowledge of a certain number of rules of acceptable conduct'⁷³ and so is a 'true social practice'.⁷⁴ Indeed, Foucault goes so far as to claim that 'the only ethic one can have with regard to the exercise of power is the freedom of others'.⁷⁵

Rethinking Normativity

Foucault's affirmation of an aestheticisation of the self is not, then, based on a model of self-absorption or asocial self-affirmation; it is a socially embedded practice that, as such, depends on individual self-expression within the parameters permitted by social circumstance. This does, however, bring us to the second issue that plagues Foucault's rethinking of ethics: the normativity inherent in it. My argument is that Foucault's description of the (sexual) practices of the ancient Greeks allows him to develop a normative conception of how we should act based the notion of openness to practices that, crucially, is consistent with his afoundationalism.

This argument is somewhat controversial in so far as it contradicts the often repeated argument that not only is there no normativity in Foucault's work, but it is also impossible to construct a normative argument from his analysis in a way that is logically consistent with his epistemic relativism. Charles Taylor, for example, argues that, for Foucault, 'there is no order of human life, or way we are, or human nature, that one can appeal to in order to judge or evaluate between ways of life'.⁷⁶ Reaffirming the foundational subject that Foucault rejects, Taylor claims that '[t]here are only different orders imposed by men on primal chaos, following their will to power'.⁷⁷ Jürgen Habermas continues in this vein, claiming that Foucault's position leads to 'an unholy subjectivism'⁷⁸ because of a logical inconsistency within his thought. On the one hand, Foucault claims that truth is power-dependent and therefore contingent and local. But, on the other hand, Foucault *implicitly* holds that his own analysis transcends any power-truth claim to be able to discern the truths of other historical discourses and power relations. This must be so otherwise his own theory would simply be an effect of particular power relations, which, on Habermas's telling, would undermine 'the entire undertaking of a critical unmasking of the human sciences'.⁷⁹ Foucault is, then, caught between his methodology, which adopts a metahistorical, transcendent, normative position – it is, after all, *the* correct way to undertake analyses of problems – and his theory of power that specifically excludes such a transcendent, normative position. As a consequence, Foucault's attempt to escape relativism 'by means of its own tools falls short'.[80]

Nancy Fraser comes to a similar conclusion by affirming that Foucault's work utilises and depends upon the normativity that his power relations reject. Having pointed to a number of apparently contradictory statements, she charges that the problem is not that 'Foucault contradicts himself. It is that he does so in part because he misunderstands, at least when it comes to his *own* situation, the way that norms function in social description.'[81] In particular, she claims that Foucault's critique implicitly holds that norms 'can be neatly isolated and excised from the larger cultural and linguistic matrix in which they are situated'.[82] This, however,

> fails to appreciate the degree to which the normative is embedded in and infused throughout the whole of language at *every* level and the degree to which, despite himself, his own critique has to make use of modes of description, interpretation, and judgement formed within the modern Western normative tradition.[83]

On Fraser's telling, Foucault's attempt to offer a non-normative account of power relations fails because he continues to use normatively expressive terms and phrases (domination, subjugation and so on) that tie him intimately to the normative tradition he rejects. Far from a neutral interpretation, Foucault's descriptions are loaded with normative judgements that he is unable to ground or justify based on his account of power relations.

In short, the fundamental problem for Fraser, Habermas and Taylor appears to be that Foucault holds that power relations generate truth. As power relations change, so too does truth. By abandoning any notion of a transcendent standpoint that could distinguish between the various truth claims of different historical epochs, Foucault simply cannot provide any grounds to legitimately criticise certain historical practices or prescribe future actions.

The basic assumption underpinning these critiques is that normativity must be tied to some form of universal practice or ahistoric rule that transcends actual historical situations so that it can be appealed to when trying to distinguish between and determine the legitimacy of various historical practices or prescribe how we should act in the future. These critics note that Foucault's notion of power rejects such an approach, with the consequence that they conclude that he cannot offer a normative position. They might also have pointed to a number of comments that he makes that confirm this: 'I am wary of imposing my own views, or of setting down a plan, or program.'⁸⁴ As noted in his rejection of any attempt to use the ancient Greeks as a straightforward model for future action, such action risks producing a universal rule that is simply inapplicable to the concrete realities of a particular situation.⁸⁵ Perhaps the most explicit support for the charge that Foucault does not offer any normative position is that he explicitly rejects the need to do so:

> I am not a prophet! I am not a programmer, I don't have to tell [people] what they have to do, I don't have to tell them: 'This is good for you; this isn't good for you.' I try to analyze a situation in all its complexity, with the function, [for] this task of analysis, of allowing at once refusal, curiosity, and invention. That's it . . . I don't have to tell people: 'This is good for you.'⁸⁶

It appears, then, that Foucault does not offer a normative programme, not only because his theory of power explicitly rejects it, but also because he does not see this as his job.

The problem with this line of critique and the conclusion it generates – namely, that there is no normativity in Foucault's thinking – is that it is based on a particularly reductionist understanding of normativity that thinks of it in terms of transcendent, universal rules that guide future action or judge past action. It is certainly true that Foucault explicitly rejects any appeal to universal laws – 'I don't accept either the notion of mastery or the universality of law'⁸⁷ – and the notion and legitimacy of a 'founding act of reason'⁸⁸ that could be used to establish a norm to programme and direct future action. However, that Foucault rejects the appeal to transcendent universal rules to guide future action does not mean that he rejects all forms of normativity. One of the key tasks that Foucault tries to undertake in his later works is to see if it is possible to develop a form of normativity based on the study of immanent historical practices. If there is no God's-eye view, are we still able to legitimately determine and point to a course of and for future action? He thinks that we can, but only if we develop a different sense of normativity and ethics. Specifically, he rejects the notion of normativity understood in terms of the establishment of universal rules – what I will call 'the normativity of universal *a priori* rules' – but affirms an alternative notion of normativity, which I will call 'normativity as an open practical principle', understood as a specific, guiding, open-ended, empty principle that is given content by the decisions of individuals based on context and circumstances. Understanding the difference between the two senses of normativity is illuminated by the distinction Foucault makes between 'morality' and 'ethics'.

Morality, for Foucault, describes 'a set of values and rules of action that are recommended to individuals through the intermediary of various prescriptive agencies such as the family (in one of its roles), educational institutions, churches, and so on'.[89] They can be made explicit in codified form or they can be 'transmitted in a diffuse manner'.[90] Importantly, these formal rules and codes of conduct come from outside the individual and outline in advance what is expected of each subject. However, that the individual is subjected to a moral code does not mean that they are determined by it. He or she contributes to the realisation of that code through their actions. How the individual actually relates to those moral codes and rules delineates their *ethics*. As Foucault explains, ethics refers 'to the real behaviour of individuals in relation to the rules and values that are recommended to them'.[91] It delineates the ways in which 'individuals are urged to constitute themselves as subjects of moral conduct'.[92] How individuals comport themselves towards the moral codes and rules recommended is not universal or based on predetermined rules. Rather, ethics is practised, in so far as it depends upon how the individual expresses him or herself as an ethical subject. So, while there are moral guidelines recommended to the individual, these do not determine his or her behaviour, nor are they as homogeneous as they claim to be. They need to be enacted through the practices of the individual.

Here, Arnold Davidson's distinction between a 'way of life' and 'style of life' is helpful.[93] The former describes the recommended moral norm that grounds a way of life, whereas the latter refers to the way(s) in which individuals express themselves in relation to that way of life. Davidson gives the example of philosophy in the ancient world. This was 'a way of life that was distinct from everyday life, and [indeed] was perceived [to be] strange and even dangerous'.[94] But philosophy was not homogeneous. There were 'different philosophies, what I shall call different styles of life, different styles of living philosophically'.[95] Similarly, while there may be one (dominant) morality of a society, there are various ethics.

By undertaking a genealogy of the subject through the sexual practices of the ancient Greeks and early Christians, Foucault points to the different ways and styles in which codified moral norms were created and affirmed by individuals; that is, the ways in which the self created itself as an ethical subject. This was not based on an abstract self-idealisation, but the practices adopted:

> A person's *ēthos* was evident in his clothing, appearance, gait, in the calm with which he responded to every event, and so on. For the Greeks, this was the concrete form of freedom; this was the way they problematized their freedom. A man possessed of a splendid *ēthos*, who could be admired and put forward as an example, was someone who practiced freedom in a certain way.[96]

The ancient Greeks did not, then, simply conflate morality and ethics, but held the two apart to affirm the importance of the latter. Rather than adhere to abstract universal rules, the ethical subject was born from a particular stylisation of freedom. It was this that defined the aestheticisation of the self.

Foucault's critics tend not to make the distinction between morality and ethics but collapse both into the standpoint of morality and so ground their critique on the notion that morality/ethics is based on the affirmation of universal formal rules or principles to determine future action. That Foucault does not and indeed cannot offer these based on his account of power relations permits the criticism that his thinking is normatively useless and/ or normatively incoherent, in so far as it cannot offer moral norms to guide future action nor appeal to such norms to underpin his critical stance.

However, rather than appeal to and depend upon universal formal rules to determine individual action, Foucault recognises and works from the contextual embeddedness of the subject to claim that agency cannot be foreclosed but *should* be defined from an on-going process of contextual experimentation that necessitates that it remain open to different practices and positions. As William Connelly explains, 'the goal is to modify an already contingent self – working within the narrow terms of craftsmanship available to an adult – so that you are better able to ward off the demand to conform transcendentally to what you are contingently'.[97] That no one practice is suitable for all circumstances means that the self must continuously make itself into an ethical subject in each moment. How it does this will be context-specific and dependent upon the self, including its use of judgement, willingness to try out alternatives, and the extent to which it is willing to challenge the dominant moral norm(s).

Foucault does, then, offer and depend upon a normative position that we might call an *ethic of practical openness*, and uses this both to judge certain practices based on the extent to which they respect this value or reject it, and to affirm how individuals are to act in the future: they are to open themselves to different practices to determine, for themselves, what works for them in that (socially embedded) moment and, indeed, what they are willing to do to create themselves in each moment. This is a radically different form of ethics than that which results from normativity understood in terms of adherence to formal universal rules. It means that the individual cannot simply close him or herself off from certain practices prior to trying them, nor can they *forever* exclude themselves from certain practices if they find them to be unsuitable in a particular moment. Individuals must engage in constant ethical self-creation and experimentation.

This is not to say, however, that Foucault does not appeal to universal formal rules; his later affirmation of human rights, for example, continues to make use of them. However, as Ben Golder notes, these appear 'as potentially useful, tactical instruments in political struggle, as political tools immanent and not exterior to the field of political combat'.[98] The issue is not to fall into an either/or situation of affirming formal moral rules or ethical practices; rather, Foucault affirms both, but emphasises that the former must be thought in terms of tactical tools of the latter, rather than as universal, ahistorical foundations. After all, what gives content to a right depends upon the way it is practised. Indeed, for Foucault, the lack of a political normative programme is not inherently negative, nor does it mean that action is directionless; 'being without a program can be very useful and very original and creative, if it does not mean without proper reflection about what is going on, or without very careful attention to what's possible'.[99]

Nevertheless, Foucault's affirmation of ethical practical openness gives rise to three questions. First, how can he justify his affirmation of an ethic of practical openness when he has rejected the notion of universal truths? The answer lies in understanding that Foucault's normative position emanates from the premises of his genealogical afoundationalism. If there is no absolute, ahistoric foundation to ground norms, it is not possible to legitimise one norm over others *a priori*. This does not, however, mean that we fall into helpless nihilism, but that we must recognise that, because we must act, the only thing we can do is simply adopt a norm to act from. That there is not one 'best' way to act means that we have to open ourselves to experimentation and the adoption of different norms to open up the practical options to us to find the one that works in a particular social situation. The *telos* of such action will depend upon the norms of the socio-historical situation and what is deemed acceptable (from both an individual and social perspective), but Foucault seems to think that the lack of any absolute foundations means that practical action can be thought to be 'good' the more it keeps open the possibility of a future ethic of practical openness. Those practices that depend upon an *a priori* discrimination against particular ways of life implicitly claim a foundation that legitimates some actions over others. In so doing, however, they violate their own (actual) afoundationalism – as outlined by Foucault's account of power relations – and are, therefore, both logically and practically incoherent.

However, second, if there are no *a priori* standards against which we can judge the ethical worth of situations, how can we know that a situation or power relation should be changed? Does Foucault not simply risk affirming change for the sake of change? What, in other words, is the *motivation* for the self to act? Foucault responds that the motivation for change arises when a situation is deemed to be 'intolerable'.[100] There is nothing universal about this; what is intolerable depends solely on the individual and the specific circumstances. If individuals judge their situation to be intolerable they will act to alleviate it. Far from dismissing that judgement or asking that it be legitimised by a universal or 'objective' standard, Foucault maintains that it is its own legitimacy: that the subject holds a situation to be intolerable makes that situation intolerable. This, however, obviously depends upon another norm, which we can term respect for the other; it is only if we respect the other that we will take his or her judgement about what he or she finds to be intolerable seriously. Unfortunately, Foucault never discusses the nature of that respect or how it is determined, although it is presumably tied to his insistence that an ethics of the self is an inherently social, rather than merely individual, undertaking.

Third, the question arises as to what end the self should act? To simply say that the self should always be open to alternative practices does not tell us in what direction the self should act. Foucault responds that if there are no universal formal rules to determine future action, and if action is contextual and practice-based, then the only option is for individuals to make it up as they go along based on the specifics of the circumstance:

> it will be up to the people to work, or to conduct themselves spontaneously in such a way that they define for themselves what is good for them ... The good comes from innovation. The good does not exist, just like that, in a timeless heaven, with people who would be like astrologers of the good, able to determine the favorable conjunction of the stars. The good is defined, practiced, invented. But this requires the work not just of some, [but] a collective work.[101]

Such reinvention cannot, however, be orientated to or from a prior model; it is and must be based on experimentation and limit experiences. Only this will break the confines of (pre-existing) moral systems, open up new practices, and allow individuals to radically express their freedom. This is an ongoing process. As Foucault puts it:

> The critical ontology of ourselves must be considered not, certainly, as a theory, a doctrine, nor even as a permanent body of knowledge that is accumulating; it must be conceived as an attitude, an ethos, a philosophical life in which the critique of what we are is at one and at the same time the historical analysis of the limits imposed on us and an experiment with the possibility of going beyond them [*de leur franchissement possible*].[102]

Therefore, the norm that conditions Foucault's thinking is that of practical openness, with the value of actions depending on the extent to which they permit future practical experimentation. Those that do are, for Foucault, 'good', those that do not are not. This is not because of a universal definition of 'good', but because, in the absence of absolute universal foundations to ground and justify moral norms, the only ethical option, he thinks, is to throw ourselves into contingency and afoundationalism by constantly remaking ourselves based on our situation.

Conclusion

Foucault's late writings on the self perform, then, at least three functions. First, having previously decentred the subject from its foundational role, he shows that the self can and must contribute to its own making. Second, he appeals to the practices of the ancient Greeks not only to undercut the (Christian) notion that ethical values are universal and ahistoric, but also, in so doing, to demonstrate that they held that ethics, far from being rule-bound, is an individual, creative, ongoing, practice-based endeavour. The discussion of different practices, in combination with his afoundationalism, brings Foucault to claim, third, that the self should affirm an ethic of practical openness, which, rather than entailing the development of an attitude of atomistic self-absorption, is a socially orientated and moderate, practice-based approach to ethics that demands that the subject continuously remake itself ethically by deciding when and how to act in each circumstance.

Foucault's ethics of the self is important, then, not only because it develops our understanding of his thinking, but also because it demonstrates that poststructuralist thought can and does offer normative standards based on context, circumstance, individual commitment and innovation that depart from the universal, rule-based variety typically meant by the term. This does not entail the affirmation of a pure egoism but a delicate and ongoing balancing act that experiments with and pushes the individual beyond their own limits and those of their society, all the while maintaining the self-control and social awareness to meet their social responsibilities.

However, for all its innovation, Foucault's account of the self lacks a certain depth, in so far as his practice-based approach is strong at emphasising the ways in which social norms and discourses structure the ethical subject, but weaker at identifying and describing the specific structures, motivations and impetuses that bring the subject to create itself (or not) in particular ways. Although Foucault comes to show that agents can and do act intentionally within the limitations of their socio-historical environments, this needs to be complemented by a more detailed explanation of why they do so (or don't) and, specifically, how they are capable of acting in this way. For this reason, it has been suggested that we need to complement Foucault's approach with a questioning of the psychic life of the agent and, in particular, the structure of, and the mechanisms that take place within, the psyche to permit intentional action; a topic about which Foucault, despite his detailed analyses of the practices of psychiatry, has little to say. In Part II, I engage with those poststructuralists who take up this approach. The next chapter starts with the response given by Judith Butler.

Notes

1. Michel Foucault, '"*Omnes et Singulatim*": Toward a Critique of Political Reason', in *Power: Essential Works of Foucault 1954–1984, Volume 3*, ed. James D. Faubion (London: Penguin, 2002), pp. 298–325 (p. 324).
2. Michel Foucault, 'Discussion of "Truth and Subjectivity"', in *About the Hermeneutics of the Self: Lectures at Dartmouth College, 1980*, ed. Henri-Paul Fruchard and Daniele Lorenzini, trans. Graham Burchell (Chicago: University of Chicago Press, 2016), pp. 93–126 (p. 102).
3. Ibid., p. 102.
4. Ibid., p. 119.
5. Ibid., p. 115.
6. Michel Foucault, 'The Ethics of the Concern for Self as a Practice of Freedom', trans. P. Aranov and D. McGrawth, in *Ethics: Essential Works of Foucault, 1954–1985, Volume 1*, ed. Paul Rabinow (London: Penguin, 2000), pp. 281–301 (p. 292).
7. Ibid., p. 292.
8. Foucault, 'Discussion of "Truth and Subjectivity"', p. 116.
9. Michel Foucault, 'Subjectivity and Truth', in *About the Hermeneutics of the Self: Lectures at Dartmouth College, 1980*, ed. Henri-Paul Fruchard and Daniele Lorenzini, trans. Graham Burchell (Chicago: University of Chicago Press, 2016), pp. 19–52 (p. 21).
10. Foucault, 'Discussion of "Truth and Subjectivity"', p. 116.
11. Michel Foucault, 'Sexuality and Solitude', in *Ethics: Essential Works of Foucault, 1954–1985, Volume 1*, ed. Paul Rabinow (London: Penguin, 2000), pp. 175–84 (p. 177).
12. Ibid., p. 177.
13. See, for example, Charles Taylor, 'Foucault on Freedom and Truth', in *Philosophical Papers 2: Philosophy and the Human Sciences* (Cambridge: Cambridge University Press, 1985), pp. 152–84 (pp. 177–84); Jürgen Habermas, 'Some Questions concerning the Theory of Power: Foucault Again', in *The Philosophical Discourse of Modernity: Twelve Lectures*, trans. Frederick Lawrence (Cambridge: Polity, 1987), pp. 266–93 (p. 279); Nancy Fraser, 'Foucault on Modern Power: Empirical Insights and Normative Confusions', in *Unruly Practices: Power,*

Discourse, and Gender in Contemporary Social Theory (Minneapolis, MN: University of Minnesota Press, 1989), pp. 17–34 (pp. 27–33). See also Nancy Fraser, 'Michel Foucault: A "Young Conservative?"', in *Unruly Practices: Power, Discourse, and Gender in Contemporary Social Theory* (Minneapolis, MN: University of Minnesota Press, 1989), pp. 35–54 (p. 50).

14. Michel Foucault, 'An Interview by Stephen Riggins', in *Ethics: Essential Works of Foucault, 1954–1985, Volume 1*, ed. Paul Rabinow (London: Penguin, 2000), pp. 121–33 (p. 131).
15. Michel Foucault, *A History of Sexuality, Volume 2: The Use of Pleasure*, trans. Robert Hurley (London: Penguin, 1985), p. 9.
16. Michel Foucault, 'Christianity and Confession', in *About the Hermeneutics of the Self: Lectures at Dartmouth College, 1980*, ed. Henri-Paul Fruchard and Daniele Lorenzini, trans. Graham Burchell (Chicago: University of Chicago Press, 2016), pp. 53–92 (p. 76).
17. Michel Foucault, 'Interview with Michel Foucault', in *About the Hermeneutics of the Self: Lectures at Dartmouth College, 1980*, ed. Henri-Paul Fruchard and Daniele Lorenzini, trans. Graham Burchell (Chicago: University of Chicago Press, 2016), pp. 127–38 (p. 136).
18. See, for example, Richard Wolin, 'Foucault's Aesthetic Decisionism', *Telos*, 67, spring 1986, pp. 71–86 (p. 85); Peter Dews, 'The Return of the Subject in Late Foucault', *Radical Philosophy*, 51.1, 1989, pp. 37–41 (pp. 39–40); Pierre Hadot, 'Reflections on the Notion of "the cultivation of the self"', in Timothy J. Armstrong (ed. and trans.), *Michel Foucault: Philosophy* (Abingdon: Routledge, 1992), pp. 225–32 (p. 230); Ranier Rochlitz, 'The Aesthetics of Existence: Postconventional Morality and the Theory of Power in Michel Foucault', in Timothy J. Armstrong (ed. and trans.), *Michel Foucault: Philosophy* (Abingdon: Routledge, 1992), pp. 233–47 (pp. 251, 253); Alexandros Kioupkiolis, 'The Agonistic Turn of Critical Reason: Critique and Freedom in Foucault and Castoriadis', *European Journal of Social Theory*, 15.3, 2012, pp. 385–402 (p. 392).
19. Foucault, 'Subjectivity and Truth', p. 21.
20. Foucault, 'Sexuality and Solitude', p. 177.
21. Ibid., p. 177.
22. Ibid., p. 177.
23. Foucault, 'Subjectivity and Truth', p. 25.
24. Foucault, 'Sexuality and Solitude', p. 177.
25. Michel Foucault, 'Technologies of the Self', in *Ethics: Essential Works of Foucault, 1954–1985, Volume 1*, ed. Paul Rabinow (London: Penguin, 2000), pp. 223–52 (p. 225).
26. Ibid., p. 225.
27. Michel Foucault, 'Sex, Power, and the Politics of Identity', in *Ethics: Essential Works of Foucault, 1954–1985, Volume 1*, ed. Paul Rabinow (London: Penguin, 2000), pp. 163–74 (p. 163).
28. Michel Foucault, 'Friendship as a Way of Life', in *Ethics: Essential Works of Foucault, 1954–1985, Volume 1*, ed. Paul Rabinow (London: Penguin, 2000), pp. 135–40 (p. 135).

29. Foucault, 'The Ethics of the Concern for Self as a Practice of Freedom', p. 294.
30. Foucault, *A History of Sexuality, Volume 2*, p. 10.
31. Ibid., pp. 10–11.
32. Foucault, 'Technologies of the Self', p. 226.
33. Foucault, 'The Ethics of the Concern for Self as a Practice of Freedom', p. 284.
34. Foucault, 'Technologies of the Self', p. 226.
35. Ibid., p. 226.
36. Foucault, *A History of Sexuality, Volume 2*, p. 48.
37. Ibid., pp. 51–2.
38. Ibid., p. 53.
39. Ibid., pp. 53–4.
40. Ibid., p. 54.
41. Ibid., p. 54.
42. Ibid., p. 59.
43. Ibid., p. 62.
44. Ibid., p. 62.
45. Ibid., pp. 14–15.
46. Ibid., p. 227.
47. Ibid., p. 238.
48. Foucault, 'The Ethics of the Concern for Self as a Practice of Freedom', p. 284.
49. Foucault, *A History of Sexuality, Volume 2*, p. 63.
50. Ibid., p. 30.
51. Foucault, 'Friendship as a Way of Life', p. 137.
52. Michel Foucault, 'On the Genealogy of Ethics: An Overview of Work in Progress', in *Ethics: Essential Works of Foucault, 1954–1985, Volume 1*, ed. Paul Rabinow (London: Penguin, 2000), pp. 253–80 (p. 273).
53. Foucault, 'The Ethics of the Concern for Self as a Practice of Freedom', p. 282.
54. Foucault, 'On the Genealogy of Ethics', p. 263.
55. Ibid., p. 263.
56. Ibid., p. 264.
57. Ibid., p. 265.
58. Ibid., p. 265.
59. Ibid., p. 265.
60. Ibid., p. 254
61. Ibid., p. 256.
62. Ibid., p. 261.
63. Ibid., p. 92.
64. Wolin, 'Foucault's Aesthetic Decisionism', p. 85.
65. Dews, 'The Return of the Subject in Late Foucault', p. 40.
66. Hadot, 'Reflections on the Notion of "the cultivation of the self"', p. 230; Rochlitz, 'The Aesthetics of Existence', p. 253; Kioupkiolis, 'The Agonistic Turn of Critical Reason', p. 392.
67. Foucault, 'On the Genealogy of Ethics: An Overview of Work in Progress', p. 271.
68. Foucault, 'The Ethics of the Concern for Self as a Practice of Freedom', p. 286.

69. Ibid., pp. 286–7.
70. Foucault, *A History of Sexuality, Volume 2*, p. 79.
71. Ibid., p. 79.
72. Ibid., p. 61.
73. Foucault, 'The Ethics of the Concern for Self as a Practice of Freedom', p. 285.
74. Michel Foucault, *A History of Sexuality, Volume 3: The Care of the Self*, trans. Robert Hurley (London: Penguin, 1985), p. 51.
75. Foucault, 'Interview with Michel Foucault', in *About the Hermeneutics of the Self*, pp. 127–38 (p. 137).
76. Taylor, 'Foucault on Freedom and Truth', p. 177.
77. Ibid., p. 177.
78. Habermas, 'Some Questions concerning the Theory of Power: Foucault Again', p. 276.
79. Ibid., p. 279.
80. Ibid., p. 281.
81. Fraser, 'Foucault on Modern Power', p. 30.
82. Ibid., p. 30.
83. Ibid., pp. 30–1.
84. Michel Foucault, 'Sexual Choice, Sexual Act', in *Ethics: Essential Works of Foucault, 1954–1985, Volume 1*, ed. Paul Rabinow (London: Penguin, 2000), pp. 141–56 (p. 154).
85. Foucault, 'On the Genealogy of Ethics', p. 256.
86. Foucault, 'Interview with Michel Foucault', in *About the Hermeneutics of the Self*, p. 137.
87. Michel Foucault, 'Interview with Michel Foucault', in *Power: Essential Works of Foucault 1954–1984, Volume 3*, ed. James D. Faubion (London: Penguin, 2002), pp. 239–97 (p. 294).
88. Michel Foucault, 'Structuralism and Poststructuralism', in *Aesthetics: Essential Works of Foucault 1954–1984, Volume 2*, ed. James D. Faubion (London: Penguin, 2000), pp. 433–58 (p. 442).
89. Foucault, *A History of Sexuality, Volume 2*, p. 25.
90. Ibid., p. 25.
91. Ibid., p. 25.
92. Ibid., p. 29.
93. Arnold I. Davidson, 'Ethics as Ascetics: Foucault, the History of Ethics, and Ancient Thought', in Gary Cutting (ed.), *The Cambridge Companion to Foucault*, 2nd edn (Cambridge: Cambridge University Press, 2005), pp. 123–48 (p. 131).
94. Ibid., pp. 131–2.
95. Ibid., p. 132.
96. Foucault, 'The Ethics of the Concern for Self as a Practice of Freedom', p. 286.
97. William E. Connelly, 'Beyond Good and Evil: The Ethical Sensibility of Michel Foucault', *Political Theory*, 21.3, 1993, pp. 365–89 (p. 373).
98. Ben Golder, *Foucault and the Politics of Rights* (Stanford, CA: Stanford University Press, 2015), p. 6.

99. Foucault, 'Sex, Power, and the Politics of Identity', p. 172.
100. Foucault, 'Sexual Choice, Sexual Act', p. 148.
101. Foucault, 'Interview with Michel Foucault', in *About the Hermeneutics of the Self*, pp. 137–8.
102. Michel Foucault, 'What is Enlightenment?', in *Ethics: Essential Works of Foucault, 1954–1985, Volume 1*, ed. Paul Rabinow (London: Penguin, 2000), pp. 303–20 (p. 319).

Part II

Turning to the Psyche

CHAPTER 5

Butler on the Subjection of Gendered Agency

In *Subjects of Desire*, her first book, Judith Butler explains that '[t]he unified subject with its unified philosophical life has served as a necessary psychological gesture and normative ideal in moral philosophy since Plato and Aristotle'.[1] Rather than follow in this vein, she continues the poststructuralist critique of the foundational subject by calling into question the foundationalism that she takes to underpin this historical affirmation of unity. As she puts it, the purpose of her 'critique of the subject is not [to offer] a negation or repudiation of the subject, but, rather, a way of interrogating the construction as a pregiven or foundationalist premise'.[2] By engaging with the processes that give rise to the notion that the subject is foundational, she aims to show that the subject is a construction and, indeed, identify the ways in which this subject is created.

To do so, Butler takes as her primary source Foucault's work on power, sexuality and the subject, but departs from him in a number of important ways. These include her claim that his historical account is too simplistic in so far as it is based on 'a single tension between the body and strategies of domination which give rise to events and values alike';[3] the identification of a contradiction between his accounts of the body and genealogical narrative;[4] her rejection of his lack of awareness and attention paid to the sexual difference;[5] and, most pertinent for our purposes, the fact that 'the entire domain of the psyche remain[s] largely unremarked in his theory'.[6] In contrast, she insists that an account of the psyche is required by his analysis of the relationship between power and the subject. After all, if the subject results from power relations, and this is not a one-dimensional hierarchical process of imposition, then the subject must participate in its own subjection. As she explains, '[p]sychoanalysis enters

Foucauldian analysis precisely at the point where one wishes to understand the phantasmatic dimension of social norms'.[7]

With this, she places her work 'in the intersection of Foucault and Freud',[8] a move that marks a major advance over previous poststructuralist analyses we have examined because it allows her to combine an account of socio-symbolic subjection with an inquiry into the ways in which this is facilitated by psychic processes that ensure that the subject participates in its own subjection. By doing so, she makes clear that purely social and purely psychoanalytic approaches are one-sided and in need of correction by the insights of the other.

Butler's approach to both Foucault's thinking and Freudian psychoanalysis is, however, troubled. I have already noted that her relationship to Foucault is marked by a certain appropriative distance, a relationship that is mirrored in her attitude towards psychoanalysis. It is certainly true that she 'works with and against the grain of psychoanalysis',[9] on the one hand, affirming its notions of the unconscious and desire, while, on the other hand, offering sustained critiques of Freud and especially Lacan, the Oedipus complex,[10] the centrality of the Phallus,[11] its heteronormativity[12] and the notion of the id.[13] Her appropriation of both Foucault and Freud is, then, largely done for and from her own purposes.

To show this, the first section of this chapter outlines Butler's critique of the essentialist foundational subject through her work on gender performativity, before the second moves to discuss the roles that social norms, language and embodiment play in the construction of the subject. From this, I note that she rejects the claim that the subject is foundational to instead hold that it is created from power relations that are manifested through socio-symbolic structures and processes. Importantly, she points out that this continuous process takes place through the reiteration of the norms by the subject constituted by them. This is relatively close to Foucault's account of the relationship between power and the subject and so, in the third section, I outline how Butler departs from Foucault by turning to her account of the psyche to show *why* the subject participates in its own subjection. In so doing, I engage with a number of readings of her work,[14] before focusing on her analyses of the roles that passionate attachments and melancholia play in subject-formation. The fourth section outlines what this means for her account of agency, by arguing that, for Butler, agency is defined by and from the disjunction between the social and psyche. Agency is not, then, a substance or essence, but a constructed site of contestation that arises from the friction between the socio-psychic-symbolic aspects that ground it.

Gendered Subjectivity

Butler's first extended discussion of subjectivity takes place in *Gender Trouble*, initially published in 1990, a book that extends Foucault's analysis of sexuality by rejecting the notion of a fixed, essential sexuality to examine the ways in which sexuality and, by extension, subjectivity are constructed. To do so, Butler engages with feminist debates regarding the nature of 'woman' to show that, contrary to the conception then dominant, this category does not have a fixed identity based in a fixed essence or natural sex.[15] It is, rather, a construction based on certain socio-symbolic conceptions of gender.

Furthermore, she insists that, while feminists have sought to reveal and undermine discrimination against women, they have tended to do so by relying on the notion of an 'essential' woman, with the consequence that their analyses are heteronormative and perpetuate a multitude of unintended exclusions and discrimination against those who do not conform to those categories. To correct this, she employs Foucault's genealogical critique to undertake '*a feminist genealogy* of the category of women':[16]

> a genealogical critique refuses to search for the origins of gender, the inner truth of female desire, a genuine or authentic sexual identity that repression has kept from view; rather, genealogy investigates the political stakes in designating as an *origin* and *cause* those identity categories that are in fact the *effects* of institutions, practices, discourses with multiple and diffuse points of origin.[17]

Following Foucault's notion of power, she argues that gender and, by extension, subjectivity are effects of power relations that give rise to designations and ways of thinking about those designations. This creates a symbolic framework through which gender is assigned and enacted. There is not, then, any notion of a fixed essence to 'woman' or universalism to that category.[18] Indeed of seeking a fixed ground from which to think gender, Butler demands 'a radical critique that seeks to free feminist theory from the necessity of having to construct a single or abiding ground which is invariably contested by those identity positions or anti-identity positions that it invariably excludes'.[19]

To develop this, Butler focuses on the sex/gender dichotomy, noting that the former is usually privileged over the latter and is normally thought to conform to some fixed biological essence. Although this is not to say that sex is understood necessarily to determine gender, it is to say that gender is placed in a subordinate position. In contrast, Butler privileges gender over sex and claims to take the constructionism inherent in the former 'to its logical limit'.[20] To do so, she notes that '[i]f gender is the cultural meanings that the sexed body assumes, then a gender cannot be said to follow from sex in any one way'.[21] Rather, 'the sex/gender distinction suggests a radical discontinuity between sexed bodies and culturally constructed genders'.[22]

This brings Butler to examine the means through which gender is constructed, which, in turn, leads her to claim that the sex/gender dichotomy has tended to be interpreted through a heteronormative framework that reduces sex and gender expression to a masculine/feminine opposition. Butler suggests, however, that even if we assume 'for the moment the stability of binary sex, it does not follow that the construction of "men" will accrue exclusively to the bodies of male or that "women" will interpret only female bodies'.[23] Indeed, 'even if the sexes appear to be unproblematically binary in their morphology and constitution (which will become a question), there is no reason to assume that genders ought also to remain as two'.[24] The problem with a binary gender system, even one that sees gender as being constructed, is that it 'implicitly retains the belief in a mimetic relation of gender to sex whereby gender mirrors sex or is otherwise restricted by it'.[25] In contrast, Butler wants not only to think sex from gender, but to remove any *a priori* framework through which to engage with the latter:

> When the constructed status of gender is theorized as radically independent of sex, gender itself becomes a free-floating artifice, with the consequence that *man* and *masculine* might just as easily signify a female body as a male one, and *woman* and *feminine* a male body as easily as a female one.[26]

This establishes the possibility that male and female bodies may, quite easily, be constructed to adopt alternative genders.

It does, however, seem to leave intact the notion of a 'natural' (or nonconstructed) sex that is culturally constructed. To tackle this issue, Butler asks '[c]an we refer to a "given" sex or a "given" gender without first inquiring into how sex and/or gender is given, through what means?'[27] In response, she explains that '[i]f the immutable character of sex is contested, perhaps this construct called "sex" is as culturally constructed as gender; indeed, perhaps it was always already gender, with the consequence that the distinction between sex and gender turns out to be no distinction at all'.[28] If so, it follows that 'gender is not to culture as sex is to nature; gender is also the discursive/cultural means by which "sexed nature" or "a natural sex" is produced and established as "prediscursive," prior to culture, a politically neutral surface *on which* culture acts'.[29] There is, then, no predefined natural sex, only the construction of a discourse that configures gender in terms of an underlying natural sex: '[the] production of sex as the prediscursive ought to be understood as the effect of the apparatus of cultural construction designated as *gender*' and, for this reason, '[w]hether gender or sex is fixed or free is a function of a discourse which . . . seeks to set certain limits to analysis or to safeguard certain tenets of humanism as presuppositional to any analysis of gender'.[30]

From these methodological deconstructions, Butler goes on to explain that, if gender and, by extension, sex are cultural products, there cannot be any appeal to an *a priori* conception of woman. Rather than being a cause for concern or distress, she suggests that '[t]he assumption of its essential incompleteness permits that category to serve as a permanently available site of contested meaning'.[31] Gender is, then, 'a complexity whose totality is permanently deferred, never fully what it is at any juncture in time' and, for this reason, 'is something that one becomes – but can never be'.[32] It should not, then, 'be conceived as a noun or a substantial thing or a static cultural marker, but rather as an incessant and repeated action of some sort'.[33]

Crucially, however, Butler holds that we should not think that the performativity of gender is a voluntary act grounded in and on the subject. Performativity refers to the process of co-constitution between power relations and the subject, wherein the subject is created from power relations but, through this creative action, perpetuates the power relations that support it.[34] As a consequence, '[t]here is no gender identity behind the expressions of gender . . . identity is performatively constituted by the very "expressions" that are said to be its results'.[35] This action is, however, prior to the formation of the subject and means that, somewhat paradoxically, 'gender is always a doing, though not a doing of a subject who might be said to pre-exist the deed'.[36]

Importantly, performativity is distinguished from constructivist accounts of gender that see it as being expressive or representative. The problem with both, for Butler, is that they are tied, however implicitly, to a prior plan or correct way to be expressed or represented. If, however, 'there is no preexisting identity by which an act or attribute might be measured [,] there would be no true or false, real or distorted acts of gender, and the postulation of a true gender identity would be revealed as a regulatory fiction'.[37] Performativity rejects precisely such pre-existing co-ordinates and, as such, holds that the body has no status apart from its acts.

Furthermore, there is no *a priori* inner/outer division according to which the (outer) body conforms to an 'inner' essence. Thinking in terms of an inner/outer division is 'an effect of a decidedly public and social discourse' through which 'acts and gestures, articulated and enacted desires create the illusion of an interior and organizing gender core'.[38] Performativity works on the surface through the doing of certain socially conditioned practices. At no point do social norms penetrate and determine any inside of the subject. Even when Butler comes to describe the workings of the psyche, she holds that the psyche does not conform to a strict 'inner' life opposed to an 'outer' one; it is immanently entwined with social norms and performative practices.

As a consequence, gender performativity is created by doing it, without this doing being grounded in a prior subject or plan. However, performativity is not free-floating; it is defined and conditioned by the social norms through which it takes place. These condition, without determining, the acceptable and unacceptable ways (which also change based on their reiteration) in which gender can be constructed and performed. This is not a one-time action: 'Gender is the repeated stylization of the body, a set of repeated acts within a highly rigid regulatory frame that congeal over time to produce the appearance of substance, of a natural sort of being.'[39]

Crucially, the process of repetition is not linear, mechanical or based on a prior movement or law. It is an immanent repetition that changes in each moment. As a result, '[t]he productions swerve from their original purposes and inadvertently mobilize possibilities of "subjects" that do not merely exceed the bounds of cultural intelligibility, but effectively expand the boundaries of what is, in fact, culturally intelligible'.[40] This swerving is crucial for the performance of new possibilities and, as we will see, is fundamental to Butler's notion of agency. To outline this further, the next section turns to the roles that social norms, language and the body play in the processes of subjectivation.

Social Norms, Language and the Body

Far from being a fully formed, unencumbered subject, Butler insists that the subject is brought into existence from and through social norms that it continues to be tied to.[41] As we saw with her discussion of gender, however, this does not mean that social norms determine the subject. Social norms are the condition for the subject's genesis *and* continue to make possible the subject's persistence:

> We do not negotiate with norms or with Others subsequent to our coming into the world. We come into the world on the condition that the social world is already there, laying the groundwork for us. This implies that I cannot persist without norms of recognition that support my persistence: the sense of possibility pertaining to me must first be imaged from somewhere else before I can begin to imagine myself.[42]

This has dramatic implications for the subject, who is no longer understood to be the foundation of social life, but, at all times, an effect of it: 'I cannot be who I am without drawing upon the sociality of norms that precede and exceed me. In this sense, I am outside myself from the outset, and must be, in order to survive, and in order to enter into the realm of the possible.'[43] At no point, then, does the subject exist apart from its social norms. For this reason, 'when [the subject] tries to give an account of itself, [this] must include the conditions of its own emergence', which, ultimately, is an endeavour that requires that the subject 'become a social theorist'.[44]

Butler explains that 'a norm is not the same as a rule, and it is not the same as a law'.[45] The former is definitive and universal, whereas the latter also conforms to a top-down model of imposition. In contrast, a 'norm operates with social practices as the implicit standard of *normalisation*'.[46] That they are linked to social practices makes norms malleable and changing. The difficulty involved in studying norms is compounded by two different, but related, issues. First, '[n]orms may or may not be explicit, and when they operate as the normalizing principle in social practice, they usually remain implicitly difficult to read, discernible most clearly and dramatically in the effects that they produce'.[47] Second, while they may be analytically differentiated from the social practices that they are attached to, it may also be the case that they make little sense without those social practices: 'the norm only persists as a norm to the extent that it is acted out in social practice and re-idealized and re-instantiated in and through daily social rituals of bodily life'.[48] The norm has, then, 'no independent ontological status',[49] but is instantiated and reinstantiated in bodily practices. The norm both conditions an individual's practice and, somewhat paradoxically, only *is* as a consequence of that practice. Therefore, in contrast to rules and laws, norms are constantly being re-enacted and, in such action, changed.

Thinking how the subject can be constituted by social norms but yet transform those norms is, for Butler, one of the challenges that we must face. To do so, she reconfigures how we understand the relation between the subject and the social norm. Rather than insisting on the division between the two so that agency results when the subject divorces itself from its constituting social norms, she asks how we can configure agency so that we understand that it takes place within and through them. In response, she makes three points. First, social norms are not static or universal; they exist in relation to 'humans, institutions, and organic and inorganic processes'.[50] This entwinement, where each aspect is itself composed of moving components and the relation between them is one of friction rather than harmony, creates the 'gaps' or tensions that give rise to unexpected consequences. Social norms do not operate in a top-down, linear fashion of imposition;

they are organic and produce unexpected results as they are performed and interact with other operationalised processes.

Second, this is complemented by the specific relationship that exists between norms and performative reiteration. As we saw, norms occur because they are enacted in social practices; they do not have an existence beyond or outside such reiteration.[51] For this reason,

> [n]orms are not only embodied ... but embodiment is itself a mode of interpretation, not always conscious, which subjects normativity itself to an iterable temporality. Norms are not static entities, but incorporated and interrupted features of existence that are sustained by the idealisations furnished by fantasy.[52]

Again, this is not a one-time action, but a continuous process whereby 'discourse produces the effects that it names'.[53]

Third, this performative reiteration is not mechanical, but an open-ended process that is created at each moment. That it must be recreated in each moment and only becomes what it is through each reiteration means that, in each moment, there exists the possibility to resignify or reinvent the norm. For this reason, Lois McNay is wrong to claim that, for Butler, the repetition of norms is a mechanical 'ceaseless repetition of the same [based on a] notion of time as a succession of self-identical and discrete acts that renders the dominant hermetic and self-sustaining and means that disruption can only come from the outside'.[54] According to Butler, 'power is not mechanically reproduced when it is assumed'.[55] The norm's relation to other aspects of social existence (institutions, language, organic and inorganic processes, and so on) in combination with the process of reiteration ensures that 'the norm does not merely reinstate social power, it becomes formative and vulnerable in highly specific ways'.[56]

However, that social norms must be performed through their reiteration means that they are tied to language and the symbolic order:[57] 'The one who acts (who is not the same as the sovereign subject) acts precisely to the extent that he or she is constituted as an actor and, hence, operating within a linguistic field of enabling constraints from the outside.'[58] The subject is introduced into language (and gender) through the iteration of a name at the moment of birth: 'to the extent that the naming of the "girl" is transitive, that is, initiates the process by which a certain "girling" is compelled, the term or, rather, its symbolic power, governs the formation of a corporeally enacted femininity that never fully approximates the norm'.[59] Through this iteration and the designation of a name, the subject is created according to a gender norm that conditions acceptable practices for it. For this reason, '[t]he sign, understood as a gender imperative – "girl!" – reads less as an assignment than as a command and, as such, produces its own insubordinations'.[60] On the one hand, this act precludes certain possibilities not socially considered to be appropriate for that name, but, on the other hand, 'by being called a name, one is also, paradoxically, given a certain possibility for social existence, initiated into a temporal life of language that exceeds power purposes that animate that call'.[61] As a consequence, the designation of a name 'may appear to fix or paralyse the one it hails, but it may also produce an unexpected and enabling response'.[62] Again, this is tied to the reiteration of the name and the possibilities that are inherent in that process.

Therefore, while other poststructuralists, such as Deleuze, Derrida and, as we will see, Lacan, hold that the function of the name imposes a constraining identity on a prior differential field, Butler holds that the 'name' is not tied to substance or a noun, nor does it simply entail the imposition of a fixed identity. Instead, she ties the symbolic to social norms to insist that the 'name' is a performative that must be continuously reiterated to be instantiated. What precisely the 'name' means changes based on its iteration, an occurrence that opens up possibilities for action rather than simply closing them down to a unitary meaning.

Crucially, 'this repetition is not performed *by* a subject [but] is what enables a subject and constitutes the temporal condition for the subject'.[63] The subject does not prefigure language, but is an effect of it:

> Where there is an 'I' who utters or speaks and thereby produces an effect in discourse, there is first a discourse which precedes and enables the 'I' and forms in language the constraining trajectory of its will. Thus there is no 'I' who stands *behind* discourse and executes its volition or will *through* discourse.[64]

This pre-subject agency occurs because the subject is born into and depends upon the continuing alterations in the socio-symbolic spheres that it is created from and continues to inhabit. For this reason, language is what structures and reveals reality. This is not, however, to say that language fully defines or controls the subjects born from it. Like social norms, the symbolic is a performative that requires reiteration. The moment of this reiteration is the site whereby norms can be recoded in ways that do not necessarily follow from what went before. This is not to point to a form of subjectivity that transcends language, but shows that *within* the structures of language itself, agency is both possible and, indeed, necessary. Symbolic transformation and, indeed, transformation of the symbolic is always taking place. How it alters depends on and is tied to (the reiteration of) social norms, which are, in turn, always tied intimately to the body: 'there can be no reproduction of gendered norms without the bodily enactment of those norms'.[65] Indeed, Butler insists that '[l]anguage sustains the body not by bringing it into being or feeding it in a literal way; rather, it is by being interpellated within the terms of language that a certain social existence of the body first becomes possible'.[66] With this, the question of the relationship between language and the body or language and materiality is brought to the fore.

To her credit, Butler notes the difficulty that she has when dealing with this topic. While she wants to maintain that the two are distinct, she also holds that they cannot be separated; material embodiment is constitutively tied to, without being exhausted by, language. This is, however, a very delicate position that, as she is aware, gives rise to the following issue:

> Every time I try to write about the body, the writing ends up being about language. This is not because I think that the body is reducible to language; it is not. Language emerges from the body, constituting an emission of sorts. The body is that upon which language falters, and the body carries its own signs, its own signifiers, in ways that remain largely unconscious.[67]

For Butler, then, 'language is not opposed to materiality, [but] neither can materiality be summarily collapsed into an identity within language'.[68] This 'overlooks the materiality of the signifier itself' in so far as 'signs work by *appearing* (visibly, aurally), and appearing through material means'.[69] It also fails to understand that materiality 'is bound up with signification from the start'.[70] The body only becomes one through the interpellation of gender in accordance with social norms. Thus, the appearance of the body is a symbolic event.

But Butler claims that such symbolic designation does not exhaust the body: 'Although the body depends on language to be known, the body also exceeds every possible linguistic effort of capture.'[71] There is a remainder to the body that language cannot capture; a pre- or non-discursivity to it that language fails to reach. For this reason, Butler can only postulate this form of embodiment because saying any more would be to describe it through language, thereby incorporating it into the symbolic. We do, however, get a sense of it when, in *Bodies that Matter*, she explains that '[t]he materiality of the body is not to be taken for granted, for in some sense it is acquired, constituted, through the development of morphology'.[72] Claiming that the body is *in some sense* acquired or constituted would seem to point to the possibility that, in another sense, a pre-discursive sense, it is not. This would appear to point to two forms of embodiment: a discursive body and a pre-discursive body that might be thought to act as the site that permits agency because it remains somehow 'detached' from language. Interpreting the non/pre-discursive body in this way would, however, be to attribute meaning to 'it', thereby reinscribing it within the discursive. As a consequence, Butler does not and cannot say anything more about this body; it acts as a necessary lacuna in her thinking, postulated to undermine the Lacanian privileging of the symbolic by affirming counter-forces – in the form of material and social norms – that exist beyond and out of reach of the symbolic.

While I will question whether Lacan does privilege the symbolic in this way, Butler's point is that there is not a linear movement from social norms to language to the body; all are entwined: social and symbolic norms create and define the forms of embodiment that are acceptable and possible, while these are re-enforced and altered by their reiteration by embodied subjects. Thus, rather than simply being an effect of socio-symbolic structures, the subject, paradoxically, participates in its own process of subjection. To understand this, Butler complements her socio-symbolic analysis with one that engages with the psychic processes of subjectivation.

Subjection and the Psyche

Butler's turn to the psyche takes place for at least three reasons. First, she notes that, for all its insights, Foucault's socio-historical analysis is partial because it does not explain how the subject participates in its own subjection. This does not, however, mean that she swaps a socially orientated analysis for a psychically orientated one. Rather, second, she insists that both work together: whereas the subject is created from and is always immersed in social norms, 'psychoanalysis enters Foucauldian analysis precisely at the point where one wishes to understand the phantasmatic dimension of social norms'.[73] Crucially, however, the psyche is not something apart from and purified of social norms because, third, the unconscious desire of the psyche is constructed by social norms.[74] Again, however, this does not conform to a simple logic of imposition, wherein social norms are imposed on and internalised by the psyche; the psyche works to subjugate itself to these norms and, indeed, in so doing, recreates and affirms them. Butler's discussion of the psyche aims to identify the ways in which the subject participates in its own subjection by showing how its psychic processes necessarily tie it to its social norms.

While Butler discusses the psyche in *Gender Trouble*, where, among other issues, she rejects the notion of 'a psychological "core"'[75] which, as we will see, distinguishes her position from Castoriadis's, and in *Bodies that Matter*, where she criticises Lacanian psychoanalysis, her most complete analysis is found in *The Psychic Life of Power*. To engage with the role of the psyche in the process of subjectivation, Butler focuses on its relation to power, 'a task that has been eschewed by writers in both Foucauldian and psychoanalytic orthodoxies'.[76] Her guiding contention is that 'power that at first appears as external, pressed upon the subject, pressing the subject into subordination, assumes a psychic form that constitutes the subject's self-identity'.[77]

Importantly, there is not a linear movement from power to the subject. Power 'is relentlessly marked by a figure of turning, a turning back upon oneself or even a turning *on* oneself'.[78] The turn is not an effect of the subject, but the process through which the subject is created from power: 'the subject is formed by a will that turns back upon itself, assuming a reflexive form, [and so] the subject is the modality of power that turns on itself; the subject is the effect of power in recoil'.[79] This is possible because, while 'power [is] *exerted on* a subject, subjection is nevertheless a power *assumed by* the subject, an assumption that constitutes the instrument of that subject's becoming'.[80] This onto-genetic turning is paradoxical because it 1) does not emanate from a moment transcendent to power but is constitutive of the expression of power, and 2) is not performed by a subject for the simple reason that the subject is an effect of the turning. Crucially, the turning constitutive of the immanent expression of power creates 'the subject [that] emerges in tandem with the unconscious'.[81] The unconscious is not, then, prior to the subject nor does it found the subject; rather, the subject is constructed at the same moment as the unconscious. Power is not, however, a transcendent function or substance, but is always a manifestation of prior reiterations of power. As we saw in previous sections, this reiteration is conducted by subjects and takes place in accordance with and through social norms. However, if the reiteration of social norms by the subject is not mechanical and so does not necessarily entail the repetition of the dominant norms, why does the subject reiterate them?

Butler responds that an innate 'desire to survive'[82] brings the child to develop passionate attachments. These do not determine the subject – the subject can always act in alternative ways to those demanded by their passionate attachments – but there is pressure to conform to them. These passionate attachments are responsible for inculcating social norms and it is in this relationship that Butler locates the genesis of psychic subordination to the other. She claims that the key moment in this process refers to the relationship between psychic *dependence* on others and psychic *subordination* to others, wherein the experience of the former brings the psyche to accept and normalise the latter, with this forming the basis for *'political* subordination'.[83] Thus, the subject's ontological dependence on others and desire to exist creates the psychic conditions through which the subject subordinates itself to the dominant social norms to blindly reiterate them.

Amy Allen criticises Butler on this point, claiming that her argument depends on a false conflation between *dependence* and *subordination,* which brings Butler to conclude that 'subjectivation is always subordinating'.[84] Allen maintains that 'Butler makes this move . . . because she equates dependency with power, and power with subordination; thus, she is led to conflate dependency with subordination'.[85] On first glance, the problem with Allen's charge is that it is not clear that Butler does this: she only says that the dependence leaves the subject *vulnerable* to political subordination – 'Although the dependency of the child is not *political subordination* in any usual sense, the formation of primary passion in dependency renders the child vulnerable to subordination and exploitation.'[86] From this, it appears that there is no necessary causal connection between the two, nor are they conflated. However, just two sentences later, Butler reaffirms the connection between dependence and subordination: 'If there is no formation of the subject without a passionate attachment to those by whom she or he is subordinated, then subordination proves central to the becoming of the subject.'[87] For this reason, Allen suggests, rightly I think, that we need to break the dependence–subordination conflation that Butler depends upon to recognise that dependency may lead, though not necessarily, to subsequent political subordination. However, in any case, this gives rise to the question as to why some subjects manifest their psychic dependence as political subordination while others do not.

To respond, Butler points out that while the subject is dependent on others to become an adult and, indeed, to survive, it must also deny this dependence to gain the illusion of autonomy that marks adulthood:

> No subject can emerge without this attachment, formed in dependency, but no subject, in the course of its formation, can ever afford to 'see' it. This attachment in its primary forms must both *come to be* and *be denied*, its coming to be must consist in its partial denial, for the subject to emerge.[88]

This dependence–denial relation creates a split within the subject between its continuing *unconscious* passionate attachment to others that permits it to survive as a subject and its *conscious* rejection of that dependence to permit the appearance of an autonomous 'I'. The two are in tension: the *unconscious* continually aims to reveal the attachments that would undermine the autonomy of the 'I', while such a move is continually denied by the *conscious* 'I'.

Crucially, the unconscious action is an act of 'agency, but not that [of] the *subject's* agency – rather, [it is] the agency of a desire that aims at the dissolution of the subject, where the subject stands as a bar to that desire'.[89] For Butler, the subject desires and so is dependent on others, who, in turn, try to break through the mirage of self-sufficiency that marks the 'I' to reveal its dependence. Because the other is a condition of the unconscious, such action is an agency but not a consequence of the subject's *conscious* action; it is a pre-subject or subjectless agency. The subject, however, continually bars that revelation because it would unravel the conscious identity that the subject has constructed for itself. For this reason, '[d]esire . . . aim[s] at unravelling the subject, but [is] thwarted by precisely the subject in whose name it operates'.[90] Through this explicit denial, the subject comes to persist because it sees itself in terms of an identity: the 'I'.

However, this is not to agree with Kirsten Campbell's complaint that, '[f]or Butler, the subject and identity are the same, [in so far as] she conceives the subject as the individual's imagined self, the seemingly coherent identity that the subject misrecognises as its being'.[91] While it is true that Butler seems to reduce each – the subject and identity – to the other, we have to remember that the subject is conditioned by the relation between its conscious and unconscious aspects. While the subject *consciously* identifies as the identity of an 'I', it can only do so because of its persisting unconscious dependence on others. The conscious subject may be synonymous with identity, but its unconscious subordination to its attachments continues to form and underpin its conscious sense of identity, while being (consciously) denied. For this reason, it is surprising to find Campbell stating that 'Butler's theory of the subject is not psychoanalytic . . . because it is not framed by the psychoanalytic problematic of that which is other to consciousness: the unconscious'.[92] As I have shown, this is simply inaccurate. For Butler, the psyche is conditioned by unconscious passionate attachments that it must affirm to persist – or, as she puts it, '[t]o desire the conditions of one's own subordination is thus required to persist as oneself'[93] – all the while consciously denying those attachments.

Crucially, the way in which the 'I' disavows its unconscious passionate attachments is not mechanical; it needs to be performed and reproduced and is in accordance with its social norms. But it must also be remembered that social norms 'are themselves vulnerable to both psychic and historical change'.[94] There is, then, an interaction between the psyche and social norms; a co-constitution. As such, the unconscious is not

> a psychic reality purified of social content that subsequently constitutes a necessary gap in the domain of conscious, social life. The unconscious is also an ongoing psychic condition in which norms are registered in both

normalizing and non-normalizing ways, the postulated site of their fortification, their undoing and their perversion, the unpredictable trajectory of their appropriation in identification and disavowals that are not always consciously or deliberately performed.[95]

That the unconscious psyche is conditioned by social norms means that the subject undergoes a subtler, but more dominant, 'internalisation' of and subordination to social norms. Because the psyche associates itself with them, they appear natural, which spontaneously re-enforces actions that reiterate them. For this reason, Butler explains that '[t]he psychic operation of the norm offers a more insidious route for regulatory power than explicit coercion, one whose success allows its tacit operation with the social'.[96]

Furthermore, the psyche's constant conscious disavowal of its unconscious passionate attachments impacts on the psyche by generating a sense of loss, mourning and melancholia. That the object (its passionate attachment) is disavowed does not mean that it disappears or is abolished. Rather, it

> preserves loss in the psyche; more precisely, the internalization of loss is part of the mechanism of its refusal. If the object can no longer exist in the external world, it will then exist internally, and that internalization will be a way to dissolve the loss, to keep it at bay, to stay or postpone the recognition and suffering of loss.[97]

Butler points out that '[c]learly, the ego does not literally take an object inside itself, as if the ego were a kind of shelter prior to its melancholy'.[98] Rather, melancholia is marked by a turning in which the response to a loss – the conscious disavowal of its unconscious passionate attachment – 'appears to initiate the redoubling of the ego as the object; only by turning back on itself does the ego acquire the status of a perceptual object'.[99]

In this moment, two alterations take place: the object is turned from a static, 'external' thing into 'the ego itself', and the ego 'is produced as a *psychic object*'.[100] The problem is that '[t]he ego is a poor substitute for the lost object, and its failure to substitute in a way that satisfies (that is, to overcome its status *as* a substitution), leads to the ambivalence that distinguishes melancholia'.[101] Indeed, 'the loss becomes the opaque condition for the emergence of the ego, a loss that haunts it from the start as constitutive and avowable', and that gives rise to 'a scene of self-beratement that reconfigures the topography of the ego, a fantasy of internal partition and judgement that comes to structure the representation of psychic life *tout court*'.[102]

There are at least three implications to this. First, melancholia is self-reinforcing, in so far as the interaction of its two psychic aspects perpetuates their relation. In reflecting on its psychic object, the psyche thinks about itself. In so doing, however, the melancholic experiences itself as 'the loss of an other or an ideal lost to consciousness', while 'the social world in which such a loss became possible is also lost'.[103] This appears to effect a split from its social world, although it must be noted that this split is only apparent because the melancholic psyche judges itself according to the social norms that have been internalised in the form of conscience. Second, the social norms that the psyche internalises in the form of conscience and that therefore form the basis for its judgement of its psychic object are idealised and so unattainable.[104] This re-enforces the sense of loss and self-beratement that characterises melancholia. Third, melancholia can be overcome, but this requires that the psyche overcome its attachment to the lost object, grieve, and pass beyond that object by facing the social world without its prior attachment to that which is lost.[105] Nevertheless, the key issues for current purposes are that, on Butler's telling, the psyche 1) participates in its own subjection through its necessary psychic subordination to passionate attachments, while consciously denying those attachments; 2) is constituted by a sense of loss as it internalises its social norm to judge its own actions; and 3) is created from its relation to social norms which it continues to be bound to in a process of co-constitution.

Conclusion: The Question of Agency

Butler's account of the subject holds it to be a consequence of a number of complex co-constituting interactions between social norms, symbolic structures, bodily reiterations and psychic attachments. With this, she extends and develops poststructuralist accounts of the decentred subject by showing what the subject is embedded 'within', that it is constructed from pre-subject structures and processes, and, indeed, how it participates in its own subjection. There has, however, been much debate regarding the conception of agency provided *and* permitted by Butler's analysis.

A particularly dominant line of critique insists that by making the subject an effect of socio-symbolic structures, Butler is unable to leave any room for individually determined intentional action. Seyla Benhabib, for example, argues that the 'death of man' thesis has two versions: a weak version that 'situate[s] the subject in the context of various social, linguistic, and discursive practices and take[s] into account a reformulated notion of the subject to preserve agency', and a stronger version in which 'the subject is dissolved into the chain of signification of which it was supposed to be the initiation'.[106] Benhabib claims that Butler affirms the latter, with the consequence that she asks 'how in fact the very project of female emancipation would even be thinkable without such a regulative principle or agency, autonomy, and selfhood'.[107]

This line of critique is also expressed by Johanna Meehan, who argues that Butler affirms an 'outside–inside' model of the self that 'accentuates the importance of constitutive processes that are initially external to the self and are then internalised'.[108] As a consequence, Butler is held to make 'what is "outside" the self – language and power – identical to the self', a conflation that brings Meehan to claim that '[i]t is inevitable that she must arrive at the claim that the subject becomes a passive conduit of power's generations'.[109] Meehan concludes that Butler 'does not [and cannot] . . . explain how what is external comes to be internal, how in the process of internalising external forces, something ontologically distinct, "the subject," is formed', with the consequence that she cannot 'explain the distinction of the self from the forces that constitute it and, thus . . . explain how human beings can think critically and act autonomously'.[110]

However, although it is certainly true that Butler decentres the subject from its foundational place and, indeed, rejects any notion of a defining essence, this does not mean that she gets rid of the subject entirely. As she explains, '[t]o refuse to assume, that is, to require a notion of the subject from the start is not the same as negating or dispensing with such a notion altogether'.[111] Instead of doing away with the subject *per se*, Butler 'ask[s] after the conditions of its emergence and operation'[112] to show that the subject is not prior to, but an effect of, socio-symbolic structures and processes.

Crucially, she holds that

> if the subject is constituted by power, that power does not cease at the moment the subject is constituted, that power is never fully constituted, but is structured and produced time and again. That subject is neither a ground nor a product, but the permanent possibility of a certain resignifying process, one which gets detoured and stalled through other mechanisms of power, but which is power's own possibility of being reworked.[113]

Rather than power merely imposing itself on a passive subject, a process that would make agency simply a reflection of dominant power relations, Butler explains that to hold 'that the subject is constituted is not to claim that it is determined'.[114] She even claims that 'the constituted character of the subject is the very precondition of its agency'[115] because she does not conceive of agency in terms of action that divorces the subject from social norms, but as a form of embodied and embedded practice that aims to reconfigure the direction of power and, by extension, the meaning and form of social norms. This is a consequence of her claim that power is not based on a top-down model of imposition, but entails a continuous twisting process wherein it enacts subjects who, in that moment, are capable of enacting power. The subject is created from the turning that is constitutive of power's expression and so is located in a particular site. In turn, power needs to be reiterated through the actions of the subjects it constitutes. The twisting constitutive of power's expression and its need to be reiterated by the subject it creates permits and necessitates that the subject act as an agent, with this being conditioned, but not determined, by previous expressions of power. As a consequence,

> 'Agency' [is] . . . the double-movement of being constituted in and by a signifier, where 'to be constituted' means 'to be compelled to cite or repeat or mime' the signifier itself. Enabled by the very signifier that depends for its continuation on the future of that citational chain, agency is the hiatus in iterability, the compulsion to install an identity through repetition, which requires the very contingency, the undetermined interval, that identity insistently seeks to foreclose.[116]

Agency is not therefore distinct from power and so cannot be considered to be unencumbered from power, but is a consequence of the turning that constitutes power's expression, and takes place during the relays of power.[117] Because the expression of power – whether in terms of social norms, language or the psyche – is dependent on its reiteration and because this does not mechanically reproduce what caused it, it is always possible for the subject to resignify the expression of power by altering the meaning of discourse or social norms. For this reason,

> [t]o enter into the repetitive practices of this terrain of signification is not a choice, for the 'I' that might enter is always already inside: there is no possibility of agency or reality outside of the discursive practices that give those terms the intelligibility that they have. The task is not whether to repeat, but how to repeat or, indeed, to repeat and, through a radical proliferation of gender, *to displace* the very gender norms that enable the repetition itself.[118]

Butler does not, then, disband the subject, nor does she annihilate forms of agency by making the subject a determined effect of the socio-linguistic structures within which it is embedded. Because agency results from the expression of power, she maintains that agency is always possible due to the constitution of power; namely, the way in which it needs to be reiterated. This does, however, bring us to a second line of critique regarding whether her account of the subject is sufficiently thick to permit the sort of agency that she affirms.

Martha Nussbaum, for example, recognises that 'Butler does in the end want to say that we have a kind of agency, an ability to undertake change and resistance', but asks 'where does this ability come from, if there is no structure in the personality that is not thoroughly power's creation?'[119] In a similar vein, Moya Lloyd argues that Butler's insistence that the subject is dependent on processes of subordination to social norms makes it difficult to see how or why the subject would challenge those norms. Because of the constitutive bond between itself and its social norms, 'it is unclear how the norms regulating the psyche can be reconfigured without threatening the subject with psychic dissolution'.[120] As a consequence, Alan Schrift concludes that '[o]ne is . . . left with the sense that a more robust notion of agency is needed to account for the decisions about which performatives to enact'.[121]

Geoff Boucher tries to defend Butler by claiming that her thinking is implicitly dependent on a moment of 'transcendental intentionality, "behind" the multiple subject-positions adopted by the empirical agent'.[122] On this reading, it is only because there is a transcendental consciousness 'behind' the conscious empirical subject that the subject can be both bound to power and divorced from it. However, Butler would, I think, reject this out of hand. Not only does she follow Nietzsche's claim that 'there is no "being" behind doing, effecting, becoming: "the doer" is merely a fiction added to the deed'[123] and so 'flatten' the subject to conceive of it as an immanent performative becoming, but she also rejects the inner/outer division that Boucher's point relies upon when she claims that such a conception of the subject is a symbolic construction to be explained, rather than a 'natural' configuration to be accepted.

As a consequence, a Butlerian response would likely claim that intentional agency is possible, not because of transcendental structures preceding power, but because the subject occupies and is a consequence of a momentary hiatus or gap between its enactment by power and the way the subject reiterates and re-enacts power. This is the paradox of subjection: the subject who is conditioned by power is distinct, in some way, from power; it is the gap between power as the condition of the subject and its subsequent expression by the subject that marks the hiatus called 'the subject' and permits what is called agency. This, however, appears to leave us on the horns of a dilemma: either we ignore Butler's objections and flesh out her theory of agency by introducing a transcendent/al dimension divorced, in some way, from power, or we follow Butler in simply accepting that agency is a paradox resulting from the turnings inherent in the subject's constitution, meaning that the best that we can do is settle for the general claim that agency is possible and that the subject acts, without being able to know precisely the mechanisms that permit this. In the following chapters, I suggest that the way out of this antinomy is to turn from Butler's focus on Freudian psychoanalysis to its Lacanian variety and, in particular, to the Lacanian strand of poststructuralist thought. It is here that the most sophisticated poststructuralist analyses of the psyche, especially as it relates to the specific psychic mechanisms that permit intentional agency, are found. Rather than merely abandoning Butler, such discussions will return us to and re-enforce her claim regarding the intimate relationship between the psyche, the social and the symbolic. It is, then, to Jacques Lacan that we now turn.

Notes

1. Judith Butler, *Subjects of Desire: Hegelian Reflections in Twentieth-Century France* (New York: Columbia University Press, 1999), p. 4.
2. Judith Butler, 'Contingent Foundations', in Seyla Benhabib, Judith Butler, Drucilla Cornell and Nancy Fraser, *Feminist Contentions: A Philosophical Exchange* (Abingdon: Routledge, 1995), pp. 35–58 (p. 42).
3. Butler, *Subjects of Desire*, p. 237.
4. Judith Butler, 'Foucault and the Paradox of Bodily Inscription', *The Journal of Philosophy*, 86.11, 1989, pp. 601–7 (p. 602).
5. Judith Butler, *Gender Trouble: Feminism and the Subversion of Identity*, 2nd edn (Abingdon: Routledge, 1999), p. xxxiii.
6. Judith Butler, *The Psychic Life of Power: Theories in Subjection* (Stanford, CA: Stanford University Press, 1997), p. 2.
7. Judith Butler, 'Competing Universalities', in Judith Butler, Ernesto Laclau and Slavoj Žižek, *Contingency, Hegemony, Universality: Contemporary Dialogues on the Left* (London: Verso, 2000), pp. 136–81 (p. 151).
8. Ibid., p. 151.
9. Penelope Deutscher, *Yielding Gender: Feminism, Deconstruction and the History of Philosophy* (Abingdon: Routledge, 1997), p. 23.
10. Butler, *Gender Trouble*, p. 100.
11. Judith Butler, 'Quandaries of the Incest Taboo', in *Undoing Gender* (Abingdon: Routledge, 2004), pp. 152–60 (p. 158).
12. Judith Butler, *Bodies that Matter: On the Discursive Limits of "Sex"* (Abingdon: Routledge, 1993), p. 141.
13. Judith Butler and Vicki Bell, 'New Schemes of Vulnerability: Agency and Plurality', *Theory, Culture, and Society*, 27.1, 2010, pp. 130–52 (p. 132).
14. See, for example, Amy Allen, 'Dependency, Subordination, and Recognition: On Judith Butler's Theory of Subjection', *Continental Philosophy Review*, 38, 2006, pp. 199–222 (pp. 207–8); and Kirsten Campbell, 'The Plague of the Subject: Psychoanalysis and Judith Butler's *The Psychic Life of Power*', *International Journal of Sexuality and Gender Studies*, 6.1/2, 2001, pp. 35–48 (p. 44).
15. Butler, *Gender Trouble*, p. 2.

16. Ibid., p. 8.
17. Ibid., p. xxxi.
18. Ibid., p. 4.
19. Ibid., p. 7.
20. Ibid., p. 9.
21. Ibid., p. 9.
22. Ibid., p. 9.
23. Ibid., p. 9.
24. Ibid., p. 9.
25. Ibid., p. 9.
26. Ibid., p. 9.
27. Ibid., p. 9.
28. Ibid., pp. 9–10.
29. Ibid., p. 10.
30. Ibid., pp. 10, 12.
31. Ibid., p. 21.
32. Ibid., pp. 22, 152.
33. Ibid., p. 152.
34. In the article 'Performative Agency', Butler explains that there are, at least, four senses to her use of 'performativity': 'first performativity seeks to counter a certain kind of positivism according to which we might begin with already delimited understandings of what gender, the state, and the economy are. Secondly, performativity works, when it works, to counter a certain metaphysical presumption about culturally constructed categories and to draw our attention to the diverse mechanisms of construction. Thirdly, performativity starts to describe a set of processes that produce ontological effects, that is, that work to bring into being certain kinds of realities or, fourthly, that lead to certain kinds of socially binding consequences' (Judith Butler, 'Performative Agency', *Journal of Cultural Economy*, 3.2, 2010, pp. 147–61 [p. 147]).
35. Butler, *Gender Trouble*, p. 34.
36. Ibid., p. 34.
37. Ibid., p. 192.
38. Ibid., pp. 185–6.
39. Butler, *Gender Trouble*, p. 45.
40. Ibid., p. 40.
41. The notion of 'social norms' ties into the question of what Butler means by 'the social', an issue that has caused much debate in the literature. Samuel Chambers ('Subjectivation, the Social, and a [Missing] Account of Social Formation: Judith Butler's "Turn"', in Moya Lloyd [ed.], *Butler and Ethics* [Edinburgh: Edinburgh University Press, 2015], pp. 193–218 [p. 210]), for example, holds that, ultimately, for Butler, 'the social simply means more than one individual', thereby concluding that her notion is a liberal one. In contrast, Emma Ingala ('From Hannah Arendt to Judith Butler: The Conditions of the Political', in Gavin Rae and Emma Ingala [eds], *Subjectivity and the Political: Contemporary*

Perspectives [Abingdon: Routledge, 2018], pp. 35–54) engages with the relationship between Butler's and Arendt's analyses of the social–political relation to argue that, while Arendt insists on the distinction between the two, Butler claims that they are entwined. This allows Ingala to show that Butler's conception of the political is based on collective action, which (while Ingala does not explicitly make this move) indicates that Butler's analysis of the social is based on a notion of collectivity rather than being defined by/as a collection of individuals.

42. Judith Butler, 'Beside Oneself: On the Limits of Sexual Autonomy', in *Undoing Gender* (Abingdon: Routledge, 2004), pp. 17–39 (p. 32).
43. Ibid., p. 32.
44. Judith Butler, *Giving an Account of Oneself* (New York: Fordham University Press, 2005), p. 8.
45. Butler, 'Beside Oneself', p. 41.
46. Ibid., p. 41.
47. Ibid., p. 41.
48. Ibid., p. 41.
49. Ibid., p. 41.
50. Judith Butler, 'Introduction', in *Senses of the Subject* (New York: Fordham University Press, 2015), pp. 1–16 (p. 6).
51. Butler, *Bodies that Matter*, p. 171.
52. Butler, 'Competing Universalities', p. 152.
53. Butler, *Bodies that Matter*, p. xii.
54. Lois McNay, 'Gender, Habitus, and the Field: Pierre Bourdieu and the Limits of Reflexivity', *Theory, Culture, and Society*, 16.1, 1999, pp. 95–117 (p. 102).
55. Butler, *The Psychic Life of Power*, p. 21.
56. Ibid., p. 21; see also Butler, *Bodies that Matter*, pp. 166–7.
57. Judith Butler, *Antigone's Claim: Kinship between Life and Death* (New York: Columbia University Press, 2000), p. 19. The intimate relationship between the social and symbolic is seen from her frequent appeal to and critical discussion of Althusser's notion of interpellation (Louis Althusser, 'Ideology and Ideological State Apparatus [Notes Towards an Investigation]', in *Lenin and Philosophy and Other Essays*, trans. Ben Brewster [New York: Monthly Review Press, 2001], pp. 85–126 [pp. 117–20]). See, for example, Butler, *Bodies that Matter*, pp. 81–2, and Butler, *The Psychic Life of Power*, pp. 106–31. For a critical analysis of Butler's treatment of Althusser's notion, see Mathew Lampert, 'Resisting Ideology: On Butler's Critique of Althusser', *Diacritics*, 43.2, 2015, pp. 124–47.
58. Judith Butler, *Excitable Speech: A Politics of the Performative* (Abingdon: Routledge, 1997), p. 16.
59. Butler, *Bodies that Matter*, p. 177.
60. Ibid., p. 181.
61. Butler, *Excitable Speech*, p. 2.
62. Ibid., p. 2.
63. Butler, *Bodies that Matter*, p. 60.

64. Ibid., p. 171.
65. Judith Butler, *Notes for a Performative Theory of Assembly* (Cambridge, MA: Harvard University Press, 2015), p. 31.
66. Butler, *Excitable Speech*, p. 5.
67. Judith Butler, 'The End of Sexual Difference', in *Undoing Gender* (Abingdon: Routledge, 2004), pp. 174–203 (p. 198).
68. Butler, *Bodies that Matter*, p. 38.
69. Ibid., pp. 6, 38.
70. Ibid., p. 6.
71. Judith Butler, 'How Can I Deny that these Hands and this Body are Mine?', in *Senses of the Subject* (New York: Fordham University Press, 2015), pp. 17–35 (pp. 20–1).
72. Butler, *Bodies that Matter*, pp. 38–9.
73. Butler, 'Competing Universalities', p. 151.
74. Ibid., p. 151.
75. Butler, *Gender Trouble*, p. 186.
76. Butler, *The Psychic Life of Power*, p. 3.
77. Ibid., p. 3.
78. Ibid., p. 3.
79. Ibid., p. 6.
80. Ibid., p. 11.
81. Ibid., p. 7.
82. Ibid., p. 7.
83. Ibid., p. 7.
84. Allen, 'Dependency, Subordination, and Recognition', p. 207.
85. Ibid., p. 208.
86. Butler, *The Psychic Life of Power*, p. 7.
87. Ibid., p. 7.
88. Ibid., p. 8.
89. Ibid., p. 9.
90. Ibid., p. 9.
91. Campbell, 'The Plague of the Subject', p. 44.
92. Ibid., p. 46.
93. Butler, *The Psychic Life of Power*, p. 9.
94. Ibid., p. 21.
95. Butler, 'Competing Universalities', p. 153; italics in the original.
96. Butler, *The Psychic Life of Power*, p. 21.
97. Ibid., p. 134.
98. Ibid., p. 170.
99. Ibid., p. 168.
100. Ibid., p. 168.
101. Ibid., p. 169.
102. Ibid., pp. 170, 180.
103. Ibid., p. 181.

104. Ibid., p. 183.
105. Ibid., pp. 195–6.
106. Seyla Benhabib, 'Feminism and Postmodernism', in Seyla Benhabib, Judith Butler, Drucilla Cornell and Nancy Fraser, *Feminist Contentions: A Philosophical Exchange* (Abingdon: Routledge, 1995), pp. 17–34 (p. 20).
107. Ibid., p. 21.
108. Johanna Meehan, 'Feminism and Rethinking Our Models of the Self', *Philosophy and Social Criticism*, 43.1, 2017, pp. 3–33 (p. 3).
109. Ibid., p. 10.
110. Ibid., pp. 14, 7.
111. Butler, 'Contingent Foundations', p. 36.
112. Butler, *Bodies that Matter*, p. xvii.
113. Butler, 'Contingent Foundations', p. 47.
114. Ibid., p. 46.
115. Ibid., p. 46.
116. Butler, *Bodies that Matter*, p. 167.
117. Butler, 'Contingent Foundations', p. 42.
118. Butler, *Gender Trouble*, pp. 202–3.
119. Martha Nussbaum, 'The Professor of Parody: The Hip Defeatism of Judith Butler', *The New Republic*, 22 February 1999, pp. 37–45 (p. 41).
120. Moya Lloyd, *Judith Butler: From Norms to Politics* (Cambridge: Polity, 2007), p. 101.
121. Alan D. Schrift, 'Judith Butler: Une Nouvelle existentialist?', *Philosophy Today*, 45.1, 2001, pp. 12–23 (p. 22).
122. Geoff Boucher, 'Judith Butler's Postmodern Existentialism: A Critical Analysis', *Philosophy Today*, 48.4, 2004, pp. 355–69 (p. 365).
123. Friedrich Nietzsche, *On the Genealogy of Morals*, trans. Walter Kaufman and R. J. Hollingdale, in *On the Genealogy of Morals and Ecce Homo*, ed. Walter Kaufman (New York: Vintage, 1969), pp. 15–198 (I:§13).

CHAPTER 6

Lacan on the Unconscious Subject: From the Social to the Symbolic

Butler recognises the importance of language to the formation of the subject, but tends to emphasise the subject's social embeddedness and dependence on social norms. Jacques Lacan, in contrast, focuses on the relationship between thought and language to insist on the fundamental importance of the symbolic realm – meaning primarily though not exclusively the differential relations that generate meaning – for the formation and continuation of the subject. This is not to say, however, that he ignores or downplays the social dimension. For Lacan, the symbolic is inherently social because it is defined by relationality and so is dependent upon the Other.[1]

This is combined with two additional points: first, Lacan holds that the subject is distinct from the ego; and, second, whereas the ego is associated with consciousness, he links the subject to the unconscious. By moving the terms of the debate away from the conscious foundational ego towards the unconscious differential symbolic relations that generate meaning, Lacan continues the poststructuralist rejection of the Cartesian *cogito* and rethinking of the subject. Schematically, his analysis fulfils at least three functions in so far as it 1) criticises any privileging of the ego, 2) undermines the notion that the subject is foundational, and 3) focuses our attention on the ways in which diachronic symbolic relations and, by extension, the Other structure and underpin the subject.

It is, then, not surprising that Lacan's theory of the subject has attracted much attention: Dany Nobus, for example, calls the subject the 'conceptual cornerstone' of Lacan's psychoanalytic edifice, while Bruce Fink relies on the fallacy that poststructuralist thought fails to offer a positive conception of the subject to claim that Lacan not only corrects this lacuna but, in so doing, also 'presents us with a radically new theory of subjectivity'.[2] Lorenzo Chiesa agrees with this assessment by maintaining that 'Lacan outlines a revolutionary theory of the subject', while Yannis Stavrakakis insists that 'this subject . . . is generally considered as Lacan's major contribution to contemporary theory and political analysis'.[3]

However, while there is agreement on the importance of Lacan's thinking on the subject, there is little agreement on what exactly the Lacanian subject actually entails or, indeed, whether it permits agency. For example, a number of commentators[4] argue that Lacan's theory cannot permit agency because he makes the subject an effect of symbolic relations to the extent that the subject is incapable of acting in alternative ways to those demanded by the symbolic relations that condition it. This conclusion is, however, based on a number of misunderstandings. First, it repeats the often made error of conflating 'condition' with 'determine', so that the claim that the subject is conditioned by the symbolic is mistakenly understood to mean that the subject is determined by it. Second, by reducing the subject to an effect of the symbolic realm, it ignores the roles that what Lacan calls the imaginary and, crucially, the real play in creating 'spaces' from the symbolic relations that condition the subject and that, so I will argue, permit agency.

Alternatively, those commentators who do not make the mistake of reducing the Lacanian subject to a determined effect of the symbolic realm fail to agree on what the subject that results looks like. For example, having affirmed the importance of Lacan's theory of the subject and agreed on the fundamental role that the real – that is, that which cannot be symbolised – plays in Lacan's thinking, Chiesa claims that 'the Lacanian subject is a *subjectivized* lack, *not a lacking* subject or subject of impossibility'[5] which, while not mentioning Stavrakakis directly, appears to be aimed at the latter's claim that Lacan affirms 'the subject as lack' and 'a politics of impossibility'.[6] Fink, in contrast, focuses on the relationship between the subject and the unconscious to explain that, far from being synonymous with one another, the 'subject of the unconscious . . . is in general excluded at the level of unconscious thought. It comes into being, so to speak, only momentarily, as a sort of pulselike movement.'[7]

A further position is staked out by Ed Pluth, who suggests that Lacan actually offers three distinct conceptualisations of the subject throughout his seminars,[8] before claiming that his 'ultimate view of the subject . . . is portrayed as something between an organised system of symbols and something that motivates or agitates that organisation in the first place'.[9] This organisational principle is not, however, a substance, but is, in a similar vein to Fink's appraisal, defined by 'a' moving function/action. For this reason, Pluth claims that, for Lacan, 'the *subject* . . . does not designate the one who acts. Instead, it designates what an act does. An act "subjects" in a new way.'[10] This trades on the dual sense of 'subject', in so far as it can refer to an *agent* or an *act*, whereby something is subjected to/by another. By affirming the latter, Pluth removes the notion of the 'subject as agent' from the equation to re-enforce the point that Lacan rejects a founding role for the subject. However, although this helpfully identifies the multidimensionality inherent in the concept 'subject', and highlights the relationship between the Lacanian subject and action, it is reductionist. Indeed, having excluded the 'agent-subject' from Lacan's schema, Pluth subsequently implicitly comes to depend on it when he claims that the Lacanian subject can and, indeed, must be able to choose how to act – which, as Alenka Zupančič points out, is 'the very condition of possibility of psychoanalysis'[11] – so as to be able to 'cure' itself as part of a psychoanalytic course of treatment.[12]

To correct this oversight and explain how such agency is possible without falling back on a substantial subject or 'a little man within a man'[13] requires, so I will argue, that we return to Fink's claim that the Lacanian subject is best thought of as a momentary, pulse-like, unconscious happening that results from, organises and joins the three registers of the symbolic, the imaginary and the real. It is here that the importance that Chiesa and Stavrakakis place on the real fits in, in so far as it is the lack of the real that means that the symbolic relations that condition the subject are never total, and thus, I will maintain, permit the subject to act in ways not conditioned by those symbolic relations. However, I conclude by arguing that Lacan's account is simply not sufficiently clear on the mechanics of agency: while the lack of the real accounts for how agency is possible for a subject conditioned by and resulting from symbolic relations, it does not adequately explain how the disruption caused to the symbolic realm by the lack of the real subsequently permits the subject to 'decide' – or whatever mechanism it takes place through – to act in a positive expressive form.

Descartes' Cogito, the Unconscious and the Imaginary Ego

In *Seminar III*, Lacan explains that 'one of the most profound characteristics of the mental foundation of the Judeo-Christian tradition [is that it] clearly profiles the being of the *I* as its ultimate ground'.[14] This reaches its clearest manifestation with the foundational role that Descartes gives to the *cogito*. Very simply, Descartes' *Meditations* searches for immutable truth. Having doubted all certainties in the first meditation, the second aims to determine whether it is possible to obtain a presuppositionless certainty. Descartes realises that his epistemological doubt provides that, in so far as to doubt requires a thought, which requires a being that thinks, and so confirms that, at the very least, he, the one thinking, exists.[15] At the ground of certainty lies, then, the existence of the thinking ego,[16] a conclusion that Lacan claims underpins subsequent thought.[17]

Needless to say, Lacan is highly critical of this development, going so far as to call it a 'joke'[18] that has led to a 'deluded'[19] anthropocentrism in which 'modern man thinks that everything which has happened in the universe since its origin came about so as to converge on this thing which thinks, creation of life, unique precious being, pinnacle of creation, which is himself, with this privileged vantage-point called consciousness'.[20] Furthermore, Lacan charges that it is based on a fallacious understanding of the ego and, indeed, the ego's role in consciousness: 'The promotion of consciousness as essential to the subject in the historical aftermath of the Cartesian cogito is indicative, to my mind, of a misleading emphasis on the transparency of the *I* in action at the expense of the opacity of the signifier that determines it.'[21]

Lacan challenges this on two fronts. First, he argues that, even if we accept Descartes' argument, it does not follow that consciousness will know itself fully. By trying to understand itself, consciousness turns itself into an object, thereby denying itself access to the non-objectivity of consciousness that truly defines it: 'If this I is in fact presented to us as a kind of immediate given in the act of reflection by which consciousness grasps itself as transparent to itself, for all that, nothing indicates that the whole of this reality . . . would be exhausted by this.'[22]

Second, Lacan points out that Descartes' analysis takes place at the level of the conscious ego and so is unable to take into consideration the fundamental Freudian discovery of the unconscious. Indeed, that discovery 'completely eludes [those] circles of certainties by which man recognises himself as ego'.[23] While admitting that the Freudian discourse on the unconscious would not have been possible without the emphasis placed on the ego by Descartes, Lacan explains that the former goes far beyond the latter in so far as it reveals that 'the full significance of meaning far surpasses the signs manipulated by the individual. Man is always cultivating a great many more signs than he thinks.'[24] To truly understand the subject, we must move away from the conscious ego to '[t]he true subject – that is, the subject of the unconscious'.[25] Therefore, far from being the foundation of knowledge, Lacan claims that the conscious ego is 'grounded' in the unconscious subject and, for this reason, is always 'the ego of the [unconscious] subject'.[26]

This is not to say, however, that Lacan abandons the ego. He rethinks it within and from the unconscious subject. For this reason, the Lacanian ego is not the same as the Cartesian one; it 'takes on an entirely different functional value'.[27] Specifically, the ego has an important structural function to do with the creation of (an imaginary) identity. The formation of this identity is *phenomenologically* fundamental, in so far as it provides the individual with the illusion of continuity that is the basis for his conscious thoughts and actions, but it also has *clinical* importance, in so far as the way in which this identity is formed – or, indeed, whether it is formed – is crucial to the individual's psychological well-being.

Lionel Bailly, for example, explains that a mother who is severely depressed or mentally ill may provide a distorting mirror, which may 'produce a narcissistic line of weakness, a "faultline" upon which identity is built', thereby causing problems for the ego's behaviour and sense of self; or, worse still, she may provide no mirror at all, resulting in the child 'remain[ing] at the fragmented body stage in its imagination for far too long, with damaging long-term effects'.[28] Specifically, and somewhat controversially, Bailly links this to '[s]ome of the symptoms commonly seen as "autistic"', in so far as in 'severe cases of autism, it appears that the "I" is not "precipitated in a primordial form" at the Mirror Stage, and the child does not make the mental leap from the fantasy of a fragmented body to that of the wholeness of the self'.[29] Without getting into the complexities of a condition such as autism, this starts to demonstrate how Lacan's theoretical formulations may play themselves out clinically and, indeed, demonstrates the importance of the mirror stage. Needless to say, in what follows I will focus on Lacan's theoretical framework, rather than its clinical implications, to identify how the ego develops from a particular stage of psychological development, before showing how it relates to the subject.

For Lacan, the child is not born with an ego, but must develop it by passing into the imaginary realm through the mirror stage. The mirror stage is important for two different, but ultimately related, reasons. First, 'it has historical value as it marks a decisive turning-point in the mental development of the child',[30] where it starts to develop a sense of individual identity. Second, 'it typifies an essential libidinal relationship with the body-image'.[31] While the child is always ensconced in a symbolic realm by virtue of being surrounded by others who talk, and, as we will see, it is the symbolic register of language, norms and rules that defines the subject, the first register that the child passes through as part of its normal development is the imaginary one, an occurrence that takes place between the ages of six to eighteen months. This stage of development is important because it marks the moment when the baby recognises itself reflected in an image and, from this, moves from its original sense of 'organic disturbance and discord'[32] to one of embodied unity. With this, the child develops a sense of mastery over itself and a body-image of itself that 'will leave its mark on every subsequent exercise of effective motor mastery' and 'entirely structures his fantasy life'.[33]

There are at least three moments of note inherent in this experience. First, the mirror does not have to be an actual mirror, but simply anything that permits the child to see itself reflected. Typically, this takes place through the mother's[34] gaze and so establishes a specific dynamic between the child and the mother in which the former sees the latter as the source of itself and its bodily satisfactions. For the child to successfully enter the symbolic realm requires that its initial privileging of the mother be replaced by the acceptance of law in the form of the Name-of-the-Father. Second, the mirror stage reveals a privileging of sight over the other senses. This is not, however, to say that blind children do not pass through this stage, only that it will take place in a different form. Third, the unity that results is defined by a moment of alienation: the child sees itself in an other and recognises itself as that which it previously took itself not to be – an object. This moment of alienation is, however, experienced joyously: the child takes a 'jubilant interest . . . at the sight of his own image in a mirror'.[35]

Importantly, Lacan explains that this

> jubilant assumption [*assomption*] of his specular image by the kind of being – still trapped in his motor impotence and nursling dependence – the little man is at the *infans* stage . . . seems to me to manifest in an exemplary situation the symbolic matrix in which the *I* is precipitated in a primordial form, prior to being objectified in the dialectic of identification with the other, and before language restores to it, in the universal, its function as subject. This form would, moreover, have to be called the 'ideal-I.'[36]

The ego is not a substance, but 'an imaginary function'[37] that provides the appearance of identity and a sense of stability. It is always linked to a phantasmatic idealisation, termed the *Idealich* or ideal-ego, that describes the imaginary unity that the child perceives when it witnesses the completeness of its body. The child will define itself in terms of the perception of its ideal-ego and, indeed, try to live up to its self-image. As an imaginary, this identity is fragile and so the child is in 'constant danger of sliding back again into the chaos from which he started'.[38]

The ideal-ego comes into contact with and is judged according to the ego-ideal (*Ichideal*) of the symbolic, which 'governs the interplay of relations on which all relations with others depend'.[39] The ideal-ego is associated with the imaginary realm and arises from the child's perception of its bodily unity; the ego-ideal emanates from the symbolic realm and regulates and dictates how the subject should act, including the validity of the ideal-ego. So, to put it somewhat schematically, the ideal-ego results from the mirror stage, but, once the child enters the symbolic register, it learns what its society expects of it in terms of body type and acceptable forms of presentation and behaviour, with the consequence that its ideal-ego becomes subject to the regulating pressure of the symbolic ego-ideal. The ego-ideal does not replace the ideal-ego; both egos operate simultaneously, with each subject struggling to reconcile them. Indeed, how the subject reconciles them plays a large role in his or her psychic life.

The Lacanian ego is not, then, a substantial 'thing', nor, like its Cartesian counterpart, is it (ontologically or epistemologically) foundational. That the imaginary ego is not primary does not, however, mean that its function is insignificant. The ego is, for Lacan, crucial to the psychological well-being and functioning of the individual. Burt Oliviers notes, however, that it does fulfil a paradoxical dual role, in so far as

> it is the very 'fictional' (and indispensable) condition for having a sense of 'self' or of a series of variations ('selves') on the initial *Gestalt*, but simultaneously *also* the condition for being alienated from this genuine capacity of fictionalisation or fantasy in so far as the subject tends to construct a kind of (no less fictional) strait jacket or carapace to 'contain' or limit its generation of images of the self.[40]

Although the identity it attains from its ideal-ego is a 'mirage'[41] based on belief in what it knows about itself,[42] this fiction is necessary for the development of a sense of self.

While this undermines the long-held notion that the ego is defined in some 'essential' way, Lacan further decentres the Cartesian ego by pointing out that the ego is not the site of agency because it is an effect of language: 'The ego is itself one of the significant elements of ordinary discourse, which is the discourse of the unconscious. As such, and in so far as it is image, it is caught in the chain of symbols.'[43] Rather than commanding its actions, the ego is a consequence of the movement of the symbolic chain subtending it. The ego does not, then, autonomously and intentionally *choose* its actions; they are a consequence of the play of signifiers of the symbolic realm. As a consequence, the ego does not initiate individual action, but is the recipient of an act that occurs prior to it. To understand agency, we have, then, to move from the conscious ego of the imaginary to its 'cause':[44] the unconscious subject of the symbolic. After all, as Lacan reminds us, rather than 'start off with an isolated and absolute subject[,] [e]verything is tied to the symbolic order, since there are men in the world and they speak'.[45]

The Symbolic

Louis Sass explains that with the symbolic register,

> Lacan presents a realm that is understood to lie beyond our conscious grasp (a realm of semiotic structures encompassing the unconscious, which is 'structured like a language'), yet which, in contrast with the illusions of the 'imaginary' realm, supposedly constitutes the actual matrix and motor of much of our experience and action.[46]

While Lacan had concentrated on the imaginary register from 1936 to 1953, the later year saw him move to focus on the symbolic one, a movement inaugurated in his famous text 'The Function and Field of Speech and Language in Psychoanalysis'.[47] In this text, Lacan insists on a return to Freud and, in particular, the role that language plays in the unconscious:

> We must thus take up Freud's work again with the *Traumdeutung* [*The Interpretation of Dreams*] to remind ourselves that a dream has the structure of a sentence or, rather, to keep to the letter of the work, of a rebus – that is, of a form of writing, of which children's dreams are supposed to represent the primordial ideography, and which reproduces, in adults' dreams, the simultaneously phonetic and symbolic use of signifying elements found in the hieroglyphs of ancient Egypt and in the characters still used in China.[48]

Claiming that there is an intimate connection between language and the subject does not, however, mean that language is controlled by the subject as if it were a tool for self-expression. On the contrary,

> [s]ymbols... envelop the life of man within a network so total that they join together those who are going to engender him 'by bone and flesh' before he comes into the world; so total that they bring to his birth, along with the gifts of the stars, if not with the gifts of the fairies, the shape of his destiny; so total that they provide the words that will make him fanciful or renegade, the law of the acts that will follow him right to the very place where he is not yet and beyond his very death; and so total that through them his end finds its meaning in the last judgment, where the Word absolves his being or condemns it – unless he reaches the subjective realisation of being-toward-death.[49]

If the symbolic precedes the subject and functions to bring 'him' into existence, the question that arises relates to the structure of those symbolic relations: how do they function to fulfil these roles?

To understand this, it is necessary to have a basic knowledge of the linguistic theory of Ferdinand de Saussure and, in particular, his claim that language is composed of signs. These are constituted by a signifier and signified that relate to one another in a particular way. As Lionel Bailly explains, for Saussure,

> the signifier (sound image/acoustic image) is not the *material* sound but the hearer's impression it makes on our senses. Also, the signified (concept) is not the object (the chair in front of you) but *the idea of the object* (any chair – the property of being a chair – of which an example may or may not be before you at the time of speaking).[50]

Because the (immaterial) signifier represents an immaterial signified, Saussure holds that signs are immaterial. Lacan, in contrast, holds that 'language is not immaterial. It is a subtle body, but a body it is.'[51] The object designated by the signifier 'dog' is not a dog apart from its signification – apart from its signification it is simply an object – it becomes a 'dog' through being named as such.

Furthermore, Lacan accepts Saussure's claim[52] that meaning arises from the relations between signifiers, but radicalises it by claiming that, if meaning is dependent on the movement between signifiers, they must take precedence over that which is signified. Meaning is not generated from the movement from signifier to *signified*, but is created from the constant and incessant movement between signifiers. It is the difference between signifiers that generates their meaning. For this reason, 'the empty spaces are as signifying as the full ones'.[53] Indeed, Lacan defines the chain of signification as 'presence in absence and absence in presence'.[54] The (presented) signifiers only attain meaning from the differences (= absences) between them:

> the sun in so far as it is designated by a ring is valueless. It only has a value in so far as this ring is placed in relation with other formalizations, which constitute with it this symbolic whole within which it has its place, at the centre of the world for example, or at the periphery, it doesn't matter which. The symbol only has value if it is organised in a world of symbols.[55]

As such, it is 'in the chain of signifier that meaning *insists*, but . . . none of the chain's elements *consists* in the signification it can provide at that very moment. The notion of an incessant sliding of the signified under the signifier thus comes to the fore.'[56] We will see that this constant sliding is contained by 'the laws of a closed order',[57] but even within that order signifiers continue to relate to others in different ways, so that meaning is constantly changing. For this reason, '[e]verything that is language proceeds via a series of steps like those of Achilles who never catches up to the tortoise – it aims at re-creating a full sense which, however, it never achieves, which is always somewhere else'.[58]

In relation to the subject, the constant sliding of the signifier 'under' the signified ensures that the subject is not a unified entity, but is defined by a constant process of becoming wherein the signifying chain that subtends the signified (name) undermines the latter to reproduce it. As Slavoj Žižek explains,

> by means of the Word, the subject finally *finds* itself, comes to itself . . . in the Word, the subject directly attains itself, posits itself as such. The price for it, however, is the irretrievable *loss* of the subject's self-identity: the verbal sign that stands for the subject, that is, in which the subject posits itself as self-identical, bears the mark of an irreducible dissonance; it never 'fits' the subject.[59]

This dissonance is not, however, an act done by the subject to itself; it does not act to subvert its own identity in a process of wilful becoming. Rather, 'this division stems from nothing other than . . . the play of signifiers'.[60] It marks the very structure of the unconscious from which the subject arises. As Lacan puts it, '[t]he unconscious is fundamentally structured, woven, chained, meshed by language. And not only does the signifier play as big a role there as the signified does, but it plays the fundamental role. In fact, what characterises language is the system of signifiers as such.'[61]

Because of the fundamental importance of the signifier, Lacan claims that 'the unconscious is structured like a language'[62] rather than by language. If it were structured by language it would be defined by both a signifier *and* signified in the same way that language is: there would be a chain of signification that culminated in a signifier obtaining a particular and definitive meaning. The unconscious, however, lacks signifieds; it is pure movement across the signifying chain. 'If there were signifieds as well, then the meaning of any particular signifier for a Subject would be quite rigid: a signifier (and its emotional load) would remain immovable, attached forever to one particular thing and not be transferable to another.'[63]

Signifiers do not, however, simply occupy a single nodal point in the field of symbols; they 'occupy' multiple positions and take on different meanings depending on the other signifier that they are, at that moment, related to and differentiated from. Indeed, the symbolic system is marked by structural criss-crossings in which 'every easily isolable linguistic symbol is not only at one with the totality, but is cut across and constituted by a series of overflowings, of oppositional overdeterminations which place it at one and the same time in several registers'.[64]

Lacan shows this clearly in his famous analysis of Edgar Allan Poe's 'The Purloined Letter'. He describes two scenes, but, for the sake of brevity, I will focus only on the first. Located in the royal boudoir, Lacan notes that the Queen receives a letter. At this point, the King enters, thereby causing the Queen some discomfort as she does not want her husband to discover the contents of said letter. It appears that she is aided in this endeavour by the entrance of a third man, Mister D, whose appearance in the room distracts the King and so allows the Queen to hide the letter. Lacan explains, however, that Mister D has noticed the Queen's attention to the letter and, having dealt with the business of the day, proceeds to 'draw from his pocket a letter similar in appearance to the one before his eyes and, after pretending to read it, places it next to the other'.[65] After a little more conversation to distract attention from the letter he dropped, 'he picks up the embarrassing letter without flinching and decamps, while the Queen, on whom none of his manoeuvre has been lost, remains unable to intervene for fear of attracting the attention of her royal spouse, who is standing at her elbow at that very moment'.[66]

There are many facets to this story, but helpfully, in *Seminar II*, Lacan explains that the

> letter, which doesn't have the same meaning everywhere, is a truth which is not to be divulged. As soon as it gets into the pocket of the minister, it is no longer what it was before, whatever it was that it had been. It is no longer a love letter, a letter of trust, the announcement of an event, it is evidence, on this occasion a court exhibit. If we imagine that this poor King, seized by some great enthusiasm which would make of him a king of greater grace, one of those kings who isn't easy-going, who isn't capable of letting something go past, and is capable of sending his worthy spouse in front of the judges . . . we realize that the identity of the recipient of the letter is as problematic as the question of knowing to whom it belongs. In any case, from the moment it falls into the hands of the minister, it has in itself become something else.[67]

There is not, then, 'one' letter; the letter takes on different forms and meanings depending on whether it is looked at in relation to the King, Queen, Mister D, Lacan or, indeed, us the reader.

However, that symbolic differential relations occur prior to the subject and, indeed, are the conditions of possibility for the subject brought Jean Hyppolite to ask whether this meant that the symbolic should be thought of as a transcendental function. Lacan responds: 'I don't think so. The allusions I have made to a completely different use of the notion of machine might well indicate that.'[68] We will see that Castoriadis criticises this emphasis on machinic production because he associates it with mechanical reproduction,[69] but, for Lacan, the metaphor of the machine simply indicates that the symbolic realm is based on a constant rhythm of differentiation; at no point does it settle into a singular, homogeneous pattern of production, nor does it produce in accordance with a prior plan or teleology.

One consequence of this is that the signifier, in a very strong sense, speaks the subject: 'language [i]s the cause of the subject', meaning that 'without [the signifier] there would be no subject'.[70] For this reason, a subject is born from the symbolic realm:

> All human beings share in the universe of symbols. They are included in it and submit to it, much more than they constitute it. They are much more its supports than its agents. It is as a function of the symbols, of the symbolic constitution of his history, that those variations are produced in which the subject is open to taking on the variable, broken, fragmented, sometimes even unconstituted and regressive, images of himself.[71]

While the child exists in a symbolic world – it is, after all, surrounded by language – it is only once the child passes from the imaginary realm to the symbolic and so starts to talk that the subject can be said to form. The naming of the child plays a fundamental role in exposing him to the symbolic:

> there's no escaping the fact that he's a human being, born in a state of impotence, and, very early on, words, language were what he used to call with, and a most miserable call it was, when his food depended on his screams. But really that is no reason to hide the fact that, no less early, this relation to the other is named, and is so by the subject. That a name, however confused it may be, designates a specific person, is exactly what makes up the transition to the human state. If one has to define the moment at which man becomes human, we can say that it is the moment when, however little it be, he enters into the symbolic relation.[72]

In being designated as/by a name, the child is defined by a signifier and so, prior to its own use of signifiers, learns their importance and, indeed, that it is designated by one. This, in turn, feeds into the construction of an imaginary identity as it comes to associate itself with that name; a signifier that, it will be remembered, emanates from other people, and so reaffirms

Lacan's claim about the alienation inherent in the imaginary realm and the importance of the symbolic Other.

However, in contrast to Castoriadis's insistence regarding the importance of a psychic core that remains autonomous from the socio-symbolic realm, Lacan dismisses the notion that there is 'a little man within a man, who makes the apparatus tick'.[73] For Lacan, the subject is always relational, constitutively tied to and dependent on the Other. As he famously puts it: 'the unconscious is the discourse of the Other'.[74] The Other is not, however, a substantial being; it, in turn, is defined by its relation to the subject, who it must be remembered is conditioned by the Other. As a consequence, the symbolic relations that generate the subject and, indeed, the subject 'itself' are conditioned by pure lack (of foundation).[75]

Whereas the child enters into the *imaginary* through its own actions – it sees and recognises itself in a mirror – its entrance into the *symbolic* comes from outside: language imposes itself on to the child at all times. It is for this reason that 'the symbolic order has to be conceived as something superimposed'.[76] This does not necessarily involve physical violence; the child is simply under constant bombardment by signifiers and the expectation that it will learn to use them correctly so as to participate in the world. Through this, the child learns to express its desires so that they are acceptable to the laws that govern each particular symbolic register.

In formal terms, the child must pass from its desire for the mother to accept the primacy of the paternal law,[77] or, as Lacan calls it, the 'Name-of-the-Father'.[78] While it cannot be named or even identified as such, the Name-of-the-Father is 'a requirement of the signifying chain. Merely by virtue of the fact that you institute a symbolic order, something corresponds to, or does not correspond to, the function defined as the Name-of-the-Father.'[79] The function of the Name-of-the-Father is 1) prohibitive because its acceptance teaches the child that it must subordinate its desire to the law, but also 2) productive because it defines the privileged norms of a symbolic system, is the key through which signifiers are combined to create a symbolic universe, and determines the structure and laws to be followed to execute a particular language. Mark Bracher also notes that it is significant 'for the larger role [it] play[s] in structuring the subject – specifically, in giving the subject a sense of identity and direction'.[80]

At this stage, it might be helpful to briefly say something about Lacan's notion of desire, particularly because it is important for his notion of the subject and reveals the roles that embodiment and the social play in his theory. Desire, for Lacan, results from the relationship between biological *needs* and the symbolic. The child starts off with certain needs that must be satisfied for it to survive. For them to be satisfied requires an other, usually but not necessarily the mother, who provides it with food, water, care, warmth and so on. Initially the caregiver knows that the child needs something by virtue of its initial screams or cries, but does not know precisely what is needed and so has to guess, thereby transforming the child's need into a symbolic function of the Other. Even when the child enters the symbolic register and can describe its needs, the demand put forth in language to articulate those needs alters them:

> With the addition of signifiers, [need] undergoes a minimal transformation – a minimal metaphor, in a word – and this makes it the case that what is signified is something beyond raw need and is remodelled through the use of signifiers. Henceforth, from this beginning, what enters into the creation of the signified isn't purely and simply the translation of need, but the recapture, reassumption and remodelling of need, the creation of a desire other than a need.[81]

The demand does not correspond exactly to the need, but alters it. The discrepancy that arises is, for Lacan, the lack that characterises desire.

Desire, for Lacan, does not, then, signify the same as it tends to mean in everyday speech. It is not a property of the subject nor is it affirmative statement ('I want x'); rather, it describes the lack that necessarily arises between the individual's biological need and its expression through the symbolic. This lack is not the fault of the subject using the symbolic incorrectly, but is a structural feature of the symbolic register; it simply cannot fully describe the biological need. Indeed, for Lacan, the biological–symbolic relationship is a problematic one: while accepting that the latter exists, he rarely talks about it for the simple reason that to do so would reduce the biological to the symbolic. As such, in *Seminar III*, Lacan points out that the symbolic can never account for the fact of biological procreation but simply has to take it for granted. The symbolic is, then, embodied in the sense that it is material and forms a body of symbols, but it is distinct from, although always related to, biological embodiment. It is this 'gap' that permits and describes the lack of desire. But the lack of desire does not just arise from the relationship between biological need and symbolic demand; it is also found in the *symbolic* construction of desire itself. This is because the unconscious desire of the subject is not orientated to an object – that is simply the superficial objective manifestation of desire[82] – but is orientated to something else: 'man's desire is the desire of the other'.[83]

This can take at least three forms: 1) desire for the other, meaning that the subject simply desires the other – this is clearly seen in sexual attraction, for example; 2) desire for the desire of the other, that is, the subject desires what the other desires simply because the other desires it; or 3) the desire to be desired by the other. The logic underpinning this last possibility is rather convoluted, but the point is actually a simple one: take, for example, the case in which I ask my partner to make me a cup of coffee. Superficially, what I desire is the cup of coffee. But what Lacan is saying is that, in asking my partner to make me a cup of coffee, I am really revealing that I desire that she show me that she desires me by foregoing everything else to try to make me happy (at that moment) by making me a cup of coffee. What I desire when I ask her to make a cup of coffee is not, then, just the cup of coffee – that which is other to me – but her *desire* for me, which is always alien and hence wholly Other to me. My desire for the cup of coffee made by her is, then, really a desire to 'obtain' her desire (for me).

The problem is that desire can never be satiated not only because the need that desire emanates from is continuous, but also because desire is conditioned by lack. In desiring the Other, the subject never desires anything substantial, but a relation in which it is the privileged point. Because it is based on a relation, the subject is returned to the difference – or, as Lacan calls it, the Other – that is constitutive of the symbolic. However, it must be remembered that the Other is defined through its relation to the subject and so, in reality, is nothing other than the lack that arises from and defines that relation. The subject's desire is not, then, an individual matter, but a symbolic relation to the Other that also entails a social relation to the other. Desire is important for Lacan not only because it reveals a crucial structure of the unconscious subject – one that also has clinical importance in so far as the structure of and attempt to satiate desire conditions the psychological well-being of the individual – but also because it shows that the symbolic register is not divorced from social norms or relations; it is intimately connected with and dependent upon them. In contrast to Foucault and Butler, Lacan privileges the symbolic register when thinking about the subject, but he holds that the symbolic does not just refer to linguistic relations or structures; it also describes and depends upon social relations and norms.

The Subject, the Symbolic and the Real

That the subject is intimately and constitutively tied to the symbolic register has, however, given rise to debate regarding what this means for the possibility of agency. If the subject is constituted by and so an effect of symbolic relations, is it possible for it to intentionally do otherwise than that permitted by those relations? A number of commentators have argued that Lacan's account of the subject–symbolic relation does not permit such agency; the subject is simply an effect of the symbolic relations subtending it and is therefore unable to choose how to act. Eve Banner, for example, claims that Lacan's symbolic account of the subject 'imposes conformity and abolishes individuality to the point where "the collective and the individual are the same thing" ... [and] leads to a situation in which "we are spoken more than we speak"'.[84] Similarly, Mikkel Borch-Jacobsen insists that, for Lacan, 'the subject *is* language' to the extent that 'the two are the *same*'.[85] As a consequence, the subject simply represents and is an effect of the symbolic relations subtending language. Finally, Jean-Luc Nancy and Philipe Lacoue-Labarthe follow a similar line of interpretation when they explain that 'the locus of the Lacanian signifier is nevertheless the subject. Fundamentally ... it is in a *theory of the subject* that the logic of the signifier settles.'[86] The subject is, then, on this reading, that which the signifier represents, with the consequence that the subject is unable to represent anything other than another signifier.[87] The subject is simply a mechanical movement along the chain of signification. While recognising that Lacan decentres *and* rethinks the subject as an effect of symbolic relations, this line of interpretation holds that he is not able to offer an account of agency – that is, action that the subject has chosen independently of its conditioning effects – that is consistent with his account of the symbolic. Instead, it claims that Lacan either makes the subject a determined effect of signifiers or, as in the case of Nancy and Lacoue-Labarthe, implicitly relies upon a 'classical'[88] notion of the subject that controls and founds the action.

Lacan certainly makes a number of statements that seem to support the idea that the subject is a passive recipient of the symbolic. He explains, for example, that 'the symbolic order can no longer be conceived of ... as constituted by man but must rather be conceived of as constituting him',[89] with the consequence that the subject 'disappears ... beneath the signifier he becomes, due to the simple fact that it addresses him, he is absolutely nothing'.[90] As an effect of the chain of signifiers, the 'subject doesn't foment this game [of the sliding chain of signifiers], he takes his place in it, and plays the role of the little *pluses* and *minuses* in it'.[91] Indeed, Lacan explains that the subject 'thinks according to laws that turn out to be the same as those that organize the signifying chain'.[92]

However, to conclude from these statements that Lacan makes the subject a determined effect of symbolic relations is to make at least two fundamental errors regarding the unconscious–symbolic relationship. First, while the subject is located in the unconscious and the unconscious is bound to the symbolic relations, it must be remembered that the unconscious and language are not synonymous: 'the unconscious is structured *like* a language'[93] rather than *by* language, in so far as it is defined by moving chains of signifiers rather than signifiers *and* signifieds. While the unconscious subject is conditioned by the symbolic, there is a distinction between the two that means that the subject cannot be said to be *determined* by (symbolic) language.

As a consequence, second, Lacan's claim that the symbolic *constitutes* the subject does not mean that the symbolic *determines* the subject, but that symbolic relations 'merely' *condition* the subject. We see this if we focus on the third register, termed the real, which Lacan maintains is part of the individual's experience and its relation to the symbolic. The real is found throughout Lacan's writing, but comes to prominence in the 1960s[94] to describe that which 'resists symbolization absolutely'.[95] More specifically, as Louis Sass explains, it designates that which

> lies beyond not just our *actual* knowledge but beyond the very *possibility* of our knowing, yet which, all the while, we also know to be there: we approach it, if at all, only in states of ecstasy or madness. In this sense the Real is also felt to be that which is most certain and most undeniable – even as we cannot grasp that which we cannot deny.[96]

Lacan also calls the real the 'ineffable', that which 'one cannot imagine' and a 'mystery'.[97] Importantly, Bruce Fink notes that Lacan describes two versions of the real: on the one hand, '[t]he real is . . . an infant's body "before" it comes under the sway of the symbolic order, before it is subjected to toilet training and instructed in the ways of the world'.[98] Through its socialisation and entrance into the symbolic world, the child learns to give meaning to its body and so turns it into something that he or she knows; 'pleasure is localised in certain zones, while other zones are neutralised by the word and coaxed into compliance with social, behaviour norms'.[99] On the other hand, the real also describes and, indeed, 'is perhaps best understood as *that which has not yet been symbolized*, remains to be symbolized, or even resists symbolization; and it may perfectly well exist "alongside" and in spite of a speaker's considerable linguistic capabilities'.[100]

While it cannot be conceptualised, Badredine Arfi notes that the real fulfils three functions within Lacan's theory. First, it designates that 'there always is *resistance* that is involved in thinking about, and in "experiencing" the effects of, the Real'.[101] It is simply not possible to think of the real as it is in-itself; doing so causes problems for the subject. Indeed, how the subject attempts to symbolise the real so as to deal with it is inherently bound up with clinical treatment. That it cannot be symbolised means that, second, 'the Real is most characteristically thought of in negative terms'.[102] And, third, 'the Real is more or less thought of as a limit to language/symbolic order, which can also be formulated as an attempt to conceptualize a totalization and closure (of sorts) of the symbolic order'.[103] Not only does this mean that symbolisation is never complete, it also ensures that the subject never is.

For this reason, the subject cannot simply be reduced to language, but is constituted by a mysterious aspect; a part that cannot be symbolised and so understood. It is a mistake therefore to reduce the Lacanian subject to a determined effect of the symbolic. The Lacanian subject is defined from the differentiation of symbolic relations, manifests itself as a conscious imaginary identity, but is always defined by a lack that prevents totality or completeness. Indeed, this creates a unique schema: the subject is distinct from the conscious ego and so is of the unconscious without being synonymous with the unconscious. Instead, the subject exists from the unconscious and 'prior' to the ego as a lack. It is not static or a substance, but a constant, momentary becoming that is continuously recreated from the movement of the symbolic chain of signification, itself disrupted by the real.

Conclusion: The Subject and Agency

Lacan's critique of the Cartesian ego and affirmation of the decentred subject entails a rethinking of the subject in terms of the unconscious that is both multifaceted and complex. While it decouples the subject from the ego and ties it to the symbolic realm, the subject is always conditioned by the lack inherent in its own desire, symbolic relations and the existence of the real. However, Lacan does not just decentre the subject from a foundational position; he rethinks the subject in terms of a function rather than substance, with this function being primarily symbolic but also linked to the identity of the ego and the lack of the real. As a consequence, he concludes that '[t]he subject goes far beyond what is experienced "subjectively" by the individual'.[104]

In relation to the question of agency permitted by this account, it must be admitted that this was a difficult issue for Lacan and continues to be so for Lacanian theory. When Jean Hyppolite questioned whether his symbolic account of the subject was sufficient to 'resolve the question of the choices man has made', Lacan initially met his question with agreement before dismissing Hyppolite's concern as just 'the problem of origins', which he claimed to care little for: 'I wasn't trying to tell you that I believed that language was in the beginning – I know nothing of origins.'[105] This response may make it appear as if Lacan has no account of agency, but simply offers a description of the subject and nothing more.

The problem is that, in a number of other places, Lacan does make statements that permit the subject to act: in *Seminar I*, for example, he explains that '[a]ll human beings share in the universe of symbols. They are included in it and submit to it, much more than they constitute it. They are much more its supports than its agents.'[106] He is of course emphasising the influence of the symbolic, but he also specifically allows room for agency so that the subject can shape and influence the symbolic. Furthermore, in *Seminar II*, he demands action and hence agency from those participating: 'What you should do, on the contrary, is open your minds to the notions being generated by another domain of experience, and turn it to your own profit.'[107] This indicates that those listening should fight against the 'resistance'[108] that they encounter when they first hear his theories, resistance that arises because his ideas are opposed to those that accord with their symbolic universe. Such action requires significant agency on the part of his listeners. And, indeed, we should not forget that the clinical practice of psychoanalysis requires agency in the form of the patient working through repressions to uncover the 'cause'. Even if this is, as Lacan claims, simply so that the patient recognises his unconscious desires,[109] such working out requires intentional participation and action by the subject.

Lacan does, then, permit and indeed demand intentional agency from the subject. The problem is that although he holds that the subject is unconscious – but not reducible to the unconscious – and conditioned but not determined by the symbolic (in no small part because of the real), thereby pointing to the possibility of intentional agency, he is not clear about what such agency actually entails or, indeed, where it is located. If it is not conscious or unconscious and is not synonymous with the symbolic Other, it is difficult to see where, within Lacan's conceptual framework, it is located. In a similar vein to Butler, his schema accounts for the *space* from the symbolic that permits agency, but does not clearly explain how the unconscious subject (if, indeed, it is the subject) of this space is able to choose – if it is, indeed, a choice – to intentionally act independently from (but always within) the symbolic, especially when he is clear that the symbolic is dominant. Remedying this necessitates a more precise explanation of how the unconscious subject acts and how symbolic relations condition those actions. This requires that we move beyond Lacan. For this reason, the final two chapters engage with two responses to his theory, first by turning to Julia Kristeva's rethinking of the subject in terms of what she calls the semiotic and agency in terms of revolt, before in the final chapter moving to the thought of Cornelius Castoriadis.

Notes

1. It is important to note that Lacan distinguishes between 'two *others*, at least two – an other with a capital *O*, and an other with a small *o*, which is the ego. In the function of speech, we are concerned with the Other' (Jacques Lacan, *Seminar II: The Ego in Freud's Theory and in the Technique of Psychoanalysis*, ed. Jacques-Alain Miller, trans. Sylvana Tomaselli [New York: W. W. Norton, 1991], p. 236). In other words, the *other* refers to a particular ego-other, whereas the *Other* refers to the differential relations inherent in language, discourse, norms and everything that Lacan calls the symbolic order.
2. Dany Nobus, 'That Obscure Object of Psychoanalysis', *Continental Philosophy Review*, 46.2, 2013, pp. 163–87 (p. 178); Bruce Fink, *The Lacanian Subject: Between Language and Jouissance* (Princeton, NJ: Princeton University Press, 1995), p. xi.
3. Lorenzo Chiesa, *Subjectivity and Otherness: A Philosophical Reading of Lacan* (Cambridge, MA: MIT Press, 2007), p. 5; Yannis Stavrakakis, *Lacan and the Political* (Abingdon: Routledge, 1999), p. 13.
4. Eve Tavor Banner, *Structuralism and the Logic of Dissent* (Urbana, IL: University of Illinois Press, 1989), p. 20; Mikkel Borch-Jacobsen, *Lacan: The Absolute Master*, trans. Douglas Brick (Stanford, CA: Stanford University Press, 1991), p. 195; Jean-Luc Nancy and Philippe Lacoue-Labarthe, *The Title of the Letter: A Reading of Lacan*, trans. François Raffoul and David Pettigrew (Albany, NY: State University of New York Press, 1992), p. 69.
5. Chiesa, *Subjectivity and Otherness*, p. 6.
6. Stavrakakis, *Lacan and the Political*, p. 35.
7. Fink, *The Lacanian Subject*, p. 46.
8. Pluth maintains that in the early seminars, Lacan defines the subject in terms of the movement of the symbolic chain rather than any form of meaning itself. In the ninth seminar, however, the subject is understood to be an organising principle that has meaning via the Other, while in the fourteenth seminar, the subject is understood as the *between* that unites the various parts of a system. See Ed Pluth, *Signifiers and Acts: Freedom in Lacan's Theory of the Subject* (Albany, NY: State University of New York Press, 2007), pp. 90–1.
9. Ed Pluth, 'Lacan's Subversion of the Subject', *Continental Philosophy Review*, 39.3, 2006, pp. 293–312 (p. 303).
10. Pluth, *Signifiers and Acts*, p. 6.
11. Zupančič, *Ethics of the Real*, p. 35.
12. Pluth, *Signifiers and Acts*, p. 94.
13. Lacan, *Seminar II*, p. 68.
14. Jacques Lacan, *Seminar III: The Psychoses*, ed. Jacques-Alain Miller, trans. Russell Grigg (New York: W. W. Norton, 1997), p. 287.
15. René Descartes, *Meditations on First Philosophy*, ed. and trans. John Cottingham (Cambridge: Cambridge University Press, 1986), pp. 16–23.

16. Jacques Lacan, 'Position of the Unconscious', in *Écrits*, trans. Bruce Fink in collaboration with Héloïse Fink and Russell Grigg (New York: W. W. Norton, 2006), pp. 703-21 (p. 705).
17. Lacan, *Seminar II*, p. 7.
18. Jacques Lacan, *Seminar V: Formations of the Unconscious*, ed. Jacques-Alain Miller, trans. Russell Grigg (Cambridge: Polity, 2017), p. 96.
19. Lacan, *Seminar II*, p. 48
20. Ibid., p. 48.
21. Jacques Lacan, 'The Subversion of the Subject and the Dialectic of Desire', in *Écrits*, trans. Bruce Fink in collaboration with Héloïse Fink and Russell Grigg (New York: W. W. Norton, 2006), pp. 671-702 (p. 685).
22. Lacan, *Seminar II*, p. 6.
23. Ibid., p. 8.
24. Ibid., p. 122.
25. Jacques Lacan, 'Introduction to Jean Hyppolite's Commentary on Freud's "Verneinung"', in *Écrits*, trans. Bruce Fink in collaboration with Héloïse Fink and Russell Grigg (New York: W. W. Norton, 2006), pp. 308-17 (p. 310).
26. Jacques Lacan, *Seminar I: Freud's Papers on Technique*, ed. Jacques-Alain Miller, trans. John Forrester (New York: W. W. Norton, 1991), p. 62.
27. Lacan, *Seminar II*, p. 13.
28. Lionel Bailly, *Lacan* (London: OneWorld, 2009), p. 38.
29. Ibid., pp. 38-9.
30. Jacques Lacan, 'Some Reflections on the Ego', *International Journal of Psychoanalysis*, 34.1, 1953, pp. 11-17 (p. 14).
31. Ibid., p. 14.
32. Ibid., p. 15.
33. Lacan, *Seminar I*, p. 79.
34. It is important to note that, despite the heteronormative language, which is found throughout Freudian psychoanalysis, the terms 'mother' and 'father' refer to functions rather than necessarily to actual individuals. To simplify dramatically, 'mother' refers to love and care, whereas 'father' refers to discipline or law.
35. Lacan, 'Some Reflections on the Ego', p. 14.
36. Jacques Lacan, 'The Mirror Stage as Formative of the *I* Function', in *Écrits*, trans. Bruce Fink in collaboration with Héloïse Fink and Russell Grigg (New York: W. W. Norton, 2006), pp. 75-81 (p. 76).
37. Lacan, *Seminar I*, p. 193.
38. Lacan, 'Some Reflections on the Ego', p. 15.
39. Lacan, *Seminar I*, p. 141.
40. Bert Oliviers, 'Lacan's Subject: the Imaginary, Language, the Real and Philosophy', *South Africa Journal of Philosophy*, 23.1, 2004, pp. 1-19 (p. 5).
41. Lacan, 'The Mirror Stage as Formative of the *I* Function', p. 76.
42. Lacan, *Seminar II*, p. 41.
43. Ibid., p. 210.

44. Lacan, 'Position of the Unconscious', p. 708.
45. Lacan, *Seminar II*, pp. 321–2.
46. Louis Sass, 'Lacan, Foucault, and the "Crisis of the Subject": Revisionist Reflections on Phenomenology and Post-structuralism', *Philosophy, Psychiatry, Psychology*, 21.4, 2014, pp. 325–41 (p. 333).
47. Jacques Lacan, 'The Function and Field of Speech and Language in Psychoanalysis', in *Écrits*, trans. Bruce Fink in collaboration with Héloïse Fink and Russell Grigg (New York: W. W. Norton, 2006), pp. 197–268.
48. Ibid., p. 221.
49. Ibid., p. 231.
50. Bailly, *Lacan*, p. 43.
51. Lacan, 'The Function and Field of Speech and Language in Psychoanalysis', p. 248.
52. Saussure, *Course in General Linguistics*, p. 118.
53. Jacques Lacan, 'Response to Jean Hyppolite's Commentary on Freud's "Verneinung"', in *Écrits*, trans. Bruce Fink in collaboration with Héloïse Fink and Russell Grigg (New York: W. W. Norton, 2006), pp. 318–33 (p. 327).
54. Lacan, *Seminar II*, p. 38.
55. Lacan, *Seminar I*, p. 225.
56. Jacques Lacan, 'The Instance of the Letter in the Unconscious, or Reason since Freud', in *Écrits*, trans. Bruce Fink in collaboration with Héloïse Fink and Russell Grigg (New York: W. W. Norton, 2006), pp. 412–41 (p. 419).
57. Ibid., p. 418.
58. Lacan, *Seminar V*, p. 92.
59. Slavoj Žižek, 'The Abyss of Freedom', in Slavoj Žižek and F. W. J. Schelling, *The Abyss of Freedom/Ages of the World* (Ann Arbor, MI: University of Michigan Press, 1997), pp. 1–104 (p. 43).
60. Lacan, 'Position of the Unconscious', p. 712.
61. Lacan, *Seminar III*, p. 119.
62. Jacques Lacan, *Seminar XX: On Feminine Sexuality, The Limits of Love and Knowledge*, ed. Jacques-Alain Miller, trans. Bruce Fink (New York: W. W. Norton, 1999), p. 15.
63. Bailly, *Lacan*, p. 48.
64. Lacan, *Seminar I*, p. 54.
65. Jacques Lacan, 'Seminar on the "Purloined Letter"', in *Écrits*, trans. Bruce Fink in collaboration with Héloïse Fink and Russell Grigg (New York: W. W. Norton, 2006), pp. 6–50 (p. 8).
66. Ibid., p. 8.
67. Lacan, *Seminar II*, pp. 198–9.
68. Ibid., p. 38.
69. Cornelius Castoriadis, 'From the Monad to Autonomy', in *World in Fragments: Writings on Politics, Society, Psychoanalysis, and the Imagination*, ed. and trans. David Ames Curtis (Stanford, CA: Stanford University Press, 1997), pp. 172–95 (p. 185).

70. Lacan, 'Position of the Unconscious', pp. 704, 708.
71. Lacan, *Seminar I*, pp. 157–8.
72. Ibid., p. 155.
73. Lacan, *Seminar II*, p. 69.
74. Jacques Lacan, *Seminar XI: The Four Fundamental Concepts of Psychoanalysis*, ed. Jacques-Alain Miller, trans. Alan Sheridan (New York: W. W. Norton, 1981), p. 131, italics in the original.
75. Ibid., p. 214.
76. Lacan, *Seminar III*, p. 96.
77. Lacan, 'The Subversion of the Subject and the Dialectic of Desire', p. 688.
78. Lacan, *Seminar V*, p. 165.
79. Ibid., p. 165.
80. Mark Bracher, 'On the Psychological and Social Functions of Language: Lacan's Theory of the Four Discourses', in Mark Bracher, Marshall W. Alcorn, Jr, Ronald J. Corthell and Françoise Massardier-Kenney (eds), *Lacanian Theory of Discourse: Subject, Structure, and Society* (New York: New York University Press, 1994), pp. 107–28 (p. 112).
81. Lacan, *Seminar V*, p. 81.
82. Lacan explains that 'I have already spoken to you about the desire for something Other – not as you feel it at the moment, perhaps, the desire to go out and eat a sausage rather than listen to me, but at any rate, and whatever it's about, the desire for something Other as such' (ibid., p. 160).
83. Lacan, *Seminar I*, p. 146.
84. Banner, *Structuralism and the Logic of Dissent*, p. 20.
85. Borch-Jacobsen, *Lacan: The Absolute Master*, p. 195.
86. Nancy and Lacoue-Labarthe, *The Title of the Letter*, p. 65.
87. Ibid., p. 69.
88. Ibid., p. 63.
89. Lacan, 'Seminar on the "Purloined Letter"', p. 34.
90. Lacan, 'Position of the Unconscious', p. 708.
91. Lacan, *Seminar II*, p. 192.
92. Lacan, *Seminar V*, p. 96.
93. Lacan, *Seminar XX*, p. 15, italics added.
94. While Lacan's writings focus on the imaginary, the symbolic and then the real, it is a mistake to hold that the three registers exist in a hierarchy. The three registers are entwined in a Borromean knot with the binding point called the 'sinthome'. See Jacques Lacan, *Seminar XXIII: The Sinthome*, ed. Jacques-Alain Miller, trans. A. R. Price (Cambridge: Polity, 2016), p. 11.
95. Lacan, *Seminar I*, p. 66.
96. Louis Sass, 'Lacan: The Mind of the Modernist', *Continental Philosophy Review*, 48.4, 2015, pp. 409–43 (p. 431).
97. Lacan, *Seminar I*, p. 86; Jacques Lacan, 'The Triumph of Religion', in *The Triumph of Religion, preceded by Discourse to Catholics*, trans. Bruce Fink (Cambridge: Polity, 2013), pp. 55–85 (p. 76); Lacan, *Seminar XX*, p. 131.

98. Fink, *The Lacanian Subject*, p. 24.
99. Ibid., p. 24.
100. Ibid., p. 24.
101. Badredine Arfi, 'Reconfiguring the (Lacanian) Real: Saying the Real (as Khôra – χώρα) qua the impossible-possible event', *Philosophy and Social Criticism*, 38.8, 2012, pp. 793–819 (p. 803).
102. Ibid., p. 803.
103. Ibid., p. 803.
104. Lacan, 'The Function and Field of Speech and Language in Psychoanalysis', p. 219.
105. Lacan, *Seminar II*, pp. 35, 36, 293.
106. Lacan, *Seminar I*, p. 157.
107. Lacan, *Seminar II*, p. 41.
108. Ibid., p. 41.
109. Ibid., pp. 228–9.

CHAPTER 7

Kristeva on the Subject of Revolt: The Symbolic and the Semiotic

While admitting that Lacan 'was brilliant' and 'a friend', Julia Kristeva offers a sustained and radical critique of his conceptual framework and, by extension, his concept of the subject.[1] She claims that, despite his protestations to the contrary, Lacan proposes 'a theory of the subject as a divided unity which arises from and is determined by lack (void, nothingness, zero, according to the context)', before going on to explain that '[t]his subject, which we will call the "unitary subject," under the law of One, which turns out to be the Name-of-the-Father, this subject of filiation or subject-son, is in fact the unvoiced part'.[2] There are two aspects to this that Kristeva finds troubling. First, while he affirms a divided subject, Lacan is charged with implicitly encasing this division within a unity, with the consequence that he remains bound to and perpetuates the privileging of unity inherent in the Cartesian tradition. Second, Kristeva points out that the Lacanian subject is an effect of the repression imposed on it by the symbolic father, a conceptualisation that radically downplays the role of the mother in fostering the child and, indeed, offers a troublingly one-dimensional account of the father that sees 'him' only in terms of authority.

To correct this, she continues to affirm the psychoanalytic division between the unconscious and conscious, but complicates the ways in which these two 'realms' are conceptualised and, indeed, how they relate to one another. To do so, she first turns away from Lacan's insistence that the unconscious is structured like language to Freud's insight that the unconscious is tied to drives.[3] These drives are differentiated and in constant, heterogeneous movement, thereby disrupting any notion of a fixed foundation for the subject. For Kristeva, it is the drives, not language, that 'introduce' difference 'into' the psyche.[4]

Second, she criticises Lacan's claim that language is tied to the symbolic, which she understands to entail conceptual signification, instead holding that symbolic language is tied to another form of non-conceptual signification, termed the 'semiotic'.[5] More specifically, this refers to 'the "unconscious" language found in children's echolalia before the appearance of signs and syntax, and especially in the discourse we receive as aesthetic (poetry, literature, painting, music, which redistribute logical categories under the pressure of oppositional processes)'.[6] Whereas Lacan holds that the symbolic, real and imaginary are intertwined, Kristeva insists that he privileges the symbolic to maintain that it 'underpins' the real and imaginary. From this (mis)reading, she inverts the relation so that the semiotic, understood to entail a combination of the Lacanian real (= what does not conform to conceptualisation) and imaginary (including what she calls the imaginary father), precedes the symbolic.[7] For Kristeva, then, the semiotic combines aspects of the Lacanian real and imaginary *and* is conceptually not just experientially prior to the symbolic. Crucially, the semiotic is tied to the distribution of drives as they attempt to manifest themselves discursively, a position that reveals that the linguistic, in both its semiotic and symbolic forms, is tied to the non-discursive.

Third, Kristeva ties the semiotic to the mother and so claims that it is the maternal, not the paternal as she holds that Lacan maintains, that is fundamental to the development of the linguistic capacity of the child.[8] This, in turn, requires a rethinking of the relationship between the mother and father functions, including a reconceptualisation of the latter. Whereas Lacan holds that the child has to learn to obey the symbolic Law/Name-of-the-Father to function properly within the symbolic realm, Kristeva objects that this not only produces a one-dimensional account of the father function, but also does not explain how the child moves from the pre-symbolic imaginary register where it lacks conceptual language to the symbolic realm where it is capable of such language. To rectify this, she insists on a mediating function between the maternal semiotic and the paternal symbolic functions, calls this the 'imaginary father', and associates it with love rather than law.[9]

The function of the imaginary father is to coax the psyche away from the abjected semiotic mother towards the symbolic paternal law. It therefore provides the mediation between the pre-symbolic and symbolic that she claims is lacking from Lacan's account. As a consequence, the psyche is marked by a threefold process of abjection (of the mother), identification (with the imaginary father and subsequently with the symbolic father) and mourning (for the loss of the abjected mother). From these, Kristeva develops the notion of the 'subject-in-process',[10] wherein the subject is defined by a continuous becoming resulting from the complex interaction between the drives, semiotic flows, symbolic relations and social norms.

Having outlined the basic parameters of her thinking on the subject to identify that it affirms a complex amalgamation, I show how this feeds through to her political analysis and, in particular, her critique of the impact that contemporary capitalist society has on the psyche. Kristeva holds that, historically, the psyche was defined by negativity, which meant that the subject was bound to social norms but was also always divorced in some way from them. This divorce was crucial to permit the subject to express itself. Kristeva warns, however, that contemporary capitalist society has undermined this negative space, with the consequence that psychic 'freedom' has shrunk. Her solution is to search for new forms of revolt to reopen the division between the psyche and social so that, in particular, semiotic, non-conceptual forms of language can find expression.

It is here that the question of agency enters her analysis. As a psychoanalyst, there is no question that Kristeva thinks that the subject is capable of agency to rectify its situation. However, within her theoretical framework, there is no explicit analysis of agency or discussion of where it fits into her schema. For example, if the subject is in constant change, where is the site of agency to direct that process? Indeed, if the subject-in-process is an effect of unconscious drives and semiotic flows, how can it choose how they are made manifest, especially if, as she claims, contemporary capitalist society is so encompassing as to close the psychic space that might permit this? This has given rise to debate in the literature between those[11] who defend Kristeva by claiming that she does *implicitly* offer a theory of agency that shows how the subject can effect social change, and those[12] who claim that she does not. I side with the latter by arguing that the former do not actually identify what agency entails for Kristeva but simply conflate it with her theory of the subject-in-process. While this reveals that Kristeva affirms a conception of agency, I conclude that her notion of the subject-in-process is too thin and conceptually blunt to adequately account for it.

Rethinking Signification and the Subject

Kristeva situates her thought firmly within the psychoanalytic tradition, explaining that she 'will make constant use of notions and concepts borrowed from Freudian psychoanalysis and its various recent developments'.[13] These include the work of Melanie Klein, but more often than not that of Lacan. Far from being Lacan's 'dutiful daughter',[14] her relationship to Lacan is one of critical appropriation that, somewhat ironically given Lacan's insistence on such a return, is premised on a return to Freud. Her engagement with Lacan is, then, one that occurs through a Freudian lens.

Specifically, she accepts Lacan's claim that Freudian psychoanalysis is tied to language, but goes beyond him by identifying three linguistic phases within Freud's work, conforming to three conceptions of signification. The first phase, corresponding to the writings from approximately 1892 to 1899, is tied to the study of aphasia and focuses on drives and psychic energy, with language being the intermediary stage that brings these drives to thought.[15] The second stage runs from approximately 1900 to 1912 and is structured around the unconscious/conscious division, with language being found in the former and expressed in the latter. Kristeva argues that '[i]t is on this theory that Lacan will later rely to construct his own theory'.[16] She points out, however, that there is a third model, found in the writings after 1912, that is orientated around what she will call *'signifiance'*.[17] This refers to the mediating movement that brings the unconscious drives to symbolic representation. Through this, '[t]he goal that Freud set himself was not to define language but to open psychoanalysis to a vaster process of symbolisation in which language had its place but was not the common denominator'.[18] This schematic and these insights set the stage for the development of her own theory in which she accepts the unconscious/conscious split, but disagrees with Lacan that the unconscious is structured like a language; following Freud, 'the unconscious is pure drive'[19] that is initially expressed non-conceptually or semiotically before potentially becoming conceptual and symbolic. To understand this, we need first to unpack the relationship between the drives and language.

For Kristeva, the child is born with drives, which are '[e]nergetic but already semiotic charges, "junctures of the psychic and somatic" [that] extract the body from its homogeneous shell and turn it into a space linked to the outside'.[20] Importantly, the drives run 'across the body and the immediate environment in a logically a-representative rhythm'.[21] While they bind and organise, the drives do 'not attain a representation of the object opposite the coagulated presence of the subject'.[22] Rather, they conform to a pre-verbal logic that 'structures the space in which the subject-object separation will be set up'.[23] For this to happen, the 'expulsion [of the drives] runs through the totalizing receptacle, the *chora* (Artaud's "gyrations of fire"), fragmenting it, cutting it up, rearranging it, and traversing the subject who is present in an "absent point," a "dead kernel," with "total lucidity"'.[24] From this, we see that not only is Kristeva's subject always embodied, but symbolic language arises from the way in which the expulsion of the drives is cut up by the *chora*.

Kristeva subsequently rejects this term, but it is key to understanding her early work on language and its relation to the drives. Borrowed from Plato's *Timaeus*, *chora* denotes 'an essentially mobile and extremely provisional articulation constituted by movements and their ephemeral stases'.[25] While she aims to describe the *chora*, Kristeva is quick to point out that 'the *chora*, as rupture and articulations (rhythm), precedes evidence, verisimilitude, spatiality, and temporality'.[26] 'The *chora* is not yet a position that represents something for someone (i.e. it is not a sign); nor is it a *position* that represents someone for another position (i.e. it is not yet a signifier either)',[27] but it is from the *chora* that all positionality, representation and signification arise and depend.

Crucially, however, the *chora* is devoid of law; it does not conform to a pre-established format. This is not to say, however, that it is simply anarchic; 'its vocal and gestural organization is subject to what we shall call an objective *ordering* [*ordonnancement*] which is dictated by natural or socio-historical constraints such as the biological difference between the sexes or family structure'.[28] The *chora* underpins representation, but its expression is channelled through and organised by the expulsion of the drives and the socio-historical constraints that it exists within. Rather than a linear progression from biology through language to the socio-historical, Kristeva points to a complex interaction between all three that is mediated through the structuring of the *chora*; a structuring that is specific to each child.

The *chora* is, however, specifically tied to language through the process of 'signifiance'[29] that describes the

> unlimited and unbounded generating process, this unceasing operation of the drives toward, in, and through language; toward, in, and through the exchange system and its protagonists – the subject and his institutions. This heterogeneous process, neither anarchic, fragmented foundation nor schizophrenic blockage, is a structuring and de-structuring *practice*, a passage to the outer *boundaries* of the subject and society.[30]

Signifiance describes, then, the heterogeneous process through which the drives find expression in and through language. It is the mediation between the two.

However, to fulfil this role requires 'a linguistics capable, within its language object, of accounting for a nonetheless articulated *instinctual drive*, across and through the constitutive and insurmountable frontier of *meaning*'.[31] It will be remembered that, for Lacan, the lack constitutive of desire arises from the 'gap' between biological need and the linguistic demand used to express that need. Kristeva, however, questions the logic subtending Lacan's conception, claiming that he relies on a one-dimensional account of language – where it is always symbolic and so conceptual – that ensures that there must be a gap between need and linguistic demand. She suggests that there is another form of linguistic expression found through the *chora* that expresses itself in the same rhythmic way as the drives. Thus, whereas she understands that Lacan limits linguistic expression to symbolic forms, which Kristeva understands to entail conceptual language, she insists that prior to conceptualisation lies another form of non-conceptual linguistic expression. With this, she distinguishes between conceptual *symbolic* signification and non-conceptual *semiotic* signification.

It is important to note, however, that the distinction between the two is not absolute. Rather, they

> designate *two modalities* of what is, for us, the same signifying process . . . These two modalities are inseparable within the *signifying process* that constitutes language and the dialectic between them determines the type of discourse (narrative, metalanguage, theory, poetry, etc.), involved.[32]

The semiotic is understood 'in its Greek sense: σημεῖον = distinctive mark, trace, index, precursory sign, proof, engraved or written sign, imprint, trace, figuration'.[33] Within the framework of Freudian psychoanalysis, '[t]his modality . . . points to not only the *facilitation* and the structuring *disposition* of drives, but also the so-called *primary processes* which displace and condense both energies and their inscription'.[34] These 'are arranged according to the various constraints imposed on the body – always already involved in a semiotic process – by family and social structures',[35] with this arrangement giving rise to the specific *chora* of each individual.

Crucially, the semiotic distribution of drives is defined by flows and marks rather than symbols. For this reason, semiotic expression is defined by 'a pre-verbal functional state that governs the connections between the body (in the process of constituting itself as a body proper), objects, and the protagonists of family structure'.[36] That it is pre-verbal does not, however, mean that it lacks signification. It is simply defined by a specific form of signification: 'Indifferent to language, enigmatic and feminine, this space underlying the written is rhythmic, unfettered, irreducible to its intelligible verbal translation; it is musical, anterior to judgement, but restrained by a single guarantee: syntax.'[37] Rather than being clear and objective, the semiotic 'introduces wandering or fuzziness into language',[38] to the extent that it 'is best realized in dance, gestural theatre or painting, rather than in words'.[39]

With the notion of the semiotic *chora*, Kristeva makes an important contribution to semiology and psychoanalytical theory, in so far as she explicitly distinguishes between conceptual and non-conceptual forms of signification and ties the latter to the drives. She also notes that the semiotic has implications for the subject: 'Our positing of the semiotic is obviously inseparable from a theory of the subject that takes into account the

Freudian positing of the unconscious.'[40] The Kristevan subject is not a 'transcendental subject'[41] or unity, because she maintains that this lacks the division between the unconscious and conscious and 'the symbolic order [and] the libido (this last revealing itself by the *semiotic disposition*)'.[42] The unconscious semiotic *chora* is a process of continuous change, both due to its own rhythms and flows and the constant interruption of the drives subtending it. There is, then, a constant disruptive flow to the semiotic, whose '*pre-meaning* and *pre-signs* (or *trans-meaning*, *trans-sign*)'[43] continuously break up static conceptual symbolic meaning. It also, of course, 'bring[s] us back to processes of division in the living matter of an organism subject to biological constraints as well as social norms'.[44] It is only because the semiotic flows continue to upset and disrupt the symbolic order that 'the speaking subject' can renew 'the order in which he is inescapably caught up'.[45] On Kristeva's telling, then, creativity and the new are tied up with the functioning of the semiotic.

Importantly, the Kristevan subject is always in-process, although, strictly speaking, the subject is only produced once the child moves from the semiotic to the symbolic. It is only in the symbolic that the hard and fast conceptual divisions that are absent from the semiotic and that allow the subject to oppose itself to an object – and so recognise itself as something (non-objective) – are created. The movement from the ill-defined rhythmic fuzziness of the semiotic to the conceptual distinctions of the symbolic arises because the psyche passes through an intermediary stage, which is termed, conceptually speaking, the 'thetic'[46] and, clinically speaking, the 'imaginary father'.[47] I will deal with the former here and the latter in the subsequent section.

The 'thetic phase marks a threshold between two heterogeneous realms: the semiotic and the symbolic'.[48] The fundamental role of the thetic function is to break the semiotic into segments to establish 'the *identification* of the subject and its object as preconditions of propositionality'.[49] In other words, while the semiotic is constantly differentiating, it operates through flows and rhythms. For these to be turned into conceptual language requires that the rhythmic division be turned into object-form, with this thereby establishing the subject/object division constitutive of conceptual thought/language. It is the thetic that performs this function and so permits the transition from pre-signifying speech to signifying symbolic speech. For this reason, Kristeva maintains that the thetic phase is key to the development of the psyche:

> [T]he Freudian theory of the unconscious and its Lacanian development show, precisely, that thetic signification is a stage attained under certain precise conditions during the signifying process, and that it constitutes the subject without being reduced to this process precisely because it is the threshold of language.[50]

Specifically, Kristeva explains that the thetic phase is organised by and orientated around 'two points: the mirror stage and the "discovery" of castration'.[51] The first is important because it 'produces the "spatial intuition" which is found at the heart of the functioning of signification – in signs and in sentences'.[52] Having seen and recognised himself in a mirror, the child must 'capture his image unified in a mirror [and] must remain separate from it'.[53] Kristeva holds that these two separations (from itself and the object posited as itself) 'prepare the way for the sign [which] can be conceived as the voice that is projected from the agitated body (from the semiotic *chora*) onto the facing *imago* or onto the object, which simultaneously detach from the surrounding continuity'.[54] The positing of the voice, including all the separations it entails, initiates a break from the rhythmic semiotic *chora* and the instantiation of 'signification . . . as a digital system with a double articulation combining discrete elements'.[55] For this reason, language learning is a violent process constituted by 'an acute and dramatic confrontation between positing-separating-identifying and the motility of the semiotic *chora*'.[56]

'Castration puts the finishing touches on the process of separation that posits the subject as signifiable, which is to say, separate, always confronted by an other: *imago* in the mirror (signified) and semiotic process (signifier).'[57] This refers back to Freud's theory of the phallus, which holds that initially the child takes its mother's body to be the source of all pleasure, with the consequence that the mother's body is the centre of its world; 'she is, in other words, the phallus'.[58] 'Phallus' in Freud psychoanalysis refers not to a bodily part but to a function designating foundationality or the centre from and to which all refers. It is the anchor point of psychic life. The problem is that, while the mother is initially taken to be the phallus, the child gradually learns that she desires another (i.e. the father), depends upon that other, and so lacks the phallus. She is, in other words, castrated. 'The discovery of castration . . . detaches the subject from his dependence on his mother, and the perception of this lack [*manque*] makes the phallic function a symbolic function – *the* symbolic function.'[59] The child recognises that the lack identified with the mother refers to an abstract rather than actual function.

Through this abstraction, the child learns to identify the phallus (desired by the mother) with an abstract father figure rather than an immediate mother figure, and so moves from identification with immediate, physical relations to identification with abstract, symbolic ones. With this, the psyche moves from the semiotic to the symbolic and so is able to distinguish 'between signifier and signified'.[60] The symbolic therefore refers to a divided unity, wherein two signs gain meaning from the difference between them and so are always united in their difference. For this reason, 'the "symbol" is any joining, any bringing together that is a contract – one that either follows hostilities or presupposes them – and, finally, any exchange, including an exchange of hostility'.[61]

The transition from the semiotic to the symbolic is not, however, a linear one, with the former disappearing once the latter is instantiated. As the condition of the symbolic, the semiotic *chora* 'disturbs the thetic position by redistributing the signifying order'.[62] This has given rise to considerable debate in the literature regarding the relationship between the semiotic and symbolic. For example, while she recognises that there is no straightforward linear movement from the semiotic to the symbolic, Judith Butler claims that Kristeva 'concedes that the semiotic is invariably subordinate to the Symbolic'[63] because it is only through the symbolic that the semiotic can be understood. On this reading, Kristeva merely complicates Lacan's privileging of the symbolic rather than fundamentally breaking from it.

Butler's reading has, however, been criticised for conflating the analytical distinction between the semiotic and symbolic with the phenomenological entwinement of both and, more specifically, reducing the latter to the former. Whereas her formulation is correct in the sense that *describing* the semiotic depends upon the symbolic, in the actual diachronic functioning of the semiotic–symbolic relation, Tina Chanter explains that

> [t]he semiotic/symbolic distinction is not offered as a mutually exclusive one. Semiotic meaning can only emerge retroactively, and can only be expressed within the terms of the symbolic. That does not mean that the semiotic can be reduced to the symbolic – it also offers resistance to symbolic expression. It erupts into and explodes onto the symbolic scene. Transgressing and destabilising the operation of language, the effect of the semiotic cannot be entirely erased, sublated, or cancelled out. Its effects will be inscribed in language, but as the other side of language – as traces, residues, marks – rather than as systems, concepts, or meanings.[64]

On Chanter's reading, therefore, the semiotic and symbolic exist in dialectical entwinement, albeit one in which the semiotic 'precedes' the symbolic.

Cecilia Sjöholm takes this one step further by rejecting the notion of a developmental progression between the two: 'The fact that the semiotic and *chora* belong to a pre-Oedipal dimension does not mean that they are to be considered developmental stages preceding the Oedipal construction of the symbolic.'[65] For Sjöholm, the semiotic and symbolic are always intimately connected and present to/'in' the psyche. Again, this seems to conflate the analytical distinction with the phenomenological one, albeit by reducing the former to the latter. After all, clinically speaking, Kristeva is clear that there is a specific developmental process that the child goes through, with entrance into the symbolic occurring from and *after* the semiotic. However, once the symbolic is instantiated, it is true that it does not lie on top of the semiotic; a dialectical relation between the two is formed wherein, as Sjöholm puts it, 'the semiotic ... indicates a resistance at work in the signifying process'.[66] Confirming this, Kristeva explains that '[a]lthough originally a precondition of the symbolic, the semiotic functions within signifying practices as the result of a transgression of the symbolic'.[67] This occurs because the semiotic is constantly changing due to the drives conditioning 'it' being expulsed in different ways to disrupt the semiotic *chora* upon which the symbolic depends.

One of the key implications of this structure is that prior to the acceptance of the paternal symbolic law lies the pre-symbolic maternal semiotic *chora*. Therefore, rather than simply holding that the maternal semiotic function is overtaken once the child enters the symbolic, Kristeva continues to emphasise the importance of the semiotic maternal. This is, as Rachel Widansky explains, because, '[f]or Kristeva, the mother represents something heterogeneous that can never be full tamed because she is the source and the aim of the drives, because she is the foundation of the object relation, and because she is at the junction of the physical and the psychological'.[68] Tying the semiotic to both the mother and chaos seems to depend upon and reinstate a long-standing patriarchal division where the symbolic father is associated with order and reason, and the semiotic mother is tied to chaos and irrationality, but Kristeva insists that the movement from the semiotic to the symbolic rests on the semiotic *chora*, with the consequence that it is where the subject-in-process 'is both generated and negated'[69] and so renewed.

Kristeva's analysis of the relationship between the semiotic and symbolic is important because it draws together the various strands that underpin her theory of the subject. The child is defined by drives that are first articulated semiotically before being thetically divided into the symbolic. The unconscious semiotic *chora*, itself continually divided and stratified by the drives, is the site from where the subject is generated and, indeed, continuously undermined and remodelled. In turn, this process is also tied to and influenced by the social norms wherein it takes place. These determine how the *chora* will find expression symbolically. From this, the subject becomes manifest at the level of the symbolic and is therefore always a 'speaking subject'.[70] However, this speaking subject is not a substance, 'a phenomenological transcendental ego nor the Cartesian ego but rather a *subject in process [sujet en procés]*',[71] defined by a continuous and complex interplay between the drives, unconscious semiotic and conscious symbolic forms of expression, and social norms.

Psychic Development: From the Semiotic to the Symbolic

Because she ties the subject to language, Kristeva's semiotic/symbolic distinction feeds through into her account of the subject and means that she differs in an important way from Lacan in terms of how the psyche develops. For Lacan, at least as Kristeva understands him, the child is born into the symbolic – language is all around – but, in terms of its own psychic development, the child first enters the imaginary mirror stage before moving into the symbolic register by accepting the authority of the Name-of-the-Father. Kristeva complains, however, that this transition depends upon a fundamental rupture between the pre-symbolic imaginary and the symbolic registers, wherein the child suddenly and simply jumps from the former to the latter.

She argues that there are at least two problems with this. First, it fails to understand that the pre-symbolic is also constituted by a linguistic registry that takes semiotic rather than symbolic form. This obviously depends on the distinction that she makes between the two systems of signification. To move from the semiotic to the symbolic is not, then, to suddenly jump into language, but requires a *gradual transition* from non-conceptual semiotic signification to the conceptual symbolic form.

Second, Kristeva charges that Lacan depends upon a one-dimensional account of the paternal function that reduces it to law. By focusing on the way that the paternal law imposes itself on to the child to force the child into the symbolic, she argues that Lacan ignores or undermines the role that paternal love plays in coaxing the child into the symbolic. That love is associated in the Lacanian schema with the mother means that Kristeva's emphasis on paternal love re-enforces, somewhat obliquely and paradoxically, the (attributes and hence role of the) mother function in a way not found in Lacan's thinking.

The thetic function of language plays the key role in this process, which, clinically speaking, is developed through the notion of the 'imaginary father'.[72] As noted, this figure is tied to love, with the consequence that the movement from the semiotic to the symbolic is constituted by both the imposition of the symbolic law on to the child *and* a tender coaxing that brings the child towards that law. In the trilogy of works published in the 1980s – *Powers of Horror, Tales of Love* and *Black Sun* – Kristeva describes how psychic development takes place through a three-stage movement of *abjection* (of the mother), *identification* (with the imaginary and symbolic fathers) and *mourning* (for the lost mother).

For Kristeva, the child is born with drives that tie it to the mother who will (normally) be the one who fulfils its desires through her body or by supplying food, warmth, love and so on. She does so by reacting to the semiotic 'cries' and rhythms of the child. As a consequence, there is an almost symbiotic bond between the two, wherein the child takes its mother to be an extension of itself. To develop its ego, the child must effect a divorce from the mother through a process of 'abjection':[73] 'The mother object is the first result of the process of expulsion of what is disagreeable in this archaic state. In this process, which I have called abjection, the mother becomes the first "abject" rather than object.'[74]

Abjection refers to 'the twisted braid of affects and thought [that do] not have, properly speaking, a definable *object*'.[75] That which is *abject* is not an *object* because, while it appears as other, it does not conform to the static, conceptual clarity of objectivity. Whereas an object places me in relation to it, that which is abject lacks that spatial definitiveness to the extent that what 'is radically excluded . . . draws me toward the place where meaning collapses'.[76] As a consequence, abjection refers to 'what disturbs identity, system, order'.[77]

There are, however, two senses to abjection, one semiotic and one symbolic. The latter occurs once the symbolic is entered into and its oppositions taken up. With this, a number of exclusions take place: Kristeva mentions that these have historically related to certain foods,[78] foreigners[79] and women.[80] The most important for present purposes is the abjection that takes place semiotically where

> the abject confronts us . . . with our earliest attempts to release the hold of *maternal* entity even before ex-isting outside of her, thanks to the autonomy of language. It is a violent, clumsy breaking away, with the constant risk of falling back under the sway of a power as securing as it is stifling.[81]

The reason for such action arises from the child's realisation that it is not desired by the mother in the way that its initial unity with the mother led it to believe it was. As Anthony Elliott explains, 'Kristeva argues that primary objectification arises, not from the child's desire for the pre-Oedipal mother, but from an affective tie with the *mother's desire for the phallus*.'[82] Having realised that the desired mother lacks something, the child comes to grasp that the mother's desire is orientated elsewhere. As a consequence, the mother is not the phallus, but desires the phallus. Initially, the child tries to become the phallus for the mother, but once that fails it learns that it is caught between the mother and that which she desires: the paternal phallus. With this, the child is first exposed to the symbolic phallic function and so *starts* to see itself as a subject opposed to an object. The next step is to fully cut the cord binding it to the mother: 'in order to become autonomous, it is necessary that one cut the instinctual dyad of the mother and the child and that one become something other'.[83]

The abjection of the maternal function is, then, '*a precondition of narcissism*',[84] in so far as it is only by abjecting the mother that the child can start to see himself as an entity opposed to another and, in so doing, gain a sense of self. Whereas she claims that Lacan moves from the abjection of the mother to the symbolic father, Kristeva maintains that the loss of the mother is too damaging to permit such a jump. Having abjected the mother, the psyche requires another support to identify with and guide it on its journey towards the symbolic father.

It is here that Kristeva introduces the figure of the imaginary father, which is not associated with the symbolic Name-of-the-Father, but is a distinct intermediary function between the semiotic and symbolic. It is, however, 'a strange father', '[e]ndowed with the sexual attributes of both parents', in so far as it is 'a coagulation of the mother and her desire', namely the father.[85] The imaginary father is not a figure, but conforms to what Freud calls 'a father in individual prehistory'.[86] It is not a transcendental aspect of the psyche, but a function that is created and defined through the abjection of the mother, and that acts as a support as the psyche moves from the abjected semiotic mother to the *symbolic* father. Crucially, however, the love (= support) associated with the imaginary father is not the same as the love provided by the semiotic mother.[87] There is a crucial distinction between the two that permits the imaginary father to provide the support that helps the child move towards the symbolic father. If the love (= function) of the imaginary father and semiotic mother were the same, the former would be collapsed into the latter, with the consequence that the movement from the semiotic to the symbolic would be one of fundamental rupture rather than transition. For this reason, Kristeva claims, it is necessary to maintain the mother/father distinction if the 'normal' development of the child is to be realised. She therefore objects to the feminist notion that fathers should become caregivers in favour of maintaining a strict division between the sexes.[88]

Importantly, Sara Beardsworth notes that the child's entrance into the symbolic is dependent upon a number of additional stages, with Kristeva, in *Sense and Non-Sense of Revolt*, mentioning two specifically.[89] Having abjected the mother and identified with the imaginary father, the child must also enter the mirror stage which permits 'identification of the self, visible through the gap that separates us from our body and the maternal body'.[90] From this 'comes narcissism, the investment of the ego: "I" love myself, me, "I" love my image, my body',[91] before a depressive stage constituted by

> the separation from the other and the investment of hallucinatory capacities [which] functions as a sort of footbridge favouring access to signs and to the linguistic capacity that replaces the earlier symbolic equivalents. We are in the presence of the first sublimation, which becomes intrinsic to the human condition; the investment of signs is translated by a surpassing of the depression, but a jubilation: 'I' invest signs; I am happy with the pleasure that signs procure for me. The investment of language therefore necessitates a certain retreat of the libido in relation to the object: 'I' do not invest the breast, 'I' do not invest mamma; 'I' invest my own capacity to produce signs. This is the beginning of intellectual pleasure, a moment of extreme importance that continues in the sublimation subjacent to all creative activity.[92]

Following the child's initial use of and identification with signs and symbols, movement through the Oedipal complex completes its transition to the symbolic. From seeing itself as the object of the mother's desire, the child recognises that the mother desires another – the father – that, in so doing, competes against him for the mother's affection. Acknowledging its weakness in front of the father brings the child to subordinate itself to the father's (symbolic) law. With this, the role of the father changes away from its previous identification with love (as with the imaginary father) towards a law to be followed, while the child finds itself caught between its necessary adherence to the symbolic paternal law and its attempts to autonomously express itself to fulfil its narcissism: '"I" must identify myself in relation to this law at the same time that "I" must separate myself from it in order to create my own place, the site of my expression: "I" have a place of my own.'[93] By accepting the symbolic paternal law, the psyche finds itself divided between its unconscious semiotic (maternal) drives and its conscious adherence to the symbolic paternal law, with the latter being necessary to establish the child as a subject opposed to an object. Importantly, while the psyche must pass 'beyond' the symbolic law, the way in which the psyche does this shapes how the symbolic (paternal) law will appear. However, because this is all made possible by the transitory 'figure' of the imaginary father, Kristeva calls the imaginary father the 'zero degree'[94] of subjectivity.

However, while the combination of the abjection of the semiotic mother and identification with the imaginary father brings the child to the symbolic and instantiates the speaking subject, the loss of the mother haunts the psyche: 'The child king becomes irreducibly sad before uttering his first words; this is because he has been irrevocably, desperately separated from the mother, a loss that causes him to try to find her again, along with other objects of love, first in the imagination, then in words.'[95] The fundamental problem is that the mother was *abjected*, not *objected*, and so never became the object that would allow the source of loss to be identified. For this reason, the lost abject takes different forms under a non-definable and non-representable 'Thing', which 'is inscribed within us without memory',[96] and so accompanies the psyche without signification. It is the semiotic mother haunting the symbolic father.

The speaking subject is, then, caught in a bind: on the one hand, 'the loss of the mother is a biological and psychic necessity, the first step on the way to becoming autonomous'.[97] The mother must be abjected so that the psyche can develop towards the imaginary father that allows it to enter the symbolic and articulate and satisfy its drives. On the other hand, this abjection always haunts it without being definable. A negativity defines the psyche and, indeed, '[t]he psychic life of speaking beings that we are is the result of a long "working out the negative": birth, separation, frustration, various kinds of lacks – so many kinds of suffering'.[98] The negativity arising from the abjection of the mother is, then, a necessary and positive moment in the psychic development of the child, in so far as it is the first stage that permits the child autonomy. It also ensures that the subject is never a substance and is always in-process.[99]

Revolt

To this point, I have focused on outlining and examining the child's psychic development, paying particular attention to the relationship between the drives and Kristeva's conception of language. This development also obviously depends upon social relations – those with the mother and father and, indeed, the Other in general – but this aspect of her 'earlier' thought is rather implicit. It is in her later writings on revolt that Kristeva makes it explicit.

For Kristeva, revolt is not simply tied to a political act of negation: 'People have reduced, castrated and mutilated the concept of revolt by turning it only into politics.'[100] Rather than follow this trajectory, she maintains that 'it is necessary to ... give the word revolt a meaning that is not just political'.[101] To do so, she emphasises two points. First, that the word 'revolt comes from a Sanskrit root that means to discover, open, but also to turn to return'.[102] This is tied to the 'revolution of the earth around the sun [and so] has astronomical meaning, the eternal return'.[103] There is, however, a second sense that is more philosophical. Found in Plato, St Augustine, Hegel and Nietzsche, it refers to 'the idea that being is within us and that the truth can be acquainted by a retrospective return, by anamnesis, by memory'.[104] Kristeva links this return to the self and explains that '[t]he return to oneself leads the individual to question his truth, much like what is accomplished with philosophical dialogues'.[105]

While noting that Plato and St Augustine pointed to this with their conceptions of reflection and prayer respectively, she insists that 'Freud gave a new meaning to this retrospective return by asking psychologically troubled patients to search for memories of their trauma and to tell their stories'.[106] This mirrors the Plato–Augustine tradition, but departs from it by rejecting the notion 'that we can stabilise ourselves in a contemplation of God or Being. Stability is provisional.'[107] Rather than a stable unity, the fundamentality of the drives means that '[t]he individual, in this return to him or herself, experiences division, conflict, pleasure and jouissance in this fragmentation'.[108] This is not a negative occurrence, but permits the subject to try out new things and to experiment.

The problem is that contemporary society does not permit such fragmentation and the resultant interrogation and originality it facilitates: 'in the automated modern world the depth of the psychic life, the liberation of psychic life, the search for truth in the interrogation and the questioning are all aspects that are overlooked'.[109] The reason for this is structural. In a culture where '[w]e are expected to be performing entities [where] we are asked to work well and buy as much as possible', the 'whole problematic of interrogation, of the return to the self, the questioning and the conflicts that are sources of human freedom have become obliterated, rejected or even destroyed'.[110] Instead, there is a 'culture of entertainment rather than one of interrogation and revolt'.[111]

Kristeva maintains that this is amplified by a threefold crisis in the values that normally (and historically) anchor(ed) and provide(d) meaning to the subject-in-process.[112] The first is 'modern human isolation: automated and computerised work prevents affective interaction with other people and subjects people to the imperatives of abstract procedures or regulations'.[113] Second, Kristeva points to 'the ruined family unit, where the father's absence or diminished authority goes along with the unavailability of the mother, if not her depression'[114] and a society in which the spectacle dominates all.[115] As a consequence, individuals cannot obtain the stability they need from the family unit. Finally, she notes that the non-familial support that used to be available to individuals has diminished:

> [T]he weakening of religions, or their worldly or fundamentalist return, has eroded educational and moral benchmarks. It has left mostly unregulated child training, the control of sphincters, sexual differentiation as well as matters of social hierarchy and behavioural codes – table manners, respect for adults and the elderly and so on.[116]

On first reading, her critique appears to be underpinned by a particularly regressive political ethos, in which she bemoans the lack of religion (and paradoxically the over-reliance on religion) and respect for traditional forms of behaviour and authority. Indeed, she claims that authority is now nothing but a fiction in which '"the new world order" confronts us with the fluctuating "authority" of banking capitals, or rather with their virtual scripture; compared to this, the authority of the politician is a fiction and, increasingly, a caricature'.[117] Somewhat paradoxically, this reduction of (parental) authority has led and continues to lead individuals to seek authority (figures), with the consequence that '[t]he ability to judge disintegrates . . . since individuals allow the judgment of a leader or the consensus of a group to be imposed on them instead of "judging for themselves"'.[118]

We should not think, however, that, with this, Kristeva is simply glorifying a return to traditional forms of patriarchal authority. Her comments on the need for interrogation and revolt reveal that her subject-in-process is not simply one of fragmentation and division; this fragmentation must also identify with static values to preserve a *sense* of unity in fragmentation. This failure to secure a sense of identity via authoritative reference points has drastic consequences: '[T]oday's men and women – who are stress-ridden and eager to achieve, to spend money, have fun, and die – dispense with the representation of their experience that we call psychic life. Actions and their imminent abandonment have replaced the interpretation of meaning.'[119] For this reason, contemporary patients 'are different from the ones Freud saw';[120] they are afflicted by *'new malad[ies] of the soul'*.[121]

The consequences of this are profound, in so far as the autonomy of psychic life 'seems to have been taken hostage between somatic symptoms (illness and the hospital) and the placing into images of his desires (reveries in front of the TV). No more psychical life then.'[122] This is problematic because psychic life is the 'interior space, this place within, that allows one to take attacks from inside and outside, that is, physiological and biological trauma, as well as social and political aggression. The imaginary metabolises them, transforms them, subliminates them, and works on them: it keeps us alive.'[123] The closure of psychic life has, then, real impact:

> The free subject has become a mirage, and we receive on our analytic couches patients afflicted with 'false selves' (Winnicott), 'borderline' personalities (Kernberg), or 'as-if' personalities (Helene Deutsch). From weeping fits to episodes of mutism, these persons go under, sometimes to the point of suicide, in the overabundance of affects that the refusal or the impossibility of verbal communication keeps from other forms of elaboration and metabolism.[124]

This diminution of psychic life does not, however, just have individual consequences – although Kristeva is quick to point out that '[y]ou are alive if and only if you have a psychic life';[125] it also has significant socio-political impact, in so far as the inability of the subject to act autonomously forestalls the possibility of revolt: 'an essential aspect of the European culture of revolt and art is in peril . . . the very notion of culture as revolt and of art is in peril, submerged as we are in the culture of entertainment, the culture of performance, the culture of the show'.[126]

While she claims that the answers to this individual and collective crisis are 'few, if truth be told',[127] she does insist that we are not completely helpless and so must revolt against contemporary society to open 'psychical life to infinite re-creation'.[128] Politically speaking, Kristeva argues for a turn to a conception of freedom that is not tied to economic liberalism, which is taken to be underpinned by an instrumental rationality that reduces action to a predetermined, abstract end; namely, to make money. While recognising 'the vastness or the benefits of this freedom measured to the logic of cause and effect, which culminates in thought-as-calculation and in science', she suggests that this form of economic logic is culturally specific and, in particular, that 'American civilization is best suited to this type of freedom', before, by extension, claiming that 'this freedom is not the only one'.[129]

In particular, Kristeva – in a similar vein to Foucault – argues that the ancient Greeks were defined by another logic, one in which freedom 'presents itself to itself and the being of speech that surrenders itself, gives itself, presents itself to itself and to the other, and in this sense liberates itself'.[130] Rather than focus on instrumental doing, there was a focus on free dialogue with the other: 'This second conception of freedom is very different from the kind of calculating logic that leads to unbridled consumerism; it is a conception that is evident in the Speech-Being, in the Presenting of the Self to the Other.'[131] Although claiming that this form of speech-being is found in the poet, the libertine and the analyst, she goes on to explain that it is inherent in the political practice of Europe and, in particular, France, which is defined by 'a different vision of freedom [to the American one], namely one that ranks the uniqueness of the individual over economic and scientific factors'.[132] While it is certainly questionable whether such a binary opposition between the two models of freedom exists or, indeed, whether her Eurocentrism and moreover Francocentrism is defensible, Kristeva maintains that this model 'is an aspiration rather than a fixed project, driven by a real concern for the uniqueness and fragility of each and every human life, including those of the poor, the disabled, the retired, and those who rely on social benefits'.[133] Indeed, she goes on to explain that '[i]t also requires special attention to gender and ethnic difference, to men and women considered in their unique intimacy rather than as simple groups of consumers'.[134] The aim, then, is not to reduce individuals to interchangeable consumers, but to respect and affirm 'the dignity of the person'.[135]

If this is her political collective goal, Kristeva also points to individual forms of revolt. Not surprisingly, these aim to liberate the semiotic drives into the symbolic. Given that the semiotic is tied to non-instrumental, creative action, she searches for those activities that permit its expression. She turns to aesthetics and, in particular, literature and modern art 'which explicitly invoke psychosis [and constitute] the sole variety of libertarian effort that tries to provide a lucid accompaniment for this destruction of Western subjectivity'.[136] The natural expressiveness of the semiotic *chora* will, then, undermine and disrupt the fixed categories of the symbolic. This will not only alter the subject, but has the potential to disrupt the instrumental rationality that Kristeva insists underpins contemporary capitalist society.

However, it is important to emphasise that her affirmation of semiotic revolt does not entail an individualistic free-for-all; to be effective, revolt needs to be channelled, which means that it must entail some form of prohibition: 'There is no revolt without prohibition of some sort.'[137] For Kristeva, there must always be some form of authority prohibiting action; 'the intra-psychic limit and prohibition are the indispensable conditions for living and for the life of language and thought'.[138] What is permitted and prohibited can, however, take different forms, and so her affirmation of revolt points to a reconfiguration of the permitted–prohibited relation rather than one in which there is only permission and no prohibition. This is part of her insistence that the individual needs authority and law: 'one needs to be able to live with the power of a boss, a politician, and at the same time question their actions. This is very difficult to imagine.'[139] As she puts it: 'Although we need power, th[e] need to revolt against the authorities is permanent.'[140]

Kristeva therefore insists on a balancing act between establishing and respecting an authority – indeed, she claims that in relation to today's 'young people . . . what they need is authority'[141] – and 'free' psychic expression through revolt which she understands to entail 'a state of permanent questioning, of transformation, change, an endless probing of appearances'.[142] Revolt and authority are bound up in a dialectical relation; both are required. As a consequence, she argues for a reordering of psychic expression within laws that permit this. Kristeva's political engagement aims, then, to release the non-conceptuality and non-instrumentality of the semiotic to counter the conceptual instrumentality of contemporary capitalist (symbolic) discourse.

Conclusion: The Question of Agency

Kristeva's affirmation of revolt as a political and individual strategy has, however, been criticised. Objections take two forms. First, her thinking on the topic is held to be politically ineffectual. Judith Butler, for example, questions whether relying on the semiotic drives can offer effective political revolt, especially given that it is unclear whether these drives can even be known by the subject.[143] However, even if they can be, Butler claims that the semiotic/symbolic distinction means that the semiotic merely interrupts the symbolic before the symbolic is necessarily reinstantiated. As such, Butler concludes that the best that Kristeva's theory can offer is 'a strategy of subversion that can never become a sustained political practice'.[144]

Of course, Kristeva would not necessarily deny this; the whole purpose of her affirmation of revolt is to undermine the symbolic order rather than establish an alternative. In this vein, S. K. Keltner points out that while 'Kristeva is a *social and political thinker* in the sense that she analyses the social and political conditions of meaning and subjectivity in the concrete life of modern societies', it is not clear that she '[i]s a *thinker of politics* in the sense of philosophically reconstructing just social and political institutions and frameworks'.[145] While calling for a socio-economic configuration that respects the dignity of the person, it is not clear that Kristeva's theory of subversion and rejection of fixed ahistorical forms of identity can consistently be used to describe the complex organisational and cultural forms and structures necessary to achieve this.

This first line of critique morphs into a second that questions whether Kristeva's theory actually permits the agency that her affirmation of semiotic revolt demands. Nancy Fraser, for example, argues that Kristeva's 'subject . . . is split between two halves, neither of which is a political agent'.[146] Whereas '[t]he subject of the symbolic is an over-socialized conformist, thoroughly subjected to symbolic conventions and norms', the semiotic 'subject' cannot be an agent of political change because Fraser claims, wrongly I have argued, that the semiotic is 'located beneath, rather than within, culture and society . . . so it is unclear how its practice could be *political* practice'.[147] Furthermore, Fraser repeats Butler's criticism that the semiotic 'is defined exclusively in terms of the transgression of social norms', before concluding that the semiotic is 'defined in terms of the shattering of social identity, so it cannot figure in the reconstruction of the new, politically constituted, *collective* identities and solidarities that are essential to feminist politics'.[148] For Fraser, the Kristevan subject-in-process simply flip-flops between its transgressive semiotic and over-socialised symbolic aspects; an oscillation that prevents it from establishing a coherent platform for individual or collective agency. For this reason, Toril Moi explains that

> [o]ne of the problems with [Kristeva's] account of the 'revolutionary' subject is that it slides over the question of revolutionary agency. Who or what is acting in Kristeva's subversive schemes? In a political context, her emphasis on the semiotic as an unconscious force precludes any analysis of the conscious decision-making processes that might be part of any *collective* revolutionary project. The stress on negativity and disruption, rather than on questions of organisation and solidarity, leads Kristeva in effect to an anarchist and subjectivist political position.[149]

The basic point underpinning these critiques is that the subject-in-process lacks the identity or firm footing necessary to permit it to choose how to act. There is no Archimedean point that permits the subject-in-process to choose to act. It is simply too indeterminate.

Others have, however, defended Kristeva by endorsing her appeal to the semiotic. Both Ewa Ziarek and Robin Goodman argue that Kristeva's affirmation of the semiotic is necessary to cut the subject-in-process off from the capitalist world to reopen a psychic space.[150] In so doing, they defend the subversive intent of Kristeva's thought. Furthermore, Noëlle McAfee takes issue with Moi's and Fraser's critiques.[151] To do so, she first reduces them to the claim that Kristeva has no socio-political critique, before showing that Kristeva does offer a theory of agency based on her notion of the subject-in-process. As a consequence, McAfee reads Moi's critique to be that Kristeva's affirmation of the semiotic is non-political, before claiming that Moi makes this claim because at the time she was writing, the political aspect of Kristeva's work was implicit rather than explicit, with this being subsequently 'corrected' in her later works.[152] However, the problem with this defence is that Moi's critique is not that Kristeva has no socio-political implication, but that her work is devoid of a questioning of agency.

McAfee deals with this in her response to Fraser's critique, which is dismissed because McAfee claims that Fraser asks for something that it is not possible to give: 'a straightforward account of how people can collectively change the world'.[153] The problem is that Fraser does not ask for a straightforward account of agency so much as *any* account of agency. There is simply no mention of it in Kristeva's thinking; she rather holds that the subject-in-process can act and so conflates the subject-in-process with agency. McAfee does the same in another text, when she claims that Kristeva's thinking on the subject-in-process allows feminists to 'avoid the thicket of essentialism by adopting a process philosophical understanding of subjectivity and feminist agency'.[154] But saying that the subject is 'a' process is not sufficient to explain how the subject that is constantly in process and so changing is able to intend change, especially given that the processes that change the subject are unconscious, multidimensional and non-linear.

The fundamental issue, then, is not that Kristeva does not offer suggestions to orientate political action, but that her conceptual framework makes no mention of how the subject-in-process – an 'entity' that is constantly changing due to its drives and unconscious semiotic structures, and that exists 'in' a society that is, by Kristeva's own admission, closing the psychic space that would permit the subject to revolt – is able to act to shape the drives and structures that subtend it. If the speaking subject is an effect of those drives and structures, how can it impact on them?

Kristeva might respond by emphasising the negativity inherent in the subject-in-process. After all, the negativity that accompanies it once it abjects its mother always permits it to divorce itself from its socio-symbolic realm and act differently to the socio-linguistic norms that condition it and from which it exists. This, rather interestingly, makes agency an effect of a particular socio-psychic developmental process, rather than a transcendental or ontological facet of the subject, but it merely conflates agency with the negativity that defines the subject-in-process. This identification is too conceptually blunt to resolve the issue of *what* psychic mechanisms take place to permit the subject to act differently to the drives and structures subtending it and *how* these relate to other aspects of the psychic apparatus.

Kristeva's problem is that she insists on the absolute, immanent development of the subject to the extent that it remains too tightly tied to the socio-symbolic framework in which it lives and develops. While she claims that this immanent development creates negativity that distinguishes the psyche from society, this makes agency dependent on a particular moment of psychic development that is unable to account for agency in those who do not pass through this moment, while it also conflates agency with subjectivity. This makes all subjectivity agential and all agency subjective, which, because she insists that the subject is the speaking subject and so conscious, means that the agency of the subject must be conscious (and symbolic). For this reason, she simply cannot account for passive forms of subjectivity, or, despite her affirmation of the unconscious, unconscious (semiotic) forms of agency. This would require a far more sophisticated and differentiated account of the psyche. In the next chapter, I argue that Cornelius Castoriadis provides this by not only distinguishing between the unconscious and conscious, but showing that the unconscious is itself split between an asocial, monadic, fluctuating core and what I will call the 'social unconscious', defined by the internalisation of social norms. This splitting allows Castoriadis to provide the most sophisticated, although not unproblematic, poststructuralist explanation regarding how agency is possible for a subject that is decentred, embodied and socio-symbolically constituted.

Notes

1. Julia Kristeva, *The Sense and Non-Sense of Revolt: The Powers and Limits of Psychoanalysis*, trans. Jeanine Herman (New York: Columbia University Press, 2000), p. 78; Julia Kristeva, 'Psychoanalysis and Politics', in *Julia Kristeva: Interviews*, ed. Ross Mitchell Guberman (New York: Columbia University Press, 1996), pp. 146-61 (p. 151). Both Anthony Elliott ('The Constitution of the Subject: Primary Repression after Kristeva and Laplanche', *European Journal of Social Theory*, 8.1, 2005, pp. 25-42 [p. 28]) and Rosemary H. Balsam ('The Embodied Mother: Commentary on Kristeva', *Journal of the American Psychoanalytical Association*, 62.1, 2014, pp. 87-100 [pp. 87-8]) claim that Lacan was Kristeva's teacher. This may be true in the sense that she attended his lectures, but it is not true in the sense that he was fundamental for her own psychoanalytical training. She purposely avoided Lacan when undergoing her own treatment (which is a necessary stage of psychoanalytical training): 'I knew Lacan very well; he was a friend, and he was intellectually important to me. But I wanted to keep my psychoanalysis apart, in a private domain of exploration, away from intellectual preoccupations. Thus Lacan was not the right person to analyse me' (ibid., pp. 151-2).
2. Julia Kristeva, 'The Subject in Process', trans. Patrick French, in Patrick French and Roland-François Lack (eds), *The Tel Quel Reader* (Abingdon: Routledge, 1998), pp. 133-78 (p. 133).
3. Kristeva, *The Sense and Non-Sense of Revolt*, p. 35.
4. Kristeva, 'The Subject in Process', pp. 164-5.
5. Ibid., p. 148.
6. Julia Kristeva, 'The Passion According to Motherhood', in *Hatred and Forgiveness*, trans. Jeanine Herman (New York: Columbia University Press, 2012), pp. 79-94 (p. 81).
7. Julia Kristeva, 'A Conversation with Julia Kristeva', in *Julia Kristeva: Interviews*, ed. Ross Mitchell Guberman (New York: Columbia University Press, 1996), pp. 18-34 (pp. 22-3).
8. Julia Kristeva, *Tales of Love*, trans. Leon S. Roudiez (New York: Columbia University Press, 1987), p. 22. It is important to note that, despite the heteronormative language, which is found throughout Freudian psychoanalysis, the terms 'mother' and 'father' refer to functions rather than necessarily to actual individuals. To simplify dramatically, 'mother' refers to love and care, whereas 'father' refers to discipline or law.
9. Ibid., pp. 26, 30.
10. Julia Kristeva, 'From One Identity to Another', in *Desire in Language: A Semiotic Approach to Literature and Art*, ed. Leon S. Roudiez, trans. Thomas Gora, Alice Jardine and Leon S. Roudiez (New York: Columbia University Press, 1980), pp. 124-47 (p. 135).
11. Robin Truth Goodman, 'Julia Kristeva's Sacrificial Murders: The Body at Work as the Work of Art', *Philosophy Today*, 56.2, 2012, pp. 183-99 (p. 192); Noëlle McAfee, 'Resisting Essence: Kristeva's Process Philosophy', *Philosophy Today*,

44, SPEP Supplement, 2000, pp. 77–83 (p. 82); Noëlle McAfee, *Julia Kristeva* (Abingdon: Routledge, 2004), p. 124; Ewa Ziarek, 'The Uncanny Style of Kristeva's Critique of Nationalism', *Postmodern Culture*, 5.2, 1995, pp. 1–28 (p. 10).
12. Judith Butler, *Gender Trouble: Feminism and the Subversion of Identity*, 2nd edn (Abingdon: Routledge, 1999), pp. 108, 110; Nancy Fraser, 'The Uses and Abuses of French Discourse Theories for Feminist Politics', in Nancy Fraser and Sandra Lee Bartby (eds), *Revaluing French Feminism: Critical Essays on Difference, Agency, and Culture* (Bloomington: Indiana University Press, 1992), pp. 177–94 (p. 189); S. K. Keltner, *Kristeva: Thresholds* (Cambridge: Polity, 2011), p. 150; Toril Moi, *Sexual/Textual Practice: Feminist Literary Theory*, 2nd edn (Abingdon: Routledge, 2002), p. 169; Beata Stawarska, 'Language as *Poesis*: Linguistic Productivity and Forms of Resistance in Kristeva and Saussure', in Sarah K. Hansen and Rebecca Tuvel (eds), *New Forms of Revolt: Essays on Kristeva's Intimate Politics* (Albany, NY: State University of New York Press, 2017), pp. 129–54 (pp. 148, 149).
13. Julia Kristeva, *Revolution in Poetic Language*, trans. Margaret Waller (New York: Columbia University Press, 1984), pp. 14–15.
14. Elizabeth Grosz, *Jacques Lacan: A Feminist Introduction* (Abingdon: Routledge, 1990), p. 150.
15. Kristeva, *The Sense and Non-Sense of Revolt*, pp. 32–8.
16. Ibid., p. 38.
17. Ibid., p. 43.
18. Ibid., p. 50.
19. Julia Kristeva, 'Language, Sublimation, Women', in *Hatred and Forgiveness*, trans. Jeanine Herman (New York: Columbia University Press, 2012), pp. 177–82 (p. 179).
20. Kristeva, 'The Subject in Process', p. 143.
21. Ibid., p. 164.
22. Ibid., p. 164.
23. Ibid., p. 164.
24. Ibid., pp. 164–5.
25. Kristeva, *Revolution in Poetic Language*, p. 25.
26. Ibid., p. 26.
27. Ibid., p. 26.
28. Ibid., pp. 26–7.
29. Kristeva, 'The Subject in Process', p. 144.
30. Kristeva, *Revolution in Poetic Language*, p. 17.
31. Kristeva, 'From One Identity to Another', p. 146.
32. Kristeva, *Revolution in Poetic Language*, pp. 23–4.
33. Ibid., p. 25.
34. Ibid., p. 26.
35. Ibid., p. 26.
36. Ibid., p. 27.

37. Ibid., p. 29.
38. Kristeva, 'From One Identity to Another', p. 136.
39. Kristeva, 'The Subject in Process', p. 165.
40. Kristeva, *Revolution in Poetic Language*, p. 30.
41. Julia Kristeva, 'The System and the Speaking Subject', in *The Julia Kristeva Reader*, ed. Toril Moi (New York: Columbia University Press, 1986), pp. 24–33 (p. 29).
42. Ibid., p. 29.
43. Ibid., p. 29.
44. Ibid., p. 29.
45. Ibid., p. 29.
46. Kristeva, *Revolution in Poetic Language*, p. 48.
47. Kristeva, *Tales of Love*, p. 26.
48. Kristeva, *Revolution in Poetic Language*, p. 48.
49. Ibid., p. 42.
50. Ibid., pp. 44–5.
51. Ibid., p. 46.
52. Ibid., p. 46.
53. Ibid., p. 46.
54. Ibid., pp. 46–7.
55. Ibid., p. 47.
56. Ibid., p. 47.
57. Ibid., p. 47.
58. Ibid., p. 47.
59. Ibid., p. 47.
60. Ibid., pp. 48–9.
61. Ibid., p. 49.
62. Ibid., p. 55.
63. Butler, *Gender Trouble*, p. 108.
64. Tina Chanter, 'Kristeva's Politics of Change: Tracking Essentialism with the Help of a Sex/Gender Map', in Kelly Oliver (ed.), *Ethics, Politics, and Difference in Julia Kristeva's Writings* (Abingdon: Routledge, 1993), pp. 179–95 (p. 184). John Lechte makes a similar point: 'Kristeva has never argued for the privileging of either the semiotic over the symbolic, or for the dominance of the symbolic over the semiotic. On the contrary, her work urges a striving for a certain equilibrium in the social and psychic experience of individuals – between language (symbolic) as meaning, and (potentially) poetic non-meaning (semiotic); that is, for what can both erase and multiply meaning' (*Julia Kristeva* [Abingdon: Routledge, 2013], pp. 208–9).
65. Cecilia Sjöholm, *Kristeva and the Political* (Abingdon: Routledge, 2005), p. 18.
66. Ibid., p. 18.
67. Kristeva, *Revolution in Poetic Language*, p. 68.
68. Rachel Widansky, 'Julia Kristeva's Psychoanalytic Work', *Journal of the American Psychoanalytical Association*, 62.1, 2014, pp. 61–7 (p. 62).

69. Kristeva, *Revolution in Poetic Language*, p. 28.
70. Ibid., p. 37.
71. Ibid., p. 37.
72. Kristeva, *Tales of Love*, p. 26.
73. Julia Kristeva, *Powers of Horror: An Essay on Abjection*, trans. Leon S. Roudiez (New York: Columbia University Press, 1982), p. 5.
74. Julia Kristeva, 'Thinking about Liberty in Dark Times', in *Hatred and Forgiveness*, trans. Jeanine Herman (New York: Columbia University Press, 2012), pp. 3–23 (p. 12).
75. Kristeva, *Powers of Horror*, p. 1.
76. Ibid., p. 2.
77. Ibid., p. 4.
78. Ibid., pp. 2–3.
79. See Julia Kristeva, *Strangers to Ourselves*, trans. Leon S. Roudiez (New York: Columbia University Press, 1991).
80. Julia Kristeva, 'The Bounded Text', in *Desire in Language: A Semiotic Approach to Literature and Art*, ed. Leon S. Roudiez, trans. Thomas Gora, Alice Jardine and Leon S. Roudiez (New York: Columbia University Press, 1980), pp. 36–63 (p. 49).
81. Kristeva, *Powers of Horror*, p. 13.
82. Elliott, 'The Constitution of the Subject', p. 30.
83. Julia Kristeva, 'Feminism and Psychoanalysis', in *Julia Kristeva: Interviews*, ed. Ross Mitchell Guberman (New York: Columbia University Press, 1996), pp. 113–21 (p. 118).
84. Kristeva, *Powers of Horror*, p. 13.
85. Kristeva, *Tales of Love*, pp. 26, 33, 41.
86. Ibid., p. 33.
87. Kristeva, 'Feminism and Psychoanalysis', p. 118.
88. On this point, Kristeva asks, 'if the fathers are always present, if fathers become mothers, one may well ask oneself who will play the role of separators' (ibid., p. 119). When asked if both sexes could be nurturers, she responds that while it would be nice, '[w]hat seems more likely is that many borderline children will be produced, and it will become necessary to find a third party, that is to say, the school, all those medical sectors of the different "psy's": psychoanalysts, psychiatrists, psychotherapists, who will play the paternal role' (ibid., p. 119). With this, she reiterates the importance of the sexual difference between (maternal) care and (paternal) law for the psychic development of children and, indeed, sees the latter as particularly important, but, in so doing, also depends upon and affirms a strict heteronormativity.
89. Sara Beardsworth, *Julia Kristeva: Psychoanalysis and Modernity* (Albany, NY: State University of New York Press, 2004), p. 269.
90. Kristeva, *The Sense and Non-Sense of Revolt*, p. 83.
91. Ibid., p. 83.
92. Ibid., p. 83.

93. Ibid., p. 84.
94. Kristeva, *Tales of Love*, p. 313.
95. Julia Kristeva, *Black Sun: Depression and Melancholia*, trans. Leon S. Roudiez (New York: Columbia University Press, 1989), p. 6.
96. Ibid., pp. 13, 14.
97. Ibid., p. 27.
98. Julia Kristeva, 'From Jesus to Mozart: Christianity's Indifference', in *The Incredible Need to Believe*, trans. Beverley Bie Brahic (New York: Columbia University Press, 2009), pp. 77–86 (p. 79).
99. Kristeva, 'The Subject in Process', p. 137.
100. Julia Kristeva, *Revolt, She Said*, ed. Sylvère Lotringer, trans. Brian O'Keefe (South Pasadena, CA: Semiotext(e), 2002), p. 99.
101. Ibid., p. 100.
102. Ibid., p. 100.
103. Ibid., p. 100.
104. Ibid., p. 100.
105. Ibid., p. 100.
106. Ibid., p. 100.
107. Ibid., p. 100.
108. Ibid., p. 100.
109. Ibid., p. 100.
110. Ibid., pp. 100–1.
111. Ibid., p. 101.
112. Julia Kristeva, 'What of Tomorrow's Nation?', in *Nations without Nationalism*, trans. Leon S. Roudiez (New York: Columbia University Press, 1993), pp. 1–48 (p. 2).
113. Kristeva, *Revolt, She Said*, p. 32.
114. Ibid., pp. 32–3.
115. For a discussion of Kristeva's views on the spectacle, see Surti Singh, 'Spectacle and Revolt: On the Intersection of Psychoanalysis and Social Theory in Kristeva's Work', in Sarah K. Hansen and Rebecca Tuvel (eds), *New Forms of Revolt: Essays on Kristeva's Intimate Politics* (Albany, NY: State University of New York Press, 2017), pp. 23–42.
116. Kristeva, *Revolt, She Said*, p. 33.
117. Ibid., p. 33.
118. Julia Kristeva, 'Europe Divided: Politics, Ethics, Religion', in *Crises of the European Subject*, trans. Susan Fairfield (New York: Other Press, 2000), pp. 111–62 (p. 128).
119. Julia Kristeva, *New Maladies of the Soul*, trans. Ross Guberman (New York: Columbia University Press, 1995), p. 7.
120. Julia Kristeva, 'Julia Kristeva in Person', in *Julia Kristeva: Interviews*, ed. Ross Mitchell Guberman (New York: Columbia University Press, 1996), pp. 3–11 (p. 10).
121. Kristeva, *New Maladies of the Soul*, p. 9.

122. Kristeva, 'Thinking about Liberty in Dark Times', p. 7.
123. Julia Kristeva, *Intimate Revolt: The Powers and Limits of Psychoanalysis*, trans. Jeanine Herman (New York: Columbia University Press, 2002), p. 267.
124. Kristeva, 'Europe Divided: Politics, Ethics, Religion', p. 129.
125. Kristeva, *New Maladies of the Soul*, pp. 5-6.
126. Kristeva, *The Sense and Non-Sense of Revolt*, p. 6.
127. Kristeva, 'Europe Divided: Politics, Ethics, Religion', p. 129.
128. Kristeva, *Intimate Revolt*, p. 6.
129. Ibid., pp. 262-3.
130. Ibid., p. 263.
131. Julia Kristeva, 'Secularism: "Values" at the Limits of Life', in *Hatred and Forgiveness*, trans. Jeanine Herman (New York: Columbia University Press, 2012), pp. 24-8 (p. 26).
132. Kristeva, 'Thinking about Liberty in Dark Times', p. 17.
133. Ibid., p. 17.
134. Ibid., p. 17.
135. Kristeva, 'Europe Divided: Politics, Ethics, Religion', p. 126.
136. Ibid., pp. 129-30.
137. Kristeva, *Revolt, She Said*, p. 31.
138. Ibid., p. 31.
139. Ibid., p. 109.
140. Ibid., p. 109.
141. Ibid., p. 91.
142. Ibid., p. 120.
143. Butler, *Gender Trouble*, p. 108. Beata Stawarska ('Language as *Poesis*', p. 149) makes a similar point.
144. Butler, *Gender Trouble*, p. 110.
145. Keltner, *Kristeva*, p. 150.
146. Fraser, 'The Uses and Abuses of French Discourse Theories for Feminist Politics', p. 189.
147. Ibid., p. 189.
148. Ibid., p. 189.
149. Moi, *Sexual/Textual Practice*, p. 169.
150. Ziarek, 'The Uncanny Style of Kristeva's Critique of Nationalism', p. 10; Goodman, 'Julia Kristeva's Sacrificial Murders', p. 192.
151. McAfee, *Julia Kristeva*, p. 124.
152. Ibid., p. 124.
153. Ibid., p. 124.
154. McAfee, 'Resisting Essence', p. 82.

CHAPTER 8

Castoriadis, Agency and the Socialised Individual

To this point, I have charted the main trajectories through which a variety of poststructuralist thinkers have both decentred the subject from its long-held foundational role *and* attempted to reconstruct the subject from what results. While the first two chapters on Deleuze and Derrida focused primarily, although not exclusively, on the former issue, the latter has increasingly come to the fore, to rethink the subject in relation to social norms (Foucault and Butler) and/or language and embodiment (Butler, Lacan and Kristeva). While these show that the poststructuralist paradigm is far more sophisticated than typically appreciated with regard to this issue – the subject is not simply decentred, but is rethought as an embodied, socio-symbolic being – they are also linked to the question of agency. The various poststructuralists engaged with do not simply make the subject a determined effect of pre-subjective structures and processes, but insist that the decentred subject is capable of intentional agency; an argument that has given rise to a variety of innovative attempts to explain how this is possible. I have argued, however, that the various 'solutions' offered to resolve this issue have been, in some way, structurally problematic because the notion of agency offered is underdeveloped, inconsistent with other aspects of that proponent's thought, or relies upon a conception of the subject that is too thin to permit such agency.

If the issue of poststructuralist agency is to be resolved, it seems that we need a thicker – meaning more substantial – conception of the subject to explain, situate and permit such agency. However, the subject cannot be too 'thick', otherwise we risk reinstantiating the ahistoric substance focus that is anathema to the poststructuralist affirmation of processes and flux. We are then left asking whether it is possible to develop, within the constraints of the poststructuralist paradigm – namely, its rejection of ahistoric, ontological substance – a conception of the subject that is 1) decentred, 2) thought in terms of fluxes and processes, 3) understood to be embodied and socially and symbolically embedded, and where the site or possibility of agency is 4) more coherently and thickly described and outlined.

In this chapter, I suggest that it *is* possible to coherently combine these components and that Cornelius Castoriadis does so within a psychoanalytic-poststructuralist framework. Castoriadis achieves this because he departs substantially from some of the major assumptions informing the work of the other thinkers analysed in this book. This has to be teased out from his theory because, with the exception of Lacan, he does not discuss, in any depth, any of the other thinkers that I have analysed and, indeed, if he does mention them at all, he tends to reject their analysis or downplay their importance. So, while recognising the importance of what he calls 'contemporary ideology: death of the subject, juggling away of the social by means of "structures" and "networks"',[1] he distances himself from it because he holds that it leads to one of two unsatisfactory options: on the one hand, as in the work of Lévi-Strauss, Althusser and Foucault, it leads to the affirmation of a '"subjectless process"'.[2] Castoriadis is dismissive of this approach: 'Big discovery! But what, then, is a galaxy but a "subjectless process?"'[3] The implication being that simply focusing on pre-subjective processes does not get us very far. On the other hand, he points to the work of Lacan, Barthes and Derrida, in which 'the human subject [is] entirely reabsorbed into the dimension of the social individual, and in particular into language'.[4] As such, one then 'say[s] that [the subject] is caught, lost, alienated in language (and in the tinsel of society), that it does not speak but is spoken'.[5] However, no sooner has agency been dissolved within the socio-symbolic than it is subsequently 'install[ed] "behind" [the subject as] a "subject of the Unconscious," which obviously cancels itself out as soon as a word is uttered'.[6] As a consequence, this line of argumentation dissolves agency, while continuing to insist that agency is possible by appealing to an unconscious subject that is immediately cancelled whenever it acts.

Putting to one side the question of whether Castoriadis's descriptions are accurate, his fundamental problem with both approaches is that they are implicitly based not only on a number of binary oppositions (subject versus society, conscious versus unconscious), but also on a reductionist understanding of the unconscious. Rather than simply seeking to ground the subject in subjectless processes/structures or an unconscious subject, Castoriadis insists that we would do better to think of the subject in terms of always fluctuating, interlinked *relations* between the social world, somatic body, symbolic realm and heterogeneous psyche. From this, he develops an embodied, socially symbolically embedded notion of the subject that, I will argue, is also sufficiently conceptually thick to offer a sophisticated, subtle and coherent analysis of how such a subject is capable of agency.

To show this, I first note that Castoriadis draws on his clinical experience to insist on a developmental account of the subject that is tied to its socialisation. Rather than engage with subjectivity from the typical poststructuralist affirmation of difference, Castoriadis starts from an initial fluctuating psychic monad – the ontological core of the psyche that he also calls the 'little screaming monster'[7] – that must be differentiated and turned into an *individual* through a process of socialisation. For Castoriadis, this process 'always entails violence'.[8] On this issue, however, a number of commentators have questioned whether 1) Castoriadis can, given the radical opposition between them, legitimately claim or explain how society can act on the psyche to socialise it,[9] and, indeed, whether 2) the psyche is, in fact, an initial closed totality that must be forcibly opened for socialisation to take place.[10] As a consequence, his critics ultimately hold that socialisation cannot and need not be violent.

In response, I first pay attention to what Castoriadis calls 'the triadic phase'[11] – which describes the process through which the psyche breaks up its initial monadic state to distinguish between the subject, the object and the other – to show that these criticisms are based on a misrepresentation of Castoriadis's position and that the socialisation process is both imposed on to the psyche and a process that it willingly engages in. The triadic phase also reveals how the somatic relates to the psyche and, in so doing, clarifies the embodied nature of the psyche.

Second, having shown that the psychic monad must be socialised, with this creating the *individual*, Castoriadis makes the point that this alteration does not annihilate the former but sublimates it. Part of the process of successfully socialising the psychic monad is to find avenues *within* the social-historical formation whereby the autonomy of the psychic monad can express itself. In this way, Castoriadis not only insists that the socialised individual must continue to act, but that such agency is integral to the well-being of the subject. This does, however, lead back to the question of whether it is logically possible for Castoriadis to claim that the socialised individual is capable of such agency.

In response, Castoriadis introduces a conceptual innovation. Whereas we have seen that psychoanalytically orientated poststructuralists, such as Butler, Kristeva and Lacan, rely on the psyche, split it between the conscious and unconscious, and focus on the latter, Castoriadis goes one step further by claiming that the socialisation process also splits the unconscious. This gives rise to a distinction between what might be called the 'socialised unconscious', describing the part of the psyche that has incorporated and internalised the social norms and values learnt from the socialisation process, and the 'primal unconscious which is the monadic core of the psyche'[12] that always remains distinct from the former. With this split, Castoriadis is able to show that, while the subject is embodied and socially embedded, there is a part of the subject's psyche – which is in constant flux rather than substance form – that is always distinct from its social norms, with this permitting and explaining how the socialised individual continues to be capable of choosing its actions. By way of conclusion, I outline the political implications of this to show that it underpins Castoriadis's affirmation of a politics of autonomy.

Being and the Radical Imaginary

Castoriadis begins with the ontological premise that '[c]haos is the ultimate depth of being; more, it is the bottomless depth of being; it is the abyss behind everything that exists'.[13] Rather than an inert substance, being as an abyssal chaos is defined as 'a magma'[14] of constant movement, producing alterations, ruptures and different forms of entities. One of these creations is what Castoriadis calls 'the social-historical element'.[15]

History, for Castoriadis, 'is not . . . determinate, but *in itself* . . . creation and destruction'.[16] This historical creation is tied to and finds expression spatially through the social, which is not defined as or by a collection of '"many, many, many" "subjects"';[17] nor is it 'an extended family'[18] or 'the unending addition of intersubjective networks (although it is this *too*) [or] their simple product'.[19] Rather, '[t]he social is what is everyone and what is no one, what is never absent and wholly never present as such, a non-being that is more real than any being, that in which we are wholly immersed yet which we can never apprehend "in person"'.[20] Putting the social and historical aspects together, we find that

> [t]he social-historical is the anonymous collective whole, the impersonal–personal element that fills every given social formation but which also engulfs it, setting each society in the midst of others, inscribing them all within a continuity in which those who are no longer, those who are elsewhere and even those yet to be born are in a certain sense present.[21]

The social-historical is not a 'thing' that is overcoded with social meaning; rather, the social-historical is an immanent becoming arising from the relationship between the material structures constitutive of the social-historical and '*that which* structures, institutes, [and] materializes'[22] it. In short, the social-historical element 'is the union *and* the tension of instituting society and of instituted society, of history made and of history in the making'.²³ Instituting society does not disappear once instituted; there will always be a distinction and distance between the two, which, far from being 'something negative or deficient . . . is one of the expressions of the creative nature of history, [t]hat prevents it from fixing itself once and for all [and] what makes a society always contain *more* than what it presents'.²⁴ As a consequence, the social-historical is never static, but is always subtended by an instituting power, which 'is the social imaginary in the radical sense'.²⁵

Importantly, the social imaginary is a manifestation of what Castoriadis calls the 'radical imaginary'.²⁶ This concept is introduced as part of his polemical critique of Lacan's symbolic account of meaning genesis which, on Castoriadis's telling, is unable to account for the radically new.²⁷ To correct this, Castoriadis insists on a fount of creative innovation that he calls the 'radical imaginary' – 'the unceasing and essentially *undetermined* (social-historical and psychical) creation of figures/forms/images, on the basis of which alone there can ever be a question *of* "something"'²⁸ – which is split into the 'radical imagination' of the psyche and the 'social imaginary'²⁹ describing the institutions and meanings of each society. As a consequence, the social imaginary is a constant 'surging forth'³⁰ that creates new configurations and manifestations of the social-historical. It is not transcendent to the human world, but is the ever-present 'background' that provides the impetus and 'support' that permits each social imaginary to renew itself. That the social-historical is a manifestation of the creativity of the radical imaginary ensures that the society created is not static, but is always in constant alteration. The dynamic between what is present and what is absent creates the conditions within which the human world exists, finds expression and institutes itself: 'The self-institution of society is the creation of a human world: of "things," "reality," language, norms, values, ways of life and death, objects for which we live and objects for which we die.'³¹ It is also, as we will see in subsequent sections, the sphere through which the individual is created.

The social-historical creates a human world by creating imaginary significations that generate meaning and values for those existing 'within' it: 'Society is [then] primarily a magma of social imaginary significations that make collective and individual life meaningful.'³² Castoriadis explains that he uses the notion of 'imaginary' because these significations 'do not correspond to, or are . . . exhausted by, references to "rational" or "real" elements and because it is through a *creation* that they are posited. And I call them social because they . . . exist only if they are instituted and shared by an impersonal, anonymous collective.'³³ That they are 'imaginary' does not, however, mean that they are abstract. Social imaginaries are inherently concrete because they are the affects, intentions, mechanisms, representations and signs that structure and dominate a society. Without them, there would be no society. They are, however, not necessarily physical, nor do they transcend the society; they are, in effect, the fabric or 'web of meanings'[34] that create and glue a society together.

As a consequence, we have 'to think of the world of social significations as the primary, inaugural, irreducible positing of the social-historical and of the social imaginary as it manifests itself in each case in a given society'.[35] These 1) consist 'of images or figures in the broadest sense of the term: phonemes, words, bank currency, jinns, statues, churches, tools, uniforms, body paintings, numerical figures, border-posts, centaurs, cassocks, lictors, musical scores ... all the totality of what is perceived in nature';[36] and 2) are particular to each society, arising from the way(s) in which each society responds to a wide variety of questions, including, but not limited to: 'Who are we as a collectivity? What are we for one another? Where and in what are we? What do we want; what do we desire; what are we lacking?'[37] These are not necessarily explicitly asked; 'it is in the *doing* of each collectivity that the answer to these questions appears as an embodied meaning; this social doing allows itself to be understood only as a reply to the questions that it implicitly poses itself'.[38]

The social doing that gives rise to social imaginary significations is not, however, unencumbered. The social world leans on the natural one, which is not to say that society is '*determined* by it in any way'.[39] The '*autonomy*'[40] of the social world distinguishes it from the natural one and ensures that, while linked, the latter can never determine the former. However, because it leans on the natural world it inhabits and acts within, each society must create imaginary significations to explain and deal with that natural world. How this occurs differs based on the society created and, of course, the natural world it leans on.

Castoriadis maintains, however, that there is one natural 'fact' that simply must be taken into account by every social imaginary: 'no society can institute itself in such a way that it totally inhibits heterosexual desire, and if it did so nonetheless it would be unobservable within a generation'.[41] This is because the continuing existence of a social imaginary depends upon the doing of individuals comprising it, which requires that children are continuously produced. As Castoriadis puts it: 'Men and women live in society; they can be unambiguously classified (biologically) as male and female. They give birth to boys and girls who are, always and everywhere, incapable of surviving unless they are cared for by adults for a rather long period of time.'[42] Each social imaginary must, then, lean on and take into account the heterosexual nature of procreation and, indeed, create a narrative and imaginary signification regarding the creation and rearing of children. This is done by turning 'the *natural fact* of being-male and being-female into an *imaginary social signification* of being-man and being-woman'.[43]

Crucially, '[n]either this transformation itself nor the specific tenor of the signification in question can be deduced, produced or derived on the basis of the natural fact, which is always and everywhere the same'.[44] So, Castoriadis is not saying that the biological male/female dualism must necessarily be mirrored in the social imaginary. He *is* saying that the perpetuation of each collective requires the continual creation of new members, which, in turn, requires the biological act of procreation. For this reason, each social imaginary must, in some way, find a way to affirm the symbolic value of having children, which requires that it, in some way, affirm the heterosexual relations through which this occurs. This is a consequence of his claim that, although not determined by the biological/natural world, social imaginary significations are nevertheless bound to, lean on and, as such, must somehow take into consideration the realities of the biological/natural world. Instead of adopting a wholly socially constructivist position, wherein being *and* its meaning are contingent social creations, Castoriadis affirms a quasi-realist position which recognises that there is a natural binary sexual division that exists beyond or 'outside' social imaginary significations, but which also holds that the *meaning* of that division is indeterminate and socially created. As such, there is a natural biological division between two sexes, but the *meaning* of each aspect and, indeed, the relation between them need not be reduced to the affirmation of a heteronormative form; nor, indeed, does Castoriadis reduce heterosexual desire to the act of procreation. As he puts it, 'to say that a minimum heterosexual desire must be tolerated by the institution of society, under pain of rapid extinction of the collectivity in question, still says nothing about the unending alchemy of desire that we observe in history – and this is what is important to us'.[45]

With this, Castoriadis follows Butler, Derrida and Kristeva in holding that sexuality is not reducible to an ahistoric, determinate essence, although there is no getting away from the fact that he continues to insist not only on a natural/symbolic division but also on a natural biological division between the sexes that they would find problematic.[46] For example, Butler would most likely argue that sexuality is never naturally binary or heterosexual, but always a consequence of symbolic construction or, in Castoriadis's language, the social imaginary. On Butler's assessment, then, Castoriadis's insistence on a natural binary sexual opposition is simply a consequence of a continuing unjustifiable heteronormative privileging on his part, or a failure to draw the correct lessons from the afoundationalism and constructivism inherent in his account of the social imaginary.

However, although Butler would probably criticise Castoriadis's continuing insistence on a 'natural' heterosexual bedrock, Luce Irigaray's later work appears to accept such a natural sexual division, as evidenced by her claims that '[t]he natural is at least two: male and female'[47] and '[t]he difference between man and woman already exists, and it cannot be compared to a creation of our understanding'.[48] Rather than ground this difference in fixed substances, Irigaray rethinks it in terms of the distinct bodily natural rhythms specific to each sex, as a precursor to reconstructing an alternative ethic of sexual difference from those sex-specific rhythms to overcome the logic of patriarchal representation that she diagnoses as being constitutive of Western thought.[49] However, while she appears to agree with Castoriadis that there is a 'natural' division between the sexes, Irigaray would probably reject the claim permitted by his theory that, because norms are creations of social imaginaries which, in turn, lack *a priori* foundations, phallogocentrism – or the privileging of the masculine position – can be justified if it is stated by a social imaginary. For Irigaray, in contrast, one sex can never be legitimately privileged over the other regardless of whether a social imaginary asserts this, because to do so would be to reduce one sex to the parameters that define the other – in the case of phallogocentrism, the female to the male – in a way that fails to respect the inherent difference(s) between the sexes; action that requires that each sex be thought on its own terms in relation to its specific natural rhythms, 'energy',[50] 'style'[51] or 'spirit'.[52]

Further engagement with this issue is beyond the scope of this book, but this brief discussion demonstrates that whether sexuality conforms to certain natural biological divisions irrespective of any symbolic constructions that might take place, or whether such divisions and by extension sexuality itself are fundamentally symbolic/social imaginary constructions, is an issue that continues to divide and, indeed, stimulate poststructuralist thinking. It also reveals the vital importance that the question of sexuality has for poststructuralist attempts to rethink the subject.

It must be emphasised, however, that while Castoriadis accepts and makes room for a pre-existing natural world, he does insist that it is the social imaginary that is overwhelmingly powerful and important in generating meaning and, by extension, social life. It achieves this because the creation of each social imaginary is intimately tied to the instantiation of a symbolic system of signification. More specifically, symbolic meaning is derived from the 'rigid tie . . . between the signifier and signified, the symbol and the thing, that is to say in the actual imaginary'.[53] As a consequence, the instantiation of a symbolic system *produces* meaning from 'the permanent connection'[54] that structures the binary oppositions of symbolic meaning.

These are not universal, but specific to each social-historical formation and the language that composes it.

Importantly, the symbolic cannot be considered primary. Without mentioning him, Castoriadis is here reaffirming his critique of what he takes to be Lacan's privileging of the symbolic. He criticises such a move because if the symbolic were primary, there would only be – on Castoridias's telling – rigid production rather than innovative creation.[55] To explain the latter, we need to recognise that symbolic production is an effect of a more primordial form of creation that Castoriadis terms the radical imaginary: the 'radical imaginary [i]s the common root of the actual imaginary and of the symbolic'.[56] Putting aside the issue of whether this is an accurate representation of Lacan's thought, Castoriadis accepts that the symbolic is a fundamental aspect of the generation of meaning *in* the social-historical, but insists that it is a second-order phenomenon dependent on the more fundamental generative power of the (radical) imaginary. This creates a social-historical and, by extension, symbolic configuration that, instead of producing meaning from a predefined schema or opposition, is defined by *open-ended creation*.

Furthermore, according to Castoriadis, social imaginary significations are not created by an individual, a group of subjects or a transcendent source. Rather, '[s]ociety must make *itself* and state *itself* in order to make or state anything'.[57] This does not follow a predetermined blueprint, but entails a spontaneous form of collective action without centre, teleology or end. That it has no definable source other than a general, ineffable form of collective action ensures that the foundation of social imaginary significations is insidious, total, yet anonymous: 'we are dealing with the power of the social-historical field itself, the power of *outis*, of Nobody'.[58] However, while their source cannot be located, social imaginary significations are sustained through the collective actions of the individuals created by and constitutive of them.

This brings us to the notion of the radical imagination, which describes the fundamental structure of the psyche. While the radical (psychic) imagination is distinct from and different to the social imaginary, the former is always tied to and embedded within the latter. However, whereas the psyche receives impressions from the social imaginary, 'it is also, and more importantly (for without this the receptivity of impressions would produce nothing) [, defined by] the emergence of representation as an irreducible and unique mode of being'.[59] That the psyche must continuously turn impressions into representations does not mean that the psyche pre-exists what it creates; it is not equivalent to a transcendental consciousness. Rather, the psyche 'is a *forming*, which exists in and through *what* it forms and *how* it forms'.[60]

Whereas Castoriadis maintains that the traditional (Western) conception conceives of the subject as an *'individual-substance'*[61] with a defined *a priori* nature, he explains that the psyche is not a substance or 'a well-oiled, rational mechanism. The psyche is essentially radical imagination, a perpetually surging flux of representations, desires, and affects. As such, it is creative, which also means that this flow and its products are as often as not undetermined.'[62] Because it is a surging flux, there is, strictly speaking, 'no "site" of the psyche properly'.[63] The psyche is indeterminate, which does not mean that it is undifferentiated or, indeed, unstructured. The structure is, however, endlessly broken up and reordered by 'a continual irruption of newness, creation, self-alteration'.[64]

In the first instance, Castoriadis explains that '[t]he human psyche is by necessity structurally divided, at least between a conscious and an unconscious level'.[65] Of the two, it is the unconscious that is key. As such, the radical imagination is unconscious, with the consequence that its fundamental creative actions occur at this level.[66] Furthermore, whereas Freud insists that the unconscious is defined by drives, Castoriadis maintains that the radical imagination precedes those drives.[67] This does not mean that there is no such thing as biology or drives for Castoriadis; only that they do not underpin the psyche. To bolster this, Castoriadis distinguishes between the radical imagination of the human psyche, 'the central nervous system and . . . the biological psyche', to explain that, in comparison with the central nervous system, the human psyche is defined by 'the emergence of meaning for the self', whereas 'in comparison to the biological psyche, the meaning that the human psyche creates or that it is by creating is defunctionalised'.[68] So, while the central nervous system relays signs based on nerve stimuli and the biological psyche is purely functional, the human psyche, defined as radical imagination, is fundamentally expressive and creative (rather than merely reactive, predefined or non-functional).

However, although the radical imagination is distinct from the drives, central nervous system and biological psyche, it is also intimately connected to them. To explain this, Castoriadis returns, once more, to the Freudian notion of *'anaclisis (Anlehnung)'*[69] – leaning on – to explain that 'psychical working out is neither dictated by biological organization nor absolutely free with respect to it'.[70] In the same way that the social world leans on but is not determined by the natural world, the psyche leans on but is not determined by the biological. Importantly, while biology does not determine or shape psychic life, the latter is not possible without the former and so the psyche must take biology into consideration. As Castoriadis explains, '[o]xygen contributes nothing to phantasies, it "allows them to exist." The mouth-breast, or the anus, have to be "taken into account" by the psyche and, what is more, they support and induce.'[71] For this reason, the psyche is not an effect of biology nor is it determined by biological need, but it *is* connected to the biological stratum and must take it into account.

Having affirmed the conscious–unconscious split, Castoriadis goes further by splitting the unconscious between what might be called the 'social unconscious', defined by the internalisation of the social imaginary significations of the society it exists within, and 'the primal unconscious, which is the monadic core of the psyche'[72] and which is inherently asocial. Castoriadis associates it with Leibniz's 'windowless monad', but, so as to secure its continuing autonomy, is quick to remind us that, in contrast to Leibniz's monads, 'there is no pre-established harmony, no harmonious integration of all monads in an overall symphony, the monad's "perception" is a perception of the self, its conatus is directed toward itself and is in no way harmonized with that of other monads'.[73] The psychic monad is also 'master of all desires, of total unification, of the abolition of difference and of distance, manifested above all as being unaware of difference and distance, which, in the field of the unconscious, arranges all the representations that emerge in the direction of its own lines of force'.[74] While it is shaped by the social imaginary, the psychic monad always remains distinct from the pressures exerted on the (social) unconscious by the social imaginary, with this permitting autonomous intentional agency against the social imaginary, and so always offering the possibility of innovative creation.

Socialising the Psyche

However, Castoriadis points out that '[l]eft to itself, the newborn dies of hunger or, in the best of cases, becomes a wild child and irreversibly loses its capacity to be truly human'.[75] Preventing this requires that the psyche socialise its asocial monadic core. In turn, because the social-historical does not exist as a transcendent substance but is dependent on the actions of those that constitute it, its continuation depends upon its inhabitants affirming the social imaginary significations that define it. Society therefore 'socializes (humanizes) the wild, raw, antifunctionally made psyche of the newborn and imposes upon it a formidable complex of constraints and limitations'.[76] These bring the psyche to 'renounce [its initial] absolute egocentrism and [the] omnipotence of imagination, recognize "reality" and the existence of others, subordinate desires to rules of behaviour, and accept sublimated satisfactions and even death for the sake of "social" ends'.[77]

Castoriadis claims that this process '*always* occurs by means of a violent break-up of what is the first state of the psyche and its requirements'.[78] It is not therefore something that the psyche voluntarily does to itself:

> the new-born will *always* have to be torn out of *his* world, without asking him for an opinion he cannot give, and forced – under pain of psychosis – to renounce his imaginary omnipotence, to recognise the desire of others as equally legitimate with his own, and taught that he cannot make the words of the language signify whatever he may want them to, made able to enter the world as such, the social world and the world of significations as everyone's world and as no one's world.[79]

By undergoing this violent break-up, the psyche is torn from its initial autism and 'force[d] . . . to enter the harsh world of reality'.[80] In exchange, however, society 'offers it . . . meaning'.[81] If successful, therefore, the socialisation process brings the psyche to identify with the social imaginary in which it exists. As such, there is a particular trajectory to the socialisation process, wherein the psyche starts as an enclosed monad, undergoes the trauma of the break-up imposed on to it by society, only to subsequently regain a sense of oneness, this time with its social imaginary rather than itself. Through its socialisation, the psyche learns to adapt to and even take pleasure in the social world that 'is mediated by a "state of affairs" which is not at the subject's disposal'.[82] The loss of its initial monadic unity will, however, continue to haunt the individual.[83]

It should also be noted that the socialisation of the psyche fundamentally alters its structure, in so far as it becomes 'characterised by . . . many agencies and by the conflict between them'.[84] Through socialisation, the psyche goes from an initial monadic totality to one that is highly stratified.[85] Castoriadis is not here referring to the conscious–unconscious split; that is integral to the psyche's existence. Rather, the experiences of the psyche and its processes of socialisation stratify that division even further by, for example, creating judgement, reflection and will, and, indeed, the ways in which these are manifested. Castoriadis does, however, remind us that the various parts of the psyche are coordinated: 'human beings, with all their inner contradictions and conflicts, are a totality, of sorts. All three are involved, therefore: the subconscious and the radical imagination as well as thinking, lucid reflection and will.'[86] This unity is secured from the drive to unity inherent in the psychic monad that continues to ground the socialised individual.

For Castoriadis then, violence plays a fundamental, necessary and, crucially, creative role in the development of the psyche and, by extension, the survival of the human being. By breaking the monadic enclosure of the psychic monad, the social imaginary imposes itself on to the psyche to ensure that the psyche exists in accordance with the values, norms and actions of that social imaginary. It should be noted that this imposition takes place both explicitly and implicitly, or consciously and unconsciously, with the latter option in each opposition being more powerful and fundamental to the process.

The role that violence plays in Castoriadis's schema has, however, been the subject of much critical debate. Joel Whitbook, for example, argues that Castoriadis's insistence on a necessary socialising violence is incompatible with the claim that the psyche is absolutely other to society. If the psyche and society are as heterogeneous as Castoriadis claims, then it is simply not clear how society could interact with the psyche at all to break the latter's asociality. For Whitbook, the absolute disjunction between the two means that 'the socialization process [sh]ould not simply be violent, it [sh]ould be impossible'.[87] In turn, it has been questioned whether the psyche is, in fact, an initial closed totality that must be forcibly opened for socialisation to take place. Eugene Wolfenstein, for example, claims that '[w]e do not come into the world, as Castoriadis would have it, enclosed within an impermeable shell'; Michel Gauchet insists that '[t]here is an original openness of the human psyche with regard to reality, and – correspondingly – an original differentiation of individuality'; and Karl Smith maintains that '[g]iven that the psyche must be formed, must be socialized by its own processes of sublimating the socio-historical, we must also allow that the relationship between the individual and society, self and other, is also embraced, desired, nurtured etc.'[88] From this perspective, then, Castoriadis's thinking is logically inconsistent and based on a conception of the psyche that is simply wrong. There must be an original openness to the psyche for the socialisation process to occur, which means that the violence that Castoriadis insists upon is not always necessary.

However, a number of commentators have argued that this line of argument is based on a fundamental misunderstanding or partial reading of Castoriadis's thought. David Curtis and Andreas Kalyvas, for example, explain that 'the old and quite false determinism of the "individual versus society"' – which underpins Smith's criticism but which Curtis and Kalyvas also attribute to Wolfenstein's – '[has] nothing to do with Castoriadis's views', which are premised on the psyche/society distinction.[89] Furthermore, Marcela Tovar-Restrepo claims that Whitbook's criticism is based on a misunderstanding of the psyche–society relation, in so far as it is unable to properly consider the way in which each leans on the other.[90] She also points out that, contrary to what Gauchet and Smith claim, Castoriadis recognises that the socialisation of the psyche is an endeavour that the psyche must open itself to and participate in; a conclusion also affirmed by Jeff Klooger.[91] The upshot of these arguments is that violence *is* necessary to socialise the psyche and so plays a fundamental role in Castoriadis's thinking specifically, and in the life and survival of human beings more generally.

My intervention in this debate takes off from those defending Castoriadis but complements their attempts by clearly outlining the component pieces of Castoriadis's actual *compatibilist* position to show that the socialisation process is both violently imposed on to the psyche and is one that the psyche willingly participates in.[92] As Castoriadis puts it: 'The process of the social institution of the individual . . . is the history of the psyche in the course of which the psyche alters itself and opens itself to the social-historical, depending, too, on its own work and its own creativity.'[93] Not only does this result from the need to ensure its own survival by satisfying its somatic needs – action that necessitates that it open itself to others – but, so Castoriadis suggests, it is also done 'much more strongly [because of] the psychical need for meaning'.[94] Clearly the need for social meaning is necessary once the psyche has been socialised, but Castoriadis seems here to be suggesting that the psyche also searches for meaning of its own accord, with this requiring that it open itself to others. Presumably, the opening resulting from this search is complemented by and entwined with the opening required to satisfy the *somatic* needs that the psyche leans on. This in-built opening is evidenced from the way in which the psyche moves through what Castoriadis calls the 'triadic phase'.[95]

The Triadic Phase

The triadic phase describes the process through which the 'great enigma'[96] that is the break-up of the psychic monad takes place. More specifically, it describes the ways through which the psyche comes to distinguish between subject, object and other, to move from a monadic to a triadic structure. The initial moment that generates the break-up of the psyche is its relation to 'somatic need'.[97] As noted, the psyche leans on without being determined by the somatic. For this reason, the somatic does not determine or shape the psyche; rather, the psyche experiences somatic need and must react to it if it is to satisfy that need and so survive. If the psyche does not respond to the somatic need 'the infant w[ill] die', but if it does respond – which it does in the overwhelming majority of cases – the satisfaction of its somatic need is 'represented as the manifestation, confirmation, restoration of the initial unity of the subject'.[98] As Castoriadis puts it: 'Hunger is normally appeased when the breast, or whatever takes the place of the breast, is offered and made available. The availability of the breast simply re-establishes, to begin, the monadic state.'[99] If pleasure is the return to its autistic, unified state, displeasure 'is the break-up of the autistic monad'.[100] By leaning on the psyche, hunger reveals to the psyche that it is not an enclosed unity, but lacks something. Because hunger is satiated through the breast, the presence of hunger reveals the absence of the breast and 'the absence of the breast is unpleasure in so far as it is the tearing apart of the autistic world'.[101] Through this, the child *starts* to distinguish between itself and its other, a division created because the psyche cannot, at this stage, recognise that the breast is both the source of pleasure and unpleasure; instead, it flits between pleasure and unpleasure depending on whether the breast is present or absent. By operating through this binary schema, the psyche takes its own pleasure to be opposed to the displeasure caused by the lack of the other.

Because the breast is so often absent, the psyche finds itself in a conundrum: if it really is the unity it insists on, it would not be able to experience the absence at the root of its displeasure. Yet absence and hence displeasure exist. To account for this and to maintain its pleasurable unity, the psyche shifts the absent breast and displeasurable state outside itself: 'an outside is *created* so that the psyche can cast off into it whatever it does not want, *whatever there is no room for in the psyche*, non-sense or negative meaning, the breast as absent, the bad breast'.[102] In so doing, the psyche creates external space: 'The psyche invents-figures an outside in order to place the breast of unpleasure there.'[103] At the same time, it objectifies the 'bad' breast to place it in the external space created. As such, the psyche comes to distinguish itself from the external object, thereby starting the process that will permit the formation of the oppositions that structure the symbolic.

Importantly, the object externalised is not yet 'a *real* object',[104] but something akin to a quasi-object; an awareness of something other than itself. 'The real object can only appear once the good breast and the bad breast begin to coincide for the subject, once the two imaginary entities appear as connected to a third entity which is the ground of both of them without being identical with either of them.'[105] Following Freud, Castoriadis claims that this takes place 'when the fact that the object "belongs" to a "person" is actually apprehended'.[106] The two breasts, pleasure and displeasure, become then tied to the same person – the mother[107] – who is forever associated with the disjunction between the two: 'Carrying the bad object, [s]he is hated; carrying the good object, [s]he is loved.'[108] Crucially, however, the other – usually the mother – is identified with 'all-powerfulness'[109] because she 'is the first person to say "no" to the infant'.[110] With this, 'the mother is construed as all-powerful, and simultaneously with the recognition that she has an existence and a desire, a will, foreign to the infant . . . that it does not control'.[111] By projecting its previous omnipotence on to the object-other, the psyche recognises the object's importance and so breaks open its own monadism.

While the triadic phase is fundamental to the socialisation process, in so far as it brings the psyche out of its monadic autism to 'recognise' an object-other – the mother – which starts to establish the differential relations that are key to the social imaginary, it still does not break up the psyche's affirmation of or dependence on omnipotence. Instead, it simply transfers the psyche's initial omnipotence to the other.[112] In so doing, the psyche, through the projection, remains at the 'root' of the other's omnipotence and, indeed, 'is able to remain shut in with its mother, which produces extremely severe, now well-known pathologies'.[113] To further its psychic development, the child must continue to be socialised, which requires that it break out of its dyadic relation with its 'omnipotent' mother by deposing her 'from the locus of her omnipotence'.[114] It is here that the Oedipus complex enters the scene, in so far as, by recognising the mother's desire for another, the child comes to see that the mother is not omnipotent; 'she is incomplete, caught up in her desire by the other, which is to say, the father'.[115] By orientating herself around the father, the mother's privileged position is toppled and the psyche learns that there is another to the dyadic relation: psyche, mother, father.

Two issues stand out at this juncture. First, it is not sufficient that the process stops here. The child must recognise that the father himself is not the source of law. Rather, '[t]he father must also be recognised as one of many fathers, as not being the source of Law in himself, but rather as spokesman for the Law, with he himself being subjected to Law'.[116] With this, the child learns that the Law cannot be identified with an individual object, but takes on ineffable, anonymous 'form'.

Second, at each stage of the psyche's movement through the triadic phase and Oedipus complex, it projects itself into the world, but at the same time introjects from its interaction with the other. From day one, the child depends on others who talk to it, name it and identify it, with the psyche introjecting the meaning imposed. This '[i]ntrojection is at the root of socialization; any communication between subjects involves the possibility of receiving and incorporating words, meanings, significations coming from an other'.[117] By introjecting the meanings that are imposed on to it by others, the psyche learns and accepts what is appropriate, how it should act, and so on. Introjection, however, can only happen if the psyche participates in the process; it does not happen simply because the social imaginary imposes itself on to the psyche.

Sublimating the Psychic Monad

Castoriadis is aware that this merely 'represents a sketch of the psyche's socialisation',[118] but it shows that, contrary to his critics, he explains how the psyche and social imaginary work together to socialise the former. It must be remembered, however, that the social imaginary is not a static substance that simply imposes itself on to the psychic monad. It is itself in constant flux based on the instituted–instituting dynamic. The socialisation process must, then, be continually adjusted to accord with the alterations in the social imaginary that are forever taking place. As a consequence, the mode of transmission of the social imaginary and the social imaginary transmitted is dynamic and fantastically complex. Nevertheless, it should be clear that, for Castoriadis, the socialisation process aims to alter the activities of the psychic monad so that they accord with the perspective and demands of a particular social imaginary.

This is not, however, achieved by reducing the psyche to society. The social imaginary must sublimate the psychic monad within its ambit so that it channels its energies in accordance with the social imaginary. At a minimum, this requires that the social imaginary 'allow . . . the individual the possibility of finding and of bringing into existence for himself a meaning in the instituted social signification'.[119] The individual must, then, be permitted 'a private world, not only as a minimum circle of "autonomous" activity (as we know, this circle can be reduced to a very narrow area) but also as a world of representation (and of affect and intention), in which the individual will always be his own center'.[120] Historically, this occurred through the emphasis that capitalism places on competition and the violence of war, each of which permits the asociality of the psychic monad to be put to use for the ends of a particular social imaginary.

That the psychic monad is sublimated within the social imaginary does not, however, mean that the former is subsumed into the latter; a disjunction continues to exist and, indeed, must exist for the autonomy of the psyche and hence creation to be possible: 'The social institution of the individual must make a world exist for the psyche as a public and common world. It cannot absorb the psyche into society. Society and psyche are inseparable and irreducible to the other.'[121] For this reason, the socialisation process is fundamental but never absolute: 'Society exceeds to an unbelievable degree (although never exhaustively)'[122] in its endeavour, 'as witnessed by the existence of transgression in all known societies'.[123] That the autism of the psychic monad is never completely extinguished but continues to exist 'in' the socialised individual means that the latter cannot completely be reduced to his social imaginary; autonomous intentional agency is still possible, although Castoriadis warns that it is extremely difficult:

> People think they have 'their original way of thinking.' The truth is that even the most original thinker owes everything but a minute particle of what she says to society, to what she learned, her surroundings, the opinions and

mood of the times, or a trivial reworking of all that, which is to say, the conclusions that may be drawn, or the underlying postulates that may be uncovered. Were we to quantify, metaphorically, the truly novel kernel in Plato, Aristotle, Kant, Hegel, Marx, or Freud, it would represent, possibly, 1 per cent of what they said or wrote.[124]

Castoriadis is able to explicitly affirm and coherently defend the possibility of autonomous intentional agency because, in contrast to the other poststructuralist thinkers who start from difference or heterogeneity to explain how (the illusion of) identity or unity becomes manifest, his clinical experience brought him to start from the unity of the psychic monad to show how socialisation leads to its differentiation. By starting from unity and, indeed, insisting that it continues, albeit in sublimated form, throughout the socialisation process, he does not reduce the subject to an effect of pre-subjective processes and structures but is able to insist on a unified psychic 'place' – the monadic core – that always transcends its social grounding. This 'place' – which, it should be remembered, is not static or a substance but pure flux – is the source of autonomous, intentional agency; it always permits the subject to 'decide' how to relate to its social imaginary.

However, while fundamental, the human subject cannot, according to Castoriadis, be reduced to the psyche; the human being is also composed of biological and symbolic aspects, both of which lean on the psyche without determining it, and through their relation shape the possibilities open to the psyche. So, while the sublimation and continuing existence of the psychic monad always permit individual agency and creation, such agency is always embodied and socially embedded and, indeed, must overcome the overwhelming dominance of the social imaginary before it can be truly creative. In turn, any creative action that arises is always situated; there is no flight to an unencumbered realm. Creative autonomous agency is '*ex nihilo* but it is not *in nihilo* or *cum nihilo*; it arises somewhere and it surges forth by means of some things'.[125] It is, as Suzi Adams puts it, 'contextual creation'.[126]

Socialisation and Autonomy

By insisting that the socialised individual 'is always haunted by the underlying psych[ic monad]',[127] Castoriadis undercuts any notion of a substantial foundational subject, while explaining how the constituted subject is capable of autonomous agency. From this, he develops a political project based on the affirmation of 'autonomy',[128] the aim of which is to assert the freedom of the psychic monad within and against the heteronomy, or 'legislation or regulation by another',[129] that defines the social individual. Heteronomy is, as noted, necessary for the psyche's survival, but, once socialised, the problem with it is 'that, ruled by this discourse [of the other], the subject takes himself or herself to be something he or she is not (or is not necessarily) and that for him or her, others and the entire world undergo a corresponding misrepresentation'.[130] Put simply, socialisation brings the subject to identify with its Other; an action that contradicts the absolute autonomy of its actual, fundamental monadism.

Clinically speaking, Castoriadis claims that this disjuncture causes the subject problems, the resolution of which requires that the psyche and social imaginary agree, but in a manner in which the latter corresponds to the former. It should be emphasised, however, that the psyche is not a thing that the social imaginary can represent; the psyche is a surging flux. Castoriadis's project of autonomy aims, then, to undermine the static categories, predetermination and otherness of the social imaginary, to affirm the alteration, change and autonomy of the psychic monad. To do so, he explains that the psyche's 'discourse is to take the place of the discourse of the Other',[131] which obviously gives rise to the issue of what constitutes a discourse that is the psyche's, especially given the capacity of the socialisation process to bring the psyche to orientate itself around the other of the social imaginary. Castoriadis responds that

> a discourse that is mine is a discourse that has negated the discourse of the Other, that has negated it not necessarily in its content, but inasmuch as it is the discourse of the Other. In other words, a discourse that, by making clear both the origin and the sense of this discourse, has negated it or affirmed it in awareness of the state of affairs, by referring to its sense to that which is constituted as the subject's own truth – as my own truth.[132]

The issue, then, is not the content of the discourse, but the sense of ownership regarding it. Only when the psyche understands the statement to come from itself can the statement be held to be autonomously given to it. Castoriadis's political project of autonomy is, then, intimately tied to self-knowledge:

> The Ego of autonomy is not the absolute Self, the monad cleaning and polishing its external-internal surface in order to eliminate the impurities resulting from contact with others. It is the active and lucid agency that constantly reorganises its contents, through the help of these same contents, that produces by means of a material and in relation to needs and ideas, all of which are themselves mixtures of what it has already found there before it and what it has produced itself.[133]

On this understanding, autonomous agency is a continuous process of self-examination and alteration. It does not conform to a prior law, nor does it aim to establish one.

For this reason, Castoriadis distances his politics of autonomy from a Kantian ethics of autonomy. Whereas he understands Kantian ethics to entail the identification with and internalisation of the universal moral law, he notes that autonomy 'does not consist in acting according to a law discovered in an immutable Reason and given once and for all'.[134] Autonomy 'is the unlimited self-questioning about the law and its foundations as well as the capacity, in light of this interrogation, *to make, to do* and *to institute* (therefore also, *to say*)'.[135] Rather than adhering to a pre-established law, Castoriadis's project of autonomy is concerned with the constant interrogation and challenging of law, with this permitting the psyche to establish its own law. The challenging of law is not to affirm anarchy, it is to question and determine, on a continuous basis, whether the law in place is the most appropriate one for the form of life desired. For this reason, '[t]o be autonomous, for an individual or a collectivity, does not signify doing "what one likes" or whatever pleases one at the moment, but rather *giving oneself one's own laws*'.[136] Castoriadis's project of autonomy is, then, a politics of continuous self-interrogation, self-alteration, self-constraint and self-moderation.

Crucially, however, Castoriadis's affirmation of autonomy does not entail a flight from the social imaginary; autonomy alters the social imaginary from *within*. For this reason, the project of autonomy refers to a form of embedded agency that always takes place within a social imaginary. It has, as a consequence, an individual *and* a social aspect. The former is, as we have seen, concerned with the relationship between the social individual and the unconscious psychic monad wherein, rather than eliminate the latter, the aim is to filter 'what of one's [unconscious] desires are to pass into acts and words'.[137] However, because the individual exists 'within' a social imaginary, his or her actions are always socially embedded. For this reason, Castoriadis explains that '[w]e therefore need institutions that favour autonomy, institutions that grant to each person an effective autonomy qua member of the collectivity and that allow that person to develop her individual autonomy'.[138] This requires 'the *ongoing, explicit self-institution of society*, meaning a state in which the community knows that its institutions are its own creation and has become able to regard them as such, to re-examine them and transform them'.[139] The entwinement of the individual and the social imaginary ensures that the project of autonomy requires both individual and social change. However, it must be noted that the first stage in affirming autonomy depends upon individuals affirming that project: 'Without autonomous individuals there is no autonomous society.'[140]

This is possible because, despite the overwhelming pressure exerted on the individual by the social imaginary, the continuing existence 'within' the individual of the 'screaming monster'[141] that is the psychic monad provides the psychic 'space' from the social imaginary for the individual to autonomously think about itself, its society and the being it wants to be. It is for this reason that the psychic monad takes on such importance in Castoriadis's thought.

Conclusion

Castoriadis therefore continues the poststructuralist deconstruction of the traditional substance-based founding conception of the subject to affirm one based on flux that is split between its psychic, somatic and socio-symbolic aspects. Furthermore, by splitting the psyche between its conscious and unconscious components *and* the latter between the primal unconscious of the psychic monad and the social unconscious defined by the social imaginary, I have argued that he is able to offer a sophisticated account of the embodied, socio-symbolically embedded subject that is also sufficiently conceptually nuanced and ontologically 'thick' to describe how such a subject is capable of agency. From this, he goes on to found a political project and so counters the long-standing objection that poststructuralists are unable or unwilling to offer logically valid, normative guidelines for ethical-political action. Castoriadis's affirmation of a political project of autonomy does, however, give rise to questions including: How, given his insistence that norms are created, can Castoriadis affirm autonomy as a grounding principle for politics? And is this affirmation not simply a reflection of his own European social imaginary?

In response, it is important to return to the distinction introduced in Chapter 4 between 'the normativity of universal *a priori* rules', in which normativity is understood in a formal, positive, juridical sense that determines in advance what is and is not acceptable, and 'normativity as an open practical principle', which describes a form of normativity based on a general principle that guides, without determining, individual action and that leaves it up to the individual to determine how to affirm that principle. Castoriadis's affirmation of autonomy is clearly tied to the latter, while its justification comes from the ontological characteristics of the psyche, the radical imaginary's afoundationalism, and Castoriadis's clinical experiences, which reveal that if the psyche is to avoid the damaging disjunction that results when its autonomy is simply made to conform to its social imaginary, then the social imaginary must be constructed to express the flux and autonomy of the psychic monad.

Because the radical imaginary is pure flux and has no foundation, what emanates from it also has no absolute ground. As a consequence, there can never be an absolute foundation for any social position or norm: 'I can only dogmatically present my own opinions ... but I beg you to bear in mind that in this field there can never be a "foundation," a priori, but only a reasonable justification, downstream, of one's positions.'[142] If no position can justify itself beforehand, the only reasonable solution, according to Castoriadis, is to permit as many positions as possible to appear so as to determine which is most appropriate based on the process of continuous practical assessment that Castoriadis claims is constitutive of the project of autonomy. This also means that, rather than being a space of rational reflection and discussion, politics is defined by conflict – 'You don't refute Auschwitz or the Gulag; you combat them'[143] – and a process of trial-and-error, wherein different ideas battle it out for supremacy and become adopted or discarded based on the results – as these are judged by the collective social imaginary – gleaned from actually doing them.

With this, Castoriadis 'grounds' the project of autonomy and, indeed, politics in general 'on' the groundlessness of the psychic monad. Because it always permits the subject to do otherwise than its social imaginary demands, each individual subject is ultimately responsible for the society created and its own form and existence generally. Rather than a transcendent principle or foundation, the type of social imaginary that a subject lives is based on nothing other than 'the desire and ability of women and men to change their social existence, to acknowledge their responsibility for their fate, and to fully shoulder responsibility'.[144] That politics is premised on the desire of individuals – as a collective – not only reveals its constitutive bond to psychoanalysis, but also shows that Castoriadis's project of autonomy is, ultimately, one of individual, ethical responsibility.

Notes

1. Cornelius Castoriadis, 'Psychoanalysis: Project and Elucidation', in *Crossroads in the Labyrinth*, trans. Kate Soper and Martin H. Ryle (Cambridge, MA: MIT Press, 1984), pp. 46–115 (p. 82).
2. Cornelius Castoriadis, 'The State of the Subject Today', in *World in Fragments: Writings on Politics, Society, Psychoanalysis, and the Imagination*, ed. and trans. David Ames Curtis (Stanford, CA: Stanford University Press, 1997), pp. 137–71 (p. 144).
3. Ibid., p. 144.
4. Ibid., p. 144.
5. Ibid., p. 144.

6. Ibid., pp. 144–5.
7. Cornelius Castoriadis, 'Power, Politics, Autonomy', in *Philosophy, Politics, Autonomy: Essays in Political Philosophy*, ed. David Ames Curtis (Oxford: Oxford University Press, 1991), pp. 143–74 (p. 148).
8. Ibid., p. 148.
9. Joel Whitbook, *Perversion and Utopia: A Study in Psychoanalysis and Critical Theory* (Cambridge, MA: MIT Press, 1996), p. 177.
10. Eugene V. Wolfenstein, 'Psychoanalysis in Political Theory', *Political Theory*, 24.4, 1996, pp. 706–28 (p. 717); Marcel Gauchet, 'Redefining the Unconscious', *Thesis Eleven*, 71.1, 2002, pp. 4–23 (p. 10); Karl E. Smith, 'Re-imagining Castoriadis's Psychic Monad', *Thesis Eleven*, 83.1, 2005, pp. 5–14 (p. 11).
11. Cornelius Castoriadis, *The Imaginary Institution of Society*, trans. Kathleen Blamey (Cambridge, MA: MIT Press, 1998), p. 300.
12. Ibid., p. 298.
13. Cornelius Castoriadis, 'False and True Chaos', in *Figures of the Thinkable*, trans. Helen Arnold (Stanford, CA: Stanford University Press, 2007), pp. 236–43 (p. 241).
14. Cornelius Castoriadis, 'Psyche and Education', in *Figures of the Thinkable*, trans. Helen Arnold (Stanford, CA: Stanford University Press, 2007), pp. 165–87 (p. 187).
15. Castoriadis, *The Imaginary Institution of Society*, p. 204.
16. Cornelius Castoriadis, 'The Social-Historical: Mode of Being, Problems of Knowledge', in *Power, Politics, Autonomy: Essays in Political Philosophy*, ed. David Ames Curtis (Oxford: Oxford University Press, 1991), pp. 33–46 (p. 34).
17. Cornelius Castoriadis, 'Individual, Society, Rationality, History', in *Power, Politics, Autonomy: Essays in Political Philosophy*, ed. David Ames Curtis (Oxford: Oxford University Press, 1991), pp. 47–80 (p. 77).
18. Castoriadis, 'Psychoanalysis', p. 88.
19. Castoriadis, *The Imaginary Institution of Society*, p. 108.
20. Ibid., p. 111.
21. Ibid., p. 109.
22. Ibid., p. 108, italics in original.
23. Ibid., p. 108.
24. Ibid., p. 114.
25. Castoriadis, 'Individual, Society, Rationality, History', p. 84.
26. Castoriadis, *The Imaginary Institution of Society*, p. 127.
27. Cornelius Castoriadis, 'The Psyche and the Society Anew', in *Figures of the Thinkable*, trans. Helen Arnold (Stanford, CA: Stanford University Press, 2007), pp. 203–20 (p. 206).
28. Castoriadis, *The Imaginary Institution of Society*, p. 3.
29. Ibid., pp. 274, 3.
30. Cornelius Castoriadis, 'From Monad to Autonomy', in *World in Fragments: Writings on Politics, Society, Psychoanalysis, and the Imagination*, ed. and trans. David Ames Curtis (Stanford, CA: Stanford University Press, 1997), pp. 172–95 (p. 183).

31. Castoriadis, 'Individual, Society, Rationality, History', p. 84.
32. Castoriadis, 'The Psyche and the Society Anew', p. 216.
33. Cornelius Castoriadis, 'The Imaginary: Creation in the Social-Historical Domain', in *World in Fragments: Writings on Politics, Society, Psychoanalysis, and the Imagination*, ed. and trans. David Ames Curtis (Stanford, CA: Stanford University Press, 1997), pp. 3–18 (p. 3).
34. Ibid., p. 7.
35. Castoriadis, *The Imaginary Institution of Society*, p. 368.
36. Ibid., p. 238.
37. Ibid., pp. 146–7.
38. Ibid., p. 147.
39. Ibid., p. 234.
40. Castoriadis, 'The Imaginary', p. 16.
41. Cornelius Castoriadis, 'Imaginary Significations', in *A Society Adrift: Interviews and Debates, 1974–1997*, ed. Enrique Escobar, Myrto Gondicas and Pascal Vernay, trans. Helen Arnold (New York: Fordham University Press, 2010), pp. 45–68 (p. 60).
42 Castoriadis, *The Imaginary Institution of Society*, p. 229.
43. Ibid., p. 229.
44. Ibid., p. 229.
45. Ibid., p. 230.
46. For example, although Castoriadis recognises that a social imaginary can affirm non-heteronormative forms of relations, the notion of an originary 'natural' binary male/female opposition ensures that his thinking appears to continue to depend upon a troubling binarism at the 'natural' level that is unable to recognise or take into consideration alternative 'natural' bodily forms, such as intersex.
47. Luce Irigaray, *I Love to You: Sketch of a Possible Felicity in History*, trans. Alison Martin (Abingdon: Routledge, 1996), p. 35.
48. Luce Irigaray, *The Way of Love*, trans. Heidi Bostic and Stephen Plukáček (London: Continuum, 2002), p. 106. Irigaray's thought is open to heterogeneous interpretation, but for a defence, albeit one that is also critical, of this realist interpretation, see Alison Stone, *Luce Irigaray and the Philosophy of Sexual Difference* (Cambridge: Cambridge University Press, 2006).
49. For example, Irigaray talks of the 'rhythms of nature' (*Sexes and Genealogies*, trans. Gillian C. Gill [New York: Columbia University Press, 1993], p. 200). For an extended discussion of Irigaray's dependence on a rhythmic, rather than substantive, account of nature and its implications for the sexual difference, see Alison Stone, 'The Sex of Nature: A Reinterpretation of Irigaray's Metaphysis and Political Thought', *Hypatia*, 18.3, 2003, pp. 60–84 (p. 77).
50. Irigaray, *Sexes and Genealogies*, p. 169.
51. Luce Irigaray, *To be Two*, trans. Monique M. Rhodes and Marco F. Cocito-Monoc (London: Athlone, 2000), p. 55
52. Irigaray, *I Love to You*, p. 25.

53. Castoriadis, *The Imaginary Institution of Society*, pp. 127–8.
54. Ibid., p. 127.
55. Castoriadis, 'Psychoanalysis: Project and Elucidation', p. 66.
56. Castoriadis, *The Imaginary Institution of Society*, p. 127.
57. Ibid., p. 269.
58. Castoriadis, 'Power, Politics, Autonomy', p. 150.
59. Castoriadis, *The Imaginary Institution of Society*, p. 283.
60. Ibid., p. 283.
61. Cornelius Castoriadis, 'The Nature and Value of Equality', in *Philosophy, Politics, Autonomy: Essays in Political Philosophy*, ed. David Ames Curtis (Oxford: Oxford University Press, 1991), pp. 124–42 (p. 128).
62. Cornelius Castoriadis, 'Psychoanalysis: Its Situation and Limits', in *Figures of the Thinkable*, trans. Helen Arnold (Stanford, CA: Stanford University Press, 2007), pp. 188–202 (p. 200).
63. Cornelius Castoriadis, 'The Greek *Polis* and the Creation of Democracy', in *Philosophy, Politics, Autonomy: Essays in Political Philosophy*, ed. David Ames Curtis (Oxford: Oxford University Press, 1991), pp. 81–123 (p. 94).
64. Castoriadis, 'Individual, Society, Rationality, History', p. 70.
65. Castoriadis, 'Psychoanalysis', p. 199.
66. Castoriadis, *The Imaginary Institution of Society*, pp. 291–2.
67. Cornelius Castoriadis, 'Life and Creation: Cornelius Castoriadis in Dialogue with Francisco Varela', in *Postscripts on Insignificance: Dialogues with Cornelius Castoriadis*, ed. Gabriel Rockhill, trans. Gabriel Rockhill and John V. Garner (London: Continuum, 2011), pp. 58–73 (p. 64).
68. Castoriadis, 'False and True Chaos', p. 241.
69. Castoriadis, *The Imaginary Institution of Society*, p. 289.
70. Ibid., p. 290.
71. Ibid., p. 290.
72. Ibid., p. 298.
73. Castoriadis, 'Psyche and Education', p. 171.
74. Castoriadis, *The Imaginary Institution of Society*, p. 298.
75. Castoriadis, 'From Monad to Autonomy', p. 187.
76. Castoriadis, 'The Social-Historical', p. 41.
77. Ibid., pp. 41–2.
78. Castoriadis, *The Imaginary Institution of Society*, p. 311.
79. Ibid., p. 311.
80. Cornelius Castoriadis, 'Psychoanalysis and Politics', in *World in Fragments: Writings on Politics, Society, Psychoanalysis, and the Imagination*, ed. and trans. David Ames Curtis (Stanford, CA: Stanford University Press, 1997), pp. 125–36 (p. 135).
81. Ibid., p. 135.
82. Castoriadis, *The Imaginary Institution of Society*, p. 315.
83. Castoriadis, 'The Psyche and Society Anew', p. 211.
84. Ibid., p. 207.

85. Castoriadis, 'The State of the Subject Today', p. 169.
86. Cornelius Castoriadis, 'A Rising Tide of Significacy?', in *A Society Adrift: Interviews and Debates, 1974–1997*, ed. Enrique Escobar, Myrto Gondicas and Pascal Vernay, trans. Helen Arnold (New York: Fordham University Press, 2010), pp. 223–9 (p. 233).
87. Whitbook, *Perversion and Utopia*, p. 177.
88. Wolfenstein, 'Psychoanalysis in Political Theory', p. 717; Gauchet, 'Redefining the Unconscious', p. 10; Smith, 'Re-imagining Castoriadis's Psychic Monad', p. 11.
89. David A. Curtis and Andreas Kalyvas, 'Fighting the Wrong Enemy: Comments on Wolfenstein's Critique of Castoriadis', *Political Theory*, 26.6, 1998, pp. 818–24 (p. 819).
90. Marcela Tovar-Restrepo, *Castoriadis, Foucault, and Autonomy: New Approaches to Subjectivity, Society, and Social Change* (London: Continuum, 2012), pp. 49–50.
91. Jeff Klooger, *Castoriadis: Psyche, Society, Autonomy* (Leiden: Brill, 2009), pp. 21–2.
92. For an extended discussion of this, see Gavin Rae, 'Taming the Little Screaming Monster: Castoriadis, Violence, and the Creation of the Individual', in Gavin Rae and Emma Ingala (eds), *The Meanings of Violence: From Critical Theory to Biopolitics* (Abingdon: Routledge, 2019), pp. 171–90.
93. Castoriadis, *The Imaginary Institution of Society*, p. 300.
94. Cornelius Castoriadis, 'The Psychical and Social Roots of Hate', in *Figures of the Thinkable*, trans. Helen Arnold (Stanford, CA: Stanford University Press, 2007), pp. 153–64 (p. 156).
95. Castoriadis, *The Imaginary Institution of Society*, p. 300.
96. Ibid., p. 301.
97. Ibid., p. 302.
98. Ibid., p. 302.
99. Ibid., p. 302. While he does not mention her, Castoriadis's description of the child's relationship to the breast is indebted to the distinction between the good and bad breast introduced by Melanie Klein in *The Psychoanalysis of Children*, trans. Alix Strachey (New York: Grove Press, 1960).
100. Castoriadis, *The Imaginary Institution of Society*, p. 303.
101. Ibid., p. 303.
102. Ibid., p. 303.
103. Ibid., p. 303.
104. Ibid., p. 304.
105. Ibid., p. 304.
106. Ibid., p. 304.
107. It is important to note that, despite the heteronormative language, which is found throughout Freudian psychoanalysis, the terms 'mother' and 'father' refer to functions rather than necessarily to actual individuals. To simplify dramatically, 'mother' refers to love and care, whereas 'father' refers to discipline or law. As previously discussed, Castoriadis notes that each social imaginary

will designate who – and, indeed, which biological sex – is primarily associated with these functions and, indeed, how they should be fulfilled. See, for example, the discussion of heterosexual desire in Castoriadis, *The Imaginary Institution of Society*, pp. 229–30.
108. Castoriadis, *The Imaginary Institution of Society*, p. 304.
109. Ibid., p. 305.
110. Castoriadis, 'The Psyche and Society Anew', p. 215.
111. Ibid., p. 215.
112. Castoriadis, *The Imaginary Institution of Society*, p. 306.
113. Castoriadis, 'The Psyche and Society Anew', p. 215.
114. Ibid., p. 215.
115. Ibid., p. 215.
116. Ibid., p. 216.
117. Ibid., p. 214.
118. Castoriadis, *The Imaginary Institution of Society*, p. 306.
119. Ibid., p. 320.
120. Ibid., p. 320.
121. Ibid., p. 320.
122. Castoriadis, 'The Social-Historical', p. 42.
123. Cornelius Castoriadis, 'Heritage and Revolution', in *Figures of the Thinkable*, trans. Helen Arnold (Stanford, CA: Stanford University Press, 2007), pp. 105–17 (p. 109).
124. Castoriadis, 'Imaginary Significations', pp. 46–7.
125. Castoriadis, 'False and True Chaos', pp. 240–1.
126. Suzi Adams, 'Interpreting Creation: Castoriadis and the Birth of Autonomy', *Thesis Eleven*, 83.1, 2005, pp. 25–41 (p. 25).
127. Castoriadis, 'The Social-Historical', p. 242.
128. Castoriadis, 'Power, Politics, Autonomy', p. 169.
129. Castoriadis, *The Imaginary Institution of Society*, p. 102.
130. Ibid., p. 103.
131. Ibid., p. 103.
132. Ibid., p. 103.
133. Ibid., p. 106.
134. Castoriadis, 'Power, Politics, Autonomy', p. 164.
135. Ibid., p. 164.
136. Cornelius Castoriadis, '*Phusis* and Autonomy', in *World in Fragments: Writings on Politics, Society, Psychoanalysis, and the Imagination*, ed. and trans. David Ames Curtis (Stanford, CA: Stanford University Press, 1997), pp. 331–41 (p. 332).
137. Cornelius Castoriadis, 'The Ethicist's New Clothes', in *World in Fragments: Writings on Politics, Society, Psychoanalysis, and the Imagination*, ed. and trans. David Ames Curtis (Stanford, CA: Stanford University Press, 1997), pp. 108–22 (p. 122).
138. Ibid., p. 122.

139. Cornelius Castoriadis, 'Why I am no Longer a Marxist', in *A Society Adrift: Interviews and Debates, 1974–1997*, ed. Enrique Escobar, Myrto Gondicas and Pascal Vernay, trans. Helen Arnold (New York: Fordham University Press, 2010), pp. 11–44 (p. 41).
140. Cornelius Castoriadis, 'Breaking the Closure: Cornelius Castoriadis in Dialogue with Robert Legros', in *Postscript on Insignificance: Dialogues with Cornelius Castoriadis*, ed. Gabriel Rockhill, trans. Gabriel Rockhill and John V. Garner (London: Continuum, 2011), pp. 93–107 (pp. 104–5).
141. Castoriadis, 'Power, Politics, Autonomy', p. 149.
142. Castoriadis, 'Psychoanalysis', p. 196.
143. Cornelius Castoriadis, 'On the Possibility of Creating a New Form of Society', in *A Society Adrift: Interviews and Debates, 1974–1997*, ed. Enrique Escobar, Myrto Gondicas and Pascal Vernay, trans. Helen Arnold (New York: Fordham University Press, 2010), pp. 103–17 (p. 116).
144. Ibid., p. 116.

Conclusion

In the preceding pages, I have attempted to show that, far from simply abandoning the subject or dissolving it as a determined effect of pre-personal structures and processes as is so often affirmed by their critics, poststructuralist thinkers not only take the question of 'the subject' seriously, but also provide a variety of remarkably rich and heterogeneous engagements with it. As I mentioned in the Introduction, this can rightly give rise to the conclusion that there is not one poststructuralism, but many *poststructuralisms*, but I have suggested that there is a style of thought common to these endeavours that justifies talk of the former. Specifically, each thinker offers a sustained critique of the historically dominant foundational subject by questioning the epistemological, metaphysical and ontological assumptions underpinning it. Generally speaking, this entails a rejection of a metaphysics of presence or fixed substance, and, instead, the affirmation of flux, non-identity, embeddedness and epistemic ambiguity; which is not to say that knowledge is abandoned, only that how we think about the subject, including what the subject is, must also change so as to 'start' from continuous flux and alteration. Rather than a foundational constituting subject, the poststructuralist approach decentres the subject to embed it – in different ways – in pre-subjective processes and forces. Of course, what this entails is contentious and accounts for the heterogeneity of the previous chapters.

The subject is not, then, incidental or contingent to poststructuralist thought; it is fundamental and, in many respects, *the* theme or lens that best brings out what is unique about its style of thought. But to say that poststructuralist thinkers do not abandon the subject even as they seek to rethink it does not do justice to the depth of their inquiries. While they challenge long-standing prejudices regarding the subject, I have also shown that they produce subtle and detailed analyses of a range of topics that result from that rethinking, most notably relating to the issue of individual intentional agency. Indeed, given their stringent critique of the founding constituting subject, poststructuralist thinkers have had to engage substantially with this topic because it is one of the key issues that results from that critique. Sometimes this is to rely on a capacity for intentional agency without fully explaining how their theories permit it, but, at least in the cases of the later Foucault, Butler, Lacan, Kristeva and especially Castoriadis, it also entails a sustained attempt to address it, albeit from and within the terms of their respective thinking.

This is not, of course, to say that all attempts are satisfactory. In particular, I have argued that it is those poststructuralists who explicitly turn to psychoanalytic theory who have had most success in explicitly dealing with this issue. The reason is not hard to determine: given that psychoanalysis sets itself the goal of understanding the subject, it must engage, to a far greater degree than non-psychoanalytical approaches, with precisely what the subject is, including the processes, structures and 'inner' workings that compose it. From this, talk of 'the subject' is replaced with a far more nuanced and differentiated conception, manifested most clearly through the turn to the psyche, which in turn is split between the conscious and unconscious. This distinction is important because it undermines the claim that the subject is transparent to itself so as to, instead, reveal that the subject is tied to unconscious processes that it does not consciously control. In so doing, the way in which the subject is founded and affected by its other, whether this is through its social or symbolic relations, is complicated.

However, as I have argued, the conscious/unconscious split is not, itself, structurally sufficient to account for how the founded subject is capable of agency, because it is still not capable of explaining how the subject, unconsciously conditioned by its other, is capable of acting in ways that run contrary to those prescribed by the other. Overcoming this problem requires, so I have argued, that we follow Castoriadis in distinguishing between the individual, the subject – the overarching 'totality' of both the social individual and the psychic monad – and the psyche, itself split between the conscious and unconscious, with the latter being further split between what I called the 'social unconscious' conditioned by the social norms and values of the social imaginary that the subject exists, and a more primordial form of the unconscious that remains autonomous from the former. With this, Castoriadis provides a *general model* that is capable of explaining how the subject, as a socialised individual, can be conditioned by its social imaginary – thereby confirming the poststructuralist affirmation of a founded constituted subject – but still be able, no matter to what degree it actually happens, to act against that social imaginary.

This does, however, require that we follow Castoriadis in reversing the primordial importance that poststructuralist thinkers have tended to accord to difference or heterogeneity, so as to instead start from the fluctuating unity of the psychic monad that is broken up through its socialisation. This does not annihilate the primordial monad but sublimates it, thereby allowing it to be the foundation from which the subject can 'push off' to act in ways other than those deemed appropriate by its founding other. It should, however, be remembered that the unified 'ground' of the psyche is not a substance but a process of continual surging flux, which brings it into line with the poststructuralist rejection of ahistoric essential substances. By starting from a primordial monad that is broken up, Castoriadis reconceptualises the identity/unity–difference relationship as it relates to the subject to, in so doing, challenge us to reconsider what we mean by 'poststructuralism'. Rather than simply affirming difference or a homogeneous unity, he argues for a compatibilist approach wherein both aspects continuously interact to create and sustain an agential subject.

The fundamental criticism levelled against this schema is, of course, that it establishes and depends upon a problematic binary opposition between psyche and society. On the one hand, Castoriadis insists that this division is necessary for autonomous agency, but, with his notion of 'leaning on', I have argued that he embeds this relationship within a wider and more nuanced understanding of the *subject* in which the psyche, somatic and social-symbolic intertwine. Focusing on the psyche–social imaginary opposition is, then, a(n) (early) stage in his theory that fails to recognise the ways in which he complicates, undermines and nuances it to offer an embodied, socially symbolically embedded notion of the subject that is also sufficiently conceptually thick to permit a sophisticated, subtle and coherent analysis of how such a subject is capable of agency. Of course, a critical engagement with Castoriadis's theory might question the specific interrelationships between the social, symbolic, somatic and psychic aspects of his thinking to suggest that they need to be developed and nuanced, but I would suggest that this would entail a further elucidation *within* his schema, rather than a fundamental reworking of it. As such, of the thinkers engaged with here, he offers the most fully developed, holistic, multidimensional and promising poststructuralist account of subjective agency.

That poststructuralist thinkers engage with the issue of agency and, indeed, through the thought of Castoriadis especially, offer a sophisticated elucidation of it does, however, bring forth the further question of how that agency is to be exercised. This is, as noted in the Introduction, related to another frequently levelled criticism of poststructuralist thought, wherein critics insist that, given the dissolution of the subject, no constructive or normative politics is possible. On the contrary, I have argued that *all* poststructuralists are deeply and extensively concerned with the question of politics, but engage with it based on their own premises. As such, the politics offered is not founded on an ahistoric principle or the constituting subject that their critics tend to assume it is and should be. Instead, poststructuralist thinkers rethink politics and political action in a processual, contingent and practice-based way. Because they hold that there are no ahistoric foundations to ground or direct action, the emphasis is placed on political experimentation and action itself, without an ahistoric rule to guide it, which is not to say that there is no normative position offered.

Understanding this requires that we reconfigure what we mean by 'normative' by distinguishing between 'the normativity of universal *a priori* rules', which describes a formal, positive, juridical sense that determines in advance what is and is not acceptable, and 'normativity as an open practical principle', which describes a form of normativity based on a general principle that guides, without determining, individual action and that leaves it up to the individual to determine how to affirm that principle in each context. By asserting (to varying degrees) the latter position, poststructuralists – such as Butler, Derrida (with his later notion of 'justice-to-come'),[1] Foucault, Kristeva and especially Castoriadis – are able to offer a normative perspective to guide political agency while remaining consistent with their rejection of *a priori*, ahistoric foundations.

Importantly, the affirmation of a contentless principle does not lead to the defence of anarchic asociality but, on the contrary, is intimately bound up with an ethics and politics of responsibility. This emanates from two different, but related, premises. First, while the embedded and embodied nature of subjectivity means that the subject is always conditioned and constrained by its other – social, symbolic, somatic and so on – it is not *determined* by its conditions and so can always act differently to them. Second, if the subject acts against its conditions, the lack of *a priori* grounding for such action means that the subject alone is ultimately responsible for its choice of action. As a consequence, poststructuralist thought offers not only a number of sophisticated and radical critiques of the foundational subject to reconstruct it in founded terms that continue to accept that the founded subject is capable of intentional agency, but also, with the notion of what I have called 'normativity as an open practical principle', offer a way to guide that agency that remains consistent with its rejection of ahistoric principles and structures. Those who seek to ground political action in predetermined universal principles or rules will probably reject this as too indeterminate, but it does identify and, indeed, recast the political nature of poststructuralist thought, while also offering a concrete, flexible, experiential and immanent account of ethical and political action. Understood in this way, we see then that poststructuralist thought continues to be a rich resource for thinking about subjectivity, agency and the ethical-political relation.

Note

1. See, for example, Jacques Derrida, 'Force of Law: The "Mystical Foundation of Authority"', in *Acts of Religion*, ed. Gil Anidjar (Abingdon: Routledge, 2002), pp. 230–98 (p. 256).

BIBLIOGRAPHY

Adams, Suzi, 'Interpreting Creation: Castoriadis and the Birth of Autonomy', *Thesis Eleven*, 83.1, 2005, pp. 25–41.
— *Castoriadis's Ontology: Being and Creation* (New York: Fordham University Press, 2011).
Adkins, Brent, *Deleuze and Guattari's A Thousand Plateaus: A Critical Introduction and Guide* (Edinburgh: Edinburgh University Press, 2015).
Allen, Amy, 'The Anti-Subjective Hypothesis: Michel Foucault and the Death of the Subject', *Philosophical Forum*, 31.2, 2000, pp. 113–30.
— 'Power, Subjectivity, and Agency: Between Arendt and Foucault', *International Journal of Philosophical Studies*, 10.2, 2002, pp. 131–49.
— 'Dependency, Subordination, and Recognition: On Judith Butler's Theory of Subjection', *Continental Philosophy Review*, 38, 2006, pp. 199–222.
— *The Politics of Our Selves: Power, Autonomy, and Gender in Contemporary Critical Theory* (New York: Columbia University Press, 2008).
Althusser, Louis, 'Ideology and Ideological State Apparatus (Notes Towards an Investigation)', in *Lenin and Philosophy and Other Essays*, trans. Ben Brewster (New York: Monthly Review Press, 2001), pp. 85–126.
Arendt, Hannah, *On Violence* (New York: Harvest, 1970).
Arfi, Badredine, 'Reconfiguring the (Lacanian) Real: Saying the Real (as Khôra – χώρα) qua the impossible-possible event', *Philosophy and Social Criticism*, 38.8, 2012, pp. 793–819.
Armour, Ellen T., 'Questions of Proximity: "Women's Place" in Derrida and Irigaray', *Hypatia*, 12.1, 1997, pp. 63–78.
Bailly, Lionel, *Lacan* (London: OneWorld, 2009).
Balibar, Etienne, 'Structuralism: A Destitution of the Subject?' *differences: A Journal of Feminist Cultural Studies*, 14.1, 2003, pp. 1–21.

Balsam, Rosemary H., 'The Embodied Mother: Commentary on Kristeva', *Journal of the American Psychoanalytical Association*, 62.1, 2014, pp. 87–100.
Banner, Eve Tavor, *Structuralism and the Logic of Dissent* (Urbana, IL: University of Illinois Press, 1989).
Bartky, S. L., 'Originative Thinking in the Later Philosophy of Heidegger', *Philosophy and Phenomenological Review*, 30.3, 1970, pp. 368–81.
Baugh, Bruce, 'Making the Difference: Deleuze's Difference and Derrida's *différance*', *Social Semiotics*, 7.2, 1997, pp. 127–46.
— *French Hegel: From Surrealism to Postmodernism* (Abingdon: Routledge, 2003).
Beardsworth, Sara, *Julia Kristeva: Psychoanalysis and Modernity* (Albany, NY: State University of New York Press, 2004).
Bearn, Gordon C. F., 'Differentiating Derrida and Deleuze', *Continental Philosophy Review*, 33.4, 2000, pp. 441–65.
Benhabib, Seyla, 'Feminism and Postmodernism', in Seyla Benhabib, Judith Butler, Drucilla Cornell and Nancy Fraser, *Feminist Contentions: A Philosophical Exchange* (Abingdon: Routledge, 1995), pp. 17–34.
— 'Subjectivity, Historiography, and Politics', in Seyla Benhabib, Judith Butler, Drucilla Cornell and Nancy Fraser, *Femininst Contentions: A Philosophical Exchange* (Abingdon: Routledge, 1995), pp. 107–26.
Bennett, Jane, *Vibrant Matter: A Political Ecology of Things* (Durham, NC: Duke University Press, 2010).
Bevir, Mark, 'Foucault and Critique: Deploying Agency against Autonomy', *Political Theory*, 27.1, 1999, pp. 65–84.
— 'Foucault, Power, and Institution', *Political Studies*, 47.2, 1999, pp. 345–59.
Bignall, Simone, 'Dismantling the Face: Pluralism and the Politics of Recognition', *Deleuze Studies*, 6.3, 2012, pp. 389–410.
Borch-Jacobsen, Mikkel, *Lacan: The Absolute Master*, trans. Douglas Brick (Stanford, CA: Stanford University Press, 1991).
Boucher, Geoff, 'Judith Butler's Postmodern Existentialism: A Critical Analysis', *Philosophy Today*, 48.4, 2004, pp. 355–69.
Bowden, Sean, '"Willing the Event": Expressive Agency in Deleuze's *Logic of Sense*', *Critical Horizons*, 15.3, 2014, pp. 231–48.
— 'Human and Nonhuman Agency in Deleuze', in Jon Roffe and Hannah Stark (eds), *Deleuze and the Non/Human* (Basingstoke: Palgrave Macmillan, 2015), pp. 60–80.
— 'Normativity and Expressive Agency in Hegel, Nietzsche, and Deleuze', *Journal of Speculative Philosophy*, 29.2, 2015, pp. 236–59.
— 'Tragedy and Agency in Hegel and Deleuze', in Craig Lundy and Daniella Voss (eds), *At the Edges of Thought: Deleuze and Post-Kantian Philosophy* (Edinburgh: Edinburgh University Press, 2015), pp. 212–28.

Bracher, Mark, 'On the Psychological and Social Functions of Language: Lacan's Theory of the Four Discourses', in Mark Bracher, Marshall W. Alcorn, Jr, Ronald J. Corthell and Françoise Massardier-Kenney (eds), *Lacanian Theory of Discourse: Subject, Structure, and Society* (New York: New York University Press, 1994), pp. 107–28.

Breckman, Warren, *Adventures of the Symbolic: Post-Marxism and Radical Democracy* (New York: Columbia University Press, 2013).

Buchanan, Ian, and Claire Colebrook (eds), *Deleuze and Feminist Theory* (Edinburgh: Edinburgh University Press, 2000).

Buchanan, Ian, and Nicholas Thoburn (eds), *Deleuze and Politics* (Edinburgh: Edinburgh University Press, 2008).

Butler, Judith, 'Foucault and the Paradox of Bodily Inscription', *The Journal of Philosophy*, 86.11, 1989, pp. 601–7.

— *Bodies that Matter: On the Discursive Limits of "Sex"* (Abingdon: Routledge, 1993).

— 'Contingent Foundations', in Seyla Benhabib, Judith Butler, Drucilla Cornell and Nancy Fraser, *Feminist Contentions: A Philosophical Exchange* (Abingdon: Routledge, 1995), pp. 35–58.

— *Excitable Speech: A Politics of the Performative* (Abingdon: Routledge, 1997).

— *The Psychic Life of Power: Theories in Subjection* (Stanford, CA: Stanford University Press, 1997).

— *Gender Trouble: Feminism and the Subversion of Identity*, 2nd edn (Abingdon: Routledge, 1999).

— *Subjects of Desire: Hegelian Reflections in Twentieth-Century France* (New York: Columbia University Press, 1999).

— *Antigone's Claim: Kinship between Life and Death* (New York: Columbia University Press, 2000).

— 'Competing Universalities', in Judith Butler, Ernesto Laclau and Slavoj Žižek, *Contingency, Hegemony, Universality: Contemporary Dialogues on the Left* (London: Verso, 2000), pp. 136–81.

— 'Beside Oneself: On the Limits of Sexual Autonomy', in *Undoing Gender* (Abingdon: Routledge, 2004), pp. 17–39.

— 'Quandaries of the Incest Taboo', in *Undoing Gender* (Abingdon: Routledge, 2004), pp. 152–60.

— 'The End of Sexual Difference', in *Undoing Gender* (Abingdon: Routledge, 2004), pp. 174–203.

— *Giving an Account of Oneself* (New York: Fordham University Press, 2005).

— 'Performative Agency', *Journal of Cultural Economy*, 3.2, 2010, pp. 147–61.

— 'Introduction', in *Senses of the Subject* (New York: Fordham University Press, 2015), pp. 1–16.

— 'How Can I Deny that these Hands and this Body are Mine?', in *Senses of the Subject* (New York: Fordham University Press, 2015), pp. 17–35.

— *Notes for a Performative Theory of Assembly* (Cambridge, MA: Harvard University Press, 2015).

Butler, Judith, and Vicki Bell, 'New Schemes of Vulnerability: Agency and Plurality', *Theory, Culture, and Society*, 27.1, 2010, pp. 130–52.

Butler, Judith, and Joan W. Scott, 'Introduction', in Judith Butler and Joan W. Scott (eds), *Feminists Theorize the Political* (Abingdon: Routledge, 1992), pp. xiii–xvii.

Cadava, Eduardo, Peter Connor and Jean-Luc Nancy (eds), *Who Comes after the Subject?* (Abingdon: Routledge, 1991).

Campbel+l, Kirsten, 'The Plague of the Subject: Psychoanalysis and Judith Butler's *The Psychic Life of Power*', *International Journal of Sexuality and Gender Studies*, 6.1/2, 2001, pp. 35–48.

Castoriadis, Cornelius, 'Psychoanalysis: Project and Elucidation', in *Crossroads in the Labyrinth*, trans. Kate Soper and Martin H. Ryle (Cambridge, MA: MIT Press, 1984), pp. 46–115.

— 'The Social-Historical: Mode of Being, Problems of Knowledge', in *Philosophy, Politics, Autonomy: Essays in Political Philosophy*, ed. David Ames Curtis (Oxford: Oxford University Press, 1991), pp. 33–46.

— 'Individual, Society, Rationality, History', in *Philosophy, Politics, Autonomy: Essays in Political Philosophy*, ed. David Ames Curtis (Oxford: Oxford University Press, 1991), pp. 47–80.

— 'The Greek *Polis* and the Creation of Democracy', in *Philosophy, Politics, Autonomy: Essays in Political Philosophy*, ed. David Ames Curtis (Oxford: Oxford University Press, 1991), pp. 81–123.

— 'The Nature and Value of Equality', in *Philosophy, Politics, Autonomy: Essays in Political Philosophy*, ed. David Ames Curtis (Oxford: Oxford University Press, 1991), pp. 124–42.

— 'Power, Politics, Autonomy', in *Philosophy, Politics, Autonomy: Essays in Political Philosophy*, ed. David Ames Curtis (Oxford: Oxford University Press, 1991), pp. 143–74.

— 'The Imaginary: Creation in the Social-Historical Domain', in *World in Fragments: Writings on Politics, Society, Psychoanalysis, and the Imagination*, ed. and trans. David Ames Curtis (Stanford, CA: Stanford University Press, 1997), pp. 3–18.

— 'The Ethicist's New Clothes', in *World in Fragments: Writings on Politics, Society, Psychoanalysis, and the Imagination*, ed. and trans. David Ames Curtis (Stanford, CA: Stanford University Press, 1997), pp. 108–22.

— 'Psychoanalysis and Politics', in *World in Fragments: Writings on Politics, Society, Psychoanalysis, and the Imagination*, ed. and trans. David Ames Curtis (Stanford, CA: Stanford University Press, 1997), pp. 125–36.

— 'The State of the Subject Today', in *World in Fragments: Writings on Politics, Society, Psychoanalysis, and the Imagination*, ed. and trans. David Ames Curtis (Stanford, CA: Stanford University Press, 1997), pp. 137–71.
— 'From Monad to Autonomy', in *World in Fragments: Writings on Politics, Society, Psychoanalysis, and the Imagination*, ed. and trans. David Ames Curtis (Stanford, CA: Stanford University Press, 1997), pp. 172–95.
— '*Phusis* and Autonomy', in *World in Fragments: Writings on Politics, Society, Psychoanalysis, and the Imagination*, ed. and trans. David Ames Curtis (Stanford, CA: Stanford University Press, 1997), pp. 331–41.
— *The Imaginary Institution of Society*, trans. Kathleen Blamey (Cambridge, MA: MIT Press, 1998).
— 'Heritage and Revolution', in *Figures of the Thinkable*, trans. Helen Arnold (Stanford, CA: Stanford University Press, 2007), pp. 105–17.
— 'The Psychical and Social Roots of Hate', in *Figures of the Thinkable*, trans. Helen Arnold (Stanford, CA: Stanford University Press, 2007), pp. 153–64.
— 'Psyche and Education', in *Figures of the Thinkable*, trans. Helen Arnold (Stanford, CA: Stanford University Press, 2007), pp. 165–87.
— 'Psychoanalysis: Its Situation and Limits', in *Figures of the Thinkable*, trans. Helen Arnold (Stanford, CA: Stanford University Press, 2007), pp. 188–202.
— 'The Psyche and Society Anew', in *Figures of the Thinkable*, trans. Helen Arnold (Stanford, CA: Stanford University Press, 2007), pp. 203–20.
— 'False and True Chaos', in *Figures of the Thinkable*, trans. Helen Arnold (Stanford, CA: Stanford University Press, 2007), pp. 236–43.
— 'Why I am no Longer a Marxist', in *A Society Adrift: Interviews and Debates, 1974–1997*, ed. Enrique Escobar, Myrto Gondicas and Pascal Vernay, trans. Helen Arnold (New York: Fordham University Press, 2010), pp. 11–44.
— 'Imaginary Significations', in *A Society Adrift: Interviews and Debates, 1974–1997*, ed. Enrique Escobar, Myrto Gondicas and Pascal Vernay, trans. Helen Arnold (New York: Fordham University Press, 2010), pp. 45–68.
— 'On the Possibility of Creating a New Form of Society', in *A Society Adrift: Interviews and Debates, 1974–1997*, ed. Enrique Escobar, Myrto Gondicas and Pascal Vernay, trans. Helen Arnold (New York: Fordham University Press, 2010), pp. 103–17.
— 'A Rising Tide of Significacy?' in *A Society Adrift: Interviews and Debates, 1974–1997*, ed. Enrique Escobar, Myrto Gondicas and Pascal Vernay, trans. Helen Arnold (New York: Fordham University Press, 2010), pp. 223–9.

— 'Life and Creation: Cornelius Castoriadis in Dialogue with Francisco Varela', in *Postscript on Insignificance: Dialogues with Cornelius Castoriadis*, ed. Gabriel Rockhill, trans. Gabriel Rockhill and John V. Garner (London: Continuum, 2011), pp. 58–73.

— 'Breaking the Closure: Cornelius Castoriadis in Dialogue with Robert Legros', in *Postscript on Insignificance: Dialogues with Cornelius Castoriadis*, ed. Gabriel Rockhill, trans. Gabriel Rockhill and John V. Garner (London: Continuum, 2011), pp. 93–107.

Cavarero, Adriana, 'Inclining the Subject: Ethics, Alterity, and Natality', in Jane Elliott and Derek Attridge (eds), *Theory after 'Theory'* (Abingdon: Routledge, 2011), pp. 194–204.

Chambers, Samuel, 'Subjectivation, the Social, and a (Missing) Account of Social Formation: Judith Butler's "Turn"', in Moya Lloyd (ed.), *Butler and Ethics* (Edinburgh: Edinburgh University Press, 2015), pp. 193–218.

Chanter, Tina, 'Kristeva's Politics of Change: Tracking Essentialism with the Help of a Sex/Gender Map', in Kelly Oliver (ed.), *Ethics, Politics, and Difference in Julia Kristeva's Writings* (Abingdon: Routledge, 1993), pp. 179–95.

— 'The Problematic Normative Assumptions of Heidegger's Ontology', in Nancy J. Holland and Patricia Huntington (eds), *Feminist Interpretations of Martin Heidegger* (University Park, PA: Pennsylvania State University Press, 2001), pp. 73–108.

Chiesa, Lorenzo, *Subjectivity and Otherness: A Philosophical Reading of Lacan* (Cambridge, MA: MIT Press, 2007).

Colebrook, Claire, 'The Trope of Economy and Representational Thinking: Heidegger, Derrida, and Irigaray', *Journal of the British Society for Phenomenology*, 28.2, 1997, pp. 178–91.

— 'Feminist Criticism and Poststructuralism', in Gill Plain and Susan Sellers (eds), *A History of Feminist Literary Criticism* (Cambridge: Cambridge University Press, 2007), pp. 214–34.

Connelly, William E., 'Beyond Good and Evil: The Ethical Sensibility of Michel Foucault', *Political Theory*, 21.3, 1993, pp. 365–89.

Critchley, Simon, 'Post-deconstructive Subjectivity?', in *Ethics–Politics–Subjectivity: Essays on Derrida, Levinas, and Contemporary French Thought* (London: Verso, 1999), pp. 51–82.

Curtis, David A., and Andreas Kalyvas, 'Fighting the Wrong Enemy: Comments on Wolfenstein's Critique of Castoriadis', *Political Theory*, 26.6, 1998, pp. 818–24.

Davidson, Arnold I., 'Ethics as Ascetics: Foucault, the History of Ethics, and Ancient Thought', in Gary Cutting (ed.), *The Cambridge Companion to Foucault*, 2nd edn (Cambridge: Cambridge University Press, 2005), pp. 123–48.

Debord, Guy, *The Society of the Spectacle*, trans. Donald Nicholson-Smith (New York: Zone Books, 1995).

Deleuze, Gilles, *Kant's Critical Philosophy*, trans. Hugh Tomlinson and Barbara Habberjam (Minneapolis, MN: University of Minnesota Press, 1984).

— *Bergsonism*, trans. Hugh Tomlinson and Barbara Habberjam (New York: Zone Books, 1988).

— *The Logic of Sense*, ed. Constantin V. Boundas, trans. Mark Lester with Charles Stivale (New York: Columbia University Press, 1990).

— 'A Philosophical Concept . . .', in Eduardo Cadava, Peter Connor and Jean-Luc Nancy (eds), *Who Comes after the Subject?* (Abingdon: Routledge, 1991), pp. 94–5.

— *Cinema 1: The Movement-Image*, trans. Hugh Tomlinson and Barbara Habberjam (Minneapolis, MN: University of Minnesota Press, 1994).

— *Difference and Repetition*, trans. Paul Patton (New York: Columbia University Press, 1994).

— 'On *A Thousand Plateaus*', in *Negotiations: 1972–1990*, trans. M. Joughin (New York: Columbia University Press, 1995), pp. 25–35.

— *Foucault*, ed. and trans. Seán Hand (London: Continuum, 1999).

— *Empiricism and Subjectivity: An Essay on Hume's Theory of Human Nature*, trans. Constantin V. Boundas (New York: Columbia University Press, 2001).

— *Francis Bacon: The Logic of Sensation*, trans. Daniel W. Smith (Minneapolis, MN: University of Minnesota Press, 2002).

— 'Bergson, 1859–1941', in *Desert Islands and Other Texts*, ed. David Lapoujade, trans. Mike Taormina (New York: Semiotext(e), 2004), pp. 22–31.

— 'How Do We Recognise Structuralism?', trans. Melissa McMahon and Charles J. Stivale, in *Desert Islands and Other Texts*, ed. David Lapoujade, trans. Mike Taormina (New York: Semiotext(e), 2004), pp. 170–92.

— *Nietzsche and Philosophy*, trans. Hugh Tomlinson (New York: Columbia University Press, 2006).

— 'Response to a Question of the Subject', in *Two Regimes of Madness: Texts and Interviews, 1975–1995*, ed. David Lapoujade, trans. Ames Hodges and Mike Taormina (New York: Semiotext(e), 2007), pp. 353–5.

— 'Letter-Preface to Jean-Clet Martin', in *Two Regimes of Madness: Texts and Interviews, 1975–1995*, ed. David Lapoujade, trans. Ames Hodges and Mike Taormina (New York: Semiotext(e), 2007), pp. 365–7.

— 'Immanence: A Life', in *Two Regimes of Madness: Texts and Interviews, 1975–1995*, ed. David Lapoujade, trans. Ames Hodges and Mike Taormina (New York: Semiotext(e), 2007), pp. 388–94.

Deleuze, Gilles, and Félix Guattari, *What is Philosophy?*, trans. Hugh Tomlinson and Graham Burchell (New York: Columbia University Press, 1994).
— *Anti-Oedipus*, trans. Robert Hurley, Mark Seem and Helen R. Lane (London: Continuum, 2004).
— *A Thousand Plateaus*, trans. Brian Massumi (London: Continuum, 2004).
Deleuze, Gilles, and Claire Parnet, 'A Conversation: What is it? What is it For?' in *Dialogues II*, trans. Hugh Tomlinson and Barbara Habberjam (London: Continuum, 2002), pp. 1–26.
— 'On the Superiority of Anglo-American Literature', in *Dialogues II*, trans. Hugh Tomlinson and Barbara Habberjam (London: Continuum, 2002), pp. 27–56.
— 'Dead Psychoanalysis: Analyse', in *Dialogues II*, trans. Hugh Tomlinson and Barbara Habberjam (London: Continuum, 2002), pp. 57–92.
Delphy, Christine, 'The Invention of French Feminism: An Essential Move', *Yale French Studies*, 97, 1987, pp. 190–221.
Derrida, Jacques, 'Différance', in *Margins of Philosophy*, trans. Alan Bass (Chicago: University of Chicago Press, 1982), pp. 3–27.
— 'The Ends of Man', in *Margins of Philosophy*, trans. Alan Bass (Chicago: University of Chicago Press, 1982), pp. 111–36.
— '"Eating Well," or the Calculation of the Subject', in Eduardo Cadava, Peter Connor and Jean-Luc Nancy (eds), *Who Comes after the Subject?* (Abingdon: Routledge, 1991), pp. 96–119.
— 'Choreographies', trans. Christie V. McDonald, in *Points . . . Interviews, 1974–1994*, ed. Elizabeth Weber, trans. Peggy Kamuf et al. (Stanford, CA: Stanford University Press, 1995), pp. 89–108.
— '"Eating Well," or the Calculation of the Subject', trans. Peter Connor and Avital Ronell, in *Points . . . Interviews, 1974–1994*, ed. Elizabeth Weber, trans. Peggy Kamuf et al. (Stanford, CA: Stanford University Press, 1995), pp. 255–87.
— *Archive Fever: A Freudian Impression*, trans. Eric Prenowitz (Chicago: University of Chicago Press, 1996).
— *Of Grammatology*, rev. edn, trans. Gayatri Chakravorty Spivak (Baltimore, MD: Johns Hopkins University Press, 1997).
— *Resistances of Psychoanalysis*, trans. Peggy Kamuf, Pascale-Anne Brault and Michael Naas (Stanford, CA: Stanford University Press, 1998).
— *Of Hospitality*, trans. Rachel Bowlby (Stanford, CA: Stanford University Press, 2000).
— *On Cosmpolitanism and Forgiveness*, trans. Mark Dooley and Michael Hughes (Abingdon: Routledge, 2001).
— 'Structure, Sign, and Play in the Discourse of the Human Sciences', in *Writing and Difference*, trans. Alan Bass (Abingdon: Routledge, 2001), pp. 351–70.

— 'Force of Law: The "Mystical Foundation of Authority"', in *Acts of Religion*, ed. Gil Andjar (Abingdon: Routledge, 2002), pp. 231–98.

— 'Letter to a Japanese Friend', trans. David Wood and Andrew Benjamin, in *Psyche: Inventions of the Other, Volume 2*, ed. Peggy Kamuf and Elizabeth Rottenberg (Stanford, CA: Stanford University Press, 2008), pp. 1–6.

— '*Geschlecht I*: Sexual Difference, Ontological Difference', trans. Ruben Bevezdivin and Elizabeth Rottenberg, in *Psyche: Inventions of the Other, Volume 2*, ed. Peggy Kamuf and Elizabeth Rottenberg (Stanford, CA: Stanford University Press, 2008), pp. 7–26.

— *Heidegger: The Question of Being and History*, ed. Thomas Dutoit with the assistance of Marguerite Derrida, trans. Geoffrey Bennington (Chicago: University of Chicago Press, 2016).

Derrida, Jacques, and Elizabeth Roudinesco, 'Politics of Difference', in *For What Tomorrow . . . A Dialogue*, trans. Jeff Fort (Stanford, CA: Stanford University Press, 2004), pp. 20–32.

Derrida, Jacques, and Antoine Spire, '"Others are Secret because they are Other"', in *Paper Machine*, trans. Rachel Bowlby (Stanford, CA: Stanford University Press, 2005), pp. 136–63.

Descartes, Rene, *Meditations on First Philosophy*, ed. and trans. John Cottingham (Cambridge: Cambridge University Press, 1986).

Deutscher, Penelope, *Yielding Gender: Feminism, Deconstruction and the History of Philosophy* (Abingdon: Routledge, 1997).

Dews, Peter, *Logics of Disintegration: Post-structuralist Thought and the Claims of Critical Theory* (London: Verso, 1987).

— 'The Return of the Subject in Late Foucault', *Radical Philosophy*, 51.1, 1989, pp. 37–41.

Dosse, François, *History of Structuralism, Volume 1: The Rising Sign, 1945–1966*, trans. Deborah Glassman (Minneapolis, MN: University of Minnesota Press, 1997).

— *History of Structuralism, Volume 2: The Sign Sets, 1967–Present*, trans. Deborah Glassman (Minneapolis, MN: University of Minnesota Press, 1997).

Dreyfus, Hubert L., and Paul Rabinow, *Michel Foucault: Beyond Structuralism and Hermeneutics*, 2nd edn (Chicago: University of Chicago Press, 1983).

Dutton, Denis, 'The Bad Writing Contest: Press Releases, 1996–1998', http://www.denisdutton.com/bad_writing.htm (accessed 22 August 2017).

Elden, Stuart, *Foucault: The Birth of Power* (Cambridge: Polity, 2017).

Elliott, Anthony, 'The Constitution of the Subject: Primary Repression after Kristeva and Laplanche', *European Journal of Social Theory*, 8.1, 2005, pp. 25–42.

Ferry, Luc, and Alain Renaut, *French Philosophy of the Sixties: An Essay on Antihumanism*, trans. Mary H. S. Cattans (Amherst, MA: University of Massachusetts Press, 1990).
Fink, Bruce, *The Lacanian Subject: Between Language and Jouissance* (Princeton, NJ: Princeton University Press, 1995).
Foucault, Michel, 'Power and Strategies', in *Power/Knowledge: Selected Interviews and Other Writings 1972–1977*, ed. Colin Gordon, trans. Colin Gordon, Leo Marshall, John Mephan and Kate Soper (New York: Pantheon, 1980), pp. 134–45.
— *A History of Sexuality, Volume 2: The Use of Pleasure*, trans. Robert Hurley (London: Penguin, 1985).
— *A History of Sexuality, Volume 3: The Care of the Self*, trans. Robert Hurley (London: Penguin, 1985).
— *A History of Sexuality, Volume 1: An Introduction*, trans. Robert Hurley (New York: Vintage, 1990).
— *The Birth of the Clinic: An Archaeology of Medical Perception* (New York: Vintage, 1994).
— *The Order of Things: An Archaeology of the Human Sciences* (New York: Vintage, 1994).
— *Discipline and Punish: Birth of the Prison*, trans. Alan Sheridan (New York: Vintage, 1995).
— 'An Interview by Stephen Riggins', in *Ethics: Essential Works of Foucault, 1954–1985, Volume 1*, ed. Paul Rabinow (London: Penguin, 2000), pp. 121–33.
— 'Friendship as a Way of Life', in *Ethics: Essential Works of Foucault, 1954–1985, Volume 1*, ed. Paul Rabinow (London: Penguin, 2000), pp. 135–40.
— 'Sexual Choice, Sexual Act', in *Ethics: Essential Works of Foucault, 1954–1985, Volume 1*, ed. Paul Rabinow (London: Penguin, 2000), pp. 141–56.
— 'Sex, Power, and the Politics of Identity', in *Ethics: Essential Works of Foucault, 1954–1985, Volume 1*, ed. Paul Rabinow (London: Penguin, 2000), pp. 163–74.
— 'Sexuality and Solitude', in *Ethics: Essential Works of Foucault, 1954–1985, Volume 1*, ed. Paul Rabinow (London: Penguin, 2000), pp. 175–84.
— 'Technologies of the Self', in *Ethics: Essential Works of Foucault, 1954–1985, Volume 1*, ed. Paul Rabinow (London: Penguin, 2000), pp. 223–52.
— 'On the Genealogy of Ethics: An Overview of Work in Progress', in *Ethics: Essential Works of Foucault, 1954–1985, Volume 1*, ed. Paul Rabinow (London: Penguin, 2000), pp. 253–80.

— 'The Ethics of the Concern for Self as a Practice of Freedom', trans. P. Aranov and D. McGrawth, in *Ethics: Essential Works of Foucault, 1954–1985, Volume 1*, ed. Paul Rabinow (London: Penguin, 2000), pp. 281–301.
— 'What is Enlightenment?', in *Ethics: Essential Works of Foucault, 1954–1985, Volume 1*, ed. Paul Rabinow (London: Penguin, 2000), pp. 303–20.
— 'What is an Author?', trans. Josué V Harari, in *Aesthetics: Essential Works of Foucault 1954–1984, Volume 2*, ed. James D. Faubion (London: Penguin, 2000), pp. 205–22.
— 'The Order of Things', in *Aesthetics: Essential Works of Foucault 1954–1984, Volume 2*, ed. James D. Faubion (London: Penguin, 2000), pp. 261–8.
— 'Theatrum Philosophicum', in *Aesthetics: Essential Works of Foucault 1954–1984, Volume 2*, ed. James D. Faubion (London: Penguin, 2000), pp. 343–68.
— 'Structuralism and Poststructuralism', in *Aesthetics: Essential Works of Foucault 1954–1984, Volume 2*, ed. James D. Faubion (London: Penguin, 2000), pp. 433–58.
— 'Truth and Power', trans. Robert Hurley, in *Power: Essential Works of Foucault 1954–1984, Volume 3*, ed. James D. Faubion (Penguin: New York, 2002), pp. 111–33.
— 'Interview with Michel Foucault', in *Power: Essential Works of Foucault 1954–1984, Volume 3*, ed. James D. Faubion (London: Penguin, 2002), pp. 239–97.
— '"Omnes et Singulatim": Toward a Critique of Political Reason', in *Power: Essential Works of Foucault 1954–1984, Volume 3*, ed. James D. Faubion (London: Penguin, 2002), pp. 298–325.
— 'The Subject and Power', in *Power: Essential Works of Foucault 1954–1984, Volume 3*, ed. James D. Faubion (London: Penguin, 2002), pp. 326–48.
— *Society Must Be Defended: Lectures at the Collège de France, 1975–1976*, ed. Mauro Bertani and Alessandro Fontana, trans. David Macey (London: Penguin, 2003).
— *Mental Illness and Psychology*, 2nd rev. edn (Berkeley, CA: University of California Press, 2008).
— *History of Madness*, ed. Jean Khalfa, trans. Jonathon Murphy (Abingdon: Routledge, 2009).
— 'Nietzsche, Geneaology, History', trans. Donald F. Bouchard and Sherry Simon, in *The Foucault Reader*, ed. Paul Rabinow (New York: Vintage, 2010), pp. 76–100.
— *The Archaeology of Knowledge*, trans. A. M. Sheridan Smith (New York: Vintage, 2010).

— *On the Government of the Living: Lectures at the Collège de France, 1979–1980*, ed. Michel Senellart, trans. Graham Burchell (Basingstoke: Palgrave Macmillan, 2014).

— 'Subjectivity and Truth', in *About the Hermeneutics of the Self: Lectures at Dartmouth College, 1980*, ed. Henri-Paul Fruchard and Daniele Lorenzini, trans. Graham Burchell (Chicago: University of Chicago Press, 2016), pp. 19–52.

— 'Christianity and Confession', in *About the Hermeneutics of the Self: Lectures at Dartmouth College, 1980*, ed. Henri-Paul Fruchard and Daniele Lorenzini, trans. Graham Burchell (Chicago: University of Chicago Press, 2016), pp. 53–92.

— 'Discussion of "Truth and Subjectivity"', in *About the Hermeneutics of the Self: Lectures at Dartmouth College, 1980*, ed. Henri-Paul Fruchard and Daniele Lorenzini, trans. Graham Burchell (Chicago: University of Chicago Press, 2016), pp. 93–126.

— 'Interview with Michel Foucault', in *About the Hermeneutics of the Self: Lectures at Dartmouth College, 1980*, ed. Henri-Paul Fruchard and Daniele Lorenzini, trans. Graham Burchell (Chicago: University of Chicago Press, 2016), pp. 127–38.

— *Histoire de la sexualité, IV: Les aveux de la chair*, ed. Frédéric Gros (Paris: Gallimard, 2018).

Fraser, Nancy, 'Foucault on Modern Power: Empirical Insights and Normative Confusions', in *Unruly Practices: Power, Discourse, and Gender in Contemporary Social Theory* (Minneapolis, MN: University of Minnesota Press, 1989), pp. 17–34.

— 'Michel Foucault: A "Young Conservative?"' in *Unruly Practices: Power, Discourse, and Gender in Contemporary Social Theory* (Minneapolis, MN: University of Minnesota Press, 1989), pp. 35–54.

— 'The Uses and Abuses of French Discourse Theories for Feminist Politics', in Nancy Fraser and Sandra Lee Bartby (eds), *Revaluing French Feminism: Critical Essays on Difference, Agency, and Culture* (Bloomington, IN: Indiana University Press, 1992), pp. 177–94.

Gauchet, Marcel, 'Redefining the Unconscious', *Thesis Eleven*, 71.1, 2002, pp. 4–23.

Golder, Ben, *Foucault and the Politics of Rights* (Stanford, CA: Stanford University Press, 2015).

Goodman, Robin Truth, 'Julia Kristeva's Sacrificial Murders: The Body at Work as the Work of Art', *Philosophy Today*, 56.2, 2012, pp. 183–99.

Grosz, Elizabeth, *Jacques Lacan: A Feminist Introduction* (Abingdon: Routledge, 1990).

— 'Ontology and Equivocation: Derrida's Politics of Sexual Difference', *Diacritics*, 25.2, 1995, pp. 115–24.

Habermas, Jürgen, 'Some Questions concerning the Theory of Power: Foucault Again', in *The Philosophical Discourse of Modernity: Twelve Lectures*, trans. Frederick Lawrence (Cambridge: Polity, 1987), pp. 266–93.

— 'Excursis on Cornelius Castoriadis: The Imaginary Institution', in *The Philosophical Discourse of Modernity: Twelve Lectures*, trans. Frederick Lawrence (Cambridge: Polity, 1987), pp. 327–35.

Hadot, Pierre, 'Reflections on the Notion of "the cultivation of the self"', in Timothy J. Armstrong (ed. and trans.), *Michel Foucault: Philosophy* (Abingdon: Routledge, 1992), pp. 225–32.

Hallward, Peter, *Out of this World: Deleuze and the Philosophy of Creation* (London: Verso, 2006).

Han-Pile, Beatrice, 'The "Death of Man": Foucault and Anti-Humanism', in Timothy O'Leary and Christopher Falzon (eds), *Foucault and Philosophy* (Oxford: Wiley-Blackwell, 2010), pp. 118–42.

Hartsock, Nancy, 'Foucault on Power: A Theory of Women?', in Linda Nicholson (ed.), *Feminism/Postmodernism* (Abingdon: Routledge, 1990), pp. 157–75.

Hegel, Georg W. F., *Phenomenology of Spirit*, trans. A. V. Miller (Oxford: Oxford University Press, 1977).

— *The Science of Logic*, trans. and ed. George Di Giovanni (Cambridge: Cambridge University Press, 2010).

Heidegger, Martin, *Being and Time*, trans. John Macquarrie and Edward Robinson (Oxford: Blackwell, 1962).

— *On Time and Being*, trans. Joan Staumbaugh (London: Harper, 1972).

— 'Letter on Humanism', trans. Frank A. Capuzzi and J. Glenn Gray, in *Basic Writings*, ed. David Farrell Krell (London: Harper, 1977), pp. 217–65.

— *The Metaphysical Foundations of Logic*, trans. Michael Heim (Bloomington, IN: Indiana University Press, 1984).

— *Hegel's Phenomenology of Spirit*, trans. Parvis Emad and Kenneth Maly (Bloomington, IN: Indiana University Press, 1988).

— *Contributions to Philosophy (From Enowing)*, trans. Parvis Emad and Kenneth Maly (Bloomington, IN: Indiana University Press, 1999).

— *Hegel*, trans. Joseph Arel and Niels Feuerhahn (Bloomington, IN: Indiana University Press, 2015).

Hernstein, Ori J., 'Justifying Subversion: Why Nussbaum Got (the Better Interpretation of) Judith Butler Wrong', *Buffalo Journal of Gender, Law, and Social Policy*, 18, 2010, pp. 43–73.

Holland, Eugene W., *Deleuze and Guattari's A Thousand Plateaus* (London: Bloomsbury, 2013).

Honneth, Axel, 'Rescuing the Revolution with an Ontology: On Cornelius Castoriadis's Theory of Society', *Thesis Eleven*, 14.1, 1986, pp. 62–78.
— 'Foucault and Adorno: Two Forms of the Critique of Modernity', trans. David Roberts, *Thesis Eleven*, 15.1, 1986, pp. 48–59.
— 'Decentred Autonomy: The Subject after the Fall', in *The Fragmented World of the Social: Essays in Social and Political Philosophy*, ed. Charles W. Wright (Albany, NY: State University of New York Press: 1995), pp. 261–71.
— 'The Other of Justice: Habermas and the Ethical Challenge of Postmodernism', in Stephen K. White (ed.), *The Cambridge Companion to Habermas* (Cambridge: Cambridge University Press, 1995), pp. 289–324.
Ingala, Emma, 'Catachresis and Mis-Being in Judith Butler and Etienne Balibar: Contemporary Refigurations of the Human as a Face Drawn in the Sand', *Literature and Theology*, 32.2, 2018, pp. 142–60.
— 'From Hannah Arendt to Judith Butler: The Conditions of the Political', in Gavin Rae and Emma Ingala (eds), *Subjectivity and the Political: Contemporary Perspectives* (Abingdon: Routledge, 2018), pp. 35–54.
— 'Of the Refrain (The Ritornello)', in Jeffery Bell, Henry Somers-Hall and James Williams (eds), *A Thousand Plateaus and Philosophy* (Edinburgh: Edinburgh University Press, 2018), pp. 190–205.
Irigaray, Luce, *Sexes and Genealogies*, trans. Gillian C. Gill (New York: Columbia University Press, 1993).
— *I Love to You: Sketch of a Possible Felicity in History*, trans. Alison Martin (Abingdon: Routledge, 1996).
— *The Forgetting of Air in Martin Heidegger*, trans. Mary Beth Mader (London: Athlone, 1999).
— *To be Two*, trans. Monique M. Rhodes and Marco F. Cocito-Monoc (London: Athlone, 2000).
— *The Way of Love*, trans. Heidi Bostic and Stephen Plukàček (London: Continuum, 2002).
Johnston, Adrian, *Time Driven: Metapsychology and the Splitting of the Drive* (Evanston, IL: Northwestern University Press, 2005).
Keltner, S. K., *Kristeva: Thresholds* (Cambridge: Polity, 2011).
Kioupkiolis, Alexandros, 'The Agonistic Turn of Critical Reason: Critique and Freedom in Foucault and Castoriadis', *European Journal of Social Theory*, 15.3, 2012, pp. 385–402.
Klein, Melanie, *The Psychoanalysis of Children*, trans. Alix Strachey (New York: Grove Press, 1960).
Klooger, Jeff, *Castoriadis: Psyche, Society, Autonomy* (Leiden: Brill, 2009).
Koopman, Colin, *Genealogy as Critique: Foucault and the Problems of Modernity* (Bloomington, IN: Indiana University Press, 2013).

Kristeva, Julia, 'The Bounded Text', in *Desire in Language: A Semiotic Approach to Literature and Art*, ed. Leon S. Roudiez, trans. Thomas Gora, Alice Jardine and Leon S. Roudiez (New York: Columbia University Press, 1980), pp. 36–63.
— 'From One Identity to Another', in *Desire in Language: A Semiotic Approach to Literature and Art*, ed. Leon S. Roudiez, trans. Thomas Gora, Alice Jardine and Leon S. Roudiez (New York: Columbia University Press, 1980), pp. 124–47.
— *Powers of Horror: An Essay on Abjection*, trans. Leon S. Roudiez (New York: Columbia University Press, 1982).
— *Revolution in Poetic Language*, trans. Margaret Waller (New York: Columbia University Press, 1984).
— 'The System and the Speaking Subject', in *The Julia Kristeva Reader*, ed. Toril Moi (New York: Columbia University Press, 1986), pp. 24–33.
— *Tales of Love*, trans. by Leon S. Roudiez (New York: Columbia University Press, 1987).
— *Black Sun: Depression and Melancholia*, trans. Leon S. Roudiez (New York: Columbia University Press, 1989).
— *Strangers to Ourselves*, trans. Leon S. Roudiez (New York: Columbia University Press, 1991).
— 'What of Tomorrow's Nation?' in *Nations without Nationalism*, trans. Leon S. Roudiez (New York: Columbia University Press, 1993), pp. 1–48.
— *New Maladies of the Soul*, trans. Ross Guberman (New York: Columbia University Press, 1995).
— 'Julia Kristeva in Person', in *Julia Kristeva: Interviews*, ed. Ross Mitchell Guberman (New York: Columbia University Press, 1996), pp. 3–11.
— 'A Conversation with Kristeva. Julia', in *Julia Kristeva: Interviews*, ed. Ross Mitchell Guberman (New York: Columbia University Press, 1996), pp. 18–34.
— 'Feminism and Psychoanalysis', in *Julia Kristeva: Interviews*, ed. Ross Mitchell Guberman (New York: Columbia University Press, 1996), pp. 113–21.
— 'Psychoanalysis and Politics', in *Julia Kristeva: Interviews*, ed. Ross Mitchell Guberman (New York: Columbia University Press, 1996), pp. 146–61.
— 'The Subject in Process', trans. Patrick French, in Patrick French and Roland-François Lack (eds), *The Tel Quel Reader* (Abingdon: Routledge, 1998), pp. 133–78.
— 'Europe Divided: Politics, Ethics, Religion', in *Crises of the European Subject*, trans. Susan Fairfield (New York: Other Press, 2000), pp. 111–62.
— *The Sense and Non-Sense of Revolt: The Powers and Limits of Psychoanalysis*, trans. Jeanine Herman (New York: Columbia University Press, 2000).

— *Intimate Revolt: The Powers and Limits of Psychoanalysis*, trans. Jeanine Herman (New York: Columbia University Press, 2002).
— *Revolt, She Said*, ed. Sylvère Lotringer, trans. Brian O'Keefe (South Pasadena, CA: Semiotext(e), 2002).
— 'From Jesus to Mozart: Christianity's Indifference', in *The Incredible Need to Believe*, trans. Beverley Bie Brahic (New York: Columbia University Press, 2009), pp. 77–86.
— 'Thinking about Liberty in Dark Times', in *Hatred and Forgiveness*, trans. Jeanine Herman (New York: Columbia University Press, 2012), pp. 3–23.
— 'Secularism: "Values" at the Limits of Life', in *Hatred and Forgiveness*, trans. Jeanine Herman (New York: Columbia University Press, 2012), pp. 24–8.
— 'The Passion According to Motherhood', in *Hatred and Forgiveness*, trans. Jeanine Herman (New York: Columbia University Press, 2012), pp. 79–94.
— 'Language, Sublimation, Women', in *Hatred and Forgiveness*, trans. Jeanine Herman (New York: Columbia University Press, 2012), pp. 177–82.
Kuiken, Kir, 'Deleuze/Derrida: Towards an almost Imperceptible Difference', *Research in Phenomenology*, 35, 2005, pp. 290–308.
Lacan, Jacques, 'Some Reflections on the Ego', *International Journal of Psychoanalysis*, 34.1, 1953, pp. 11–17.
— *Seminar XI: The Four Fundamental Concepts of Psychoanalysis*, ed. Jacques-Alain Miller, trans. Alan Sheridan (New York: W. W. Norton, 1981).
— *Seminar I: Freud's Papers on Technique*, ed. Jacques-Alain Miller, trans. John Forrester (New York: W. W. Norton, 1991).
— *Seminar II: The Ego in Freud's Theory and in the Technique of Psychoanalysis*, ed. Jacques-Alain Miller, trans. Sylvana Tomaselli (New York: W. W. Norton, 1991).
— *Seminar III: The Psychoses*, ed. Jacques-Alain Miller, trans. Russell Grigg (New York: W. W. Norton, 1997).
— *Seminar XX: On Feminine Sexuality, The Limits of Love and Knowledge*, ed. Jacques-Alain Miller, trans. Bruce Fink (New York: W. W. Norton, 1999).
— 'Seminar on the "Purloined Letter"', in *Écrits*, trans. Bruce Fink in collaboration with Héloïse Fink and Russell Grigg (New York: W. W. Norton, 2006), pp. 6–50.
— 'The Mirror Stage as Formative of the *I* Function', in *Écrits*, trans. Bruce Fink in collaboration with Héloïse Fink and Russell Grigg (New York: W. W. Norton, 2006), pp. 75–81.
— 'The Function and Field of Speech and Language in Psychoanalysis', in *Écrits*, trans. Bruce Fink in collaboration with Héloïse Fink and Russell Grigg (New York: W. W. Norton, 2006), pp. 197–268.

— 'Introduction to Jean Hyppolite's Commentary on Freud's "Verneinung"', in *Écrits*, trans. Bruce Fink in collaboration with Héloïse Fink and Russell Grigg (New York: W. W. Norton, 2006), pp. 308–17.
— 'Response to Jean Hyppolite's Commentary on Freud's "Verneinung"', in *Écrits*, trans. Bruce Fink in collaboration with Héloïse Fink and Russell Grigg (New York: W. W. Norton, 2006), pp. 318–33.
— 'The Instance of the Letter in the Unconscious, or Reason since Freud', in *Écrits*, trans. Bruce Fink in collaboration with Héloïse Fink and Russell Grigg (New York: W. W. Norton, 2006), pp. 412–41.
— 'The Subversion of the Subject and the Dialectic of Desire', in *Écrits*, trans. Bruce Fink in collaboration with Héloïse Fink and Russell Grigg (New York: W. W. Norton, 2006), pp. 671–702.
— 'Position of the Unconscious', in *Écrits*, trans. Bruce Fink in collaboration with Héloïse Fink and Russell Grigg (New York: W. W. Norton, 2006), pp. 703–21.
— 'The Triumph of Religion', in *The Triumph of Religion, preceded by Discourse to Catholics*, trans. Bruce Fink (Cambridge: Polity, 2013), pp. 55–85.
— *Seminar XXIII: The Sinthome*, ed. Jacques-Alain Miller, trans. A. R. Price (Cambridge: Polity, 2016).
— *Seminar V: Formations of the Unconscious*, ed. Jacques-Alain Miller, trans. Russell Grigg (Cambridge: Polity, 2017).
Lampert, Mathew, 'Resisting Ideology: On Butler's Critique of Althusser', *Diacritics*, 43.2, 2015, pp. 124–47.
Lechte, John, *Julia Kristeva* (Abingdon: Routledge, 2013).
Lloyd, Moya, *Judith Butler: From Norms to Politics* (Cambridge: Polity, 2007).
Lumsden, Simon, *Self-Consciousness and the Critique of the Subject: Hegel, Heidegger, and the Post-structuralists* (New York: Columbia University Press, 2014).
Lundy, Craig, 'From Structuralism to Poststructuralism', in Benoît Dillet, Iain MacKenzie and Robert Porter (eds), *The Edinburgh Companion to Poststructuralism* (Edinburgh: Edinburgh University Press, 2013), pp. 69–94.
McAfee, Noëlle, 'Resisting Essence: Kristeva's Process Philosophy', *Philosophy Today*, 44, SPEP Supplement, 2000, pp. 77–83.
— *Julia Kristeva* (Abingdon: Routledge, 2004).
McNay, Lois, *Foucault and Feminism: Power, Gender, and Agency* (Cambridge: Polity, 1992).
— 'Gender, Habitus, and the Field: Pierre Bourdieu and the Limits of Reflexivity', *Theory, Culture, and Society*, 16.1, 1999, pp. 95–117.
— *Gender and Agency: Reconfiguring the Subject in Feminist and Social Theory* (Cambridge: Polity, 2000).

Marx, Karl, 'Theses on Feuerbach', in Karl Marx and Frederick Engels, *Marx and Engels Collected Works*, Volume 5 (London: Lawrence and Wishart, 2010), pp. 6–8.
Massumi, Brian, *Parables for the Virtual: Movement, Affect, Sensation* (Durham, NC: Duke University Press, 2002).
May, Todd, *The Political Philosophy of Poststructuralist Anarchism* (University Park, PA: Pennsylvania State University Press, 1994).
Meehan, Johanna, 'Feminism and Rethinking Our Models of the Self', *Philosophy and Social Criticism*, 43.1, 2017, pp. 3–33.
Memos, Christos, *Castoriadis and Critical Theory: Crisis, Critique, and Radical Alternatives* (Basingstoke: Palgrave Macmillan, 2014).
Michel, Johann, *Ricoeur and the Post-structuralists: Bourdieu, Derrida, Deleuze, Foucault, Castoriadis*, trans. Scott Davidson (New York: Rowman and Littlefield, 2015).
Moi, Toril, 'Power, Sex, and Subjectivity: Feminist Reflections on Foucault', *Paragraph*, 5, 1985, pp. 95–102.
— *Sexual/Textual Practice: Feminist Literary Theory*, 2nd edn (Abingdon: Routledge, 2002).
Nancy, Jean-Luc, and Philippe Lacoue-Labarthe, *The Title of the Letter: A Reading of Lacan*, trans. François Raffoul and David Pettigrew (Albany, NY: State University of New York Press, 1992).
Newman, Saul, *Power and Politics in Poststructuralist Thought: New Theories of the Political* (Abingdon: Routledge, 2005).
Nietzsche, Friedrich, *Will to Power*, ed. Walter Kaufmann, trans. Walter Kaufmann and R. J. Hollingdale (New York: Vintage, 1968).
— *On the Genealogy of Morals*, trans. Walter Kaufman and R. J. Hollingdale, in *On the Genealogy of Morals and Ecce Homo*, ed. Walter Kaufman (New York: Vintage, 1969), pp. 15–198.
Nobus, Dany, 'That Obscure Object of Psychoanalysis', *Continental Philosophy Review*, 46.2, 2013, pp. 163–87.
Nussbaum, Martha, 'The Professor of Parody: The Hip Defeatism of Judith Butler', *The New Republic*, 22 February 1999, pp. 37–45.
Oliviers, Bert, 'Lacan's Subject: the Imaginary, Language, the Real and Philosophy', *South Africa Journal of Philosophy*, 23.1, 2004, pp. 1–19.
Patton, Paul, *Deleuze and the Political* (Abingdon: Routledge, 2000).
Patton, Paul, and John Protevi (eds), *Between Deleuze and Derrida* (London: Continuum, 2003).
Pluth, Ed, 'Lacan's Subversion of the Subject', *Continental Philosophy Review*, 39.3, 2006, pp. 293–312.
— *Signifiers and Acts: Freedom in Lacan's Theory of the Subject* (Albany, NY: State University of New York Press, 2007).

Rae, Gavin, *Realizing Freedom: Hegel, Sartre, and the Alienation of Human Being* (Basingstoke: Palgrave Macmillan, 2011).
— 'Anthropocentrism', in Henk ten Have (ed.), *Encyclopedia of Global Bioethics* (Dordrecht: Springer, 2014), pp. 1–12.
— *Ontology in Heidegger and Deleuze* (Basingstoke: Palgrave Macmillan, 2014).
— 'Traces of Identity in Deleuze's Differential Ontology', *International Journal of Philosophical Studies*, 22.1, 2014, pp. 86–105.
— 'Authoritarian and Anthropocentric: Examining Derrida's Critique of Heidegger', *Critical Horizons: A Journal of Philosophy and Social Theory*, 16.1, 2015, pp. 27–51.
— *The Problem of Political Foundations in Carl Schmitt and Emmanuel Levinas* (Basingstoke: Palgrave Macmillan, 2016).
— *Critiquing Sovereign Violence: Law, Biopolitics, Bio-juridicalism* (Edinburgh: Edinburgh University Press, 2019).
— 'Taming the Little Screaming Monster: Castoriadis, Violence, and the Creation of the Individual', in Gavin Rae and Emma Ingala (eds), *The Meanings of Violence: From Critical Theory to Biopolitics* (Abingdon: Routledge, 2019), pp. 171–90.
Rajan, Tilottama, *Deconstruction and the Remainders of Phenomenology: Sartre, Derrida, Foucault, Baudrillard* (Stanford, CA: Stanford University Press, 2002).
Rochlitz, Ranier, 'The Aesthetics of Existence: Post-conventional Morality and the Theory of Power in Michel Foucault', in Timothy J. Armstrong (ed. and trans.), *Michel Foucault: Philosophy* (Abingdon: Routledge, 1992), pp. 233–47.
Rozmarin, Miri, 'Living Politically: An Irigarayan Notion of Agency as a Way of Life', *Hypatia*, 28.3, 2013, pp. 469–82.
Rushton, Richard, 'What Can a Face Do? On Deleuze and Faces', *Cultural Critique*, 51, spring 2002, pp. 219–37.
Sartre, Jean-Paul, 'Jean-Paul Sartre Répond', *L'Arc*, 30, October 1966, pp. 87–96.
Sass, Louis, 'Lacan, Foucault, and the "Crisis of the Subject": Revisionist Reflections on Phenomenology and Post-structuralism', *Philosophy, Psychiatry, Psychology*, 21.4, 2014, pp. 325–41.
— 'Lacan: The Mind of the Modernist', *Continental Philosophy Review*, 48.4, 2015, pp. 409–43.
Saussure, Ferdinand de, *Course in General Linguistics*, ed. Charles Bally, Albert Sechehaye and Albert Riedlinger, trans. Roy Harris (Chicago: Open Court, 1986).
Schrift, Alan D., 'Judith Butler: Une Nouvelle existentialist?' *Philosophy Today*, 45.1, 2001, pp. 12–23.

Singh, Surti, 'Spectacle and Revolt: On the Intersection of Psychoanalysis and Social Theory in Kristeva's Work', in Sarah K. Hansen and Rebecca Tuvel (eds), *New Forms of Revolt: Essays on Kristeva's Intimate Politics* (Albany, NY: State University of New York Press, 2017), pp. 23–42.

Sinnerbrink, Robert, 'Power, Recognition, and Care: Honneth's Critique of Poststructuralist Social Philosophy', in Danielle Petherbridge (ed.), *Axel Honneth: Critical Essays* (Leiden: Brill, 2011), pp. 177–206.

Sjöholm, Cecilia, *Kristeva and the Political* (Abingdon: Routledge, 2005).

Smith, Daniel W., 'A Life of Pure Immanence: Deleuze's "Critique et Clinique"', in *Essays on Deleuze* (Edinburgh: Edinburgh University Press, 2012), pp. 189–221.

Smith, Karl E., 'Re-imagining Castoriadis's Psychic Monad', *Thesis Eleven*, 83.1, 2005, pp. 5–14.

Söderbäck, Fanny, 'Being in the Present: Derrida and Irigaray on the Metaphysics of Presence', *Journal of Speculative Philosophy*, 27.3, 2013, pp. 253–64.

Soper, Kate, 'Feminism, Humanism, and Postmodernism', *Radical Philosophy*, 55.1, 1990, pp. 11–17.

Stark, Hannah, *Feminist Theory after Deleuze* (London: Bloomsbury, 2016).

Stone, Alison, 'The Sex of Nature: A Reinterpretation of Irigaray's Metaphysis and Political Thought', *Hypatia*, 18.3, 2003, pp. 60–84.

— *Luce Irigaray and the Philosophy of Sexual Difference* (Cambridge: Cambridge University Press, 2006).

Taylor, Charles, 'Foucault on Freedom and Truth', in *Philosophical Papers 2: Philosophy and the Human Sciences* (Cambridge: Cambridge University Press, 1985), pp. 152–84.

Tovar-Restrepo, Marcela, *Castoriadis, Foucault, and Autonomy: New Approaches to Subjectivity, Society, and Social Change* (London: Continuum, 2012).

Van Leeuwen, Anne, 'Sexuate Difference, Ontological Difference: Between Irigaray and Heidegger', *Continental Philosophy Review*, 43.1, 2013, pp. 111–26.

Whitbook, Joel, *Perversion and Utopia: A Study in Psychoanalysis and Critical Theory* (Cambridge, MA: MIT Press, 1996).

Widansky, Rachel, 'Julia Kristeva's Psychoanalytic Work', *Journal of the American Psychoanalytical Association*, 62.1, 2014, pp. 61–7.

Widder, Nathan, *Political Theory after Deleuze* (London: Continuum, 2012).

— 'How Do We Recognise the Subject?' in Benoît Dillet, Iain MacKenzie and Robert Porter (eds), *The Edinburgh Companion to Poststructuralism* (Edinburgh: Edinburgh University Press, 2013), pp. 207–26.

— 'Year Zero: Faciality', in Jeffrey A. Bell, Henry Somers-Hall and James Williams (eds), *A Thousand Plateaus* (Edinburgh: Edinburgh University Press, 2018), pp. 115–33.

Williams, Caroline, *Contemporary French Philosophy: Modernity and the Persistence of the Subject* (London: Continuum, 2001).

— 'Structure and Subject', in Benoît Dillet, Iain MacKenzie and Robert Porter (eds), *The Edinburgh Companion to Poststructuralism* (Edinburgh: Edinburgh University Press, 2013), pp. 189–206.

Wolfenstein, Eugene V., 'Psychoanalysis in Political Theory', *Political Theory*, 24.4, 1996, pp. 706–28.

Wolin, Richard, 'Foucault's Aesthetic Decisionism', *Telos*, 67, spring 1986, pp. 71–86.

Ziarek, Ewa, 'The Uncanny Style of Kristeva's Critique of Nationalism', *Postmodern Culture*, 5.2, 1995, pp. 1–28.

Žižek, Slavoj, 'The Abyss of Freedom', in Slavoj Žižek and F. W. J. Schelling, *The Abyss of Freedom/Ages of the World* (Ann Arbor, MI: University of Michigan Press, 1997), pp. 1–104.

— *Interrogating the Real* (London: Continuum, 2005).

Zupančič, Alenka, *Ethics of the Real: Kant and Lacan* (London: Verso, 2011).

INDEX

abandonment, 20, 43, 54, 77–8, 107, 207
abjection, 192, 201–5, 216
absence, 39, 66, 71, 73, 134, 175, 233
aesthetics, 110–11, 119, 125–6, 138, 209
afoundationalism, 127, 132, 134, 225
agency, 6, 14–24, 26, 35–6, 49–53, 55–6, 117, 144, 156, 158–62, 168–9, 181–2, 184–5, 193, 210–12, 219–21, 229–31, 235–7, 239, 248–51
   autonomous, 9, 108–9, 236, 238, 249
   intentional, 8, 15–16, 18–20, 22–3, 35–6, 51–2, 248, 250
   subjective, 10, 14, 34–6, 55, 107, 109, 249
   subjectless, 156
alienation, 26, 172, 179
Althusser, Louis, 77, 164, 220
ancient Greeks, 117, 121–3, 125–7, 129–31, 134, 208
anthropocentrism, 7, 9, 20, 26, 170

archaeology, 29, 88, 90, 94, 111
assemblage, 35, 54
author, 93–4
authority, 69, 77, 85, 191, 201, 207, 209, 251
autonomy, 23, 29, 109, 113, 155, 159, 202, 207, 221, 224, 235–41, 243–6
   project of, 238, 240

Bacon, Francis, 41, 48, 58, 60
becoming, 37, 39–40, 42–3, 48, 50, 58, 68, 70, 154–5, 161, 176
Benhabib, Seyla, 12, 28, 158, 162, 166
biology, 195, 228–9
body, 35, 41–4, 47–50, 73, 75, 94–8, 119–20, 143, 146–8, 152–4, 164–6, 175, 194, 196, 202–4
Bowden, Sean, 35, 50–3, 56, 60
breast, 204, 232–3, 244
Butler, Judith, 4, 12–14, 18–19, 21–2, 24–5, 27–8, 143–67, 210, 214–15, 218–19, 221, 225–6, 248, 250

Castoriadis, Cornelius, 4–5, 9, 18–19, 23–4, 26, 29, 178, 185, 188, 212, 219–46, 248–50
chaos, 49, 172, 200
children, 17–18, 154–5, 171–3, 178–80, 183, 191–2, 194–5, 197–8, 200–5, 224–5, 233–4
chora, 194–6, 199–200
Christianity, 121, 123, 125
consciousness, 68, 80–1, 92, 94, 156, 158, 167, 170
  transcendental, 161, 227
creation, 44, 52, 54, 56, 120, 170–1, 180, 222–3, 225–8, 235–6, 238, 242–4
critique, 3–4, 6, 10–16, 20–2, 27, 55, 57, 112–13, 118–19, 126, 128–9, 131, 135–6, 158–60, 211
culture, 89, 146, 162, 164, 206, 208, 210, 214

Dasein, 63–4, 70–8, 80–1, 83
  neutrality of, 71, 73–4
death, 89–90, 92–3, 107–10, 116, 164, 220, 223, 229
deconstruction, 16, 20, 24, 62, 69, 76–7, 81, 162
Deleuze, Gilles, 18, 20–1, 26, 29, 33–45, 47–63, 65, 82, 86–8
Derrida, Jacques, 20, 25, 29, 62–3, 83–5, 251
Descartes, René, 33, 119, 169–70, 186
de-territorialisation, 40, 42–3, 48
Dews, Peter, 83, 107–8, 111, 114, 126, 136–7
différance, 20, 62–70, 76–80, 82–5

difference, 2–4, 20, 22, 36–40, 42–3, 49, 62–9, 75, 82–3, 88–9, 175, 198–9, 214–15, 226, 229
  conceptual, 36–7
  -in-itself, 37–8, 62
  ontological difference, 12, 62–4, 70, 74–6, 83
  politics of, 84–5
  sexual, 10, 12, 62, 69–76, 78, 83, 85, 242
differentiation, 38–9, 67–8, 178, 184, 231, 236
discourse, 9–10, 12–13, 75, 77, 79, 81, 88, 90, 93–4, 102–8, 136, 145–7, 150–1, 189, 237
domination, 10–11, 96, 101–3, 110, 117–18, 120, 126, 128

earth, 42–3, 205
economy, 65–6, 77, 83, 125, 163
ego, 7, 44, 157, 167, 170–3, 184, 186–7, 202–3
embodiment, 95, 144, 150, 152–3, 179, 219
entities, 6, 11, 38–9, 64, 66–8, 70, 203, 212
epistemes, 91, 94, 102
essence, 3, 6, 37, 39–40, 43, 66–7, 71, 74
ethics, 25–6, 110, 115–19, 121, 123–7, 129–31, 133–9, 215, 217–18
event, 10, 45, 51–2, 56, 60, 130, 143, 177

faciality, 34, 36, 40, 45–6, 49, 59
facticity, 70, 73, 75
father, 187, 191, 198, 203–5, 213, 216, 234, 244
  imaginary, 192, 197, 201, 203–5
  symbolic, 191–2, 200–1, 203, 205

Fink, Bruce, 167, 183, 186–9
Foucault, Michel, 9–12, 18–19,
  21, 24–9, 88–121, 123–39,
  144, 181, 219–20, 244,
  248, 250
foundationalism, 3, 19, 33,
  117, 143
Fraser, Nancy, 28, 128, 135–6, 162,
  166, 210, 214
Freud, Sigmund, 22, 144, 187–8,
  191, 193–4, 206–7, 228,
  233, 236

gender, 12, 28, 111, 145–8, 150–2,
  160, 163–4, 208
genealogy, 9, 88, 94, 112, 117,
  130, 145
God, 45–6, 66, 91, 93, 122–3,
  129, 206
ground, 4, 7, 124–5, 128, 131,
  134, 144–5, 220, 226, 230,
  233, 249–50
group, 26, 94, 101, 104, 109, 207,
  209, 227

Habermas, Jürgen, 5, 9–10, 26–7,
  106–7, 111, 114, 119, 127–8,
  135, 138
Hegel, G. W. F., 26, 37, 56–7,
  59–60, 63, 83, 205,
  236
Heidegger, Martin, 57, 60, 62–5,
  70–8, 80–1, 83–7
heterosexual, 224–5, 245

identity, 3–4, 10, 14, 20, 33–4,
  36–8, 40, 47–9, 64–5, 73–4,
  76, 81–2, 156, 160, 171–3,
  176–7, 210–11
images, 40, 171–3, 178, 198, 204,
  207, 224

imaginary, 168–9, 171–4, 178–9,
  187, 189, 192, 223, 225, 227
  radical, 222–3, 227, 240
  significations, 223–5, 242, 245
  social, 223–7, 229–31, 234–40,
    242, 244, 248–9
Imagination, 171, 188, 204, 227,
  229, 240–3, 245
  radical, 223, 227–8, 230
individuation, 38, 54–5
Irigaray, Luce, 4, 27, 83, 226, 242

judgement, 95, 99, 128, 131, 133,
  157–8, 196, 230

knowledge, 89–93, 95, 99, 111,
  119, 121, 127, 133, 241, 247
Kristeva, Julia, 18–19, 21–5, 27,
  185, 191–203, 205–19, 221,
  225, 248, 250

Lacan, Jacques, 4–5, 18–19, 22,
  24–6, 77, 151, 153, 167–96,
  201, 203, 213–14, 219–21, 223
language, 2, 66, 90–2, 148, 150–3,
  159–60, 167, 171–6, 178–80,
  182–4, 186–97, 199, 201–2,
  204–5, 213–16, 218–20
law, 95, 97, 101, 103–4, 122–3,
  148–9, 172, 174, 179, 191–2,
  201, 204, 209, 234, 238
life, 13, 16, 58, 119, 121–2,
  127, 130, 132, 136–7, 170,
  174, 218
love, 120, 187–8, 192, 201–4, 213,
  215–17, 242, 244

madness, 29, 48, 55–6, 58, 111,
  183
materiality, 96, 152
melancholia, 144, 157–8, 217

metaphysics, 65, 72–3, 78, 83, 247
mirror stage, 5, 171–3, 179, 187, 198, 203, 206
morality, 129–31
mother, 171–2, 179–80, 187, 191–92, 198, 200–6, 212–13, 216, 233–4, 244
multiplication, 73–5
multiplicity, 2, 37, 39–41, 49, 54, 73–5, 104, 120

name, 68, 70, 78, 118, 122, 150–1, 156, 176, 178
 -of-the-Father, 172, 179, 191, 201
nature, 44, 63, 68, 76, 78, 89, 93, 99–100, 122, 145–6, 242–3
negativity, 22, 59, 72, 75, 193, 205, 211–12
neutrality, 70–5
Nietzsche, Friedrich, 36, 56–7, 60, 91, 112, 205
normativity, 116–19, 121, 123, 125, 127–9, 131, 133, 135, 137, 139, 239, 250
norms, 11, 13, 118, 122, 128–9, 131–4, 148–53, 156–7, 161, 223, 226, 239–40
number, 6, 14, 34–6, 44, 50–2, 76, 78, 80–1, 119, 126–8, 143–4, 168, 181–2, 202–3, 220–1

object, 38, 43, 74, 98–9, 157–8, 170, 172, 175, 194, 196–8, 202–5, 221, 223, 232–3
omnipotence, 99, 229, 233–4
ontic, 64, 71–3, 80

ontology, 16, 26, 33, 57, 60, 67, 85–7
 differential, 34, 36, 40, 47, 49, 54–5
opposition, 19–20, 37, 67–8, 72–3, 81, 227, 231, 233
 binary, 9, 66–7, 72, 75, 77, 81, 220, 226
origin, 16, 68, 71, 73, 145, 170, 184, 237

perception, 14, 172, 198, 229
performativity, 21, 147–8, 163
phallus, 144, 198, 202
Plato, 143, 205–6, 236
Pluth, Ed, 168–9, 186
political
 action, 8–9, 13, 16, 49, 69, 89, 118, 250–1
 change, 11, 15–16, 33–4, 36, 82, 90, 210
 regimes, 34, 44
politics, 13, 15–16, 24–5, 28–9, 34, 36, 55–6, 99–101, 164, 166, 215, 217–18, 238–43, 245–6, 250
poststructuralism, 1, 3–7, 11–12, 14–15, 17, 24–8, 247, 249
potency, 71–2, 91
power, 6–7, 9–11, 25–9, 41–2, 88–91, 93–117, 120, 126–8, 135–6, 138–9, 143–5, 154–5, 159–62, 164–5, 209, 227, 241, 245–6
 disciplinary, 101, 103
 expression of, 154, 160
 relations, 9, 11, 13–14, 21, 89–90, 94–7, 99–110, 116–17, 120, 127–8, 132, 143–5, 147

procreation, 123, 224–25
psyche, 18–19, 21–5, 141, 143–4, 148, 153–4, 156–8, 160–2, 191–3, 197–9, 203–5, 212, 221–3, 227–39, 248–9
 biological, 228
psychiatry, 29, 90, 135, 188
psychic, 13, 19, 156–7, 193–4, 227, 239, 249
 dependence, 154–5
 development, 201, 205, 212, 216, 234
 life, 135, 157, 162, 173, 198, 205–8, 228
 monad, 19, 23–4, 221–2, 229–32, 234–7, 239–40, 248–9
 space, 23, 193, 211–12
punishment, 94, 96–8, 103

Real, 26, 181, 183, 186–7, 190
reality, 3, 5–7, 58, 65, 99, 160, 163, 170, 223, 225, 229–31
reiteration, 144, 148, 150–4, 160
repetition, 36, 40, 47, 56–60, 148, 150–1, 154, 160
resistance, 8, 11, 13–14, 97, 103–5, 109, 183, 185, 199–200
revolt, 185, 191, 193, 195, 197, 199, 201, 203, 205–18

Sass, Louis, 174, 183, 188–9
Saussure, Ferdinand de, 1–2, 25, 66, 84, 175, 188, 214
self, 12–13, 21, 78–81, 89–90, 110, 114–21, 123–7, 129–39, 159, 171, 173, 203, 205–6, 208, 228–9
semiotic
 chora, 196, 198–200, 209
 mother, 200, 203–4

sense, 35, 37–8, 50–3, 56, 60, 66, 96, 148–9, 152–3, 163–5, 171–3, 175–6, 210, 213, 237
sexuality, 20–1, 63, 70–6, 83, 99, 103–5, 111, 113–14, 120, 122–3, 125, 136–8, 143, 145, 225–6
signification, 2, 5, 41–2, 44–5, 48–50, 118–19, 123, 175, 193–6, 198, 223, 225–6
 chain of, 158, 175–6, 182
 conceptual, 42, 192
 non-conceptual, 22, 192, 196, 201
signifiers, 1–2, 41, 44, 152, 160, 170, 173, 175–6, 178–80, 182–3, 186, 195, 198
signs, 2, 43, 45–7, 151–2, 170, 175, 192, 195, 198, 204
singularities, 54–5, 62, 79–80
socialisation, 18, 23, 183, 221, 230–1, 236–7, 249
 process, 24, 221–2, 230–2, 234–7
society, 44, 88–90, 97–100, 103, 105, 110, 112–13, 162, 164, 188–9, 212, 220–5, 229–31, 235, 238–46
soul, 54, 119, 207, 217–18
sovereign, 5, 94, 97–8, 104
 power, 102, 105
sovereignty, 97, 99, 101, 103
 juridical, 101–2
space, 7, 11, 66–8, 92–3, 98, 185, 194, 196, 239–40
speech, 66, 174, 186, 188, 190, 208
structuralism, 2–5, 10, 24, 26, 28, 55, 186, 189

subject, 6–28, 49–50, 53–6, 62–3,
    76–81, 83–4, 86–99, 101–3,
    105–11, 115–17, 119–20, 143–4,
    147–51, 153–62, 167–74,
    176–87, 191–201, 203–13,
    219–22, 247–50
  classical, 77, 79
  constituted, 19, 63, 90, 102,
    110, 236
  constituting, 17–18, 63, 101,
    105, 110, 119, 248, 250
  decentred, 18, 21, 26, 55, 77,
    117, 158, 184
  ethical, 117, 123–5, 130–1,
    134
  foundational, 8, 12, 16, 34, 36,
    127, 143–4, 236
  founding, 16, 93, 107, 109–10
  -in-process, 23, 192–3, 200,
    206–7, 211–12
  speaking, 200, 204–5, 212,
    215
  unconscious, 167, 169–71, 173,
    175, 177, 179, 181, 183, 185,
    187, 189, 220
subjection, 14, 143–4, 153–4, 158,
  161–2
subjectivation, 124, 154–55, 163
subjectivity, 7–9, 15–16, 20, 25–8,
    33–5, 41, 43–7, 49, 53–7, 61–2,
    69, 77–83, 108–10, 145, 186,
    210–12, 250–1
  ethical, 125
  post-deconstructive, 77–8,
    82, 87
subordination, 69, 154–7, 161–2,
  165
substance, 144, 148, 151, 154, 168,
  172, 184, 200, 205
subversion, 13, 69, 187, 189, 210

symbolic
  law, 200–1, 204
  order, 150, 173, 179, 182–4,
    186, 197, 210
  register, 171, 173–4, 180–1, 201
  relations, 22, 167–9, 174, 178–9,
    181–4, 192, 199, 248

time, 7, 37, 40–1, 67–8, 70–1, 74,
  76, 78, 80, 82–4, 90–1, 98–9,
  122–3, 147–8, 150
transcendent, 35, 65, 127–9,
  154, 223
transformation, 16, 46, 48–9, 152,
  209, 225
triadic phase, 221, 232, 234
truth, 42–3, 64, 67, 69, 111, 114,
  118–20, 127–8, 135, 138,
  205–6, 208, 235, 237

unity, 39, 73–4, 79, 191, 197, 230,
  233, 236

values, 121, 129–31, 134, 175, 218,
  222–3, 243, 248
violence, 97, 104, 114, 230–2,
  235, 244
virtuality, 39, 41, 48–9

war, 99–101, 235
woman, 10–13, 71, 75, 117, 122,
  145–7, 202, 207, 209, 214,
  224, 226
world, 6–7, 12, 15, 17, 148,
  173–5, 179, 183, 188, 230–1,
  234–5, 237
  human, 223
  natural, 123, 224, 228
  social, 148, 158, 220, 224, 230

Žižek, Slavoj, 26, 162, 176, 188

EU representative:
Easy Access System Europe
Mustamäe tee 50, 10621 Tallinn, Estonia
Gpsr.requests@easproject.com

www.ingramcontent.com/pod-product-compliance
Lightning Source LLC
Chambersburg PA
CBHW050211240426
43671CB00013B/2293